A Freethinking Cultural Nationalist

A Freethinking Cultural Nationalist

A Life History of Rahul Sankrityayan

ALAKA ATREYA CHUDAL

OXFORD
UNIVERSITY PRESS

OXFORD
UNIVERSITY PRESS

Oxford University Press is a department of the University of Oxford. It furthers the University's objective of excellence in research, scholarship, and education by publishing worldwide. Oxford is a registered trademark of Oxford University Press in the UK and in certain other countries.

Published in India by
Oxford University Press
YMCA Library Building, 1 Jai Singh Road, New Delhi 110 001, India

First Edition published in 2016

ISBN-13: 978-0-19-946687-0
ISBN-10: 0-19-946687-4

Typeset in ScalaPro 10/13
by Tranistics Data Technologies, New Delhi 110 044
Printed in India by Replika Press Pvt. Ltd

timrai lāgi

CONTENTS

List of Tables ix
Acknowledgements xi
Notes on Transliteration, Translation, and Citation xv

Introduction: Rahul Sankrityayan in the Context of His Age 1

1 Rahul Sankrityayan's Autobiography: The Product of a Prison Cell 40

2 The Arya Samaj: A 'New Light' 89

3 Buddhism: A Source of Indian Pride 131

4 Hindi: An Indian Voice 189

Afterword: Rahul Sankrityayan—A Freethinking Cultural Nationalist 243

Appendices 258
Selected Bibliography 304
Index 318
About the Author 324

TABLES

1.1 The Volumes of *MJY* 52

A.1 Theses/Dissertations on Rahul Sankrityayan 296

ACKNOWLEDGEMENTS

Biography has been a subject of personal interest since my childhood. This interest led naturally to a second interest, namely Indian nationalism; for during the 1990s, the years of my childhood, many biographies were made available for me to read in Banaras (present Varanasi), where I grew up. I read many stirring life histories in the form of whole volumes or essay-length sketches, along with fictionalized accounts, such as short stories or comics, about various Indians and a number of men and women of great international renown. The impressions such accounts left upon my young imagination are still alive in my memory. They invariably contained moral episodes illustrative of admirable conduct on the part of a son, daughter, student, wife, king, or patriot. Many figures became my ideals, and some I felt particularly influenced by. I have never been an Indian by nationality, but I automatically took the side of Indians, be it a Chatrapati Shivaji or a Jhansi ki Rani Lakshmibai, to the point of crying whenever I read of their suffering. I easily imagined myself as one of Chatrapati Shivaji's children dealing with the trials of life in the jungle. One fruit of this upbringing was writing a childhood memoir of my own, *Bālyakālsãga lobhīdai bālyakālmā* (On being fascinated by childhood in childhood [2006]). The present study is the second fruit of this fascination.

My childhood days on the premises of Banaras Hindu University, on the bank of the River Ganga (where I learnt to swim), and at the city's many temples (where I had the first elements of Sanskrit instilled in me) left me indelibly moulded by Hinduism and Indian nationalism. But my family eventually left India for our own country, Nepal, where I continued my Sanskrit studies and where I gained a new perspective from which to view the objects of my enthusiasm.

During my Master's study (*ācārya* level in the field of *sarva darśana*, 'eastern philosophy') at Nepal Sanskrit University, Kathmandu, I borrowed the book *Tibbat mẽ bauddha dharm* (Buddhism in Tibet) from the campus library and read it during bus rides home. My immediate impression of this book was: What a straightforward way the author has of explaining things! I had not even thought of who might have written it, the title having been enough to get me to start reading. At some point I leafed back to the title page and found Rahul Sankrityayan's name. Some years later I stumbled upon the first part of his autobiography, which whetted my appetite to read the rest and I bought all the volumes. It took me some time to realize that the author of the autobiography and of *Tibbat mẽ bauddha dharm* was one and the same person, but when I did I felt a pleasant surprise at being able to connect the two to what was clearly a single voice.

Some years later, and now enrolled at Vienna University, I was looking for a topic related to ancient Indic studies, one of my major subjects at the Master's level. Sankrityayan, who was both a Buddhist scholar and a Sanskritist, was looming in the background as one appealing subject. But I was still unsure. Finally Professor Martin Gaenszle, who would eventually become my supervisor, provided the needed inspiration for me to plunge into the ocean of Sankrityayan's writings, dotted with the islands of his multiple personalities. It was not an easy task to navigate my way around them and to make some sense of how they all formed a related group. Professor Gaenszle's supervision kept me properly on course and away from the shoals. I am very much obliged to him for his patience and kind guidance over the last several years. Professor Hans Harder also helped me forward by kindly reading the draft version and providing valuable feedback, and to him too I am much obliged.

There are many persons that I can never forget for helping me to overcome sometimes short and sometimes long periods of so-called doctoral phobia and anxiety. Professor Abhi Subedi was my inspiration, a person whom I could always write to knowing that I would receive a prompt and encouraging response. I am thankful to Dr Diwakar Acharya, who was regularly in touch with me during the entirety of my study period to provide needed suggestions, inspiration, or consolation.

At the Department of South Asian, Tibetan and Buddhist Studies, I am also thankful to Professor Karin C. Preisendanz, Professor Chlodwig H. Werba, Professor Michael Torsten Wieser-Much, Professor Bergit Kellner, Dr Johanna Buss, and my colleagues. Special thanks also go to Professor Danuta Stasik for her inspiration, and in particular for her words of wisdom: 'You are not alone.'

I remember with a sense of gratitude Professor Ulrike Stark, Professor Heinz Werner Wessler, Alankar Atreya Aryal (my brother), Anil Sigdel, Pratibha Chelaparampath, Preety Atreya Gyawali (my sister), and Ursula Lindenberg reading, early on, various parts of my draft and commenting on them. Professor Eli Franco, Dr Ines Fornell, Dr Hannelore Lötzke, Jacques Huynen, and Dr Simron Jit Singh also took interest in the subject of the dissertation and shared their expertise and book collections. I gratefully acknowledge Gautam Liu and Dr Sonja Stark-Wild at the South Asian Institute, University of Heidelberg, for their help in finding sundry items of literature.

I greatly appreciate help received in Nepal from Prakash A. Raj, Rochak Ghimire, Poet Laureate Madhav Ghimire, Ratna Sundar Shakya, Vidhan Ratna Yami, Basanta Kumar Sharma, Shyamdas Vaishnav, Dr Suman Dhakal and his family, Dr Pratyoush Onta, Gyanmani Nepal, Modnath Prashrit, the late Govinda Bhatta, Shyam Prasad Sharma, Bipin Rijal, Krishna Prasad Parajuli, Vishnu Prabhat, and many more persons too numerous to mention, for helping me in one way or another, particularly by discussing my topic with me with keen interest.

I feel greatly indebted to Professor Manager Pandey, Professor Vijaya Sati, and Dr Anil Kumar Pandey in Delhi for their help.

My meetings with Dr Kamala Sankrityayan and her daughter, Jaya Parhawk, in Vienna provided truly unforgettable moments of the period of research. I am particularly thankful to Jaya didi for her valuable suggestions sent via email.

I am very grateful to Philip Pierce for proofreading the final draft and thereby helping me, a non-native English speaker, put this study into a more readable shape. I take entire responsibility for any errors that may remain in spite of all the attention given to the text.

My parents (Professor Vishnu Raj Atreya and Arya Atreya), my children (Nandita and Dhawal), my parents-in-law (Laya Prasad Chudal and Nilakshi Chudal), who always looked forward to the day when my dissertation would be completed, inspired me constantly, and I can only hope that they are pleased with the result.

Finally, I would like to express my gratitude to the numerous other institutions, libraries, and individuals, whose names I have not mentioned for lack of space, for their help and encouragement without which this study would not have been possible.

To my husband, Rudra Chudal, who left behind his career as a radio journalist to come to Vienna to be with me, I say: I often could not be with you because of my ambitious academic goals and heavy teaching responsibilities, whether in the frozen nights of winter, flowery spring, warmly awaited summer, or golden autumn. For seven long years you were often alone in an unfamiliar city among unknown people speaking an incomprehensible language. To you (*timrai lāgi*)—it is only you who made it possible—I dedicate this study.

Alaka Atreya Chudal
Vienna, Austria

NOTES ON TRANSLITERATION, TRANSLATION, AND CITATION

The primary sources for this study are in the Hindi, Nepali, Newari, and Sanskrit languages. Direct quotations from any of these languages are presented in Devanagari. All the accompanying English translations, unless otherwise stated, are my own, and aim at literal accuracy rather than literary effect. Sanskrit, Hindi, and Nepali words which have become common in English language—for instance, Brahmin, sadhu, satyagraha, and bhikkhu—have been written in roman and without diacritical marks. The proper names of the authors that appear in the Sanskrit, Hindi, Nepali, and Newari sections of the bibliography, along with words in these languages other than ones well established in English, are transliterated with diacritics throughout. The transliteration of Hindi words for the most part follows R.S. McGregor's *The Oxford Hindi–English Dictionary* (2006).

Place names appear in their usual English form; thus Bihar and Kathmandu rather than Bihār and Kāṭhmāḍauṃ. Names of famous persons (for instance, Jawaharlal Nehru, Mahatma Gandhi, and Anagarika Dharmapala) and famous social organizations (for example, the Arya Samaj, Brahmo Samaj, and the Congress party) have also been cited in their anglicized form. The same applies to Rahul Sankrityayan himself, the subject of this thesis. Names of Nepalese persons are cited according to norms common among scholars. Certain crucial Hindi, Sanskrit, and Nepali words (for example, *rājguru, ghumakkaṛ*) that have no precise English synonym or are more expressive in the original language have been transliterated throughout the main body of the text. Their meanings are offered in brackets or footnotes, or by other appropriate means.

Books and journals published in Nepal are generally dated (and here cited) according to the Vikram Saṃvat (VS) era, which is (depending on the month) fifty-six or fifty-seven years ahead of the Common Era.

INTRODUCTION

Rahul Sankrityayan in the Context of His Age

Mahāpaṇḍit Rahul Sankrityayan (1893–1963) is a well-known figure in the field of Buddhist studies and Hindi literature, and is perhaps best known for his adventurous journeys to Tibet in search of lost original Buddhist texts. Born a *sanātanī* Brahmin,[1] he lived variously the life of a sadhu, an Arya Samajist, a Buddhist monk, a lay Buddhist, a secularist, a wanderer, a progressive writer, and a scholar who eventually embraced Marxist socialism. He was also a political activist, and was arrested and even jailed several times for such activities as delivering anti-British speeches (1922 and 1923–5), participation in the *kisān* (peasant) satyagraha campaign in Bihar (1939), and involvement in the banned Communist Party of India (1940–2).[2] Sankrityayan 'became quite a legendary figure and exercised great allure in the Hindi literary sphere for his vast scholarship' (Orsini 2010: 428). At a later stage in his life, his opinions on *bhārtīyatā* (Indianness) called for making Hindi the national language and Indianizing Islam, for which stance he was dismissed from the Communist Party of India.

Sankrityayan was such a frequent traveller that he came to be known as *ghumakkaṛ-rāj* (king of wanderers). He got into his wandering habits at the age of fourteen (1907), when he ran away

[1] That is, '[born into] the immemorial [dharma]', Hinduism, involving acceptance of *śruti* (heard—that is, revealed—truth) and *smṛti* (remembered—that is, received—truth).

[2] The years in brackets here indicate the period of Sankrityayan's imprisonment.

from home. His wanderlust never died and, given his frequent journeys and other pursuits in life, it is amazing that he found time to write such a large number of books (often at the same time).

Sankrityayan's numerous works are highly regarded. Prabhakar Machwe (1978: 7) totals up Sankrityayan's output as '125 published titles in five languages: Hindi, Sanskrit, Pali, Tibetan and Bhojpuri. The spectrum of subjects they cover includes philosophy, history, sociology, science, travelogue, biography, fiction, drama, essays, lexicography, grammar, textual editing and research, Tibetology, Buddhism, folklore, politics and even pamphleteering.' He further (1998: 29) notes that he 'has nearly 50,000 published pages to his credit [...].'[3]

Sankrityayan appears to those who have studied and written about him in a number of contradictory guises:

> Sāṅkr̥tyāyan, Rāhul (Kedārnāth Pāṇḍe, alias Baba Rāmodar Dās) (1893–1963) Occupation: Scholar, Political activist.
>
> (Orsini 2010: 427–8)

> I know only one Rahula and he is a very delightful and learned scholar who is a Buddhist monk and knows any number of out-of-the-way languages.
>
> (Jawaharlal Nehru, cited in S. Gandhi 2004: 75–6)

> He changed his name and orthodox Sanatani Hindu belief to Baba Ram Udar Das, a wandering mendicant, and to Arya Samaj. Not satisfied with the Vedic dogmatism of Arya Samaj, he took to yellow robe and became a regular Buddhist *bhikkhu* (monk) after his tours to Nepal and Sri Lanka. [...] Marxism attracted him to such an extent, that after his journey to Soviet Russia, in 1935, he turned into a socialist zealot.
>
> (Machwe 1978: 9)

> Besides as a mahāpaṇḍit, Rahul was also known in Nepal as a dogmatic communist leader.[4]
>
> (Janaklāl Śarmā, cited in Pokhrel and Dhakāl 2060 VS: 69)

[3] Some of his works were posthumously published by his wife Kamala Sankrityayan. These are not included in this reckoning.

[4] 'नेपालमा राहुलको नाम महापण्डितबाहेक कट्टर साम्यवादी नेताका रूपमा पनि लिइन्थ्यो।' (The translations of all foreign language passages into English appearing herein are mine, unless otherwise noted.)

> The influence of Marxist school was quite strong on Hindi novel, the most noted exponents being Yashpal (1903–76) and Rahul Sankrityayan (1893–1963).
>
> (Das 1995: 284)

As a sadhu, Sankrityayan donned a long black *alphī* (tunic worn by ascetics); as an Arya Samajist, a white dhoti and kurtā; as a Buddhist, a yellow or maroon robe; as a peasant leader, a khaki shirt and shorts; or as a communist, a formal Indian dress. Some persons have been drawn to one or the other of Sankrityayan's identities, as the statements above by Jawaharlal Nehru, Janaklāl Śarmā, Francesca Orsini, and Sisir Kumar Das indicate. Others, however, like Prabhakar Machwe, focus not on any one persona but on the full palette of personas. As Urmileś notes (1994: 7): 'He resembles an Indian image of the renowned thinker Antonio Gramsci's idea of an "organic intellectual".'[5]

Who was Sankrityayan? Was he at once everything mentioned above, or, at different times, a scholar, political activist, Buddhist monk, and communist? What lay behind these multiple identities?[6] Was there any link between them? These queries were the initial motivation for this study, which started out with the aim of finding crucial motives for the emergence of Sankrityayan's diverse masks.

5 'प्रख्यात विचारक अन्तोनियो ग्राम्शी की "आर्गेनिक इंटेलेक्चुअल" की धारणा के वे भारतीय प्रतीक लगते हैं।'

6 The word 'identity' in this study is not used in accordance with any specific personality theory but rather simply with the meaning supplied by the Oxford Dictionary (accessed online on 7 December 2011 at http://www.oed.com/view/Entry/91004?redirectedFrom=identity#eid): 'Who or what a person or thing is; a distinct impression of a single person or thing presented to or perceived by others; a set of characteristics or a description that distinguishes a person or thing from others.' *Vyaktitva* is the corresponding word used by Hindi-speaking scholars. For instance, A. Bhaṭṭācārya (2005) with reference to Sankrityayan employs the term *vyaktitvāntaraṇ* (changes in identity), and V. Siṃh (1995) *navjāgraṇkālīn vyaktitva* (Renaissance personality).

SANKRITYAYAN STUDIES AND A FORMULATION OF THE PROBLEM

Sankrityayan's life and work have been viewed from various perspectives. Extensive studies[7] have been published on his literary works. To date, twenty-six doctoral dissertations on him and his literary output have been written in India and abroad. A review of each dissertation was not possible during my own research. However, I was able to read a select number and to collect information about almost all of them.[8] Twenty-three of them are devoted to Sankrityayan's literary writings, and mainly concentrate on his contribution to different fields in the Hindi idiom. Another two (Pāṇḍeya 2011 and Urmileś 1978–80[9]) are concerned with his involvement in the Bihar peasant movement and non-cooperation. One dissertation (A. Bhaṭṭācarya 2005) deals with Sankrityayan's vyaktitvāntaraṇ.

Not only Sankrityayan's works but also his life are no longer quite the enigma they once were. From being an author of numerous biographies in the first half of the 20th century in India, Sankrityayan

7 The following list represents the major work published to date:

1. Biographies: Prabhakar Balvant Machwe, *Rahul Sankrityayan* (New Delhi: Sahitya Akademi, 1978); Guṇākar Mule, *Mahāpaṇḍit Rāhul Sāṅkr̥tyāyan: jīvnī aur kr̥titva* (New Delhi: National Book Trust, 1998); Viṣṇu Candra Śarmā, *Samaya sāmyavādī* (New Delhi: Vani Prakashan, 2002).
2. Literary Studies: Vīrendra Siṃh, *Mahāpaṇdit Rāhul samagra mūlyaṅkan* (Jayapur: Panchashil Prakashan, 1995); Madan Rāy, *Rāhul ke kathā-sāhitya kā sāmājik sandarbh* (New Delhi: Radhakrishna Prakashan, 1997); Kaśmīrī Lāl, *Rāhul Sāṅkr̥tyāyan kā kathā sāhitya* (Ludhiyana: Unistar, 2006; Abhijīt Bhaṭṭācārya, *Mahāpaṇdit Rāhul Sāṅkr̥tyāyan ke vyaktitvāntaraṇ kī prakriyā* (Calcutta: Anand Prakashan, 2005); Urmileś, *Rāhul Sāṅkr̥tyāyan: sr̥jan aur saṅgharṣ* (New Delhi: Vani Prakashan, 1994); Harerām Pāṇḍeya, *Rāhul Sāṅkr̥tyāyan: bhārtīya mukti āndolan ke apratim yoddhā* (Delhi: Mekhala Prakashan, 2011); Hildegard Fischer, *General Simha: Interpretation und Ubersetzung Eines Historischen Romans von Rāhul Sāṅkr̥tyāyan* (Wiesbaden: Harrassowitz, 1990).

8 See Appendix 5 for details of the dissertations.

9 Unpublished dissertation.

has himself now become a subject of choice for biographers and researchers in the late 20th and early 21st centuries. He has also earned a niche for himself in school and university curricula. Hindi school textbooks in India have included a chapter containing a short biographical sketch of him,[10] while at the university level he has become a standard part of the syllabus for students of Hindi literature. In addition, numerous memoirs and articles have been published in newspapers, journals, and books.

Academic studies of Sankrityayan's life have been coming out regularly for a long time now. These biographies are necessarily based mainly on their subject's own autobiography, *Merī jīvan yātrā* (*MJY*),[11] as their primary source, a huge work with such an inexhaustible fund of information that students of Sankrityayan studies can easily select a specific period or strand of narrative from it to focus on. For instance, Ratna Sundar Śākya (1992 and 2046 VS) and Bhikṣu Sudarśan (2022 VS) have confined their attention to Sankrityayan's Nepal and Tibet journeys and his activities relating to Buddhism. Guṇākar Mule (1998: 1–3) follows his quest for knowledge as a ghumakkaṛ-rāj and as a virtual *svayaṃbhū* (self-arisen) scholar (Mule: 1993). Of those who have attempted complete biographies of Sankrityayan, Prabhakar Machwe (1978) offers a very compact one, while also briefly analysing his scholarly writings and contributions to literature. Viṣṇu Candra Śarmā (2002) has written a comparatively comprehensive biography in five sections: Sankrityayan's early life of imbibing *sipāhī saṃskṛti* (soldierly culture) under the guardianship of his grandfather, an army man; his recourse to the Arya Samaj and Buddhism to build up his personality—*mānav vikās kā tal* (the basis of human development); the period of his social commitment to *kisān rājnīti* (peasant politics);

[10] A short biographical sketch of Sankrityayan and a portion of *MJY-2*, which describes his first visit to Tibet via Nepal, have been selected as a course text by the Central Board of Secondary Education (CBSE) for the class 9 Hindi curriculum: Nareś Yādav, *Kṣitij: Bhāg 1*, 3rd ed. (New Delhi: National Council of Educational Research and Training, 2009), pp. 23–9.

[11] Sankrityayan's autobiography is titled *Merī jīvan yātrā* (henceforth *MJY*). Numbers after the abbreviation will refer to its different parts. *JY-6* will denote the last part of *MJY* written by Sankrityayan's wife. For details of the writing and publishing of this work, see sub-section 'The Structure of *MJY*' in Chapter 1.

extending his *kāryakṣetra* (zone of activity) to Tibet; and finally *krānti* (revolution), the longest section, rounding out his life. Less ambitious but still informative are the biographical sketches by R.P. Chaturvedi (2010) and Diwan C. Ahir (1993), portraying Sankrityayan's personality, with an emphasis on his literary writings and service to Buddhism.

Many studies survey Sankrityayan's total output in Hindi (for instance, Lāl [2006]; Pāṇḍeya [2011]; Rāy [1997]; V. Siṃh [1995]; and Urmileś [1994]). Others consider individual works or individual themes; Sanjay Srivastava (2005: 391), for example, explores three works[12] for their treatment of the themes of 'home', 'belonging', and 'attachment', and also the space marked out for itself by the theme of *ghumakkaṛī* (wandering) throughout Sankrityayan's writings. Similarly, Hildegard Fischer (1990) has interpreted his historical novel *Siṃh senāpati* and translated it into German.

Sankrityayan has also been the subject of a more hands-on kind of research. Kazuo Kano travelled to Tibet in 2007[13] to retrace Sankrityayan's footsteps (as described in *MJY*) and did a comparative study (of monasteries, libraries, routes, and so on) between the time of Sankrityayan's and his own journey. An exhibition of photographs taken during that visit was organized at the University of Vienna.[14]

There are other works in progress on Sankrityayan. In Sweden, Mirja Juntunen is currently working on a research project titled 'The Buddhist-Modernist Thinker Rahul Sankrityayan and His Influence on Contemporary Indian Writing', focusing on ancient Indian Buddhist societies and the similarity they bear to primitive communist societies as described in Sankrityayan's historical novels. Similarly, Birgit Kellner has also started a project of translating the section in *MJY*-2, devoted to the Tibet visits, into German.[15] In Belgium, Jacques Huynen is currently translating Sankrityayan's book *Ghumakkaṛ śāstra* into French.[16]

12 *Ghumakkaṛ śāstra*, *Volgā se Gaṅgā*, and *Madhya Eśiyā kā itihās*.

13 Personal communication, Vienna, December 2007.

14 During a symposium titled 'The Peregrinations of Mahāpaṇḍita Rāhula Sāṅkṛtyāyana (1893–1963): Buddhist Scholar, Political Activist, Writer', 14–15 December 2007.

15 Email correspondence, 11 July 2012.

16 Email correspondence, 8 May 2012.

The major interest of both completed and ongoing research in Sankrityayan studies has been his work in the literary field. His communist and indeed Marxist leanings, the historical and social aspects of his fiction, his travel literature, and his historical writings have been studied extensively. His life, too, has attracted great interest among scholars. His most popular books have already been (and are still being) translated into other languages. A number of scholars have retraced Sankrityayan's visits to Tibet. What has yet to be written, though, is a detailed study of his multifaceted life in the historical context of the Indian subcontinent during his own time. Against this backdrop, then, the present study, rather than rehearsing Sankrityayan's literary or political attainments once again, will analyse through his writings his development of separate identities throughout the different stages of his life and within the historical context of 20th-century India.

For all the extensive work done in Sankrityayan studies, the simple query about a possible single track that the subject may have been following throughout his life as the underlying cause behind the multiplicity, ambivalence, and turning points in it has yet to be answered. The study of Sankrityayan's multiple identities by Abhijīt Bhaṭṭācārya (2005) seriously addresses the necessity of studying his multifaceted personality. He advances a new explanation for Sankrityayan's multiple identities. He treats Sankrityayan's life as a journey—a journey that involved stopping and shifting directions at four different *paṛāv*s (halts).[17]

I would argue that paṛāv in the sense of a stopping place or camping ground occupied for a limited time before being abandoned for good as the next stage of the journey beckons is an unsuitable metaphor in this case. Sankrityayan's life does not really divide neatly into four different paṛāvs that he subsequently never looked back on. Rather, his ideas and ideals overlapped, and in many cases reflected a sense of ambivalence.[18]

[17] Sankrityayan's life would seem to fall into a well-ordered chronology, based on his affiliation to successive religious or political organizations, during which he figured as a sanātanī, *ārya samājī*, *tripiṭakācārya* (master of the Tripitaka) and *sāmyavādi* (communist), corresponding to the four paṛāvs.

[18] See section 'Ambivalence in the Interstices between the Arya Samaj, Buddhism, and Communism' in Chapter 3 of this volume.

Even before Bhaṭṭācārya, Satyavrat Sinha had similarly traced Sankrityayan's *dhārmik vikās kā kram* (stages of religious development) as being 'from *sanātan dharm* to Arya Samaj, from Arya Samaj to Buddhism, from Buddhism to *mānav dharm*' (cited in R. Tivārī 2007: 623; italics mine). *Mānavdharm* (humanism) may here be taken to refer to communism, which Sankrityayan embraced after Buddhism. During the corresponding period, he consequently looked upon religion as one main obstacle to development and social harmony. To say, then, that the different phases of Sankrityayan's life amount to his religious development is somewhat inexact. To be sure, as I shall argue, religion does play a part in the turnings[19] in Sankrityayan's life, but it was not the only major factor.

Madan Rāy, another scholar of Sankrityayan studies, writes in his study of the latter's fictional literature. Rāy here fails to mention the Arya Samaj or Buddhism in the making of Rahul Sankrityayan, which raises the question: Were these two less important influences on Sankrityayan's vyaktitva?

R.S. Sharma (2009: 283) has posited rationalism as the moulding force behind Sankrityayan's multifaceted personality: 'Rahul's thirst for knowledge was insatiable and his rationalism firm. Rationalism came to him through the process of constant questioning. This led to his conversion to Arya Samaj following Buddhism and finally to Marxism. The intellectual making of Rahul could be a subject for in-depth investigation.' He further states (2009: 286): 'Rahul was completely dedicated to the cause of rationalism and socialism on which he did not make any compromise.' According to him, Sankrityayan's adaptation to the life of a sadhu, his admission to a school run by the Arya Samaj, his stay at Vidyālaṅkāra Pariveṇa, a vihara in Sri Lanka, his travels to Tibet, and the rest were all the result of a quest for knowledge and a coherent form in which to pack it, and while one can hardly argue with this, one may question whether it gets to the bottom of the matter. By themselves, rationalism or dedication to select causes would not seem to effectively account for the

[19] Cf. Mandelbaum's (1973) theoretical comments concerning the study of life history and, in particular, the significance of 'turnings' for it; see note 46 of this chapter.

making of Rahul Sankrityayan. In my opinion, studying Sankrityayan within the narrow terms of his own personal impulses does not yield the key to his life story. He needs to be studied more carefully within the historical, social, and political context of his period.

As noted above, Vīrendra Siṃh (1995: 1–2), a scholar of Hindi literature, has called Sankrityayan a *navjāgraṇkāl* (renaissance) personality. A renaissance period in his words is 'a period of new awareness and the churning up of thought, and secondly a period of reforms and political movements meant to bring about change in social, economic, and political arenas'. It is such a period in Indian history that, in his opinion, formed Sankrityayan's vyaktitva. Concerning it he states (1995: 2) that 'one other main characteristic of [this] renaissance period is its explanation of Indian history and myth, which motivated Sankrityayan to approach Indian history and the history of Central Asia'.

Although Siṃh properly terms Sankrityayan a Renaissance personality, his work does not clearly define how that period led to the development of Sankrityayan's multiple identities. Is there a thread running through Sankrityayan's life? Or was he just randomly testing out new values to replace old ones with? This study will take its starting point from Siṃh's insight that Sankrityayan's personality was indeed a product of the renaissance period in Indian history, but will attempt to delve into the details of just how exactly it managed to fashion his multiple identities. It will observe Sankrityayan's life and work critically, then, within the wider frame of the Indian subcontinent during the first half of the 20th century.

Among studies to date, Sankrityayan has generally been evaluated merely as a writer, the reasons for the mutability of his personality—his transformed identities—having been shunted aside. In this study the attempt has been made to view Rahul Sankrityayan as he passes through the struggle of a life of changed identities and relating this to his status as a nationalist.

The time in which Sankrityayan flourished roughly corresponded with the age of nationalism in India, namely the late colonial and early post-independence period. Nationalism as such, however, did not die out once independence was achieved, since other issues immediately arose involving the concrete forms the nation would take, not least being the issue of official languages. Nationalism, then, is a pervasive feature of the period, and one that at the very least serves as an ever-present landmark, as it were, providing a good point of orientation for such research as the present study. Indeed, in attempting to sound the depths of Sankrityayan's genius and multifaceted life, we may find that it harbours insights into and even reasons for them, and may account for links between those different identities. With the objective of this study in mind, it will first be necessary to delineate Sankrityayan's conception of nationhood by placing him within the context of his own 20th-century India.

SANKRITYAYAN IN THE AGE OF INDIAN NATIONALISM

Studies of recent Indian history tend to conclude that the rise of nationalism was inevitable in the colonial period. No less a person than Jawaharlal Nehru wrote that his visceral emotional attitude towards India during his lifetime was one of nationalistic pride—something people inhaled with every breath. If that is true, then one may argue, as this study will do, that Sankrityayan's nationalist sentiments were a form of consciousness acquired from the colonial Indian context itself. In the heyday of nationalism in India—in the years after 1915—it was natural for politically conscious persons like Nehru or Sankrityayan to be nationalists; and both have said as much.[20] To quote Nehru:

> My reaction to India thus was often an emotional one, conditioned and limited in many ways. It took the form of nationalism. In the case of many people the conditioning and limiting factors are absent. But nationalism was and is inevitable in the India of my day; it is a natural and healthy growth. For any subject country national freedom must be the first and dominant urge; for India, with her intense sense of individuality and a past heritage, it was doubly so. (Nehru 1996: 52)

Indian nationalism developed with a sense of cultural superiority. It was believed that India could modernize itself while at the same time retaining its cultural identity. The rise of nationalism in India was coupled with the rise of anti-British sentiment. The people of India, speaking different languages, professing different creeds,

[20] For Sankrityayan's statement, see Chapter 2.

and belonging to different castes and classes, would slowly come together to fight for the sovereignty of their country. Depicting the changes during the British Raj in India, A.R. Desai (1954: xxiii–xxiv) writes:

> The advanced British nation, for its own purpose, radically changed the economic structure of the Indian society, established a centralized state, and introduced modern education, modern means of communications, and other institutions. This resulted in the growth of new social classes and the unleashing of new social forces [...] [T]hese social forces by their very nature came into conflict with British Imperialism and became the basis of and provided motive power for the rise and development of Indian nationalism.

Indian nationalism developed as a result of the interaction between the colonizer and the colonized—actions followed by reactions under a rising tide of dissatisfaction with the oppressive British rule. From the very beginning, nationalist sentiment was viewed by the Indian elite as a prerequisite for gaining independence and restoring national pride. Foreshadowing the national democratic awakening were many social reform–minded religious organizations that were established during the period—for example, the Brahmo Samaj, Prarthana Samaj, Arya Samaj, Ram Krishna Mission, and Theosophical Society. Concerning them Desai (1954: 247) notes: 'These movements represented attempts to revise the old religion in the spirit of the new principles of nationalism and democracy which were the conditions for the development of the new society.'

The Brahmo Samaj[21] and Arya Samaj, the two most prominent Hindu social reformist organizations, were indeed the breeding ground of Indian nationalism. Henrik Berglund has called their stance 'proto-Hindu nationalism' (2004: 62): 'The process started already in the late 19th century, much related to the development of Arya Samaj and the activities of its individual members. The patriotic, nationalist,

[21] Kopf (1979: xxi) highlights the most important dates in the chronology of the Brahmo Samaj:

1823 Established as Calcutta Unitarian Committee

1828 Ram Mohan Roy founds the Brahmo Sabha

1843 Birth of Brahmo Samaj when Debendranath Tagore institutionalizes Ram Mohan Roy's ideology of Hindu reform

and militant elements were very much present in the ideology of the organization, to some extent in the form of the expressed intolerance against other religions, especially Islam. Arya Samaj was not a political party, but its ideological content was used for political purposes.' The next Hindu revivalist after Ram Mohan Roy (1772–1833) and Swami Dayananda Saraswati (1824–83, founder of the Arya Samaj) was Swami Vivekananda (1863–1902, founder of the Rama Krishna Mission), who followed in the footsteps of his illustrious preceptor Ramakrishna (1834–86) by emphasizing the oneness of all mankind and the essential unity of all religions, including Christianity and Islam.

According to Ācārya Narendra Dev (2010: 11), in the beginning the Indian National Congress (INC) was not established with a purely political aim either. It had as an objective every kind of reform. In 1885, 'a number of Indian lawyers and professionals formed the Indian National Congress in its first session, held in Bombay in the presidency of Womesh Chandra Bonnerji' (Aiyar and Bhandare 1945: 9). Its members, of various religions, had come from all parts of India. They debated political and economic reforms, the future of India, and ways for Indians to achieve equal status with the British. One year later, in 1886, Dadabhai Naoroji, a founding member of the INC, expressed the opinion that Congress should be a political organization unconcerned with controversial social questions (Ācārya Narendra Dev 2010: 11).

The organizations established during this period were of two kinds. Some took the form of political organizations (for example, the INC), while others remained under the banner of social and religious reform (such as the Brahmo Samaj and Arya Samaj). However, some members of these socio-religious organizations did become involved in political activities on the side. This was particularly true in the case of the Arya Samaj.

Slowly, both the social and political movements started assuming communal forms, giving Muslims cause to believe that the Congress was a Hindu organization aiming for Hindu rule. In 1906, in reaction, several Muslim leaders formed the All-India Muslim League. To be sure, the INC, the major political party of 20th-century India, was from the start mainly dominated by Hindus. However, those with the most fervent Hindu nationalist sentiments eventually separated from it. In 1915 the All-India Hindu Sabha[22] was formed specifically with the purpose of protecting the Hindu community. By 1937 it had become a full-fledged political party in thrall to the concept of Hindutva being propagated by V.D. Savarkar (1883–1966). Indians, in search of a collective self-identity, cast their glances back on the glories of history, religious doctrine and myth, and literary narratives, hoping to find symbolic ideas or icons representative of a common culture. Among Hindus, this was only bound to increase dissatisfaction with the Muslim invasion of India. Their cultural heroes came out of the Vedas, the epics (most prominently the Ramayana and the Mahabharata, portraying respectively Rama and Krishna), and other sacred texts, including the more clearly historical texts centring on the human figure of the Buddha. A multitude of other personalities down through history stood as beacons in their fields of endeavour (such as literature, history, religion, politics, and social reform): for example, Kalidas, Shankaracharya, Chatrapati Shivaji, Swami Dayananda, Bal Gangadhar Tilak, Gandhi, and Nehru. All became national heroes in 19th- and 20th-century India. People readily felt a sense of pride at being citizens in a land where such figures had been born, lived, and taught.

Another element, language, became an instrumental factor in Indian nationalism. Linguistically many modern Indian languages are strongly linked to Sanskrit; therefore the prestige of Sanskrit also increased. Persian and its literature too had influenced vernacular literature, but its absence from the ancient past of Indian history and the partition it formed between Hindus and Muslims (as reflected in Hindi and Urdu vocabulary) disqualified it as a rallying point for all. Hindi became the language of Hindus, and Urdu of Muslims (C.R. King 1995).

The heritage of literary Sanskrit united the south and north of India, and both could be proud of the canon of Sanskrit, Pali, and the other ancient Indian literary vehicles. The glorious past served as the inspiration of the present, even as the European Renaissance had looked back upon Greece and Rome. The great men of history

[22] It re-christened itself as the All-India Hindu Mahasabha (Akhil Bhārtīya Hindū Mahāsabhā) in 1921 (Bapu 2013: 21).

provided the footsteps to follow in. Such cultural nationalism resonated not only in India, but also in Sri Lanka and Nepal, given their common culture based on Buddhism and Hinduism. (The education and ordination of Indian and Nepalese Buddhist monks in Sri Lanka, the interest of Sri Lankan Buddhists in 'rebuilding Buddhism'[23] in India and Nepal, and the demand to hand over the Maha Bodhi Temple to Buddhists are good examples.[24]) However, for all that India was an important melting pot, cultural differences between Hindus and Muslims divided it internally.

A hunger developed all over the country for cultivating what was thought to be the peculiar Indian identity. In the words of Vasudha Dalmia (1997: 27): 'The burning issue of the day was the establishment and maintenance of an indigenous cultural identity, whether in matters of food, clothing or language.' It was not only politicians; the impact of nationalism was also felt keenly by intellectuals of 19th- and 20th-century India. This search for selfhood and the re-interpretation of Indianness has been a major focus of scholarly interest. For instance, Dalmia's cited work concentrates on Bharatendu Harishchandra (1850–85) and his activities in the field of Hindi language and literature, analysing the confluence of nationalism and Hinduization in Banaras (present Varanasi) during the 19th century. Francesca Orsini (2010) has showed how the press, education and schools, literature, associations, and political activities contributed to redefining Hindi as a symbol of nationalism in the early 20th century. Similarly, Shobna Nijhawan (2012) has analysed the role of Hindi-language women's periodicals in shaping nationalist–feminist thought in early 20th-century India. Lata Singh (2012), concentrating her studies in Bihar, has demonstrated how nationalism became a call to save the culture of the nation (its religion, traditions, moral values, and so on) during the non-cooperation movement. Ananya Vajpeyi (2012) has focused on five important Indian figures (Mahatma Gandhi, Rabindranath Tagore, Abanindranath Tagore, Jawaharlal Nehru, and B.R. Ambedkar), describing how each of them turned to classical Indian texts to recover an original sense of Indian selfhood.

[23] Levine and Gellner's 2008 study is devoted to this topic.

[24] For details, see Chapter 3.

Against this background, a study of the nationalist sentiments of another prominent Indian intellectual, Rahul Sankrityayan, and the impact of that age on his multifaceted life is worth adding to the list.

Rahul Sankrityayan developed his nationalist sentiments through his involvement with the Arya Samaj and through his other socio-religious activities within the wider political and cultural framework of 20th-century India. The present study, however, will attempt to define Sankrityayan as a nationalist sui generis, as someone who distanced himself from the ordinary trends of his time. For though he was a Buddhist and an Arya Samajist, his basic motives were not religious, nor were they internationalist, even though he became a communist. The political, economic, and social conditions of India in the first half of the 20th century formed the nationalist sentiments in Sankrityayan, but he did not blindly follow the whims of his age; rather, he developed in ways of his own. He supported Hindi and imagined it as one day becoming the national language of India, but this was not because he was a Hindu. He developed into what can only be called an irreligious person, but he still respected everything Indian. Indian cultural identity was indeed his major concern. Having felt the impact of an intensely religious form of nationalism (Arya Samaj) on him, Sankrityayan turned towards Buddhism. In the latter's egalitarianism he recognized in turn similarities with communism and he became a communist. From there he passed on to Hindi nationalism.[25]

The primary focus of this study is the period between 1915 and 1961, that is, between Sankrityayan's admission to an Arya Samaj school and the year he lost his memory. The former year, it is safe to say, was when nationalist sentiment first took root in him, while the latter was unambiguously the end of his creative life, at which time Hindi nationalists were still devoting themselves to the spread of Hindi and its adoption as the sole official language after India's independence in 1947. History had given Hindi fifteen years to prove itself as a viable choice for being crowned as India's national language. Sankrityayan had been an active campaigner in this struggle. As things turned out, the Official Language Act was passed on 10 May 1963, recognizing Hindi as an official language, but with English as an 'associate

[25] To borrow a term from Rai (2007), but not in a negative sense.

additional official language'. Hindi nationalists continued to be committed to their cause up to the very end and the passage of the act. For the man who forms the subject of this study, though, the age of nationalism had ended in 1961. Sankrityayan died on 14 April 1963, shortly before the act came into force.

SANKRITYAYAN'S CONCEPTION OF A NATION

> भारत जैसी मातृभूमि पाकर कौन अभिमान नहीं करेगा? यहाँ हजारों चीजें हैं जिन पर अभिमान होना ही चाहिए।
>
> Who cannot but be proud in having a *mātṛbhūmi* (motherland) like India? There are thousands of reasons why one ought to be proud. (Sankrityayan 2004b: 86)

Nationalism has long been a subject that scholars have studied and tried to define.[26] On the basis of such studies, we have gained a rough understanding of how nationalist sentiment makes persons and groups bond around an image of shared nationhood and state, for which they join movements, agitate, and even sacrifice their lives. Nationalism is virtually omnipresent, if often only latently so, in any society. It is an ingrained feature of modern human life, whether in specifically political or more broadly cultural manifestations (for example, language, religion, and ethnicity). It offers itself as a satisfying ideological framework within which to view, understand, and partition the surrounding world, the result inevitably being that 'we' feel superior to 'them'.

It is against the backdrop of the previous section—which noted that language and religion, along with other areas of culture, have been

[26] Among the most notable contributions are: Anderson (2006); Billig (1999); Chatterjee (2011a and 2011b); E. Gellner (1987); Hobsbawm (1990); Hutchinson (1987a, 1987b, and 1999); Jaffrelot (1999 and 2007); Kohn (1948); Renan (1939 [1882]); Shafer (1955 and 1974); Smith (1975, 1998, and 2010); and van der Veer (1994). This study will not enter into the academic discourse relating to nationalism. It will seek neither to describe nor explain how nationalism arose and has developed to date, nor will it in particular consider the various explanations of anti-colonial nationalism in India and how it played out.

important driving forces of nationalism in India—that I now set off to analyse Sankrityayan's own conception of nationhood. I shall tap mainly into the works of Anthony D. Smith, Clifford Geertz, John Hutchinson, and Benedict Anderson, whose seminal theorizing on nationalism would seem to have the greatest relevance to the present study. I have pointed out the importance, for understanding Sankrityayan's multiple identities, of cultural fixtures that caused the major turnings in his life. These are: the Arya Samaj, Buddhism, communism, and the Hindi language. What was it about them that created emotional legitimacy for him? This was the question that I hoped would lead to a better understanding of his various life pursuits, including his voluminous writing, his becoming an Arya Samajist, a Buddhist, a communist, his visits to Tibet, and his relationship with Nepal.

According to Smith (1975: 26), nationalist sentiment is '[a] consciousness of belonging to a nation and feeling of solidarity with its members; also aspirations for the nation's strength, liberty and unity', while nationalism is '[a]n ideological movement for the attainment and maintenance of autonomy and individuality for a social group, some of whose members conceive it to constitute an actual or potential nation'. To translate this into Sankrityayan's (2004b: 86) terminology, nationalist sentiment could be called *mātr̥bhūmi kī sugandh* (the motherland's aroma), which was the source of his own *abhimān* (pride) in being an Indian. It was this general sentiment, I argue, that guided Sankrityayan throughout the various endeavours of his life. It stood for *hazārõ cīzẽ* (thousands of [individual] reasons) why Indians could be proud of their country. He did not draw up a separate list of those reasons, but it is clear what some of them were. Identifying them will be the concern of this study further below.

Among the possible different meanings of nationalism, Smith (2010: 6–7) highlights that of a socio-political movement. Nationalism in this sense is directed towards the gestation and representation of a culture. Prominent activities of such a movement include the rediscovery of national history and the cultivation or revival of vernacular languages (through such disciplines as philology and lexicography), literature, and arts and crafts (including native dance and folk songs). Such nationalist movements, then, do not take off with protest rallies or armed resistance but with the appearance of literary societies, historical research, music festivals, and cultural journals. Accordingly, the term 'nationalist sentiment' in this study will be taken in Sankrityayan's understanding of it as pride in a particular culture, and 'nationalism' as the deeds or activities inspired by that sentiment.

In the quest for a link between Sankrityayan's multiple identities, it was abhimān that I felt held the key to a solution. Guided by his pride in being an Indian, Sankrityayan plunged into various socio-political movements. It became even clearer to me that much of what he did in his life was guided by this emotion. He became an Arya Samajist because he believed that the Arya dharma enjoyed special authority in India, whose progress and unity was only possible through it. He became a political activist because the Arya Samaj sparked a desire for nation-building work in him. He visited Tibet to bring back lost artefacts of Indian heritage. He became a communist because its aims were comparable with the economic equality practised by Buddhism. He stood up for Hindi and Devanagari script because they represented the best linguistic means of unifying the Indian people and representing their identity. He himself wrote extensively in Hindi in order to sow his ideas among the general public. In sum, it can be argued that it was his nationalist sentiment that guided him towards socio-political movements.

Anderson (2006: 6) defines the nation as a socio-culturally constructed field in his pioneering work, *Imagined Communities: Reflections on the Origin and Spread of Nationalism*: '[I]t is an imagined political community and imagined as both inherently limited and sovereign. It is imagined because the members of even the smallest nation will never know most of their fellow-members, meet them, or even hear of them, yet in the minds of each lives the image of their communion.' In other words, the agent of this imagined construction, the nation, is its own people acting as members of a larger community that none of them knows in full. The process involves defining borders with external groups of peoples, in part by attempting to create a national identity as a unifying bulwark within. Anderson stresses that this sense of national coherence is achieved through genuine communal interaction and shared cultural representations of nationality.

Sankrityayan's notion of community was born and bred in the Arya Samaj. It was there that anti-British sentiments first sprouted up in him, eventually leading him to become a *garam rāṣṭrīyatāvādī* (fervent nationalist). During that time, his nationalist sentiment was informed wholly by the Vedic religion propagated by the Arya Samaj, to the point where he was even ready to sacrifice his life if need be. The Arya Samaj, in short, represented a new light for Sankrityayan (see Chapter 2).

Sankrityayan's ideas broadened during his participation in politics between 1921 and 1927. After leaving the Arya Samaj, he was exposed to a host of new social and political experiences, the most outstanding being the joint demonstration of Hindus and Muslims against the Rowlatt Bills on 6 April 1919 in Lahore and the start of the satyagraha campaign. All this served to widen the confines of the narrow Vedic religious community he had earlier imagined as his ideal. Still later, his introduction to Buddhism demolished for him whatever boundaries were left among religions, and he started regarding religion as an artificial problem blocking the unity of Indians.

The nation as conceived by Sankrityayan was a society that presented a completely secular and casteless face, with equal rights for every caste and each gender (here strains of Marxism are already apparent). He was not happy with the use of the word 'Hindu' in a restricted sense as a synonym of Bhrāhmaṇśāhī (Brahmanism) to indicate a particular religion and its culture. 'Hindu', in his opinion, was a name that could be applied to the entire country and its thousands of years of culture. It applied in particular, for example, to the Buddha as a great thinker and representative of India, whose influence has served to promote Indian culture, art, literature, and philosophy around the world. The attraction Buddhism had for him, then, was due not to its being a religion but to its being a source of Indian pride (see Chapter 3).

His broader understanding of a Hindu nation has remained a significant definition of bhārtīyatā, which was the most important touchstone of true nationalism for Sankrityayan. He imagined a nation that satisfied the conditions it imposed as consisting of people from every religion, be it Islam, Hinduism, Jainism, Christianity, or Buddhism. He accepted, that is, even religions that were unknown to ancient Indian history (such as Islam and Christianity) as parts of his nation, but on condition that they manifest an Indian character. He expected that Islam for one could be Indianized. Addressing the 35th Akhil Bhārtīya Hindī Sāhitya Sammelan (All-India Congress on Hindi Literature) in 1947, he said:[27]

[27] For details about this speech, see Chapter 4.

इस्लाम को भारतीय बनना चाहिए

Islam should become Indian. (Sankrityayan 2004d: 31)

What he meant by becoming Indian in concrete terms was that followers of non-native Indian religions would accept the use of a national language, dress, cuisine, and literature, and, above all, a shared sense of *bhārat kā gaurav pūrṇ itihās* (India's glorious history). Bhārtīyatā would be the cultural force that united the adherents of India's different religions.[28]

Sankrityayan proposed the novel concept of *ek jātīyatā* (single cultural identity) for all of India. This involved widening and liberalizing the conventional meaning of *jāti*, that of 'a common cultural identity',[29] so as to encompass the whole citizenry within one cultural community. Throughout his lifetime, jāti[30] generally referred to common religious and linguistic communities, whereas his new conception of it dropped all religious and linguistic criteria, leaving in their place pride in Indian history, its ethos, and its civilization (including its languages and the like).

SANKRITYAYAN AND THE PRINTED WORD IN HINDI

Benedict Anderson (2006: 36) has argued that the most important factor in modern times in making people think of themselves as an 'imagined community' in profoundly new ways has been 'print-capitalism'. He gives the example (2006: 75) of 'professional intellectuals' in 19th-century Europe, whose energetic activities and widely disseminated views shaped nationalism on that continent. '[L]exicographers, philologists, grammarians, folklorists, publicists and composers' found a ready outlet for their products in the silent bazaar of a print market that served an avid consuming public.

[28] The examples of Samual Aijak (a Christian Indian) and Mahmud (a Muslim), cited by Sankrityayan, are treated in Chapter 4.

[29] Orsini (2010: 5).

[30] See Orsini (2010) and Chalmers (2003) for detailed discussions of jāti. Orsini focuses on a cultural community of Hindi-speaking Hindus, while Chalmers turns his attention to a Nepali-speaking community that has been treated as a jāti.

Within the history of print-capitalism in North India,[31] printed material in Hindi occupies a special place. The Hindi print market laid a base upon which national consciousness in that region could easily intensify.[32] Indeed, printing presses were not established with merely commercial profit in mind, as Ulrike Stark argues:

> If not for material gains, what then motivated Indian pioneers of print? For many, editing a vernacular paper constituted an intellectual pursuit rather than a commercial activity. Journalism, in Sudhir Chandra's telling phrase, was a mission rather than a profitable business [...], inspired by a variety of reformist, religious, educational, social, and political concerns. [...] To the aspiring literate classes, print opened up new possibilities of cultural and political participation, of voicing individual and collective concerns. [...] Print afforded an opportunity to spread information, knowledge, and reformist thought on a supra-regional level. To many, it was a means of entering the fray of political, rationalist, and religious discourse and shaping public opinion, be it in the name of a particular community, class, sect, or the general public. (Stark 2007: 74)

To be sure, educational institutions and religious and social organizations also contributed profoundly to constructing a national consciousness, but the printed word played an even greater role. Even religious leaders, who traditionally relied on oral transmission, eventually recognized its power. For instance, during his tour of Punjab in the 1870s, Dayananda Saraswati observed missionaries busy

[31] See Stark (2007: Introduction and Chapter 1), for details of the early history of print material in Hindi and Urdu in the North-Western Provinces and Oudh. She closely analyses the period after 1857 following the emergence of printing presses—in her words, the 'Age of Commercialization', which saw the growth of print-capitalism in colonial India take off. Taking the Naval Kishore Press in Lucknow as the subject of a case study, she explores social, cultural, and material aspects of book production in 19th-century north India, and in particular the growth of an indigenous paper industry, which made books an affordable commodity for a large section of the urban literate class.

[32] See Orsini (2010) for the ways in which Hindi intellectuals and publishing industries reshaped group identities and provided the necessary historical discourse that allowed Hindi to become a hegemonic means of socially transmitting knowledge in northern India.

translating and selling cheap editions of the Bible in every regional language, but could not find a single printed copy of the Vedas; so he established his own press and started transcribing his lectures and teachings and having them printed (Stark 2007: 22–3). In the long run, the Arya Samaj supplemented the oral with the written method of transmission, and later established its own educational centres.

In describing different organizations' contributions to creating the standard-bearers of nationalistic consciousness, Orsini (2010: 7) notes: 'Institutions create actors. If, for example, the idea of writing as 'service' (*sevā*) to literature, to the people, and to the nation provided writers with a new identity, it was institutional spaces like the press, publishing houses, literary associations, and the education system that directed their activities and defined their social positions.' She further points out that the literary associations created scholar-activists; the press and print market, independent writers, journalists, and editors; and schools, nationalist-minded teachers. 'Such actors came to these institutional spaces bringing their own diverse background, attitudes, and beliefs' (Orsini 2010).

Sankrityayan assessed the power of print very perspicuously and stepped onto the Hindi-speaking public arena with a set of personal ideas, attitudes, and beliefs he was bent on purveying. As a scholar-activist, he was quite aware of the power his writing could exert—a mixture combining his idea of nationhood with the political philosophy of Marxism—when circulated through the Hindi print-bazaar. He consciously avoided adopting Marxism directly, modifying it instead to accord with his country's current situation. The political works he wrote were in very simple Hindi so as to make them easily understandable to the general public, most of whom had only completed a primary education.[33] And while Sankrityayan was not always happy with the high prices set for his books by the print capitalists, he considered writers helpless in such a situation, and so continued to write extensively in Hindi, utilizing the space the market provided to disseminate his views (see section titled 'Print: Progress, Pleasure, Profit, and Propagation' in Chapter 4 of this volume).

[33] *Bhāgo nahī̃ (duniyā ko) badlo* (*BNDB*) represents a particularly good example of rural Hindi.

As a Buddhist, Sankrityayan also produced works in Hindi with Buddhist themes (including his edited and collected scholarly output relating to Buddhism). His aim was to introduce the *mahāpuruṣ* (great man) Buddha, his teachings, Buddhist philosophy, and original Buddhist texts to the general public and scholars worldwide, as well as to Buddhists. His deeply rooted Indian pride led him to believe that the Buddhist concept of the *saṅgh* (monastic community of Buddhist monks) represented a communist-like political system. In his famous Buddhist–communist utopian novel, *Siṃh senāpati*, he imagined a primeval communist[34] *gaṇtantra* (republic) of 500 BC. Its decline from AD 350 to 400 and replacement by a monarchy is portrayed in another such novel, *Jay yaudheya*.

Hindi, in Sankrityayan's opinion, had earned the right to be the lingua franca of India, the language that would unify its citizens. To be sure, his imagined nation would have different languages, spoken in different states. However, the language of communication beyond state borders, the language which would facilitate all Indians' engaging in a similar act of imagining an imagined community among people of different mother tongues, would be Hindi.

Making Hindi the leading print language and Devanagari the common print script were key parts of Sankrityayan's nationalism. The print market he foresaw for his own books, moreover, would not be limited to India but would also cover Nepal.[35] Thus he suggested that not only the Urdu-speaking community adopt Devanagari, but also that Newars[36] in Nepal abandon their use of the *rañjanā* script for the Newari language. The purpose of such standardization, I argue, was a desire, not openly declared, to expand the reach of the print-bazaar (see Chapter 4).

The logic behind making Devanagari the national script was that if Hindi indeed became the lingua franca of India and every language were written in Devanagari, the Hindi print market would

34 'Utopie einer ursprunglichen urkommunistischen Gesellschaft' (Fischer 1990: 53).

35 For further consideration of Nepal's status in this regard, see the section below.

36 Newars are the dominant ethnic group of the Kathmandu Valley.

attract more readers throughout the country. Sankrityayan realized that the printed word was becoming more powerful than its spoken counterpart, no matter how big the crowd. As a *sāhitya sevī* (servant of literature), he regarded writing as his *dāyitva* (duty), not only in order to propagate Marxism, but also to prove the value of the Hindi-speaking community to the world. Moreover, from the very beginning of his writing career, he had understood that the print capitalists in northern India preferred Hindi as their language of choice, given the imposing number of its speakers. This is clear from his first book, *Bāisvī̃ sadī* (*BS*), originally in Sanskrit, which he translated into Hindi for publication (although he was equally well versed in Urdu). Das (1995: 82) notes that Sankrityayan wrote an article in Sanskrit on communism in 1922, but it must have been his first and last such writing on political matters in the language. Similarly, he started writing a book in Sanskrit as an introduction to Islam in 1922, but it too ended up being published in Hindi (in 1957, with some revision to the 1922 manuscript).

Sankrityayan accepted Hindi and Urdu as one language (jointly known as Hindustani) or two different dialects of the same language, each tapping into separate sources (respectively Sanskrit and Arabic or Persian) for their vocabulary. However, he would not have accepted Urdu (or Hindustani) as the national language, precisely because its sources lay beyond the boundary of his imagined nation (see section titled 'Hindi Nationalism' in Chapter 4 of this work). He cites the example of East Bengal (present-day Bangladesh), where Islam did not suffer discrimination, since the language spoken there was not Urdu but Sanskritic in its roots. Islam would suffer throughout India, he argued, were Hindi not to be made the national language (Sankrityayan 2004d: 32). Sankrityayan's strong support of the Hindi language, particularly through his scholarly activity, is the subject of 'Hindi: An Indian Voice' (Chapter 4).

Sankrityayan always enjoyed writing, and the proofreading process prior to publication only doubled his pleasure. He took delight in watching his ideas spread among the huge public masses and eventually seep over the political boundary into what he thought of as 'his nation', Nepal.

Nepal, where Hindi was widely understood, was indeed an important print-bazaar for Sankrityayan's books. Moreover, it was the birthplace of the Buddha and a country where Buddhism, an integral element of Indian culture in Sankrityayan's (1984: 134) opinion, continued to thrive after it had disappeared from India. It would also be the transit station that led on to Tibet in search of lost Indian heritage later in life. It was a land too, significantly, where few distinctions were made between Buddhism and Hinduism—where, for instance, the Buddha was worshipped as an incarnation of Vishnu.

One particularly promising paradigm for explaining Sankrityayan's nationalist sentiment and the activities he engaged in under its sway is what is known as 'cultural primordialism' (or simply 'primordialism'). Often favoured by historians, it regards culture as what most truly binds people together into larger communities. The most prominent primordialist is the anthropologist Clifford Geertz, who, along with his colleague Edward Shils, argues that each culture structures the beliefs and indeed the basic identity of all individuals born into it (cf. Joireman 2003: 24–5). According to Geertz (1973: 52–3): 'Culture has its impact on the concept of man [...] culture provides that link between what men are intrinsically capable of becoming and what they actually, one by one, in fact become. Becoming human is becoming individual, and we become individual under the guidance of cultural patterns. [...] To be human here is thus not to be Everyman; it is to be a particular kind of man.' Religious schools and socio-cultural associations are two examples of powerful transmitters of a society's culture for the individuals who come under their influence. How did Sankrityayan's multiple identities take shape on such cultural foundations? What was their impact on him? Geertz's paradigm may help us to understand that culture was indeed the most important factor in the formation of Sankrityayan's identities. The Arya Samaj's role in awakening Sankrityayan's nationalist sentiment, his relationship with the Vidyālaṅkāra Pariveṇa and Mahabodhi Sabha, and his Buddhist leanings can all be submitted to the explanatory power of this theory.

Primordialists regard language as something that faithfully encapsulates a culture. Language choice, according to Geertz (1973: 241) is 'a good, even a paradigmatic, example [of culture]'. It is an obvious marker of ethnic borders (sometimes religious like in the case of Hindi and Urdu) and is thus highly relevant to any study of nationalism. India is a country of many languages and much language overlap, but Hindi and English are the two official languages of the Government of India.[37] Before India's independence in 1947 and up to the Official Language Act of May 1963, the campaign to make Hindi the sole *rāṣtra bhāṣā* (national language) was fiercely conducted. Sankrityayan, whose mother tongue was Bhojpuri, nevertheless took up the cause for Hindi, arguing that it was the most common and emblematic link among Indians and that, unlike English, it had originated in their homeland. A similar sentiment underlies the appeal Buddhism had for him. Some scholars of Sankrityayan studies have contended that he was fundamentally a communist who, in searching for a similar Indian philosophy, found it in Buddhism. I shall argue the reverse: that he, a Buddhist, was searching for something similar to communism that could be applied to modern-day India. The crucial point for him was the fact that Buddhism, a religion practised in many other countries (some of which he would visit), was a product of his own homeland.

Anthony Smith (2010: 14), a 'soft primordialist',[38] believes that the key defining feature of any nation is that it has a distinct public culture. It is just such a public culture rooted in history that, as Sankrityayan's life history reveals, was his deepest aspiration for his nation. We have seen, concerning his literary pursuits, that—as Sharma (2009: 284–5) writes—'[h]is main subject was ethnic, social, economic and cultural history'. He fully appreciated the fact, of course, that much of Indian history presented a dissatisfying picture of feudal exploitation extending up into his own time. That was why, while in the Arya Samaj, he had imaginatively relived the Vedic golden age, and later underwent the same sort of experience with regard to what he thought of as a Buddhist–communist republic. In both cases, the yearning and pride he felt for the past is remarkable.

However, criticisms have been leveled against primordialists and proponents of cultural nationalism. Competing paradigms of nationalism exist that claim to be better explanations of it within the context of the modern globalizing world. Anderson for one has embraced the constructionist approach, a modernist paradigm. I shall not enter into a detailed discussion of it, but merely note its relevance to this

[37] Indian states each have their own official state languages.
[38] Joireman (2003).

study, since, to quote Smith (2000: 58), '[f]or Anderson himself, the idea of the imagined political community was historically embedded'. Along with Smith and in line with Hutchinson's notion of cultural nationalism, which 'may look back to a presumed glorious past, but ... repudiates both traditionalism and modernism' (Smith 1998: 178), I believe, in the case of Rahul Sankrityayan, primordialism to be an effective paradigm, and the one most applicable to this study.

OBJECTIVE AND SCOPE OF THE STUDY

There is a need for further research within Sankrityayan studies into the fundamental reason for its subject's multiple identities. Starting with the oft-repeated fact of the *sāmyavādī* (communist) and ghumakkaṛī proclivities in Sankrityayan's life, this study will consider whether something deeper underlay them. I shall part with the popular conception of Sankrityayan as a ghumakkaṛ in search of a satisfying philosophy—one who, having tried on many masks, finally embraced something on the order of communism. Instead, I shall argue in the following pages that Sankrityayan was a nationalist from the beginning and remained so till the end, his seeming changes of identity being simply the result of an ongoing process of trying to fulfil his nationalistic yearnings. I show that *rāṣṭrīya kārya* (the work of building a nation) was the common thread that ran throughout the diversity in Sankrityayan's life. I place Sankrityayan at the very centre of developments on the Indian subcontinent during his lifetime, and conversely attempt to re-identify him in terms of the influences that period had on him.

To be sure, recognizing that Sankrityayan was a nationalist is not an entirely new insight, as can be seen in the words of Lata Singh (2012: 73). To date, however, no careful study of Sankrityayan's views on nationhood and his nationalist sentiment—of what nationalism meant for him—has been done, so it has yet to be determined just what sort of a nationalist he was, how he became one, and why. This research will seek to provide answers to these questions.

Against the claim that all the different turnings, activities, and affiliations in Sankrityayan's life had one common link, namely nationalist sentiment and nationalism, one can put forward the counterargument that, as a communist, he was an internationalist, not a nationalist. While Sankrityayan was unquestionably a communist, his notion of communism was dissimilar to that of his fellow party members in India, for which reason he was eventually expelled from the party. His imagining of a socialist community shot through with Indianness was what placed him for them beyond the pale.

Sundry competitive studies of Indian nationalism and its impact on Hindi literature and the country's public life have been carried out; but the space that Sankrityayan occupied within that discourse has still to be more fully investigated. It is obvious that a person with the temperament and heightened consciousness of Sankrityayan, who lived in the period of great social, political, religious, and cultural upheaval leading up to his country's sovereignty, could not remain aloof from events; indeed, he contributed significantly to them. Earlier studies of Hindi writers and Indian intellectuals, and especially research on nationalism in Bihar (for example, Orsini 2010, Pāṇḍeya 2011, Singh 2012, and Urmileś 1994), have taken note of such contributions. However, his own nationalist sentiment has not been sufficiently taken into account up to now.

I have had three major aims in my research. The primary goal has been to pay close attention to the expression of nationalist sentiment in Sankrityayan's writings and to assess such sentiment as possibly most faithfully reflective of his truest intentions when he underwent the turnings in his life. How were the Arya Samaj, Buddhism, communism, and the Hindi language able to spark these turnings? What was his real motive in immersing himself in those fields of action? By exploring the nationalist sentiment embedded in his writings, I will seek to demonstrate how this mental outlook was in each case instrumental in bringing about the major turnings in his life. The works that I have selected for a closer reading do not cover Sankrityayan's entire output. They mainly comprise the four larger volumes of his autobiography, *Merī jīvan yātrā*, along with a number of other works, including biographies, travelogues, novels, and several political writings and speeches. *MJY* is the mostly widely used primary source in Sankrityayan studies and has been subject to much interpretation. However, no study up to now has focused critically on the nationalist sentiment expressed in it as a possible key to the entire span of its author's creative life.

Second, I will present Sankrityayan as a Hindi-language nationalist. Given that he was a writer of numerous titles, I shall try to pinpoint the reasons for his prolificness and for the importance he attached to the printed word. This will be preliminary to tackling the question of why Hindi was a *premāspad* (labour of love) for him.

Finally, Sankrityayan's intimate ties with Nepal,[39] as shown in his writings, including the Nepalese response to him, is another focus of this research. A concerted attempt will be made to search for echoes of him and his books in Nepal, both past and present, in order to determine what it was that drove this relationship. Besides being helpful for his visits to Tibet, what else did Nepal represent for him?

There are at least three good reasons why Nepal will figure so prominently in the coming pages: first, because that country played a role in Sankrityayan's every major turning; second, because the study of Sankrityayan's relationship with Nepal affords an entirely new vantage point from which to broaden the scope of Sankrityayan studies—namely one lying outside India; third, because Nepal represents a good basis for elaborating the concepts of 'print market' and 'nationalist kinship'.

I will explore Sankrityayan's relationship with Nepal from different perspectives: first, I will present the picture Sankrityayan draws of Nepal in his first novel, *Bāisvī̃ sadī* (see Chapter 2) and the Nepalese response to it; second, the extent to which this relationship was built up around Buddhism will be examined, particularly as regards his Tibet trips and his relations with members of the Theravada movement in Nepal; third, I shall analyse the concept of 'nationalist kinship' between certain nations, which led him to assert a sense of 'brotherhood' between India and Nepal (and specifically between himself and Nepal), whose populations he thought of as sharing 'one cultural soul' (Chapter 3); finally, I will view Nepal as an essential print market for the dissemination of Sankrityayan's works and analyse the Nepalese response to them (see Chapter 4).

39 Rocak Ghimire's (January–February 1994: 29–33) article 'Mahāpaṇḍit Rāhul Sāṅkr̥tyāyan ko Nepāl Sambandha' (Mahāpaṇḍit Rāhul Sāṅkr̥tyāyan's Relationship with Nepal) has been a primary reference source in this regard.

Nepal was Sankrityayan's second home. Though it was a different country with a different polity, he never thought of Nepal as a *videś* (foreign country). One clear reason for this was that he understood that the country was an important place on the Indian subcontinent where his works were being read. These propagated his ideas there with the same force as they did in India. During his creative period, India was in conflict with the British over the question of sovereignty, while the Nepalese for their part were struggling against the Ranas.[40] Every work was censored by the Rana government, so that there was no question of the legal import of Sankrityayan's popular political works in Hindi. His Tibet travelogue too faced censorship. Therefore, he had to tone down the passages relating to Nepal in it in order to ensure that his other, non-political works were legally accessible to Nepalese readers. Still, Sankrityayan's banned political books did reach the Nepalese public secretly and were instrumental in the promotion of communism there.

Rhoderick Chalmers (2002, 2003) has studied the early development of Nepali publishing in Banaras and unravelled the story of nascent print capitalism in that language. He explores how Nepali publishing took off alongside its Hindi counterpart in Banaras, expanded its readership, and helped to form a Nepalese public culture by addressing fundamental questions of communal identity during the few decades from the end of the 19th century up to at least the 1920s. However, I shall be exploring the Nepalese readership from another perspective, namely that of the role Sankrityayan's Hindi works played in Nepal itself—their effect, that is, in a distant zone outside the Hindi heartland, particularly in regard to education, political consciousness, and scholarship. This study will provide confirmation in these three areas and of Chalmers' (2003: 20) depiction of the Hindi printed word as 'Nepali readership's staple diet'.

In this context, I may refer to Abhi Subedi's (1999) notion of the 'trespassing insider'. He uses this expression to characterize the

40 The Ranas ruled the kingdom of Nepal from 1846 to 1951. 'Rana' was a title that Janga Bahadur Kunwar took after seizing power through the 1846 Kot massacre. He used it as a family name instead of Kunwar and passed it on to his sons and brothers.

Buddhist monk Ekai Kawaguchi who secretly entered Nepal and went on to Tibet in search of manuscripts at the beginning of the 20th century. Sankrityayan, too, during his earliest visits to Nepal, was a trespassing insider, along with his works of a non-Buddhist nature that entered the country clandestinely during the same period of Rana rule. Sankrityayan's relationship with Nepal was something out of the ordinary then, and, for this reason alone, deserves to command special attention in this study (see Chapters 3 and 4).

The objectives and aims of this study can be summarized, then, as testing the nationalist sentiment expressed throughout Sankrityayan's life and writings as a possible reason for his multiple identities. My research has drawn its main strength from the familiarity I have gained with his works, with his relationship with individual Nepalese, and with his supple use of Hindi as a language of scholarship in Nepal. I shall sketch a picture of Sankrityayan from a vantage point beyond the Hindi heartland. Sankrityayan studies have already yielded extensive results relating to his literary output, his political life, and his contributions to retrieving, translating, and editing old Buddhist texts from Tibet. This study, while building on them, will seek to add a new dimension to what has gone before.

RESEARCH METHODOLOGY, SOURCES, AND QUESTIONS

This study will use a combination of methodologies. It will apply methods of textual criticism when reading Sankrityayan's own works and those of others who have interpreted him, while also drawing on the results of fieldwork. This will call for a close reading and analysis of content, with exploratory and interpretive methods being applied to test the hypothesis. It will interpret Sankrityayan's writings against the backdrop of contemporary history, whose depths will need to be more carefully plumbed so as to elicit as much implicit meaning of the sources as possible. My translations of important passages from Sankrityayan's works will serve as a platform for engaging in the process of interpretation.

My actual research first focused on Sankrityayan's works that bore traces of his association with Nepal (and particularly on those specific parts of them). Fieldwork was carried out in India (Delhi)[41] and Nepal (Kathmandu)[42] during some three months of the monsoon season of 2008. The main objective of the fieldwork was to conduct interviews and collect material. I took both recorded and non-recorded interviews of persons who had read Sankrityayan's works, experts in the field of Sankrityayan studies, people who had met Sankrityayan or attended his lectures, communist leaders and supporters, and his family members and friends. I consulted archives for relevant letters and journals and newspaper articles. An attempt was also made to collect copies of historical documents, such as pamphlets, diaries, letters, and photos. A questionnaire was produced targeting the readers of Sankrityayan's works and people who had met Sankrityayan in Nepal. This fieldwork in Nepal both sharpened my view of how Sankrityayan looked from an outside perspective and clarified the ways in which Hindi functioned as a language of both agitation and scholarship in Nepal during that time.

Sources

The student of Sankrityayan studies has access to a wealth of published sources in Hindi, first and foremost the host of Sankrityayan's books and articles themselves. Kamala Sankrityayan (1971: 57–64) has counted 127 books written by Rahul Sankrityayan (both published

[41] The visit to Delhi was mainly used for collection of material. I visited the library of Jawaharlal Nehru University, the Sahitya Akademi, and such publishing houses as Vani Prakashan and Rajkamal Prakashan. I met Manager Pandey, an expert in the field of Sankrityayan studies, and with his help arranged an interview with Sankrityayan's nephew Anil Kumar Pandey and his wife, Usha Pandey. Earlier, in 2007, I also had had an opportunity to meet, in Vienna, Sankrityayan's wife, Kamala Sankrityayan, and their daughter Jaya Parhawk.

[42] In Kathmandu, I visited the families of Hemraj Sharma, Dharmaratna Yami, Dharmaman Sahu, Mandas Tuladhar, Citta Harsha Bajracharya, and Janaklāl Śarmā and interviewed them. I also visited places in Kathmandu mentioned in *Merī jīvan yātrā*, such as libraries (Hemraj Sharma's collection, now part of the National Library in Lalitpur, and Keshar Library in Keshar Mahal), Buddhist viharas, and Dharmaman Sahu's and Dharmaratna Yami's houses, where Sankrityayan had stayed. I met and interviewed people who had met, talked to, or just seen Sankrityayan in their youth, such as

and unpublished) on various subjects.[43] In addition, many secondary sources, including dissertations, letters, articles, and memoirs by other writers, are also available in Hindi, if much less so in other languages.

Primary Sources

The majority of primary sources examined in this thesis have already been discussed in previous studies. Here they will be studied from different perspectives, namely with a view to eliciting the embedded significance of nationalism in them. Therefore, it is Sankrityayan's Hindi writings among the primary sources that will come under closest scrutiny. And among the large number of these, only those presented in the bibliography were chosen to focus on. These include Sankrityayan's autobiography, biographies, letters, novels, political writings, articles, and speeches. The interviews I conducted between 2007 and 2009 in India, Nepal, and Austria with his family members and personal acquaintances, and with scholars of Sankrityayan studies and modern-day readers of his works, are also considered as primary sources. The languages of these sources are Hindi, Nepali, and, in a very few cases, Sanskrit and English.

Secondary Sources

The studies on Sankrityayan and his writings by other writers constitute the secondary sources. I have restricted these to what has

---

Vasanta Kumar Sharma, Rochak Ghimire, Madhav Ghimire, Purna Harsha Bajracharya, Rajeshwar Devkota, Krishnachandra Singh Pradhan, Bhavani Prasad Ghimire, Jñānmaṇi Nepāl, Shyamdas Vaishnav, and Prakash A. Raj. I interviewed persons who had read, and booksellers who had marketed, Sankrityayan's works. During the fieldwork in Kathmandu, a questionnaire was also prepared targeting the persons who met Sankrityayan and were familiar with his name and works.

43 The categories she has identified are: (*a*) novels and stories, (*b*) dictionaries, (*c*) biographies, (*d*) philosophy, (*e*) country studies, (*f*) Buddhism, (*g*) Bhojpuri plays, (*h*) travelogues, (*i*) politics, (*j*) science, (*k*) literature and history, (*l*) Sanskrit commentaries and translations from Sanskrit, (*m*) language studies and grammar, and (*n*) Sanskrit manuscript editions of philosophical and religious texts.

appeared in Hindi, Nepali, English, Newari, and German. They take the form of dissertations and other scholarly studies, memoirs, journals, newspaper articles, diaries,[44] or pamphlets.

It was only after I came back to Vienna from the 2008 fieldwork and reviewed the collected material and secondary sources that I realized that a whole new area within Sankrityayan studies was waiting to be explored. The study then shifted its focus so as to make Sankrityayan's relationship with Nepal one of its key concerns. This new focus would, I felt, prove relevant to the understanding of Sankrityayan's multiple identities.

Further research was then undertaken that involved a rereading of the sources so as to reconstruct the growth in Sankrityayan's development of his conception of nationalism (that is, each turning represented a new stage in that development).

This rereading was undertaken with the tools for autobiographical reading recommended by Sidonie Smith and Julia Watson[45] and within the analytical framework for studying life histories proposed by

[44] Those of Hemraj Sharma, Rochak Ghimire, and Prakash A. Raj.

[45] These scholars have divided the 'autobiographical I' into four components: (*a*) the real or historical I, (*b*) the narrating I, (*c*) the narrated I, and (*d*) the ideological I. As Smith and Watson (2003: 58–62) explain, the first of these is the historical person assignable to a particular period and geographical setting, who matches the name on the title page. In our case, it is 'Mahāpaṇḍit Rāhul Sāṅkr̥tyāyan', the well-known figure in Hindi literature and Buddhist studies and sometime sadhu, traveller, Arya Samajist, Buddhist, and communist. His real I is now an unchangeable relic of history, but the other three—the narrating, narrated, and ideological I's—continue to exist in the readerly present, and thus admit of change. The narrating I is the I who speaks, the autobiographical first person, directly accessible to readers, who wants to tell own life history. The narrated I is distinguished form the narrating I in being a projection of the latter, the protagonist of the narrative and the version of the self that the narrating I chooses to constitute. In our case, the narrated I is seen to be a ghumakkaṛ, someone adept at moving about both physically and intellectually, and at assuming new identities. The ideological I is a particular concept of personhood selected by the narrator, among all the ones culturally available to him, for the telling of his life story. This study will suggest that Sankrityayan's different turnings were the products of his ideological I.

D.G. Mandelbaum.[46] This rereading has fed into the second chapter of this study, where the different turnings in Sankrityayan's life are analysed. It was during this time that the idea first took shape to observe these turnings through the lens of nationalism as it expresses itself in his writings. Again the sources were reread, and only after this closer look into his life and his turnings did the following hypothesis take concrete shape, namely that *Sankrityayan was a committed Indian nationalist, and the different turnings, adaptations, and other aspects of his life could be put down as due to his nationalist sentiment.*

The guiding questions that were formed during the early stages of study were the following:

> Towards a conceptual foundation of the study:
>
> In what sense or senses did Sankrityayan conceive of himself as a nationalist?
>
> Towards an explanatory superstructure of the study:
>
> How did he become a nationalist?
>
> What kind of nation did he imagine India becoming?
>
> What kind of nationalist was he?
>
> How could nationalist sentiment, acting uniformly throughout his creative life, have shaped his multiple identities?
>
> Did perhaps, alternatively, different forms of nationalist sentiment inform the different turnings of his life? If yes, what were they?

[46] D.G. Mandelbaum (1973) elaborates a threefold scheme for studying life histories, which he proceeds to apply to the study of Gandhi, namely dimensions, turnings, and adaptations. A dimension is made up of the biological, cultural, social, and psycho-social experiences a person undergoes and their effects on subsequent actions. Turnings are the principal periods in a life, the major transitions the person goes through (striking new roles undertaken or new relationships entered into). Adaptation is any alteration of established behaviour which has a major effect on a person's life. Sankrityayan's life history is significant for being filled with many turnings and adaptations, but in his case they occurred with an unusually great sense of deliberateness; Sankrityayan consciously fashioned his own self.

Towards the findings that cap the study:

How is he to be judged as a nationalist, not in his own terms but historically, from our present perspective?

To answer these questions, the sources were analysed for the tracks they have left of Sankrityayan's nationalist sentiment. These were analysed in turn for any major shifts they display. Thereupon the attempt was made to correlate these results with the major turnings of his life, by applying Mandelbaum's theorizing. It will be shown that his nationalist sentiment did indeed undergo significant shifts, and that these can be assigned, with causal force to them, to the different phases of his life. Three further chapters (Chapters 2 to 4) will be devoted to cementing this conclusion.

The major part of the study has necessarily focused on the primary sources that provide insight into the turnings in Sankrityayan's life, his nationalist concerns, and his relationship with Nepal. An effort was made to conduct as close a reading as possible of these texts in order to document significant shifts in opinion from one period to another in his life. Secondary literature was consulted as independent sources of confirmation for posited arguments. Indeed, each step of the way led ever more insistently towards the overall aim of the research, providing cumulative evidence in support of the starting hypothesis.

AN OUTLINE OF THE STUDY

The present study attempts to chart Sankrityayan's nationalist sentiment in terms of three major turnings in his life, each of which, as will be shown, was fuelled by that sentiment. It consists of the present introduction, four chapters, a conclusion, and appendices.

Chapter 1 reviews the course of Sankrityayan's life through a critical study of *Merī jīvan yātrā*. The basic facts of Sankrityayan's autobiography provide the necessary background information for proceeding further. This chapter will then analyse the genres of autobiography and biography within the literary landscape of 20th-century India as popular literature and the unique space that Sankrityayan's autobiography occupies within it. It will move on from that to consider why Sankrityayan felt such an imperative to write his autobiography in a large number of thick instalments, and why he also engaged in writing biographies of many other persons. Finally, an outline of his life will be proposed to serve as a preliminary basis for linking our study of nationalism to the three major turnings of his life.

Chapter 2 looks into the first major turning by posing the question: Why did the Arya Samaj represent a *nav prakāś* (new light) for Sankrityayan? It will explain how the revival within Indian society envisaged by Sankrityayan might take place and how the Arya Samaj came to be regarded by him as instrumental for the emergence of nationalist sentiment in him personally, in its fostering of *deś bhakti* (nationalism, patriotism) and the desire for *rāṣṭrīya kārya* (national work). This is the period of Sankrityayan's first 'inarticulate glimpse' (*asphut jhãkī*) of the ideal he saw the nation striving to attain: a mixture of the Arya Samaj's principles and his own vague understanding of the Russian Revolution. The different ways Sankrityayan understood the word 'Hindu' at different stages of his life will also be taken up.

Chapter 3 considers the second major turning in Sankritayayan's life, the one connected with Buddhism. It searches out the meaning Buddhism had for him as a source of great enthusiasm. The sentiments aroused in him by it and the actions it aroused him to will be explained as being due to its importance for him not so much as a religion but as a product of Indian culture. The adoption of Buddhism occurred during the central period of Sankrityayan's life. He had moved away from Arya Samaj, and communism was still wholly in the future. Therefore, Sankrityayan will be presented as now caught between ambivalent views. The chapter then briefly deals with Sankrityayan's contributions to the field of Hindi literature, and specifically with the Buddhist themes woven into them. Sankrityayan's links with members of the Theravada movement in Nepal and his more general relationship with Nepal will also be explored in this chapter. Finally, it will turn to the concept of 'nationalist kinship' or 'brotherhood' between India and Nepal (that is, the more generalized form of Sankrityayan's own relationship with Nepal); this kinship between the two nations and its citizens was posited on the basis of their sharing 'one cultural soul' (see van der Veer 1994: 85).

The final major turning of Sankrityayan's intellectual journey will be presented in Chapter 4. After a brief discussion on Sankrityayan's involvement in the peasant movement and the Communist Party of India, it discusses Sankrityayan's own notion of the Indian nation, one that set him apart from his fellow communists. He imagined this nation as being based on pride in the common Indian culture and having Hindi as the lingua franca. How this difference of opinion led to his dismissal from the Communist Party will be a further subject of discussion. The reasons behind his esteem for Hindi will also be looked into. The chapter will then explore Sankrityayan's response to the printed word and how it came to be one of the main concerns in his life, tying in as it did to *sāhitya sevā* (service to literature), considered by him a dāyitva. His many printed works were a means of fulfilling that duty, and also of providing pleasure, a livelihood, and an outlet for his ideas. The mixed response to Sankrityayan's contraband books in Nepal will be the final focus of this chapter.

At the end of this volume I have provided a number of Appendices. Appendix 1 gives brief background information on Nepalese who were either associated with Sankrityayan in one way or another or are otherwise mentioned in this study. Appendix 2 contains English translations of the pamphlets in which Muralidhar Bhattarai publicizes his challenge to Sankrityayan, along with their responses. Appendix 3 encloses Lakshmi Prasad Devkota's poem *Pāgal* (The madman). Appendix 4 contains Sankrityayan's felicitation certificate awarding him the title of 'mahāpaṇḍit' and an English translation of the same. Appendix 5 encloses a list of dissertations having Sankrityayan as their subject, together with details of birth centenary volumes, centennial anniversary celebrations, and prizes given in Sankrityayan's name. Appendix 6 contains a chronology of prominent events in Sankrityayan's life.

The general impression Rahul Sankrityayan's life history gives is of a man who tried on sundry and wholly dissimilar masks one after the other: a religious sadhu, an Arya Samajist, a Buddhist monk, a secularist, a communist, a fiction writer, a cultural critic, and a Hindi activist. However, a closer analysis undertaken in the following pages will reveal an underlying coherence among all these seemingly contradictory identities—in the form of an unwavering, if malleable, nationalist sentiment. Within the historical context of the first half of 20th-century India, Sankrityayan stands out as an Indian nationalist sui generis, each of whose major stages in life represented a link in the process of his striving to fulfil his nationalist ideals. The subsequent chapters will present Sankrityayan's major turnings in life as being in tandem with the development of his nationalist sentiment. Before these major turnings are addressed individually, the following chapter presents a critical study of Sankrityayan's autobiography, *Merī jīvan yātrā*, an extraordinary work of Hindi literature that captures his life as an aggregation of continual self-renewal.

CHAPTER ONE

Rahul Sankrityayan's Autobiography

The Product of a Prison Cell

यहाँ न पढ़ने के लिए पुस्तकें थीं, न बात करने के लिए कोई आदमी। सारा समय बेकार जाते देखकर मैंने सोचा, अपनी 'जीवन-यात्रा' ही लिख ड़ालूँ।

Here there were neither books nor anyone to talk to. When I realized that the time was passing unproductively, I thought of writing my *Jīvan-yātrā*.

—Rahul Sankrityayan (1998b [*MJY-2*]: 339)

The prison as an institution figured prominently in the Indian middle-class imagination and experience between the 1890s and 1940s (Arnold 2004: 29). During that period, imprisonment for political offences could only enhance one's reputation, symbolizing as it did the oppressive nature of colonial rule. Sankrityayan wrote: 'Being a prisoner of the Indian government, not of a regional government, was a matter of pride. Coming to prison as a *śāhī kaidī* [royal prisoner] is much more prestigious than being caught as a thief' (1998b [*MJY-2*]: 337). And further: 'The prison is a second *sasurāl* [parental house of one's wife] for *krāntikārī taruṇ* [revolutionary youths]' (1998b [*MJY-2*]: 349). During the independence movement, 'jail-going' (Arnold 2004: 29) was regarded as one standard means of resistance. The sasurāl is customarily a place where great respect and much hospitality are shown to sons-in-law and brothers-in-law, so that one can correspondingly gauge the degree of honour attached to political prisoners.

Sankrityayan was one such prisoner, and during his stay in jail he found himself with an abundance of time on his hands—a difficult situation for a diligent person of his nature. In similar cases, revolutionaries often turned to writing. The literature produced in Indian prisons during this period ranges from jail diaries, newspaper articles, and autobiographies to novels, plays, and other literary works. While some of the prisoners in colonial India, such as Manabendra Nath Roy (M.N. Roy), deliberately refused ink, pen, and paper, and even books and newspapers (Arnold 2004: 30), others, like Sankrityayan, insistently demanded reading material and writing facilities (1998b [*MJY-2*]: 337). During his imprisonment in the Hazaribagh jail in 1923, Sankrityayan had a copy of the *Majjhima nikāya* in Pali, which he used to read for an hour every day. When it was taken from him, he managed to get it back only by engaging in a hunger strike.[1] In this he was helped by Śaṅkarācārya Swami Bharti Krishnatirth, who convinced the authorities that it was the Buddhists' most important collection of texts.[2]

Krishnatirth was the Śaṅkarācārya[3] of Govardhan *math* in Puri from 1925 to 1960. A mathematician famous as the author of *Vedic Mathematics*,[4] Krishnatirth was imprisoned in the same jail as Sankrityayan for having delivered a lecture on *rāj-dharm* (political ethics) and *prajā-dharm* (public ethics). That lecture was considered to be instrumental in instigating a public rebellion. Although prisoners were not allowed to keep any paper or writing instrument, Sankrityayan had managed to obtain a slate to revise his knowledge of algebra and geometry under the guidance of Krishnatirth. Sankrityayan took responsibility for preparing the *phalāhār* (fruit diet) and *pūjā pāṭh kā sarjām* (worship paraphernalia) for his teacher, which brought them even closer (Sankrityayan 1998b [*MJY-1*] 277–8; Machwe 1978: 19). Shortly before the latter's release, Sankrityayan managed to get approval for the needed paper, pen, and ink. Indeed, it is fair to say that

[1] Sankrityayan also had occasion to fast for two days during his first imprisonment (1922), as part of a hunger strike conducted by all prisoners in protest against the mistreatment of prison employees.

[2] This is one indication that Sankrityayan had already become interested in Buddhism by 1923.

[3] Śaṅkarācārya is a title of heads of monasteries called maths in the Advaita Vedanta tradition. The title derives from Ādi Śaṅkara (9th century), the first such head. Govardhan math in Puri is believed to be one of the maths established by Ādi Śaṅkara.

[4] Krishnatirth culled a set of sixteen Sutras and thirteen sub-Sutras from the *Atharva Veda* and developed methods and techniques for calculation, and called it *Vedic Mathematics*.

Sankrityayan's writing career began in earnest during his prison stay. He wrote his first published work, *Bāisvī̃ sadī*, there in 1923.[5] His other works produced during later periods of imprisonment are: *Tumhārī kṣaya* (1939), *Jīne ke lie* (1939), *Viśva kī rūprekhā* (1941), *Mānav samāj* (1941), *Vaijñānik bhautikvād* (1941), *Volgā se Gaṅgā* (1942), *Japaniyā̃ rāchach* (1941), *Darśan digdarśan* (1942), and his autobiography.[6]

The writing of autobiographies in India had commenced before Indians had thought to write about their prison experience, but Arnold (2004: 30) notes that India's most celebrated autobiographies were produced in prison, including Gandhi's *Satyānā prayōgō* (*The Story of My Experiments with Truth*) and Nehru's *Autobiography* (first published in 1936). Gandhi started to write his autobiography in Yerawada prison near Pune in the early 1920s. Nehru wrote his autobiography for reasons similar to those of Sankrityayan, as he notes in the preface of the first edition (2004: xiv): 'The primary objective in writing these pages was to occupy myself with a definite task, so necessary in the long solitudes of gaol life [...].'

Arnold (2004: 30) remarks that it became a convention among political prisoners to write prison memoirs, even as it came to be a patriotic duty for newspaper editors and book publishers to see them into print. This accounts for the many such celebrated autobiographies in both English and vernaculars. Sankrityayan recounts in the foreword to the first volume of his autobiography (Sankrityayan 1946: 5–6) that his friends and publishers had urged him to write and publish an autobiography both during and following his periods of imprisonment,[7] but he had repeatedly postponed doing so. It was only after the publication of his other works written

[5] It was mainly written in the prison hospital, where he had been admitted for treatment of dysentery.

[6] He also translated English novels into Hindi during his second imprisonment (1923–5): *Śaitān kī ā̃kh* (The eye of a devil [1923]), *Nirāle hīre kī khoj* (The search for a unique diamond [date unavailable]), *Vismṛti ke garbh mẽ* (In the womb of forgetfulness [1923]), *Jādū kā mulk* (The land of magic [1923]), and *Sone kī ḍhāl* (A shield of gold [1923]). Sankrityayan (2006: 3) writes in the foreword of *Sone kī ḍhāl* that he failed to record the names of the authors and so was unable to locate the original works later on.

[7] He was imprisoned for two years from 14 March 1940 to 23 July 1942. The first part was written during this imprisonment.

in prison[8] that the first part of *Merī jīvan yātrā* (*MJY*) was finally published. It meant more for Sankrityayan, apparently, to see those books circulating on the market, while perhaps the Indian wariness of displaying *ahammānyatā* (pride, conceit) also held him back.

AUTOBIOGRAPHY IN HINDI LITERATURE

During the period from 1940 to 1944 in which Sankrityayan's *MJY-1* was written and published, the autobiographies of 'common people' were not a widespread phenomenon in South Asia, though autobiography itself was not something unknown. Banarsidas Jain's *Ardhkathānak*, considered the first autobiography in Hindi literature, was indeed written by a commoner, a Jain merchant, in 1641 at the age of 55, during the heyday of the Mughal Empire. Its author believed that humans have a lifespan of 110 years, and as he had just reached the halfway mark, he named his memoirs *Ardhkathānak* (Half the story). However, he did not live much beyond its completion (Caturvedī 2011: 47). *Ardhkathānak* is written in Brajbhāṣa, in the famous *dohā*[9] and *caupāī*[10] verse style of that time. It also displays fine Brajbhāṣha prose in the preface (Snātak 2004: 183). Bharatendu Harishchandra, 'who brought literature from the palaces of kings and nawabs to the public' (Snātak 2004: 219), and so is known as the father of modern Hindi prose, attempted to write an autobiography in the guise of a novel under the title *Ek kahānī kuch āp bītī, kuch jag bītī* (A story, partly experienced by [my]self and partly by the world), narrated in the first person. Parts of it were published in 1877 in the magazine he edited, *Kavivacanasudhā*, but in the strict sense it cannot be regarded as a true autobiography due to its novelistic nature. Ambikadatt Vyas's *Nij vṛttānt* (A personal account [1901]) and Sudhakar Dvivedī's *Rām kahānī* (A long story[11] [1908]), are examples of more conventional autobiographies of this period, written by two scholars. It was Satyanand Agnihotrī's *Mujh mẽ dev-jīvan kā vikās* (The development of spiritual

8 *Viśva kī rūprekhā* (1942), *Mānav-samāj* (1942), *Darśan digdarśan* (1942), *Vaijñānik bhautikvād* (1942), *Volgā se Gaṅgā* (1942), and *Siṃh senāpati* (1944).

9 Written in couplets, with 13+14 *mātrās* (the total sum of syllabic vowel lengths) in each line.

10 A verse of four lines, each containing sixteen *mātrās*.

11 This is a collection of various episodes in his life. A literal translation would be: 'The story of Ram'.

life within me [1910]), Bhāi Parmānand's *Āp bītī* (An experience of life [1921]), Shri Ramvilas Shukla's *Maĩ krāntikārī kaise banā* (How I became a revolutionary [1939]), and Babu Shyamsundar Das's *Merī ātm kahānī* (A story of my own [1941], however, that were the first autobiographies in Hindi to gain true popularity. They were followed by Gulab Ray's *Merī asfatāẽ* (My failures [1941]) and Sankrityayan's *MJY-1* (1944). In 1946, Rājendra Prasād's *Ātma kathā* (An autobiography) was published as the 'first autobiography written by a political leader in Hindī' (Caturvedī 2011: 54), and it, too, happened to be a product of the prison cell.

An issue of *Haṃs*[12] devoted to autobiography in January–February 1932 was an important milestone in the history of Hindi autobiography. The editor of the journal, Premchand,[13] had requested both established and young writers to contribute to it. Until that time life histories or autobiographies tended to have great or at least famous persons—be they kings, saints, scholars, or warriors—as their subject. By the time Gandhi's autobiography was published, for instance, he had already become a celebrated figure. Autobiography was regarded as a kind of moral tale, from which people could learn valuable lessons to apply to their own lives. Nand Dulare Bajpeyi, a young and competent critic, staunchly refused to write for the issue of *Haṃs*, stating that autobiography was not something for any *aire-gaire* (stranger, Tom, Dick, or Harry). The correspondence between Premchand and Bajpeyi marked a turning point in how biography and autobiography were viewed among the Indian reading public.

Traditionally, not just (auto)biography but every other kind of literature was expected to offer practical guidance to readers. Literature, in other words, was meant not only to provide entertainment, but also to expand one's knowledge.[14] Furthermore, Indian culture

[12] A literary-political magazine launched by Premchand in 1930, it still comes out as a monthly Hindi literary magazine.

[13] Munshi Premchand was a pioneer of Indian fiction who wrote in the realist tradition, thematizing the poor and urban middle classes and the social issues they faced. He was strongly influenced by Gandhi's non-cooperation movement.

[14] Cf. the verse from the *Kāvyaprakāśa*, a classical guide to poetry:

काव्यं यशसेऽर्थकृते व्यवहारविदे शिवेतरक्षतये।
सद्यः परनिर्वृतये कान्तासम्मितयोपदेशयुजे। (Mammaṭa 1981: 9)

downplayed the importance of individual everyday consciousness, of the type usually cultivated in the autobiographical tradition. The first-person singular pronoun *aham* (I) in Sanskrit had always tended to be considered as standing for something insubstantial, the ego, an obstacle to be overcome. Autobiography, whose authors typically wish to make a good case for themselves, was therefore regarded as foreign to Indian culture. Steeped in this traditional belief, Bajpeyi had asked Premchand in a letter (cited in Caturvedī 2011: 23), '[H]ow many people are able to write an autobiography in Hindi? How many great characters are there, whose life could be a *path-niyāmikā* [guideline] for Hindi [-speaking] people?' Premchand, a progressive writer of realistic fiction, politely replied to Bajpeyi by saying: 'Even a sweeper who works in my house has some secrets in his life which can enlighten us.... No one's life is so *tucch* [insignificant] that it does not have something [to teach] to the *mahaccarit* [greatest people]. That is how great people are made' (cited in Caturvedī 2011: 23).

The eventual success of the autobiographical issue proved that Premchand knew where Hindi literature was heading. That issue itself helped to open up the door to autobiography for every Hindi writer. This influence continues even today, with autobiographies of Dalits and women having now become a matter of course. The autobiographical issue of *Haṃs* featured fifty-two writers, some established and some new, who contributed by writing short autobiographical sketches or poems. They included such reputed names as Jaya Shankar Prasad (poetry), Ramcandra Shukl, Jainendra Kumar, Śivrānī Devī, Radheshyam Kathavachak, and Munshi Ajmeri.

Rājendra Prasād was one of those who at first harboured doubts the propriety of writing his autobiography but later cast such doubts to the wind:

> कभी-कभी दिल में यह विचार भी उठता कि इस संस्मरण की जरूरत या उपयोगिता ही क्या है। [...] मेरा संस्मरण लिखना केवल अहम्मान्यता है, इससे दूसरों को कोई लाभ नहीं पहुँच सकता। तो भी, जब एक बार काम शुरू कर दिया तो उसे पूरा कर देना ही ठीक जँचा; [...]

Poetry [conduces] to fame, wealth, knowledge of moral/social conduct, fortune, instant pleasure and instructions as sweet as [those of one's] beloved.

> Sometimes thoughts arose in my mind about the need and usefulness of these memoirs [...]. Writing one's memoirs is an act of *ahammānyatā*, and they would not profit anyone. But later, having once started the work, I decided it would be well to complete it. (Prasād 2007: 845–6)

The tradition of Indian biography rooted in the lives of 'great men' (*mahāpuruṣ* or *vīr puruṣ*) continued to prevail during the independence movement, when such figures served the cause of nationalism. In this context, Bajpeyī's objection to Premchand's request to write something autobiographical was understandable; Premchand was simply ahead of his time, and it took some time for writers and the general public to catch up.

The famous autobiography of Gandhi was not written by someone who thought of himself as great, but by a man who felt that he had simply found a way of life that others might find worth imitating. This is why he avoided calling the work an autobiography, titling it instead *My Experiments with Truth*. Responding to doubts raised by one of his friends regarding autobiography as being a practice peculiar to the West, he (Gandhi 2003: 6) wrote: 'I do not attempt to write an autobiography. I simply want to tell the story of my numerous experiments with truth. It is true that my life consists of those experiments, so that the story will take the shape of an autobiography.' (Later, however, Gandhi's autobiography became popular under the conception that it was indeed one of a great man.) It is in this same spirit that Sankrityayan set about writing *MJY*: to present his own life as a ghumakkaṛ and thereby to encourage others who in the future might feel inspired to engage in a similar way of life. After his death, his wife Kamala Sankrityayan published the remaining parts of *MJY* along the lines of the lives of 'great men'.

Sankrityayan's numerous contributions to the field of biography and autobiography in Hindi literature are remarkable, and these, along with travelogues, were genres in great demand by readers and publishers in 20th-century India.

The Demand for Biography and Travel Literature

Mahavir Prasad Dwivedi, the editor of the prominent Hindi journal *Sarasvatī*, had early on noted the need for biographies and travelogues in Hindi literature. In his article, 'The Present State of Hindī' (1911), he wrote:

Biographies also comprise an extremely important branch of literature. Young people and old people, men and women, everybody can understand the books in this branch. All can benefit from them and be entertained by them. It does not require any exceptional thought or expertise to comprehend the overall significance of these books. There are only a few books in Hindi that belong to this readable, entertaining, and generally useful branch of literature [...] [and] I can tell you from personal experience that people like this kind of literature. Therefore, everyone, including publishers and readers, would benefit if good biographies were to be published.

[...] Every year, several Indian students travel abroad. If even one or two of them published descriptions of their travels every year, then this branch of literature would develop very quickly. Unfortunately, even gentlemen who have maintained their love for Hindi while travelling or living abroad, who have tirelessly written articles in Hindi, and who have been kind enough to send them home, when they return to this country they, too, turn their backs on writing in Hindi. What can we expect from others? (Dwivedi 2010: 361–2)

It was *Sarasvatī*[15] that published Sankrityayan's series of articles on Sri Lanka in 1927, which he had written during his stay there. These articles, in a well-known and reputed literary magazine, Sankrityayan felt, constituted the start of his literary career, even though he was already the author of a published novel and many published articles.[16]

एक तरह 1927 ई. में ही मेरे साहित्यिक जीवन का आरम्भ होता है।

In a way, my literary carrier starts from 1927. (Sankrityayan 1998b [*MJY*-2]: 23)

Das (1995: 247) describes two kinds of biographies prevalent in Indian literature at the time, one featuring 'cultural heroes' of linguistic and religious communities who have for centuries served as sources of inspiration, and the other contemporary 'eminent men', including those who have made a mark politically. Das's categories could be termed respectively 'spiritual' (or 'cultural') and 'political'

15 Dwivedi was the editor of *Sarasvatī* from 1903 to 1920.

16 His first article was published in 1915.

biographies. The first category would include such sages, poets, writers, or religious leaders as the Buddha, Mahavir, Dayananda, and Shankardev, or from beyond the Indian border, Mohammed. The second would include nationally important political leaders like Mahatma Gandhi, Jawaharlal Nehru, Vallabhai Patel, and Maulana Azad, and internationally important ones like Lenin, Stalin, and Marx.

The 20th century, then, was an age in which biography was used as a means of propagating the rich and ancient national history of Indian culture. In the words of Orsini (2010: 208–9), '*Vīr-rasa* (heroic) literature was considered, in the reformist view, one of the necessary features of a national literature. Narratives of heroes and heroines were seen as the most appropriate means of carrying the message of valour, virility, and strength.' She (2010: 210) further states: 'Whereas Maharana Pratāp, Raja Chattrasāl, Śivājī, and Amar Singh Raṭhaur represented evident ideals of masculinity, heroines like Ahalyābāi, Durgāvatī, and Lakṣmībāi transcended gender. They became the perfect nationalist icons for the present, in that they synthesized self-less activism, heroism, wisdom, good rule, freedom, Sarasvatī, and Mother India.'

These biographies, written in Hindi, resonated not only in India but in neighbouring Nepal as well. Although they were not easily accessible there, owing to the strict censorship imposed by the Rana government, people did find ways to get their hands on them, and read them as a similar source of encouragement, in the struggle to free their own country from the yoke of the Ranas. Rewanta Kumari (b. 1918), the wife of a later Nepalese prime minister, Tanka Prasad Acharya (1912–92), recounts her reading habits:

> I was very much influenced by the female Indian revolutionaries, like Laxmibai, Vijaya Laxmi Pandit and others. I had read what they had written. Later I also had a book about the Rani of Jhansi. I used to get these books from members of the Nepali Congress. (Fisher 1997: 151)

The book that most stirred her was *Viśva kī mahān mahilaẽ* (Great women of the world), which contained biographical sketches of Kasturba (Gandhi's wife), Sarojini Naidu, Vijayalakshmi Pandit, Amrita Shergil, Mahadevi Varma, and other Indians, along with similar ones of foreigners, such as Helen Keller and Madame Curie (Fisher 1997: 152–3).

Thus, even before *MJY* was written (1940) and published (1944), there were many autobiographies, in a diversity of forms and languages, which had already found a ready audience on the subcontinent. Surely the most widely read autobiography of the century, though, was Mahatma Gandhi's *Satyānā Prayōgō* (1927), originally written in Gujarati but later translated into many other languages.

MERĪ JĪVAN YĀTRĀ: BIOGRAPHY–AUTOBIOGRAPHY–LIFE HISTORY

Sankrityayan started writing his autobiography on 16 April 1940 in Hazaribagh Jail and wrote the first part of it, covering the period between 1893 and 1927 (1998b [*MJY*-2]: 339), based on memory. It was first published in 1944 by Kitab Mahal, Allahabad. The second part (taking his life forward from 1927 to 1944) was dictated by him in 1944 in India while waiting for a Russian visa to come through. It was published in 1950.

MJY is in six parts, and presents Sankrityayan's life from his birth to his funeral (and also includes much background family history). The extraordinary nature of the work has in part to do with the fact that it extends from the cradle to the cremation ground. In part, too, it has to do with its having two authors, a husband and wife, both writing in the first person as narrating I's. The last (the sixth) part was written by Kamala Sankrityayan and describes the last seven years of her husband's life, from 10 April 1956 to his death and funeral, based on his diaries and letters and on her own diaries (Sankrityayan 1998b [*MJY*-1]: 26). The part written by Kamala Sankrityayan is in the form of day-to-day entries with dates, whereas Sankrityayan's writing is structured more imaginatively, under different section headings. The sixth part, therefore, is a collaborative autobiography, a term coined by Smith and Watson (2003). In the sixth part, the narrating I shifts from Rahul to Kamala Sankrityayan, but the narrated I has given way to a real (or historical) I. This latter is referred to as Paṇḍitjī, or Rāhuljī, polite forms of address used when he was still alive. The first-person narrating I in the first to fifth part of *MJY* is now in the third person in the sixth part.

The definitions of *biography* and *autobiography* given by Brian Roberts are as follows:

> Autobiography: An account by an individual of their life in written or oral form.

> Biography: An account of an individual life written by another. It is the practice of writing about a person. (Roberts 2002: 177)

To judge by these two definitions, *MJY* seems to be a combination of both a biography and an autobiography. One alternative would be to call it a 'life history'. *Life story* and *life history* are common concepts of contemporary research, and different definitions have been given of them. The definition of *life story* given by R. Atkinson is: 'The story a person chooses to tell about the life he or she has lived, told as completely and honestly as possible, what is remembered of it, and what the teller wants others to know of it [...]. A life story is a fairly complete narrating of one's entire experience of life as a whole, highlighting the most important aspects' (cited in Roberts 2002: 3). Under these criteria, *MJY* might well be considered a life story. Arnold and Blackburn (2004: 9), following J.L. Peacock and D.C. Holland, similarly prefer the term *life story* to *life history*, but their reason for doing so is precisely because *story* does not imply that the narration is true, that the events narrated necessarily happened, or that it matters whether they did or they did not. In the case of *MJY*, the autobiography-cum-biography does not consist of imaginary events and could therefore probably be accepted by them as a life history.

In 1940, when Sankrityayan started writing his autobiography, he was forty-seven years old and had already accumulated a wide range of experience in life. He had written a number of books on various subjects and had travelled to many places in and outside of India. He had lived through different phases in his life, as a Brahmin boy, a sadhu, an Arya Samajist, a Buddhist monk, and a wanderer. By then, too, he had become an active communist, but one still with leanings towards Buddhism, and had married a Russian woman, who in 1938 bore him a son, Igor. Therefore his own life history, written while an imprisoned political activist, can be described as a narration about a village boy who wants to explore first his country and later the world, and to live a kind of life an ordinary villager of his time would not have lived.

The Structure of *MJY*

The most recent editions of *MJY* (1994, 1998, 2006, edited by Kamala Sankrityayan) have been published in four volumes with a total of six parts (*bhāgs*).[17] Sankrityayan had originally conceived *MJY* as being in three parts: *MJY-1* and *MJY-2* were published during his lifetime, and he wrote in the foreword to *MJY-2*: 'A third part needs to be written, but readers will have to wait till I turn sixty (9 April 1953).' When that day rolled around, however, he was at the point of death. In 1968 Kamala Sankrityayan published *MJY* in five parts: she converted Sankrityayan's travelogue *Rūs mẽ paccīs mās* (Twenty-five months in Russia) into *MJY-3*, and brought out *MJY-4* and *MJY-5* compiled from material Sankrityayan had penned with the aim of publishing them as part of the third part of *MJY*. *MJY-5* ends on the day of his 64th birthday, 9 April 1956, which he did not celebrate but went about business as usual.

Sankrityayan kept a diary every day until 8 December 1961. It is not clear when exactly he started it, but as indicated in *MJY*, it was sometime in 1927 (*MJY-2*: 339). He mainly wrote in Hindi, with the occasional expression in Sanskrit. On 8 December 1961 he wrote: 'Today we are leaving home at five early in the morning. By the afternoon we will reach the airport. I am leaving the diary here.'[18] On that day Sankrityayan visited Calcutta (now Kolkata) with his family. Three days later, on 11 December 1961, he woke up at midnight with his memory gone, and was unable to write ever again.

Responding to requests from Sankritryayan's readers to learn more about him, Kamala Sankrityayan edited, wrote, and published *JY-6* on the occasion of her husband's birth centennial. *JY-6* thus rounds out Sankrityayan's autobiography, filling in the last years of his life and taking leave of him at his funeral in 1963.

MJY breaks down volume-wise as follows:

17 Bhāg is here translated as 'part'. These bhāgs are termed 'volumes' by Machwe (1978), but this leads to confusion, given that Kamala Sankrityayan published only four volumes. This study cites from the 1998 edition, appending numbers to the title to indicate the parts (*MJY-1*, *MJY-2*, *MJY-3*, *MJY-4*, *MJY-5*, and *JY-6*). The size of the volumes is double crown 30″ x 20″. The number of pages in each volume is as follows:

- *MJY-1* (Volume 1): 364 pages
- *MJY-2* (Volume 2): 475 pages
- *MJY-3* and *MJY-4* (Volume 3): 496 pages
- *MJY-5* and *JY-6* (Volume 4): 717 pages

18 'आज पाँच बजे सबेरे घर से जा रहे हैं। दोपहर तक विमान के अड्डे पर होंगे। डायरी यहीं छोड़ रहा हूँ।' (*JY-6*: 592–4)

Table 1.1 The Volumes of *MJY*

Volumes (as they appear now)	Bhāg (Part) and Details	Publisher and Original Year of Publication
Vol. 1	*MJY-1:* • contains the life history from 1893 to 1927 • written in Hazaribagh jail, from 16 April to 14 June 1940 (*MJY-2:* 339) • *MJY-1* has 5 appendices: • Appendix 1: Some diary entries dating back to 1922 • Appendix 2: Sankrityayan's genealogy • Appendix 3: A biographical sketch of his maternal grandfather Ramsharan Pathak • Appendix 4: A biographical sketch of his father Govardhan Pandey • Appendix 5: An account of a visit to his birthplace after 34 years	Calcutta: Adhunik Pustak Bhavan, 1944
Vol. 2	*MJY-2:* • contains the life history from May 1927 to September 1944 • dictated to Satyanārāyan in Prayāg, September 1944	Allahabad: Kitab Mahal, 1950
Vol. 3	*MJY-3:* • contains the life history from 1944 to 1947 • originally published as a travelogue, *Rūs mẽ paccīs mās* • dictated to Hariścandra Puṣp in 1951, Masuri	• published as *Rūs mẽ paccīs mās*. Bikaner: Alok Prakashan, 1952 • published as *MJY-3*. New Delhi: Rajkamal Prakashan, 1963
	MJY-4: • contains the life history from 1947 to 1950 • written in 1956 for the third part of *MJY* by Sankrityayan	New Delhi: Rajkamal Prakashan, 1968
Vol. 4	*MJY-5:* • contains the life history from 1951 to 1956 • written in 1956 for the third part of *MJY* by Sankrityayan	New Delhi: Rajkamal Prakashan, 1968

(*Cont'd*)

Table 1.1 (*Cont'd*)

Volumes (as they appear now)	Bhāg (Part) and Details	Publisher and Original Year of Publication
	JY-6: • contains the life history from 10 April 1956 to the end • written by Kamala Sankrityayan, and therefore the pronoun *merī* (my) is removed from the title • the life history from 10 April 1956 to 8 December 1961 is based on Sankrityayan's own diary • the life history from 8 December 1961 to 28 May 1963 is based on Kamala Sankrityayan's diary	New Delhi: Radha Krishna Prakashan, 1994

Source: Compiled by author.

The life of Sankrityayan portrayed in the first two parts of *MJY* is that of a village boy who develops into adulthood on his own, without any family (or any other kind of) support, in a struggle for food, shelter, clothes, money, education, guiding philosophy and, above all, the sovereignty of his country. These two parts give insight into the social, political, educational, and economic situation of 19th-century India. The third part, originally published as *Rūs mẽ paccīs mās,* is mainly about his two years of living in Russia (1944–7). The remaining parts focus more on both his personal and public activities as a now famous writer.

The making of Mahāpaṇḍit Rahul Sankrityayan, starting out as Kedarnath Pandey, is described in the first and second parts of *MJY*, published during his lifetime as part of a more broadly conceived autobiography. These two parts are significant, therefore, if one is to understand the whole process of his changing identity against the social background of his time. The other four parts, published posthumously, describe the life of an established scholar.

The Autobiographical Imperative

Paul John Eakin (2008: 152) has coined a phrase to denote the motivation to write about one's own self or life for others' consumption: 'I called the impulse to self-expression—rather grandly as it now seems to me—"the autobiographical imperative".' To borrow his expression, Sankrityayan's urge to write his life history so as to be an inspiration for other ghumakkaṛs is what constituted the autobiographical imperative for him. In his own words:

> मेरी 'जीवन-यात्रा' मैंने क्यों लिखी? मैं इसे बराबर महसूस करता रहा, कि ऐसे ही रास्ते से गुजरे हुए दूसरे मुसाफ़िर यदि अपनी जीवन-यात्रा को लिख गए होते, तो मेरा बहुत लाभ हुआ होता–ज्ञान के ख्याल से नहीं समय के परिमाण में भी। [...]
>
> मैंने अपनी जीवनी न लिखकर जीवन-यात्रा लिखी है, यह क्यों? पाठक इसका उत्तर पुस्तक को पढ़कर ही पा सकते हैं। अपनी लेखनी द्वारा मैंने उस जगत की भिन्न-भिन्न गतियों और विचित्रताओं को अंकित करने की कोशिश की है, जिसका अनुमान हमारी तीसरी पीढ़ी मुश्किल से करेगी।[19]
>
> Why did I write *MJY*? I felt frequently that if other travellers who had passed over similar paths had written of their life's journey, it would have been very useful to me—in terms of not only what I could have learned, but also the time I could have saved [...].
>
> I did not write my life history but the journey of my life. Why is that? The readers can get an answer to this only by reading it. I have tried to present various ways and wonders of that world, which the third generation [from now] will hardly believe. (Sankrityayan 1946: 5)

The leitmotif of Sankrityayan's life is one of movement or of journeying. He never stayed in any one place for a long time, being ever drawn to experience new societies, people, and circumstances. This constant travel was what led him in 1940, when it came time to find a name for his autobiography, to call it 'The journey of my life'. As a ghumakkaṛ rāj, Sankrityayan was not simply interested in travelling for its own sake; he (2004b: 7) held the belief that ghumakkaṛs have

[19] According to the modern rules for writing Hindi, postpositions in Sankrityayan's texts are written under a separate upper horizontal line (except when joined with pronouns), but they are written together with the nouns in the 1946 edition of *MJY-1* and in other published works of him as well. Another deviation from modern rules is the infrequent use of the *nuktā* (a dot below a Devanagari consonant to signal its foreign origin and pronunciation, for the most part in words borrowed from Arabic or Persian).

created the present world and that they are its pride.[20] The work he titled *Ghumakkaṛ śāstra* (The wanderer's manual [1948]) makes the case for the importance of the wandering life and provides guidelines on how to go about it. Divided into sixteen chapters, it attempts to inspire not only men but also women to take to the road. The basic qualifications it sets forth are: indifference to family life, aged between 16–18 and 23–4, and the equivalent of a high-school education in order to have acquired a basic knowledge of history, geography, and mathematics. Further, he urged that languages such as English, Russian, Chinese, and French be learned. The most important requirement can be said to be the lack of romantic attachments, whether in the form of marriage or love affairs. Sankrityayan justifies his views on the basis of his own experience from the age of sixteen, when he himself began his first journey. The influence of this way of life can be seen not only in *Ghumakkaṛ śāstra* but in many other of his writings.

Das (1995: 100) notes that '[i]t was possible for a scholar of the eminence of Rahul Sankrityayan to create almost a new genre of historical writings that exploited travelogues as one of the major devices of narrative'; and further (1995: 252), that 'Rahul Sankrityayan is indeed the most fascinating figure of Modern Indian Travelogues'. Most of his works are in one way or another the product of his travels, in that they either incorporate the data collected during them or describe their actual course. Almost all the characters of his novels, too, are travellers.

Sankrityayan names Swami Dayananda and the Buddha as India's great ghumakkaṛs. The special place the wandering life occupies within Buddhism, and more generally within Indian culture and beyond, as a world religion, is pointed up in the Buddha's teaching 'चरथ भिक्खवे! चारिकं' (Dear monks, practise ghumakkaṛī).[21] He went so far as to blame the vanishing of Buddhism, the *mahān ghumakkaṛ-dharm,* (great ghumakkaṛ religion) from India for having created conditions for the country's political dependency. This came about when, in a later period, religious gurus such as Ramanuja, Madhvacharya, and other Vaishnava sages cast disapproval upon travelling and turned it for many into a taboo. In his opinion, this hindered the consolidation

[20] 'घुमक्कड़ क्यों दुनिया की सर्वश्रेष्ठ विभूति हैं? इसीलिए कि उसी ने आज दुनिया को बनाया है।'

[21] A translation of Sankrityayan's Hindi translation (Sankrityayan 2004).

of a pan-Indian identity, making it vulnerable to outside interference. He regarded the ghumakkaṛ dharm as the greatest religion, of which he was a follower. Ghumakkaṛī, as described by Sankrityayan, can be set off against the modern notion of tourism. Tourism in the 21st century is a luxurious holiday activity, whereas until the 20th century it was an undertaking that promised and demanded adventure, discovery, and personal achievement.

Abhi Subedi (1999: 19) notes: '[…] [one] important point regarding travel literature, or the travel narrative is the writer's conscious construction of the self as the protagonist within that construct. The writer puts himself or herself in the narrative in such a way that the travelogue, though it spans a short period of his or her life can be valorized as a biographical structure and it becomes something usable as reference in life.' Sankrityayan's autobiography is indeed a form of travel literature, or a travel narrative, the protagonist of which he builds up as he 'travels along'. It is a life history in the guise of a travelogue and vice versa. Subedi (1999: 19) terms Ekai Kawaguchi's travelogue a 'travel biography'. Sankrityayan's work is something similar but on a much grander scale: Kawaguchi narrates only a segment of his life, whereas Sankrityayan presents a string of seemingly disjointed episodes from his own life to produce a tale that nevertheless hangs together.

To conclude, it can be said that travel was the autobiographical imperative for Sankrityayan's having written his life history. *Ghumakkaṛ śāstra* sets forth the art of ghumakkaṛī, and *MJY* serves as a concrete illustration of one man's practice of it. The passion felt for ghumakkaṛī was Sankrityayan's excuse for neglecting his grandfather's wishes, refusing an arranged marriage, running away from home, and leaving his father, who had rushed to the railway station to bring him back, crying on the platform—all in the name of following the greatest religion, ghumakkaṛī.

Biographies as Expressions of Gratitude

One of the motives of Sankrityayan's remarkable contributions to the field of biography and autobiography was to show his gratitude towards the persons he considered heroes. This is clear from the foreword to his 1957 work titled *Jinkā maĩ kr̥tajñ* (To whom I am grateful, henceforth *JMK*): 'By writing *JMK*, I wish to pay back a debt and to be clear of debts.' His debt here was not a financial but rather an emotional one, for, as he further writes: 'These persons are not only the ones from whom I have learnt something or have been guided by, but there have also been many persons, relations with whom have been of help to me in my life's journey—as my *mānsik sambal* [intellectual mainstays]. I have learnt much from many people without their being aware of it—from their conduct and manners.'[22]

Bhaṭṭācārya (2005: 206) lists sixteen biographical volumes (both collective and single) written by Sankrityayan. This list includes biographies of Karl Marx, Stalin, Lenin, and Mao-Tse-Tung, all written in 1954. These were all figures of popular interest in India (Das 1995: 247) during Sankrityayan's lifetime. In the foreword to the work on Karl Marx, Sankrityayan writes:

> हिन्दी में छोटी-मोटी पुस्तकों का बिल्कुल अभाव नहीं है, लेकिन जिसमें पर्याप्त रूप से मार्क्स की जीवनी, सिद्धांत और प्रयोग मौजूद हों, ऐसी पुस्तक का अभाव जरूर खटक रहा था, केवल इसी की पूर्ति के लिए यह पुस्तक लिखी गई।
>
> There is no absolute absence of such biographies in Hindi, but the absence of books with sufficient details of Marx's life, his philosophy, and the application [of his philosophy] has been rankling. This book has been written merely to make up for this lack. (Sankrityayan 2004c: Foreword)

Apart from the biographies of these four internationally well-known communists, Sankrityayan wrote—under the first distinct series of biographies listed by Das (1995: 247)—one of the Buddha (*Mahāmānav Buddha* 1956), wherein he is specifically described as a cultural hero. Beside all these popular subjects, he wrote many biographical sketches and books about persons closely involved with him at some point during his life. Besides the above-mentioned *JMK* (1957), these include *Mere asahyog ke sāthī* (My friends from the non-cooperation movement [1956]), *Naye bhārat ke naye netā* (New leaders of new India, two volumes [1942]), *Bacpan kī smṛtiyā* (Memories of childhood [1953]), *Atīt se vartamān* (From the past to the present [1953]).

[22] 'जिनका मैं कृतज्ञ' लिखकर मैं उस ऋण से उऋण होना चाहता हूँ, जो इन बुजुर्गों, बन्धुओं, और मित्रों का मेरे उपर है। [...] इनमें सिर्फ वही नहीं हैं, जिन से मैंने मार्ग दर्शन पाया या कुछ सीखा, बल्कि ऐसे भी पुरुष हैं, जिनका सम्पर्क मेरे मानसिक सम्बल के रूप में जीवन यात्रा में सहायक हुआ। कितनों से बिना उनकी जानकारी, उनके व्यवहार और बर्ताव से मैंने बहुत कुछ सीखा।"

These four books represent a combination of biography and autobiography, with the narrating I in the first person sharing his personal experiences and impressions about the narrated person in question.

As Sankrityayan's relationship with Nepal is a major focus of this study, it is important to consider at this point the Nepalese he chose to write about. Separate sketches were devoted to Hemraj Sharma, Dharmaratna Yami, Lakshmi Prasad Devkota, Dharmaman Sahu, and Baba Paramhams. All of these were originally written as articles either for books or newspapers, but the life of Dharmaratna Yami was later expanded into a book. Short sketches of Hemraj Sharma, Baba Paramhams, and Dharmaman Sahu appear in *JMK*. Hemraj Sharma was respected by Sankrityayan for his scholarly achievements; Baba Paramhams, while not having helped him directly, was considered by him as a mānsik sambal; and Sahu Dharmaman helped make his first visit to Tibet possible by offering generous support, including funds and accommodations in Kathmandu and Lhasa.

However, for all his gratefulness, Sankrityayan ran into some misunderstandings and dissatisfaction in two cases. The first one had to do with the biography of Dharmaratna Yami, which was criticized by Muralidhar Bhattarai.[23] Bhattarai published a written *hũkār* (challenge) directed at Sankrityayan, calling upon him to prove what he had written about him, and at the same time inviting him to take part in a public *śāstrārth* (debate on the *śāstras*) in either Hindi, Nepali, or Sanskrit, as he wished.[24]

The second case involved the *mahākavi* (great poet) Lakshmi Prasad Devkota, which was misunderstood by the poet himself. This article was published in the Indian magazine *Ājkal* in 1953, after his visit to Nepal in the same year. Sankrityayan wrote it as a show of respect to someone he had come to greatly admire, and in order to introduce Indians to him. Devkota, however, was upset by it and lay awake the entire night after reading it. Later he wrote a satirical poem, *Pāgal* (The madman), containing unmistakable allusions to Sankrityayan. It is now regarded as one of Devkota's most important poems.[25]

[23] Muralidhar Bhattarai was involved in the anti-Rana movement in Nepal and was jailed together with Dharmaratna Yami. He was not happy with certain statements Sankrityayan made about him which he says were not true.

[24] See Appendix 2.

[25] See Appendix 3.

It is clear from Sankrityayan's own statements that he wrote of the lives of persons whom he admired or had reason to be grateful to. Apart from persons he actually met, he also wrote about the lives of persons who served as his ideals. In particular, he wrote short biographical sketches of the five Buddhist scholars—Nagarjun, Asanga, Vasubandhu, Dignaga, and Dharmakirti (Sankrityayan 1994).

Sankrityayan's Lineage

Sankrityayan composed very short biographical sketches of his maternal grandfather, Ramsharan Pathak, and father, Govardhan Pandey, in Appendices 3 and 4 of *MJY-1*. He also wrote a short but detailed introduction to the Sāṅkṛtyāyan lineage (Sankrityayan 1998b [*MJY-1*]: Appendix 2), containing a history of his ancestors and very short biographical sketches of some of the main ones. In it he demonstrates that he is a descendant of the legendary sage Saṅkṛti, whose birth year he gives as 1440 BC. Building on the latter's name, he created for himself a secondary name, Sāṅkṛtyāyan (descendant of Saṅkṛti), Sāṅkṛtya being his *gotra* (lineage) and Pandey his family name.

The composition was written in 1939 under the title Sāṅkṛtyāyan-*vaṃś*. The historical part of it is divided into four periods: (*a*) Vedic, (*b*) Buddhist, (*c*) middle, and (*d*) modern. In addition, it provides precise details of the procedure for performing a *kuldevtā pūjā* (worshipping the family god), traces the family's roots back to northern India, and identifies the period when his ancestors migrated to the village of Kanaila in Azamgarh district (in present-day Uttar Pradesh).

The work is a good example of what Indian cultural nationalism meant to Sankrityayan, linking him as it does to the golden Vedic period and following the lineage down to his own generation. In footnotes, he quotes from Vedas, Puranas, Upanishads, and Sanskrit epics, and many other old texts, as references to support his arguments. These include showing that his roots go back to the Vedic rishi Aṅgirā,[26] that King Bharat and the Pandavas and Kauravas of the Mahabharata were his ancestors, inasmuch as they were all descendants of the sage Bhāradvāja, the great-grandfather of Saṅkṛti (King Bharat was the son of Bhāradvāja's eldest grandson, Suhotra).

26 Aṅgira or Aṅgiras.

AN OUTLINE OF SANKRITYAYAN'S LIFE

A review has already been made of the literature devoted to studying Sankrityayan's life (see Introduction above) and of the major segments of his life such studies tend to define. Now, mainly based on his autobiography, a more detailed examination of his life will be attempted. There is a pragmatic reason for this: this study, being in the main biographical in nature, strongly demands a solid acquaintance with the biographical facts. The major goal of this work is to analyse the three major turns in Sankrityayan's multifaceted life. Before these are presented individually, though, it is essential to observe Sankrityayan's life in aggregate, across all of his turnings, and this will be done in the following pages.

An Unsuccessful Cultural Life Plan during Childhood

> ऐसा लड़का मेरा होता तो मैं उसे अंग्रेजी पढ़ाता।
>
> If I had such a son, I would have taught him English.
> (Sankrityayan 1998b [*MJY-1*]: 129)[27]

Rahul Sankrityayan was born as Kedarnath Pandey on Sunday, 9 April 1893 into a Brahmin family (the highest order in the varṇa scale), who lived in the village of Pandaha, Azamgarh district (Uttar Pradesh). He was born in his maternal grandparents' house and spent most of his childhood there. Neither of his parents' families were involved in priestly or education-related pursuits, although traditionally these were the main occupations of Brahmins. For seven generations his ancestors had been landowners who practised farming as their way of life.

Sankrityayan was the eldest child of his parents. His mother went on to bear other children after him, and he was left with his maternal grandparents in Pandaha, for in India's society, parents pinned their

[27] This quotation from *MJY* exemplifies the Indian craze for learning English throughout the 20th century. Since a command of English was important for getting a government job, people wanted their children to be educated in that medium. Teaching English to gifted students usually bore results. The quoted sentence was uttered by someone who had been treated to a display of Sankrityayan's intelligence.

hopes in old age upon having a son to look after them. Sankrityayan's mother was her parents' only child, and so his grandparents took him in lieu of a son of their own, having been left alone after their daughter's marriage. At his grandparents' house he received good care, and he long regarded his grandmother as his own mother.

Sankrityayan's primary- and middle-school education was seen to by his maternal grandfather, Ramsharan Pathak, who wanted to give him the best education possible. In November 1898 (Sankrityayan 1998b [*MJY-1*]: 7) he entered the Urdu primary-level madrasa in the village of Rani ki saray. Madrasas were mainly attended by Muslims and *kāyasthās* (the caste of government clerks). Pathak's ambitions for his grandson dictated the choice, for there he would learn Urdu. Urdu's status as the court language raised it above that of any of the other vernaculars, including Hindi, and it was an essential qualification for obtaining administrative jobs in British India. After making his grandson proficient in Urdu, Pathak had plans to send him on to a missionary school in Azamgarh district. Pathak had a cousin who was a munsif, and he himself dreamt of something like that for his grandson. As it turned out, though, his plans never materialized.

Sankrityayan attended a Hindu school in Badauda for some time in 1899, and there he learnt the Devanagari alphabet from a book published by the Khaḍgavilās Press with a picture of the goddess of learning, Saraswati, as a frontispiece.[28] In the summer of 1902 Sankrityayan was sent to his father's village, Kanaila, to escape a cholera outbreak in Pandaha. According to Hindu belief, performing various religious activities to please the goddess Durga would restore normalcy. Thus his parents organized a Śatcaṇḍī-pāṭh[29] at their home. Sankrityayan's uncle Mahadev Pandit,[30] a well-known scholar of Sanskrit, was invited to perform the recitation as a priest. After the completion of that ritual, Sankrityayan went along with Mahadev Pandit back to Bachval, where he started studying Sanskrit together with his uncle's students. A desire to further his Sanskrit education soon sprouted up in him.

[28] Khaḍgavilās Press of Bankipur had a monopoly on textbook production in Bihar until 1930 (Orsini 2010: 96).

[29] This involved reciting the religious work *Durgāsaptaśatī* one hundred times.

[30] The husband of his father's sister.

Even in the 20th century some teachers, following old tradition, were still teaching Sanskrit in their homes in villages and cities. Sankrityayan's uncle arranged *muṭhiyā* (formalized alms-begging)[31] in the village for students to obtain their food. Once the students acquired a certain level of knowledge they would go to Banaras for further studies. Banaras was the centre of Sanskrit education in the North India, and since it was close to Bachval, it naturally attracted students from the latter, and often to the latter's detriment.

During the 19th and beginning of the 20th century, Urdu's status as a court language may have given it the edge over Hindi, but neither Urdu nor any of the other vernaculars bore comparison with classical languages like Arabic, Persian, or Sanskrit in the eyes of traditional Indians (C.R. King 1995: 91). A love for one's language was one of the most significant forms nationalism took in India, and Sankrityayan, under the influence of his uncle, was falling into this mould. However, his urge ran against the wishes of his grandfather, and he was eventually forced to return to Pandaha. When Sankrityayan passed out of middle school in 1909, his grandfather insisted on further English-medium education for him. Sankrityayan for his part was set on pursuing Sanskrit studies. The impression his uncle had made on him and a desire to study Vedanta were overpowering. He resisted his grandfather's request with the argument:

> अंग्रेजी म्लेच्छ भाषा है, मैं तो संस्कृत पढ़ूँगा, उसी में स्वर्ग-मोक्ष का मार्ग रखा है। घरवालों के जिद करने पर एक दिन वह चुपके से निकल भागा।
>
> [']English is an alien language. I'll study Sanskrit. It contains the path to heaven and salvation.['] When his family insisted, he ran away. (Sankrityayan 1998b [*MJY-1*]: 348)[32]

Sankrityayan's grandfather had one and only one means of support left for him on the earth, and that was his grandson Kedarnath. But Sankrityayan did not take to this idea. In the brief biographical sketch of his grandfather in the appendix to *MJY-1*, Sankrityayan looks back at

[31] Every household was expected to put aside a handful of rice grains or other edible items to distribute to the poor or give to beggars once a day.

[32] One symptom of Indian nationalism was a firm belief in the superiority of Eastern culture.

this episode in his life with objective eyes and movingly presents his grandfather's state of mind, while relegating himself to the third person.

To a certain extent, though, Sankrityayan had a happy childhood. A diary entry in Sanskrit in an appendix to *MJY-1* provides evidence for this:

> शैशवं धन्यं। आजन्ममधुरं शैशवं कथं नाभूत्। बृद्धानां तत्कथाश्रावणम्।
>
> Childhood is a blessing. How could childhood, from birth onwards, not be sweet? It consists in elders telling stories. (Sankrityayan 1998b [*MJY-1*]: 318)

As the only form of security his grandparents had in old age, Sankrityayan was, if anything, too well cared for. They did not allow him to play in the water, climb trees, and so on, which they thought might be dangerous for life and limb. This was against the freedom-loving instincts of the young Sankrityayan, who always enjoyed being in his parental home in Kanaila more, where there were no such restrictions.

Sankrityayan got into the habit of fleeing from home at the age of fourteen. His mother and grandmother had both died by that time, leaving him with his grandfather, who, having mapped out his future for him, was bent on seeing that he stuck to the plan. The grandfather's combination of love and self-interest, however, was a burden to his longing to be free.

Sankrityayan's desire to travel was in part due to the stories his grandfather had been telling him all through his childhood, based on the experiences he had had working as a constable in south India and during his own many travels. These were stories that his grandfather used to tell to his wife in the evening while Sankrityayan lay in her lap on the point of falling asleep. It is clear from the above quotation that their content formed the stuff of his dreams.

Sankrityayan's father and grandfather always fetched him back home and tried to steer him towards a normal boyhood. But Sankrityayan had a mind of his own. He married in 1904,[33] but his relations with his first wife are not described in *MJY*, even if the marriage itself is

[33] He was married at the very young age of eleven to a twelve-year-old girl. She is called different names by different persons. Snātak (2004: 295) states that her name was Santoṣī; Kamala Sankrityayan, that it was Ramdulari (*JY-6*). Sankrityayan never mentions her name in *MJY*, but he did dedicate one of

mentioned. In it he blames society for this forced custom, but it could not keep him in the village for long either. He flew the coop for the first time in 1907, and a second time in 1909, in both cases to Calcutta. In the first case, he gives as his reason being afraid of his grandfather's reaction to his having accidentally poured ghee on the floor; in the second case, he offers no reason beyond a desire to wander.

The self-image presented by Sankrityayan during his childhood was of a youth determined to do what he wanted—to live his own life. The paths chosen for him by his father (the traditional married life of a villager) or by his grandfather (a minor judge) were both unacceptable to him. Every attempt to domesticate him failed. He did not care for others' points of view or emotional needs, but only followed his own heart's tugging. This was the lesson he had learned from his grandparents' rearing. His own force of character won out over all constraints imposed by the world, and he geared his life to his own wishes. Sankrityayan's psychological makeup, then, was radically different to that of other young men of his time, culture, and class.

Distinctive Adaptations in Youth

Following the two journeys to Calcutta, Sankrityayan next headed out on a pilgrimage to the western Himalayas. His uncle Mahadev Pandit

---

his books, *Kanailā kī kathā* (1998a [1957]), to her: 'To my first spouse, whose entire life became the victim of my ambitions.' [उसी प्रथम परिणीता को जिसका सारा जीवन मेरी महत्वाकांक्षाओं का शिकार हुआ]. In the foreword he writes about meeting her on 13 February 1957: 'I had decided that I would see my first spouse before leaving Kanaila. She was now confined to bed. It was natural to feel compassion at the sight of her. In the end, I was the reason why a half century of this woman's life was empty and insufferable. How would my penance help her at this stage? I saw her once. She could not hold back her tears. Then I came out.' [कनैला छोड़ने से पहले अपनी प्रथम परिणीता को देखने का निश्चय कर चुका था। अब वह चारपाई पकड़े थी। देखकर करुणा उभर आना स्वाभाविक था। आखिर मैं ही कारण था जो इस महिला का आधा शताब्दी का जीवन नीरस और दुर्भर हो गया। मैं प्रायश्चित करके भी उनको क्या लाभ पहुँचा सकता था? एक बार देखा। वह अपने आसुओं को रोक नहीं सकीं। फिर मैं घर से बाहर चला आया।]

The book consists of short stories on Kanaila, his parental village, where his first wife spent her life with the family of his brother. (Information received during a conversation with Sankrityayan's nephew Anil Kumar Pandey and his wife, Usha Pandey, in New Delhi, August 2008.)

and a later *darśan* of (visit to) Baba Paramhams[34] awakened a desire in him to study Sanskrit and Vedanta. He had started regularly showing up at the hermitage of Baba Paramhams near Kanaila and established a close friendship with his disciple Harikarandas, who further fuelled his desire to study Vedanta, while at the same time urging him to go on a pilgrimage to the Himalayas. Sankrityayan followed his counsel and set off to the mountains: to Haridwar, Rishikesh, Badrinath, Kedarnath, Devaprayag, Gangotri, and Yamunotri. Afterwards he went to Banaras and started his studies there in 1911.

When his grandfather heard about his Himalayan journey, he set off in pursuit but could not find him. Later, when his grandson was in Banaras, he could only hope that by allowing him to study Sanskrit there, he could eventually convince him to settle down in the village. This was not to be, though, for in 1912 he heard that his grandson had become a sadhu. Not long afterwards, in 1913, while his grandson was going about ascetic practices in Madras, and unbeknownst to him, Ramsharan Pathak breathed his last.

In his autobiography, Sankrityayan accepts that his grandfather loved him dearly, but he himself was not sure if he would have visited him during his final days, even if he had known of his condition. Any stirrings to do so were doubtless only a velleity, for later he did not attend his father's funeral either, even though he had heard of his death. His excuse was a vow he had by then taken not to re-enter Azamgarh district until he was fifty.

By 1912 Sankrityayan was fully devoted to his studies and wanted to become fully versed in Sanskrit and English. Sanskrit education was free of cost and even came attached with a possible *vṛtti* (scholarship). He was, however, not satisfied with Sanskrit studies alone but hoped to earn some money for an English-language education, having seen that even sadhus and renunciants attached importance to knowledge of the language.[35] In the long run Sankrityayan was never able to carry his institutional study of either Sanskrit or English up to a conclusion. He was a person 'who had no formal education' (Machwe 1978: 8)—no university degree—even if he did learn Sanskrit and other languages

34 See the biographical sketch of Baba Paramhams in Appendix 1.

35 'साधुओं और त्यागियों के समाज में भी अंग्रेजी जानने वाले की कदर होते देख, मैंने तय किया, कुछ समय उसके लिए देने को।' (Sankrityayan 1998b [*MJY-1*]: 115)

well enough to later edit texts, translate, produce literary works, and do professional research. He kept learning on his own and was largely self-taught.

A formal education was not in Sankrityayan's stars. After three days of English classes in Banaras, he was requested to read a court letter in English and translate it for Lachumandas, the *mahant* (head of an ashram) of Parsa, a Vaishnava maṭh. The mahant was very impressed by him and wished to groom him as his successor. Sankrityayan for his part was attracted to the educational facility. He was not utterly destitute, but still it would have wounded his pride to have had to ask for money at home (1998b [*MJY-1*]: 120). Job openings to earn the school fee were few and far between, so he agreed to become the disciple of the mahant, whose personality he found agreeable. Apart from the financial security this offered, he was attracted to the possibility life in Chapra[36] would have of maintaining his distance from his home (1998b [*MJY-1*]: 121).

Keeping the journey a secret, Sankrityayan arrived at Chapra in September 1912, but his father and uncle discovered him after three months. In the meantime, he had been initiated as a sadhu and given a new name: Sadhu Ramudar Das. Sankrityayan eventually came to dislike the new cosy life of an heir and would-be master of the monastery, and saw little incentive to continue his studies. He now set his sights on south India. Without informing anyone, he fled Chapra in July 1913. After visiting many places as a sadhu, he arrived at Tirumishi and lived there for about four months. The head of Uttarārdhī monastery, too, succumbed to him and requested him to become his successor. Sankrityayan was again initiated, this time as a Śri Vaishnava[37] sadhu and was given the name Damodarachari (Sankrityayan 1998b [*MJY-1*]: 12). His main aim in staying in the monastery, however, was his studies, and after a few months he again felt that he was wasting his time.

He headed back north, to Ayodhya, and after some days got admitted to a *vedānt pāṭhśālā* (Vedanta school). There, too, he found trouble fitting in, as he attests to in the following lines:

[36] Chapra, a city of the Saran district in the state of Bihar, later became a base for his political activity.

[37] The Śri Vaishnava sect is a sub-branch of Vaishnavism, one that follows the Viśiṣṭādvaita philosophy espoused by Rāmānujācārya.

मुझे अब अयोध्या के रहने में अरुचि होने लगी–अपने सहपाठियों और सहकारियों की मनोवृत्ति में अन्तर आ गया था। आर्य समाज के अतिरिक्त अखबारों द्वारा बाह्य जगत की हवा भी मुझे लग रही थी। मैं अपने अन्तस्तल में एक संकीर्ण गड़हिया से निकलकर विशाल जलाशय में जाने की मूक वेदना को अनुभव कर रहा था, यद्यपि अब भी मुझे यह नहीं मालूम था, कि वह जलाशय किस दिशा में है, कैसा है?

I began to be dissatisfied with my stay in Ayodhya. The difference between my friends' mental outlook and my own had come to the surface. Along with the Arya Samaj, it was through newspapers that I was exposed to the outer world. I was in silent agony to get out of what was a narrow pit and to enter a wide lake. However, I had no idea in what direction the lake lay or what it looked like. (Sankrityayan 1998b [*MJY-1*]: 170)

In his confusion, Sankrityayan was forced to write a letter to his uncle. His father, informed of his whereabouts, fetched him back home. It was October 1914, and Sankrityayan's family was now hopeful that he had turned a corner. His maternal grandfather had already died, and his father was confident that his son would become a proper householder. His family took heart at seeing him abandon the strange ways of a sadhu, for he indeed no longer performed the strict observances at home. He passed his days instead reading newspapers about the world war. He was slowly being drawn ever closer, though, to the Arya Samaj, through the lectures that he occasionally attended. He still had plans of earning some money and continuing his studies. He applied for a proofreader's position at the Indian Press in Allahabad, the publishing house that brought out the prominent Hindi journal *Sarasvati*, of which Sankrityayan was a regular reader. As it turned out, he had applied too late, but he did get some information about the Ārya Musafir Vidyālaya in Agra, where he could study free of cost and be trained for delivering the Arya Samajist lectures. This sent Sankrityayan off on a new trajectory; he left Allahabad for Agra in January 1915.

During Sankrityayan's stay in Agra, he won for himself the reputation of being a zealot Arya Samajist and an iconoclast. For two years he learnt Sanskrit, Arabic, the theology of various religions, and a nationalist version of India's history. This disciplined life in the school left an indelible urge in him for simple living. He also progressed well in lecturing, and upon occasion was sent outside Agra for that purpose. During this time Sankrityayan (1998b [*MJY-1*]: 178) confesses: 'I was slowly becoming indifferent towards the Vaishnava *vairāgī* [ascetic] cult.' This inner change was mirrored in a change of name: from Sadhu Ramudar Das he became Kedarnath Vidyarthi.

After two years of education in Ārya Musāfir Vidyālaya, Sankrityayan was asked to commit himself to the school and to the Arya Samaj, but he demurred, saying (1998b [*MJY-1*]:), 'I want to work for the Arya Samaj, but I cannot perform satisfactorily under the present imperfect situation. In order [to be able] to perform successfully, I wish to study further.' This demand was acceded to, and the door of the DAV (Dayanand Anglo Vedic) school in Lahore opened up for him. At that time Lahore was the stronghold of the Arya Samaji movement. In 1916 Sankrityayan got admitted in a *viśārad śreṇī* (advanced class) of the Sanskrit department (Sankrityayan 1998b [*MJY-1*]: 266). From Lahore, too, he frequently travelled to many places to propagate the Arya Samaj agenda.

His education and participation in the activities of the Arya Samaj instilled in Sankrityayan the desire to engage in social reform. Gradually, too, he waded into politics and became interested in Buddhism. The social environment and activities of the Arya Samaj was a suitable breeding ground of nationalistic sentiment. They meshed well with the ideas Mahatma Gandhi was sowing at the time. As Gupta (2005: 122) notes: 'In the matter of social reform, Dayanand comes closer to Gandhiji. Gandhiji has himself praised the work done by Dayanand [...] [and taken] up the work of the up-liftment of the depressed classes and dedicated his whole life to it. He also advocated the cause of widow remarriage. But he could not give it a revolutionary character. Dayanand and his followers spearheaded this movement to such an extent that it created [a] stir in the country.'

Sankrityayan, now under the spell of persons who were devoting their life to their country, made up his mind to take a vow of *prānotsarg* (sacrificing one's life) for *deś kī āzādī* (the country's freedom) if need be.[38] Although Sankrityayan had not yet read any books on communism, only newspaper articles, he began thinking a lot about it. Later he would analyse his adoption of the Arya Samaj's ideals as the beginning phase of his interest in communism:

38 See Chapter 2 for more details on the role of Arya Samaj in Sankrityayan's life.

अखबारों को पढ़ना, देश-विदेश की राजनीतिक खबरों को गौर से देखना, भारत में राजनीतिक क्रान्ति की चाह, रूसी क्रान्ति और साम्यवाद-ये मेरे प्रिय विषय थे। साम्यवाद पर किसी ग्रंथ के पढ़ने का अब भी अवसर न मिला था, किन्तु उस पर काफ़ी चिन्तन और तर्क-वितर्क किया करता था, तो भी अभी मेरा साम्यवाद आर्य समाज के धर्म की एक उदार व्याख्या में सम्मिलित होने लायक था। कुछ सालों तक अच्छी तरह पढ़ाई करके पूर्वीय देशों-चीन या जापान-में वैदिक धर्म प्रचार के लिए जाना, बस यही धुन थी। अपने इस प्रोग्राम में जब मुझी को सन्देह नहीं था, तो दूसरे को सन्देह कैसे होता। नये तजर्बे के बिना पर आदमी बदलता रहता है-इस तत्त्व पर मेरा विचार अभी नहीं गया था।

Reading newspapers, observing the political happenings in and outside the country, the wish for revolution in India, the Russian Revolution and communism—these were my favourite concerns. I had not had the opportunity to read any book on communism yet, but I had thought a lot and used to discuss a lot about it, even if my [idea of] communism would have been [more] suitably included under the liberal philosophy of the Arya Samaj. I had only one ruling passion: to complete my studies well and go to eastern countries—China or Japan—to propagate the Vedic dharma [that is, Arya Samaj principles]. I did not have any doubts about this course of action, [and could not have imagined] how anyone else could have had. I had not yet considered the truth that a person is constantly changing in virtue of new experiences. (Sankrityayan 1998b [*MJY-1*]: 213)[39]

Sankrityayan, then, during his many travels within India, was keeping close tabs on ongoing political developments within the country. In 1920 he visited Sarnath, Kasaya (the former Kushinara or Kushinagara), and Matha Kuar, all holy places for Buddhists. His journey continued north to the border area of Nepal. He crossed the border to visit Lumbini (the birthplace of the Buddha) and Kapilavastu (the kingdom of his father Śuddhodana). He tried to enter the Kathmandu Valley, which was still called Nepal, but was not allowed to, so he turned back towards Bihar.

39 The last sentence is grammatically problematic. The Hindi word *binā* has two meanings: the first one is as an adverb signifying 'without', while the second is as a feminine noun signifying 'cause or plea'. The preposition *ke* before binā is inconsistent with a feminine noun, while *par* after it is inconsistent with an adverb. On the basis of the context, however, I consider the noun to have more likely been the author's intent.

This was a time when Sankrityayan was slowly turning to Buddhism, and his interest in Vaishnavism and the Arya Samaj was waning, even if the Arya Samaj's philosophy still strongly resonated in him. He was no longer a sadhu at heart; he merely travelled about dressed up as one in order to obtain easy accommodations and food in maṭhs. He continued his journey south and in September 1920 again reached Tirumishi, where he spent two more years studying the Mīmāṃsā and Vedanta philosophies, and also learning Tamil. In 1921, after completing his studies, he joined the Arya Samaj mission in Coorg and travelled about delivering lectures on the philosophy of Arya Samaj for four more months.

Coorg was then in the midst of the *asahyog āndolan* (non-cooperation movement) against British rule. Sankrityayan received summons from his friends to participate in it. He was keenly interested in politics, and in the asahyog āndolan in particular, about which he was well informed through the newspapers. Despite his inclinations, he could not leave the Arya Samaj mission, owing to commitments made to it at the time of his admission. When a letter from one of his cousins informed him of his father's demise, however, the news offered him a valid reason to leave the mission. The vow Sankrityayan had taken in 1917 not to return to his home district of Azamgarh until he was fifty had been meant to call a halt to his father's repeated requests to put down roots there. The last meeting with his father had been in that same year, when his father went to the train station after learning that his son would be passing through. Now, true to his vow, he did not go home for the final rituals. The letter, however, had paved the way for his political engagement.

June 1921 found Sankrityayan in Chapra with politics at the top of his agenda. The death of his father had somewhat unsettled him, but he was soon occupied with his new raison d'être (1998b [*MJY-1*]: 375). Sankrityayan's involvement with the Arya Samaj was now pretty much over.

Turning to Politics

The year 1921 was one of triple identities for Sankrityayan. At the beginning of it he was active in Chapra as a sadhu, but one for whom society and its problems were constantly pricking his conscience. Later he returned to the Arya Samaj and was able to engage in social reform, if only within the framework that that organization supplied for it. Later still he completely devoted himself to politics, with the main objective of securing political autonomy for his country.

In June 1921, when the asahyog āndolan was at its height, thousands of students left schools and colleges, and many lawyers their practices. Gandhi had succeeded in collecting much money for the Tilak Memorial Swaraj Fund.[40] In that same month a young sadhu holding a *kamaṇḍalu*[41] in his hand, with shaven head and bare feet, entered the office of the District Congress Committee in Chapra and sat down in a corner. The committee was introduced to what would be its newest member, Ramudar Baba. Sankrityayan had gone to Chapra to get initiated into the world of politics, wanting to start off in a backwater. Following the example set by Gandhi, he delivered lectures against alcohol and hemp consumption and against animal sacrifice; he also helped flood victims during a particularly bad monsoon season. He travelled far and wide to extol the ideal of satyagraha. On 31 January 1922 he was arrested while chairing a meeting of the District Congress Committee in Chapra and sent to Baksar jail for six months.

After being released from jail, Sankrityayan plunged back into politics, but he was not as active as before. The title of the chapter in *MJY* which takes up from this point, 'Rājnītik śithiltā' (Political laxity), is indicative of this. He was dissatisfied with the situation in

[40] After Gandhi became involved in politics and the Congress party, he introduced three main changes. First, he made Congress a mass organization by opening its membership to all; second, he got it to adopt the policies of non-cooperation and civil disobedience; and third, he had it launch a countrywide organizing and propaganda campaign in favour of Congress. To finance these activities on behalf of Swaraj, the Tilak Memorial Swaraj Fund was established at Gandhi's initiative to collect Rs 10,000,000 in memory of Bal Gangadhar Tilak. Contributions to this fund came from all sources, in small and large amounts, and the target was reached within three months. For more details, see Krishna (1966).

[41] A pot or vessel with a handle, and sometimes a spout, used by ascetics to receive alms in the form of grains.

the party. The lull brought about by Gandhi's imprisonment and his abandoning of satyagraha after the Chauri Chaura incident[42] divided the Congress into two groups. One, the supporters of Gandhi's decision, were ready to wait till his six-year sentence expired. A second group, which opposed it, was unwilling to remain idle for that length of time. The first group within the Indian National Congress were called 'status quoists' (*aparivartanvādī*), while the second group, which in 1923 went on to form the Swaraj Party, were known as 'changers' (*parivartanvādī*). The Swaraj Party's main leaders were Motilal Nehru, Bittal Bhai Patel, and Deshbandhu Chittaranjan Das. Unhappy with the decision made by Gandhi, Sankrityayan became a Swarajist, although following his release from jail in 1925, after the Congress party had split, he never confessed in writing his affiliation to the new party.[43]

Sankrityayan participated in the Gaya congress in 1922 and campaigned on behalf of the future Swaraj Party, while also pushing

[42] Chauri Chaura is a village in Gorakhpur district, Uttar Pradesh, where on 5 February 1922 police fired at a group of demonstrators gathered to picket the liquor shop at the local market, killing three and wounding several. Infuriated, the crowed took revenge by setting the chowki ablaze, and many officers were killed, trapped inside. In response to these killings, the British authorities declared martial law in Chauri Chaura. Gandhi decided that the Indian people were still ill prepared for satyagraha, and the Indian National Congress halted the non-cooperation movement at the national level. Gandhi himself was arrested and sentenced to six years of imprisonment but was released early, in February 1924, on grounds of ill health. For details on Chauri Chaura incident, see Amin (2003).

[43] Jawaharlal Nehru's sentiments, too, were mixed; his father Motilal was the leader of the group, but Nehru himself did not support it, writing (Nehru 2004: 112): 'Deshbandhu Das tried, soon after my discharge from prison, to convert me to the Swarajist creed. I did not succumb to his advocacy, though I was by no means clear as to what I should do. It is curious and remarkable, but characteristic of him, that my father, who was at the time very keen on the Swaraj Party, never tried to pressure me or influence me in that direction. It was obvious that he would have been very pleased if I had joined him in his Campaign.'

to have the Bodh Gaya temple handed over to the Buddhists (Sankrityayan 1998b [*MJY-1*]:).[44] He delivered many lectures on the temple, and indeed the proposal to hand it over was his own. The debate between status-quoists and changers was so heated, though, that the issue surrounding the temple could not be resolved. Still, Sankrityayan had the opportunity to build very good relations with the Buddhist monks, and this would facilitate his later visits to Sri Lanka and Tibet, and conduced to his embracing Buddhism. He remained regularly involved in politics after the Gaya congress, taking time out for a break in the form of a one-and-a-half-month trip to Kathmandu (during those days the capital was known as Nepal) in March–April 1923 to participate in the Śivarātri festival.[45]

After his return to Chapra from Nepal in April 1923, he found a warrant for his arrest, leading to a two-year jail term awaiting him for having delivered a speech in Patna on 26 January 1923 against the Chauri Chaura incident. He was released on 18 April 1925, having utilized his confinement for studying and writing. He had written his first book (the Utopian novel *Bāisvī̃ sadī*), translated three nomadic adventure novels into Hindi, and studied astrology, some French, and the Avesta.

Gandhi's call for an asahyog āndolan had attracted Sankrityayan to politics, further fortifying the nationalist sentiment that had sprouted in him in the Arya Samaj. He started engaging in political activity in 1921, and by 1927 he had been imprisoned two times for a total of two-and-a-half years. The conflict within the Congress party, understandably, dampened Sankrityayan's spirits. His nationalist sentiment, nevertheless, found another outlet, namely the historical Buddha and his philosophy, which he hoped could be used to advance his country's cause. He ended up going to Sri Lanka to study Buddhism, with further plans of visiting Tibet.

44 For details of Sankrityayan's involvement in the Maha Bodhi Temple restoration, see the section titled 'Initial Endeavours Relating to Buddhism' in Chapter 3 of this volume.

45 Although the Kathmandu Valley during these years was not easily accessible, Hindu pilgrims could obtain visas during the Śivarātri festival. Utilizing this opportunity, Sankrityayan visited the valley a few times in the guise of a sadhu.

Turning to Buddhism

After Sankrityayan's release from prison in 1925, travelling, politics, and lecturing still ran along parallel to one another, but his main focus had shifted to Buddhism. During his travels he occasionally resided in Arya Samaj centres. He was no longer a devoted Arya Samajist, but he did continue to participate in their functions. During his lectures for the Arya Samaj in 1926 he started extolling the Buddha:

> मैंने कई जगह व्याख्यान दिये जो आर्य समाजी ढ़ग के थे, किन्तु उनमें बुद्ध की बहुत अधिक प्रशंसा होती थी।
>
> In a number of places I delivered lectures that, while in the style of the Arya Samaj, contained inordinate praise for the Buddha.
> (Sankrityayan 1998b [*MJY-1*]: 288)

He was delivering lectures as well as travelling to various parts of northern India, but he was no longer very interested in doing so. During the period when he was back in Bihar he entered again into active politics, attending, for example, the Gauhati congress in 1926. He helped to arrange Gandhi's trip to Saran in 1927, and met him for a few minutes there. All in all, though, Sankrityayan found little excitement in politics now that his interest had turned to Buddhism, as he himself wrote:

> कांग्रेस के सामने कोई नया कार्यक्रम न था। मेरे साम्यवादी विचार बाइसवीं सदी लिखकर रख रखने ही तक सीमित थे, और उनके प्रचार के लिए साथी और अनुकूल वातावरण नहीं था। उधर बौद्ध धर्म के विशेष अध्ययन की मेरी इच्छा जो लद्दाख यात्रा से जग उठी थी, अब मुझ पर भारी जोर दे रही थी।
>
> The Congress [Party] did not have any new program. My communist philosophy was limited to [what] I had written [in] *Bāisvī̃ sadī*, and neither friend nor favourable situation there was to propagate it. A desire to make a special study of Buddhism had awoken in me after my trip to Ladakh, and now was pressing heavily upon me.
> (Sankrityayan 1998b [*MJY-1*]: 311)

In this state of mind, Sankrityayan took up a teaching post in Sanskrit at Vidyālaṅkāra Pariveṇa in Sri Lanka, where he immersed himself in Buddhist texts for nineteen months. He renounced his salary in exchange for books, food, clothes, accommodation, and, above all, the excellent opportunity to study Pali (Mule 1998: 37).

Sankrityayan earned the title Tripiṭakācārya (master of the Tripitaka) before leaving Sri Lanka for Tibet in 1928. He was convinced that such a trip was obligatory if he was to gain a full knowledge of Buddhism, and in particular of the history of Indian Buddhism. He did not want to become a monk right off, for that would have meant scratching his travel plans. Entering Tibet was no easy thing for Indians at that time. After going over maps, he realized that he could only enter Tibet via Nepal, and penetrating Nepal up to Kathmandu was only possible for Indians during the Śivarātri festival. He left Sri Lanka on 1 December 1928 with the aim of utilizing the three months before Śivarātri by making pilgrimages in India to a number of historical places associated with the Buddha.

Sankrityayan entered the Kathmandu Valley as a Hindu pilgrim-sadhu on 6 March 1929. There he remained for two months disguised as a Tibetan, before hazarding the onward journey to Tibet under the alias Khunnū Chevaṅ. The ploy worked and, after one year, six months, and twenty days, Ramudar Das was back in Sri Lanka with copies of the Tibetan *Kanjūr* and *Tanjūr*, many 'pictures' (*citrapaṭ*), and one palm-leaf manuscript of the *Vajraḍākatantra* in Sanskrit. In terms of the writing that came out of it, his first visit was not that remarkable, but he did learn Tibetan and at the same time compiled a dictionary (unpublished) of it, *Bhot-Sanskrit śabdkoś*, containing 16,000 words. He obtained nine Sanskrit grammar books preserved in Nepalese temples and started reading them with the help of their Tibetan translation. Later he was also able to get *Tanjūr* from Muru monastery which helped him learning Tibetan as well as collecting Tibetan words with their Sanskrit synonyms.

On arriving back in Sri Lanka on 22 June 1930, Sankrityayan was 'initiated' (*pravrajit*) as a Buddhist monk. Prior to the renaming ritual, he himself suggested changing his name from Ramudar to Rahul. At first he had not wanted to change his name, since he was already well known as a writer, but the head of the vihara, Mahapad Nayak Mahastavir, insisted that he do so, so he chose Rahul because it started with the same syllable as his previous name. Thus he came to be addressed as Rahul Sankrityayan, combining his Buddhist monastic name with his Hindu *gotra*[46]. When he was accorded the title 'mahāpaṇḍit' by the Kāśī Paṇḍit Sabhā from Banaras in February 1930 while still in Tibet, he was addressed by his former name, Ramudar Das Sankrityayan.[47] But the final one, the one which he himself adopted and became famous under, was Mahāpaṇḍit Rahul Sankrityayan.

Sankrityayan himself does not say much about the title besides mentioning it in his autobiography. The title of 'mahāpaṇḍit' (great scholar) was given to him in his absence. Sankrityayan had not achieved the scholarly height yet in 1930, for which this title would get its meaning and the image of Mahāpaṇḍit Sankrityayan we have. In time, this title would be made meaningful. Furthermore, Sankrityayan had already changed his family name and had foreseen himself as Rāmodār Sankrityayan before going to Tibet for the first time. Later, after coming back, he did not continue with the first name, for which the title was given, rather continued the family name and the title.

Sankrityayan had turned to Buddhism, but his social conscience did not leave him in peace. During his stay in Lhasa, he impatiently followed the *namak* (salt) satyagraha. But even after returning to India, he was unable to jump back into politics immediately. He first had to arrange storage for all the things he had bought from Tibet (Sankrityayan 1998b [*MJY*-2]: 76), and then, after his initiation, Mahapad Nayak Mahastavir refused to let him leave. Sankrityayan obeyed and used his time from 7 October to 14 December to write the *Buddha caryā* (The Buddha's way of life) in Hindi, based on the Tripitaka. Thereafter he took permission from Mahapad Nayak Mahastavir to leave for Chapra on 15 December 1930 to take part in the satyagraha. He returned to Sri Lanka on 28 November 1931, having visited many historically important places along the way, including Karachi, Mohenjo-Daro, Harappa, and Sarnath.

In July 1932, Sankrityayan and Bhikkhu Ānand Kauśalyāyan went to London as *dhammadūta*s (religious messengers) representing the Maha Bodhi Society.[48] In Sankrityayan's words: 'The main propagator

46 'Gotra' is an exogamous sub-division of a caste group (named after risihis) according to the Hindu religion (McGregor 2006).

47 See Appendix 4 for the felicitation certificate.

48 Anagarika Dharmapala had bought a four-storey house near Regent's Park in London. This became a centre for promoting Buddhism in London, with a temple, lecture room, library, kitchen, and rooms to accommodate Indian and Sri Lankan students.

was Ānand Kauśalyāyan, and I was merely accompanying him' (1998b [*MJY-2*]: 95). At regular Sunday sessions at the Maha Bodhi Society in London, Ānand Kauśalyāyan was often the main speaker, but Sankrityayan, too, spoke on a number of occasions. Sankrityayan returned within a few months via France and Germany, while his companion stayed on in Europe for over twenty months. Sankrityayan had been requested by the society to remain longer in London and then to visit the United States to promote Buddhism there, but he demurred. He wrote about his London journey: '[...] I find the capitalist life very dreary. I have observed and understood what I wanted to; there are similar things in America; so I do not want to waste my time.' (Sankrityayan 1998b [*MJY-2*]: 109). This statement proves that Sankrityayan saw himself in England not for the main purpose of promoting Buddhism but to size up a different form of society, in this case one embodying a capitalist system. He admits that, for all his being a great lover of journeys, his reluctance in this case was due to the journeying being too easily facilitated by the society; to the comfortable travelling by train, bus, and ship; and to the residing in bungalows. All forms of wealth vexed him, and he yearned to be back among the misery of the poor. Indeed he was so keen to visit Russia to experience communism being put into practice that he had already started learning Russian in London. He had also tried to meet some people who might make a Russian visit possible, but nothing came of this. In any case, he had saved two hundred German marks for such a journey and had met many Indian and German communists. Finally he returned to Sri Lanka and then, in January 1933, went on to India, with Russia still very much on his mind.

Sankrityayan spent the year 1933, before his second visit to Tibet, engaging in literary pursuits and visiting different places in India: Patna, Ladakh, Lahul, Kullu, and Lahore. By the end of the year, he was back in the Ganges plain. His literary works published in that year were: *Tibbatī bāl śikṣā* (Tibetan children's education [1933]) and *Tibbatī vyākaraṇ* (A Tibetan grammar [1933])—two books on the Tibetan language for Ladakhi Buddhists; a Hindi–Sanskrit translation of the *Dhammapada* (1933); a Hindi translation of the *Majjhimnikāya* (1933); and many articles about his travels. Such deep involvement in writing, however, could not dampen Sankrityayan's eagerness for travel. He continued travelling throughout to different parts of India, and then in March 1934 set off for Tibet via Kalimpong. His book about the first journey, *Tibbat mẽ savā varṣ* (One and a quarter years in Tibet [1933]), had just come out.

He went thrice to Tibet between 1934 and 1938, and also visited Burma, Hong Kong, Japan, Korea, Manchuria, the Soviet Union, Afghanistan, and Iran. As fruits of his four hazardous journeys to Tibet in 1930, 1934, 1936, and 1938, he brought back more than eighty Sanskrit Buddhist works to India, some of which he himself later edited and published.

The unsatisfactory course of Congress politics had driven Sankrityayan to channel his nationalist sentiments through Buddhism. The study of the Tripitaka in Sri Lanka, the Tibet visits in search of lost Buddhist texts and their subsequent editing, the Europe trip as a *dhammadūta* of the Maha Bodhi Society, and his stay in Russia, the land of his dreams, were the most important events of this phase. Up to then he had lived the life of a single man. His aim in becoming a Buddhist monk and adopting Buddhism had been fulfilled. His second visit to Russia led to a marital life and a more fervent devotion to communism.

The Visits to Russia and Turning Away from Buddhism

Sankrityayan was one of many writers throughout the world who had been inspired by the Russian Revolution of 1917, and he was keen to visit the Soviet Union. In 1935, at the earliest opportunity after his second Tibet visit, he set foot on its soil. He reached Moscow by train from Manchuria on 4 September and spent a fortnight in Russia. He hoped to meet Theodor Ippolitovich Stcherbatsky, the Russian Indologist and author of the famous work *Buddhist Logic*, but the latter was in Leningrad, where Sankrityayan was not permitted to go.[49] Therefore he went on to Iran and by 21 December was back in India. He had the chance to visit Russia for a second time in 1937, at the invitation of the Soviet Academy (on Stcherbatsky's initiation) to teach Sanskrit at Leningrad University. He stayed in Leningrad from 17 November 1937 to 13 January 1938. There he met a young Russian lady, Ellena Narvertovna Kozerovskaya,[50] the secretary of the Indo-Tibetan department. She

[49] For details on Sankrityayan's relationship with Stcherbatsky, see the section 'The Different Trips to Tibet and Their Different Aims' in Chapter 3.

[50] Sankrityayan uses the name Lola when referring to her in his writings.

could speak French, Russian, English, and Mongolian, and started learning Sanskrit from Sankrityayan, while at the same time teaching him Russian. Both quickly fell in love and married on 22 December 1937. Sankrityayan discarded the robes of a monk and reverted to the status of a lay Buddhist. Although he no longer professed the Buddhist religion, he continued to admire its philosophy. This, combined with his commitment to the communist ideology, was what he remained true to throughout the remainder of his life.

After his return from Russia in 1938 and a short visit to Tibet, and following eleven years of relative retirement from political life, Sankrityayan again threw himself fully into the peasant movement. He had devoted those intervening years to studies, research, and travel, fulfilling a number of cherished wishes. In December 1938 he became a member of the Congress Socialist Party. He organized a *kisān* (peasant) satyagraha at Amvāri and was jailed for a few months. The Bihar Communist Party was established in October 1939, and Sankrityayan became a member. Being a communist was a risky affair, requiring, for instance, knowing how to dodge police surveillance. In February 1940, he presided over a *kisān sammelan* (peasants' meeting) held at Motihari, and for his provocative speech there was re-arrested and forced to spend the next twenty-nine months, stretching from 1940 to 1942, in the Hazaribag and Deoli jails. While incarcerated, he fell sick many times during the numerous hunger strikes. Still, he managed to devote much of his time to enriching Hindi literature. He wrote his monumental work *Darśan digdarśan* (Philosophical bearings) (1942), providing a critical exposition and Marxist interpretation of Indian, European, and Islamic philosophies. He also wrote *Viśva kī rūprekhā* (An outline of world [history] [1942]) and *Mānav samāj* (Human society [1942]), in both of which he traced the development of humanity through the ages. *Vaijñānik bhautikvād* (Scientific materialism [1942]) is another work from this period. The most important fictional works published during these years were *Volgā se Gaṅgā* (From the Volga [to] the Ganges [1942], a collection of twenty historical short stories) and *Siṃh Senāpati* (General Singh [1944] a historical novel), and eight political plays[51] in the language

[51] These were (a) *Japaniyā rāchach* (A Japanese demon), (*b*) *Deś-racchak* (The protector of the country), (*c*) *Jarmanvāṃ ke hār nihicay* (Germany's

spoken in Chapra, called *Malikā*. To these were added a flesh-and-blood creation, for while in jail he received news of the birth of his son Igor (on 5 September 1938) in Russia. After being released from jail, Sankrityayan travelled to different parts of India during the years from 1942 to 1944 for both political work and literary meetings.

In July 1945 the Russian government invited Sankrityayan to take up a professorship at Leningrad University. Professor Scherbatsky wrote in his memoirs that the only person in the world who could teach Buddhology authoritatively after him was Rahul Sankrityayan (Machwe 1978: 21). Sankrityayan served in this post from July 1945 to July 1947. During his stay he recorded many books in his own voice. Guṇākar Mule quotes one Dr Kalianof: 'Rahulji was always sensitive to correct pronunciation. Therefore stories from the *Nalopākhyān* and Kauṭilya's *Arthaśāstra* in Sanskrit, and the *Setubandha* in Prakrit, were recorded in his voice. Many of them are still preserved, and the well-known dulcet voice of Rahulji could be listened to at the university' (Mule 1998: 102; italics mine). His wife Lola and son Igor were also with him in Leningrad. It was his first experience of a household of his own, and it came at the age of fifty-two. He has described his days in Russia in detail in *Rūs mẽ paccīs mās* (1951), the work which was re-assembled into the third part of *MJY*. On 15 August 1947 India became independent, and a few days later, on 17 August 1947, he set off back to his home country by ship and landed in Bombay.

The years between Sankrityayan's first visit to Russia in 1935 and his return from his third Russian sojourn in 1947 were eventful ones for him, covering political activities, twenty-nine months of prison life, the creation of many monumental written works, the birth of a son, two years of family life in Russia, and the experience of teaching at Leningrad University. As described in *MJY*, a visa problem meant that Sankrityayan could not live in Russia indefinitely, while it proved

defeat is certain), (*d*) *Ī hamār laṛāī* (This is our war), (*e*) *Ḍhunmun netā* (Fickle-minded leaders), (*f*) *Naikī duniyā* (The new world), (*g*) *Joṅk* (The bourgeois), (*h*) *Mehrārūn kī durdasā* (The poor condition of women). All these plays were written in 1942 and printed in Chapra in 1944 (Mule 1998: 202). They were published in two volumes; the first volume contained the first five stories, and second volume the last three.

impossible on the other hand for his wife and son to get permission to live in India. Therefore, the family was consigned to live apart from one another. This period further strengthened his commitment to communist philosophy, while his nationalist sentiments attained their finest expression. He could have lived on in Russia for the rest of his life, had he wanted to, but his love for his motherland drew him back to India, where, he thought, he still had much to contribute to the Hindi language and its literature.

Adaptation to a Household Life and His Final Days

After August 1947, Sankrityayan remained in India except for one journey to China, three to Nepal, and a teaching assignment in Sri Lanka. He was elected president of the Akhil Bhārtīya Hindi Sāhitya Sammelan (All India Hindi Literary Conference) in Allahabad and served from 1947 to 1948. His speech at the 35th conference of the organization in Bombay on 27 December 1947 was criticized because he spoke against accepting Urdu and its script as the national language and national script. This went against the policy of the Communist Party of India, and he therefore faced expulsion from it. He was requested to retract his words, but he did not do so, raising his voice all the louder for Hindi and Devanagari script. In December of 1947, then, he was dismissed from the party. At the same time he learned that he was suffering from diabetes.

Somewhat later he was nominated by the Government of India as a member of the Constitution Translation Committee. Along with the busy schedule this required, he continued to write and travel to different parts of India. His health weakened, though, and he cut back on his travels and went in search of a permanent assistant to whom he could dictate. He appointed a number of scholars and other helpers too, to aid him in compiling a dictionary of administrative terms at his Mussoorie residence. One of them, Kumari Kamala Pariyar, whom he had taken on as a typist, also assisted him by administering insulin. Both became close and in December 1950 took marriage vows.

While Sankrityayan was staying at Mussoorie, he also wrote another monumental work, *Madhya Eśiā kā itihās* (The history of Central Asia [1952]), dictated over a period of four months. This work, published in two volumes, earned him the Sahitya Akademi Award in 1958.

He continued writing and travelling occasionally. A daughter, Jaya, and son, Jeta, were born in 1953 and 1955. In 1959 the Vidyālaṅkāra Pariveṇa (VLP) in Sri Lanka, where he had taught Sanskrit, was upgraded to a university, and it invited him to head its Department of Philosophy. Accordingly, he took up this new assignment in September 1959. While in Sri Lanka, he fell ill and had to return to India in August 1961. By December the overwork and his weak health had aggravated his diabetes to an acute stage. On 11 December he lost his memory in Calcutta, which he was visiting together with his family in order to act as the chief guest at a commemorative function for Pundit Kishoridas Vajpeyi. He was taken to Russia[52] for treatment but showed no improvement. After seven months, he was brought back to India. On 14 April 1963, at the age of seventy, he breathed his last at his Darjeeling house, where he had always intended to end his days. Political struggle, writing, and ghumakkaṛī had been synonyms for him of life's meaning, but it was such relentless activity that at the same time steadily undermined the physical foundations of his life.

* * *

The popularity of autobiography or biography as a literary genre in 20th-century India had been one reason for the publication of *MJY*. Besides the interest that he knew existed among readers and publishers, Sankrityayan was also responding to requests of his friends when he took to writing it. Up till then, biographies (including those of historically important figures) could be classified as falling either under the spiritual (cultural) or political category. *MJY*, however, does not really fit under either of these. It is neither spiritual or cultural, in the sense of Paramahansa Yogananda's *Autobiography of a Yogi* and Purohit Swami's *The Autobiography of an Indian Monk*, nor political in the manner of Nehru's or Prasād's widely read autobiographies.

In *MJY* the narrative I is able to define the narrated I by shifting direct attention away from it and onto its surroundings: onto, for

[52] Sankrityayan was accompanied by his wife, Kamala. His Russian wife and son also visited him in the hospital, but Sankrityayan was unable to recognize them.

instance, the geography and society of India and the importance it feels must be attached to Indian culture. It presents an energetic young Indian who wants independence for himself and who realizes that he can achieve this only when his country as a whole has achieved independence for itself. Towards that end he joins religious and political organizations, disregarding all responsibility for his family. His many journeys to famous Hindu pilgrimage sites, as recounted in the travelogues that came out of them, are metaphors of the country's own quest for its true place in the world. For, like Sankrityayan, it too had spent many years as a political prisoner to a foreign power. Like him, it bided its time, soaked up experience, and remained literarily creative. *MJY* thus mingles the spiritual, literary, social, and political substance of 20th-century India, showing how what was transpiring on the national level was a summation of what was taking place on a personal level. It was a narrative, then, that every kind of reader could identify with, providing as it does a vicarious self for all of them. In this, it is uniquely representative of its time, both in terms of the diversity of its scope and the archetypical meanings it conveys.

Why did Sankrityayan write *MJY*? This is a question readers will naturally ask themselves, but it was one, too, that the writer would certainly have asked himself. The answers that first come to mind with regard to the first part of it are: first (and more superficially), in order to make better use of otherwise unproductive time in prison, and second (and more fundamentally), to provide an account of a ghumakkaṛ's life that might serve as an example to other would-be ghumakkaṛs. He elsewhere sets limits to the utility any guidelines afford, stating that 'any two lives by necessity cannot be the same, but [nevertheless] every life has to face the same internal and external waves of the world' (Sankrityayan 1994a: foreword). The second part of *MJY*, too, was written to utilize the otherwise idle time of waiting for his Russian visa in Allahabad. He submitted the manuscript to the publishers before leaving the country. Sankrityayan saw only these two parts of *MJY* published, but lived to write a third part (reworked into the fourth and fifth parts of the final edition). The complete *MJY* in our hands today is not what Sankrityayan had envisioned, for while the aim of the first and second parts was to inspire other ghumakkaṛs, the remaining parts, posthumously published by Kamala Sankrityayan, were meant to present Sankrityayan as a luminary in Hindi literature.

MJY is a life history of a self. Now the question arises, what kind of self-perception does Sankrityayan convey in it? It is one that, throughout the first two parts, Sankrityayan is consciously working on to construct, and the picture he presents of it is at once distant and strongly purposeful. The narrated I presented in *MJY* is determined to fulfil its aims, and thus bent on overcoming any obstacles that might get in its way, even if this means seeming distant to those in its immediate proximity.

Sankrityayan's life history unfolds against the backdrop of contemporary history—its political, social, and educational arenas—and provides a starkly vivid picture of these spheres of activity as experienced by the narrator. The narrating I has taken pains to be as neutral as possible in presenting the narrated I, and at times provides an almost clinical analysis of it. All the seminal transformations in Sankrityayan's life took place between 1907 (when he first left home for Banaras) and 1944 (when he wrote *MJY-2*). Therefore the first two parts of *MJY* can be considered to present the quintessence of his life history, a fully self-aware account of how the Brahmin boy Kedarnath developed himself into Rahul Sankrityayan.

If Sankrityayan's autobiography is compared with the two popular autobiographies of Gandhi (2003) and Nehru (2004), it will be seen that all share some similarities. All of them paint a picture of India and Europe from the end of the 19th to the middle of the 20th century. Unlike Gandhi and Nehru, however, Sankrityayan was not born into a wealthy family and did not find himself raised to the ranks of a national political leader. It is therefore, in that sense, less circumscribed. Nehru's description of his life, in particular, is largely limited to the political arena in which he was active, whereas Sankrityayan's autobiography covers many more facets of life and society beyond the political realm, ones seen through the eyes of a struggling village student, a sadhu, a Buddhist monk, a writer, a traveller-scholar, and a teacher. Gandhi's autobiography, to be sure, examines the self from within, but it is there that his 'experiments with truth' are largely conducted, so that again the perspective is intentionally narrowed down. Gandhi's and Nehru's autobiographies, then, introduce their readers to individuals that follow a fairly straight line of development and establish logically successive and well-defined niches for themselves within society, and their picture of society is correspondingly bounded within the limits of vision these niches afford. Sankrityayan, by contrast, experiments not only with politics and with inner truth, but more characteristically with the whole spectrum of experience life offers. Sankrityayan's *MJY* situates itself somewhere between the two poles represented by Gandhi's and Nehru's autobiographies, while at the same time implicitly acknowledging the legitimacy of both their subjects' aims. For it, too, recognizes the absolute need for independence along with the attendant struggle required to attain it. But unlike them, it insists on the self's right to be free from any kind of family, social, organizational, or philosophical compulsion. Sankrityayan's frequent running away from home, his vow not to return to his home district until the age of fifty, his affiliation to and separation from a string of organizations, culminating in his expulsion even from India's Communist Party, were all part of an ongoing experiment to try to make the self independent. The seriousness with which he approached ghumakkaṛī and writing were touchstones of the struggle. How successful was the struggle—how successful Sankrityayan in achieving independence? The mass of his writings contains the evidence relating to his struggle, while the unique picture it presents suggests that he gained a measure of the independence that comes by—according to the Buddhist philosophy he espoused—successfully avoiding attachment and by meditating upon one's life dispassionately.

An autobiography is written to introduce a self to others, so that they may share, and perhaps profit from, its experiences vicariously. Gandhi's autobiography records the paths that his struggles to be led by truth took him on, in the hope that others will be convinced of the power and superiority of truth. Sankrityayan for his part wrote *MJY* for prospective ghumakkaṛs, for those, that is, out to forge an independent self, again through the hard path trod. At a definite point along the way, the ghumakkaṛ Sankrityayan became Mahāpaṇḍit Rahul Sankrityayan, by which point he had achieved a goodly measure of independence. The major theme recurring in his writings is ghumakkaṛī and the independence that comes with simply striking out towards some beckoning destination.

The saying, 'Life is an open book,' can be turned around and used as a gauge to measure the success of an autobiography. For if an autobiography is open—that is, honest—it will necessarily acquire a life and meaning of its own. *MJY*, compared with most other autobiographies and biographies, is huge in size, but at the same time it stands out for its minuteness of detail (one characteristic feature being the exactness of dates). Thus one quickly comes to feel that the author is indeed being honest with his readers. Shivachandra Sharma evaluates *MJY* thus: 'It is a virtual encyclopedia of political, social, literary and historical conditions created by individuals and groups in India and abroad. It has very little about Rahul, more about others' (Machwe 1978: 31). This sums up the importance of *MJY* as an historical document of India's path to independence in the 20th century written by someone who prefigured that achievement with a similar one of his own.

An autobiography is written for a specific audience, whereas a diary is written for the self alone. The fact that Sankrityayan early on started keeping a diary, though, meant that he was able, when he came to write an autobiography, to use it when filling in the details of his life. For the last part of his autobiography (until 8 December 1961), of course, which he was no longer able to write himself, his diary entries provide the only means for him to express himself directly to the reader. The role played by Sankrityayan's diaries in the making of his autobiography only serves to enhance its truthfulness, and indeed to raise it to the status of a life history.

MJY-1 and *MJY-2* represent Sankrityayan's own retrospective of his life history up to the time of their writing. In them Sankrityayan presents himself as a communist, for just prior to the time he wrote *MJY-1* he had been imprisoned for communist activities, while he wrote *MJY-2* while waiting for a visa to visit Russia right after being released from jail. He was and remained a devoted communist, but he was, as the later parts of the autobiography make clear, a communist sui generis, who shaped his beliefs to the contemporary Indian context.

MJY confirms Machwe's (1978: 28) characterization of Sankrityayan: 'Rahul is not romantic or sentimental. His relations with other human beings, superiors or seniors, equals or even juniors are those of a friend and a questing soul. He is neither cynical nor carping.' Sankrityayan was devoted to his chosen ideals and determined to realize them. He did upon occasion cause hurt to others in pursuit of his aims, but shows little inclination to dwell over such incidents:

दूसरों के साथ रूखे बरताव के मेरे बहुत कम उदाहरण हैं।

There are only a very few examples of my treating others rudely. (Sankrityayan 1998b [*MJY-1*]: 162)

He knew that at times he seemed distant to others and points out his mistakes, but having done so, he also finds good reason for having so acted. In this way, he suggests, he was able to move on in life, free from mental pressure. Typical examples include his flouting his father's desire to keep him in the village, life with his first wife, leaving the Arya Samaj on the pretext of attending his father's funeral, and his defence of his book on Dharmaratna Yami in Nepal.

For all the exactness of detail in *MJY*, Sankrityayan's own psychological disposition is not always clear. The narration is more focused on social and cultural phenomena than on the author's own state of mind. Personal emotions, be they sorrow, happiness, excitement, or boredom, tend to be covered over. In the Indian context, such an attitude could well serve to illustrate the *ādarś saṃyamit jīvan* (ideal of the self-controlled life). The veil is lifted, however, in the sixth part of *JY*, where Kamala Sankrityayan, by including citations from his letters, demonstrates that Sankrityayan was in fact an emotionally sensitive husband and father.

After the memory loss, his family tried to restore him to health by reading to him from *MJY*, but for the most part this did not help. To be sure, he showed intense interest in having *MJY* read to him. His childhood name drew a response from him, and he showed the mark branded with hot iron on his arms during the initiation as a sadhu (*JY-6*: 600–36). Before going for treatment to Moscow, Sankrityayan was in Delhi for some days. One of the visitors at Delhi's Constitution House has described his condition:

राहुल जी चौपाई पर चित लेटे हुए थे। अपनी आत्मकथा के दोनों भाग छाती पर रखे हुए थे। वे उन्हें सस्नेह सहला रहे थे और मुस्करा रहे थे जैसे पिता अपनी संतान को प्यार करते और लोरी देते हुए मुस्कराता है।

Rāhul-jī was lying supine on the bed. He had placed both parts of his autobiography on his chest. He was stroking them lovingly and smiling, as when a father smiles when doting on and singing a lullaby to his child. (Rahbar, December 2006–November 2007: 281)

The relevance of *MJY* to the 21st century is the factual picture of 20th-century India—its religious, cultural, and political life—sketched in it and the figure that sketches itself in the process. It was a figure that helped to define, and in turn was defined by, the age of nationalism in the India of its time. Through the vicissitudes of life, it avoided feelings of distress or regret by maintaining the spirit of adventure that it thought life called for. This was why Sankrityayan could successfully nurture nascent modern Hindi literature in the years between 1923 and 1960 with such an astounding number of indelible contributions to it. In 'The journey of my life', life and journeying have become synonyms of each other. Sankrityayan's life history, while the life history of an individual, has made of that individual an icon of the nomadic life, one who lived and journeyed from 1893 to 1963 in much the same way the characters in his novels and stories do.

CHAPTER TWO

The Arya Samaj

A 'New Light'

उस वक्त ग्यारह वर्ष की अवस्था में मेरे लिए यह तमाशा था। जब मैं सारे जीवन पर विचारता हूँ, तो मालूम होता है, समाज के प्रति विद्रोह का प्रथम अंकुर पैदा करने में इसने ही पहिला काम किया।

At the age of eleven it [that is, marriage] was a *tamāśā* [farce] for me. When I think about the whole of [my] life, then it becomes clear that it caused the first bud of revolt against society to sprout.

—Sankrityayan (1998b [*MJY-1*]: 53)

Sankrityayan has admitted that the first stirrings of the sense of a need for revival within Indian society commenced with his rejection of a marriage arranged for him at the age of eleven. This was not yet bound up with any nationalist sentiment, but it can be considered as having ignited a certain feeling of anger in him; he began his life of revolt by criticizing the custom of child marriage in north Indian society. Sankrityayan wrote in *MJY-1* that he had irrevocably rejected his marriage by 1908, at the age of 15, and by 1909 was making preparations to leave home. From 1910 or 1911 onwards, he completely avoided all marital responsibilities imposed upon him. Later he said that the vow he made in 1917 provisionally not to re-enter his home district was the final nail in the coffin of his forced marriage (1998b [*MJY-1*]: 53).

Desai (1954: 242–3) notes that '[c]hild marriage had been one of the principal evils from which Indian women, more even than men, suffered. Due to the efforts of Ishwar Chandra Vidyasagar, the Act of 1860 was passed raising the age of consent for married and unmarried girls to ten. [...] However, it was only in 1929 [...] The Child Marriage Restraint Act passed [...] [which] raised the marriage age for girls to fourteen and for boys to eighteen'. Not only had social reformers struggled to raise the legal minimum age for marriage, but widow remarriage was also legally permitted from 1856 on. Child marriage was one of the main items on the social reform agenda of the Arya Samaj. Swami Shraddhananda[1] had presented a strategy for reviving the ancient *āśram dharm*[2] and settled on a minimum marriageable age of twenty-five years in the case of males and sixteen for females (see Jaffrelot 2007: 79). One can therefore surely argue that the Arya Samaj served to strengthen Sankrityayan's opposition to his own child marriage. This starting point of Sankrityayan's own rebellion against key features of Indian society can thus be seen as part of the larger social reform movement in the early 20th century.

Sankrityayan clearly believed that the stance he took against his first marriage was justified, for he wrote: 'It would be a mistake to blame me for this unsuccessful marriage instead of blaming society' (1998b [*MJY-1*]: 53). And when he goes on to characterize his marriage at the age of eleven as a tamāśā (farce), he was implying that it was something so absurd as to be laughable. Besides fleeing home, he had also planned to become a sadhu,[3] that is, someone who leads the very opposite of a married life. These plans were carried out during the years between 1910 and 1914, from the age of seventeen, when he set out on a Himalayan pilgrimage: 'I had decided that, having studied

[1] Lala Munshi Ram (1857–1926), later Swami Shraddhananda, was a prominent leader of the Indian National Congress and a loyal Arya Samajist, the one indeed generally considered most faithful to Swami Dayananda's ideals. He was also an educationalist (the founder of Gurukul Kangri in 1902), a founder of several newspapers, and an activist in the non-cooperation and Khilafat movements. He was killed by an enraged Muslim in 1926. For details, see Orsini (2010) and Jaffrelot (2007).

[2] The division of the whole life of an individual into four stages, called *āśrams*: *brahmacarya*, *grihastha*, *vānaprastha*, and *sanyāsa*.

[3] Fleeing from home was not only an act of rebellion but also the means of fulfilling a desire to visit new places. From 1912 to 1914 Sankrityayan travelled widely in south India as a sadhu and lived in free lodgings called *chatrams*, which he regarded as a boon to the roaming way of life: 'These places are hotels that provide food and shelter free to travellers. This proves how easy travel is made for sadhus by these institutions' (Sankrityayan 1998b [*MJY-1*]: 151).

Sanskrit and Vedanta, I would become a sadhu' (1998b [*MJY-1*]: 81). Having chosen not to study what his grandfather had hoped he would, he left home and became involved with the Arya Samaj. When his father came to take him back home, he made a vow not to set foot in his home district until he had turned fifty. He kept his vow and did not even attend his father's funeral—something unheard of among Hindu Brahmin families, especially in the case of an eldest son. Indeed he used the mourning period for his father to start engaging in political activities. His nationalist sentiment, nascent during his involvement with the Arya Samaj, was now what guided his decisions. His duties to his family yielded to those he felt he owed his nation and society.

Sankrityayan's father's continual attempts to bring him back home, then, were all to no avail. In 1917, when he heard that his son was passing through Azamgarh, he ran nine or ten miles without delay to the train station. Finding him there waiting for a train, he began pleading with him either to come back home or to take him along too. But his son, on his way to Maheshpura to establish an Arya Samaj school, would not listen. His recorded reply was:

> मेरा जीवन भी किसी भविष्य की लालसा रखता है, जिसकी जो अस्फुट झाँकी मुझे मिल रही है, उसके कारण जबर्दस्त से जबर्दस्त खतरे, मृत्यु के साक्षात् दर्शन तक भी अब मुझको अपने पथ से विचलित नहीं कर सकते।
>
> My life also has a certain desire relating to the future, an indistinct glimpse of which I can see, [and] for that reason the most horrifying dangers, even a direct confrontation with death, cannot now deflect me from my path. (Sankrityayan 1998b [*MJY-1*]: 199)

What was this *lālsā* (desire) and this *asphuṭ jhā̃kī* (indistinct glimpse)? The context makes it clear that it was an imagined future form of his own nation, for which he was ready, if need be, to sacrifice his life. This raises the question of what exact form it took in his imagination. Trying to create a picture of Sankrityayan's vision in this context will be the main objective of this chapter. Before proceeding, however, it is essential to realize just how much Sankrityayan credited the Arya Samaj with the development of his nationalist sentiment.

In this chapter, I will sketch the notion of true nationhood that Sankrityayan formulated by mixing the Arya Samaj's principles with his own still vague understanding of the Russian Revolution.

Defining Sankrityayan's relationship with the Arya Samaj is basic to understanding the emergence of his nationalistic sentiment. The aim here will not be to enter into a discourse on the terms Aryan or *ārya*, either as to their origin or definition. It will be limited, rather, to showing how the Arya Samaj helped to form a conception of self and other in Sankrityayan's mind. It may suffice to say that Sankrityayan held the opinion that Aryans entered India around 1500 BC.[4] He proudly claimed them as his ancestors and saw himself as their descendants.[5] The following pages will seek to elucidate Sankrityayan's conception of *rāṣṭrīyatā* (nationalist sentiment) and his notion of nationhood, as influenced by his understanding of the Arya Samaj's principles and the Russian Revolution.

Before embarking on the main discussion of this chapter, I need to make clear the meaning of the word rāṣṭrīyatā, which I have translated as 'nationalistic sentiment'. Rāṣṭrīyatā can mean simply 'nationality', in the sense of the status or identity conferred by a nation. An Indian citizen will respond to the question: 'What is your rāṣṭrīyatā?' with the answer: 'I am an Indian.' Sankrityayan uses this word in *MJY* in its second meaning of 'nationalism', that is, nationalist sentiment, implying for him a spirit of sacrifice and service to the nation. He invariably uses the word in the immediate context of India, and later—a reflection of this fact—replaced it with *bhārtīyatā* (Indianness). Sankrityayan's opinion, then, was that rāṣṭrīyatā was something that inspired people to devote themselves wholeheartedly to the advancement of their nation. I would therefore argue that, during the first half of the 20th century, this word came to be increasingly used in its secondary meaning, in response to an urgent need of the times. Indeed, all instances of

[4] In *R̥gvaidik ārya* (Aryans in the *Rig-Veda* [2004e]), Sankrityayan describes the Aryan way of life, including their origins and practices relating to administration, education, health, dress, sports and entertainment, gods, science, women, language, and literature. For detailed information on the Aryan debate, see further: Trautmann (1997), Sotī (2006), and Trautmann (2005). Fischer (1990) has explored the theme of ārya in Sankrityayan's novel *Siṃh senāpati*, while at the same time discussing how the Indian reform movement is reflected in it.

[5] See section 'Sankrityayan's Lineage' in Chapter 1 of this volume.

rāṣṭrīyatā throughout this study are meant in the sense of 'nationalist sentiment' and 'nationalism'. For example, when Sankrityayan uses the expression *rāṣṭrīyatā kā vidyālaya*,[6] I have rendered this as 'a school of nationalist sentiment'. Such a school would have been successful in inculcating service to the nation among its students, to such an extent that they would have even been willing to sacrifice themselves for it. Similarly, when Sankrityayan saw the crowd of people on 6 April 1919 in Lahore agitating against the Rowlatt Bills, he describes the scene as *rāṣṭrīyatā kī pahlī bāḍh* (the first flood of national sentiment). Such spontaneous engagement on the part of people was something, he felt, that nationalist sentiment encouraged. This is what Sankrityayan logically means, too, when he calls himself a *rāṣṭrīyatāvādī* (nationalist). Rāṣṭrīyatā, then, or the more literal *rāṣṭrīya bhāv*, are the terms he uses to denote nationalist sentiment.

SANKRITYAYAN'S TURNING TO THE ARYA SAMAJ

The Arya Samaj earned the right to be called Hinduism's most important socio-religious reform movement by abandoning the system of hereditary endogamous castes (the jātis) and the principle of untouchability, and by opposing Brahmanism (which it believed to have led to the corruption of the knowledge of the Vedas), and thereby initiating a process of returning to Vedic philosophy. Previous studies of Indian history have traced the beginnings of social reform in India back to Raja Ram Mohan Roy (1772–1833), the founder (in 1828) of the Brahmo Samaj. He tried to show that the worship of idols was not originally part of Hinduism. He also campaigned in favour of the abolition of all caste distinctions and pernicious social customs such as sati. The Brahmo Samaj attracted Hindu reformists from various regions, including the Bombay Presidency. Swami Dayananda Saraswati (1824–83), who hailed from that region,[7] founded the Arya Samaj in 1875, which developed into a powerful organization in northern India. He did not propose to do away with the caste system

[6] A literal translation: 'a school of nationality'.

[7] He was born in Tankara, a small town in central Kathiawar, Gujarat. For comprehensive account of Dayananda's life, see Jordens (1978).

but rather to reinterpret it as a merit-based division of labour. Parting from Brahmo Samaj doctrine, Dayananda asserted that the Vedic religion was superior to all other religions, including Christianity and Islam. He wrote and preached in Hindi and regarded Sanskrit as the mother of all languages. Dayananda's tone, then, was more nationalist than Ram Mohan Roy's.

Dayananda stated his ideas and beliefs in *Satyārthprakāś* (early on translated into English: *The Light of Truth*), first published in 1875. Primarily, he argued that the Vedic religion was monotheistic and thus rejected idol worship. Secondly, he attacked the caste system and rejected the common social divisions known as varṇas.[8] According to him, everyone in the Arya Samaj, no matter what their caste, would enjoy equal status and could become priests and perform the organization's principal rites and the Vedic sacrifices. Dayananda directly attacked the ritual hegemony of Brahmin priests. The *śuddhi* (purification) ritual was devised to allow those who had converted to other religions to return to the Hindu fold, and also to allow those who were not originally Hindus to become ones. It could be organized for a single person, for a family, or for a large group of people.[9] Another important innovation of the Arya Samaj was the great emphasis it laid upon education, while it also took up the revolutionary issue of protecting cows against the British and the Muslims. Arya Samaj preachers organized *śāstrārth*s (doctrinal debates) to compare their philosophy with other religious beliefs (especially Islam and Christianity) in an effort to demonstrate its superiority. These became their major tool for proselytizing. All of this activity attracted many Hindus to what would become the most important reform organization in early 20th-century India.

But while the Arya Samaj was originally established with the aim of achieving social and religious reform, it moved far beyond this goal from the early 20th century onward. Many members became involved in politics, and the organization itself strongly identified with the Indian National Congress, which hardened its nationalist stance in the

[8] The broader fourfold division of all castes: *brāhman* (priestly class), *kṣatriya* (martial or royal class), *vaiśya* (merchant class), and *śūdra* (labour class).

[9] 'On 3 June 1900, the Samaj conducted a public ceremony of *shuddhi* in the city of Lahore for 200 Rathias' Jones (1989: 113).

country as the independence movement gained momentum. Śuddhi and the cow protection movement of the Arya Samaj could easily be turned to political ends, and indeed they were, providing the occasion for collaboration between the Arya Samaj and the Congress party.[10] It was against this background that Sankrityayan in January 1915 joined the Arya Samaj, while a student of the Ārya Musāfir Vidyālaya in Agra.

To be sure, Sankrityayan's first impression of the Arya Samaj had not been so positive:

> मैंने आर्यसमाज का नाम पहिले-पहल 1901 या 1902 में [...] सुना था। इतना ही जानता था, कि वह देवी-देवता की निन्दा करते हैं। बनारस में दयानन्द स्कूल (वर्तमान डी. ए. वी. कॉलेज) का मैं कई महीनों तक विद्यार्थी था, किन्तु वहाँ बराबर जल में कमल की तरह रहा, कभी उनकी बातें न सुननी चाहीं न सुनीं। यहाँ अयोध्या में [...] स्वामी दयानन्द के 'सत्यार्थप्रकाश' का नाम सुना। मैं भी पहले इसे 'मिथ्यार्थप्रकाश' ही कहता था। [...] पढ़ भी रहा था [...] खंडन ही की दृष्टि से [...] इधर देवकाली के मामले में अयोध्या के सब-इन्सपेक्टर, तथा बा. बलदेवप्रसाद वलीक आदि- जिन्हें आर्यसमाजी कहकर मुझे बतलाया गया था- के बरतावों नें आर्यसमाजियों के प्रति मेरा भाव बदल दिया; और इस प्रकार सत्यार्थप्रकाश [...] को मैं सिर्फ़ खंडन की दृष्टि से पढ़ने वाला नहीं रह गया।
>
> I first heard about the Arya Samaj in [...] 1901 or 1902. I only knew that they criticized the gods and goddesses. For several months I had been a student of the Dayananda School [present-day DAV College] in Banaras, but I was always like a lotus in water [that is, indifferent]. I never wanted to listen to them, nor did I listen. In Ayodhya, [...] I heard about *Satyārthprakāś*. At first I called it *Mithyārthprakāś* [that is, The light of lies]. [...] I read it with an eye to criticizing it. [....] During the Devkali incident, the conduct of the Ayodhya sub-inspector and the lawyer Bā[bu] Baldev Prasad–who, I was told, were Arya Samajists–changed my attitude, and accordingly I stopped being a reader who read *Satyārthprakaś* [...] only with an eye to criticizing it. (Sankrityayan 1998b [*MJY-1*]: 170)[11]

[10] For details of the Samaj–Congress collaboration, see Gould (2005). On the Arya Samaj's contribution to strengthening Hindu religious nationalism, see van der Veer (1994). For more details about the Arya Samaj, see Jones (2006).

[11] Sankrityayan participated in a group which protested against animal sacrifice in a temple in Devakali, near Ayodhya. The protest turned violent and the police had to intervene.

Thus, through his more sympathetic reading of the *Satyārthprakāś*, he turned into an ardent devotee of Dayananda. Dayananda's every sentence became a *ved-vākya* (Vedic utterance) to him.[12] During his time in the Arya Samaj, Sankrityayan first learned through newspaper reports about the Russian Revolution. He stated that his extracurricular reading during these years was meant to serve as a base for his *bhaviṣya jīvan nirmāṇ* (construction of the future) (1998b [*MJY-1*]: 175–6). Indeed, the Arya Samaj and printed matter represented for him two beacons of what he called *nav prakāś* (new light) in his life. We may preface a discussion of the nature of this new light by first considering the Arya Samaj and its quest for a system of national education and Sankrityayan's own schooling under the organization.

The Arya Samaj and Its Quest for National Education

Education was not very widely available in pre-British India. Sanskrit education existed, but was restricted to the upper castes among Hindus. In the case of Muslims, any Muslim could study in madrasas, but any higher education was conducted in both Arabic and Persian. There were, to be sure, some vernacular schools in towns and villages, but again they tended to serve a limited group, mainly the sons of traders, sent to learn reading, writing, and the rudiments of arithmetic.

Desai (1954: 119–43) has credited three parties with spreading modern education in colonial India: foreign Christian missionaries, the British government, and progressive Indians. The missionaries were inspired by their proselytizing aim to spread Christianity among the Indian people. The education sponsored by the British government mainly served to meet their own administrative and economic needs. The third party, however, progressive Indians, had objectives that contrasted sharply with those of the other two, namely progressive

[12] 'मेरा रोआँ-रोआँ आर्यसमाज तथा स्वामी दयानन्द के प्रति कृतज्ञ था। [...] मैं दयानन्द के एक-एक वाक्य को वेद वाक्य मानता हूँ।'

I was deeply indebted to Swami Dayananda. [Lit.: Every part of my body was grateful to Swami Dayananda.] [...] I regarded Dayananda's every utterance as a Vedic utterance [that is, as something commanding instinctive belief] (Sankrityayan 1998b [*MJY-1*]: 189).

modern education for all of India. Raja Ram Mohan Roy, regarded as the pioneer of progressive modern education in India, hailed the English education system (as practised in England) as the key to accessing the treasures of scientific and democratic thought of the modern West. He, in collaboration with his colleagues, established the Hindu College in 1817 and the Anglo-Hindu College in 1822, both in Calcutta. Subsequently, numerous groups, including the Arya Samaj, the Ramkrishna Mission, and the Aligarh movement, and individuals like Bal Gangadhar Tilak, Gopal Krishna Gokhale, Madan Mohan Malaviya, and Mahatma Gandhi, worked further towards establishing other educational institutions for both males and females. Indian nationalists criticized the education systems promoted by the government, the Christian missionaries, and others as being divorced from the realities of Indian life and as purveying a distorted account of India's past history, one that tended to weaken national pride and individual self-respect. Moreover, education was conducted in English, a foreign language. The intent of Indian nationalists was:

> [...] to 'Indianize' education by preparing textbooks with a different cultural content and by pressing for the use of the vernacular, or they founded independent educational institutions. Noteworthy in north India in this respect were the schools founded by the Ārya Samāj and those established during the nationalist movement, the so-called 'national' schools. Such independent schools became [...] important symbolic 'places' and rearing grounds for nationalists. (Orsini 2010: 95)

It is clear, then, that education and the character building it entailed were integral parts of the nationalist reform movement in India. This can be observed throughout, from the establishment of the Hindu College by Roy to that of the national schools, called Gandhi Vidyālaya (Gandhi schools), during the independence movement. Such schools focused on moulding students' character and simultaneously inculcating a spirit of sacrifice and service to the nation, and firmly grounding students in other aspects of nationalist sentiment.[13] Sankrityayan

[13] See Singh (2012: Chapter 3) for the role of national schools in Bihar in forging a new national identity. Some of Sankrityayan's political activity in Bihar centred on such schools.

actively engaged in establishing and running such schools under the Arya Samaj and Gandhi Vidyālaya network. He himself had been, of course, a student at one such Arya Samaj school.

The founder of Arya Samaj, Swami Dayananda, seeing in Vedic education the main method of regenerating the country, called upon people to open Vedic *pāṭhśālās* (schools). By 1870 three *pāṭhśālās* had been established, in Mirzapur, Kas-Gang, and Chhalesar, although these schools, opened by Dayananda himself, were later dissolved (Gupta 2005: 143). R.K. Pruthi (2004: 4) writes: 'The leaders of the Ārya Samāj realized, from the very beginning, the vital importance of education in opening the eyes of the people to their true cultural heritage.'

After Dayananda's death, his followers built an English-medium high school in his name as a fitting means of commemorating him. Classes in this DAV school, located in Lahore, commenced in 1886. The college combined a study of Western literature and science with lessons in Hindi and Sanskrit. DAV College gradually grew into a network of similar institutions. Some Arya Samajists, including Swami Shraddhananda (Lala Munshi Ram), felt that the system adopted by DAV deviated from the ideals of Vedic education. He thus established Gurukul Kangri in 1902 near Haridwar. Harald Fischer-Tiné notes:

> The institution was to become the blueprint for a whole network of schools and colleges modeled in its image, [...] the school soon became an icon of early Hindu nationalism [...] and one of the main motives for its foundation was the desire to provide an institution at which an intensive study of Sanskrit and the Vedas was combined with a 'modern' curriculum. [...] Among the measures undertaken in Kangri that were supposed to foster a national identity, the spread of Arya Bhasha (a 'purified' style of Hindi) as a national language, [and] the rewriting of Indian history and the reorganization of society on the basis of equality and social mobility were prominent. [...] The extraordinary emphasis placed on 'character-formation' is certainly the most striking feature of the school. From the outset, physical training, fencing, horseback riding and drill formed an important part of the daily programme students were called, in the allusion to ancient educational practices. (Fischer-Tiné 2004: 232)

He further writes:

> In 1908 police officers and other officials speculated that the school was actually used as a training camp of terrorists. [...] The students, they suspected, would be ideologically equipped and physically prepared to take up arms against the British because of the emphasis [...] on rigid physical exercise and paramilitary training. There were rumors about an alleged subterranean bomb-factory supposedly situated under the *yagyashala*,[14] [...] (Fischer-Tiné 2004: 233)

Besides DAV College and Gurukul Kangri, which were prominent Arya Samaj educational institutions, many other schools were established by members of the organization. Some were branches of these schools, whereas others—such as Ārya Musāfir Vidyālaya, where Sankrityayan studied—were independent.

Ārya Musāfir Vidyālaya: A School of Nationalist Sentiment

It is clear from *MJY* that Sankrityayan had had great hopes that his desire to pursue uninterrupted studies would be fulfilled in Chapra, and therefore he had become a Vaishnava sadhu, but the reality there gave the lie to his expectations. He had also stayed in Ayodhya for three months to study in a Vedanta pāṭhśālā. Eventually he realized that his future lay neither in a monastery nor in Vedanta, and so he returned to his village, Kanaila. But remaining at home idle was not an option either, and when he heard about the Arya Samaj and the free education in its school in Agra he decided to try out Ārya Musāfir Vidyālaya.

Ārya Musāfir Vidyālaya had been established by Pandit Bhoj Datt in memory of an Arya Samajist, Pandit Lekh Ram. A former police officer in Peshawar, Pandit Lekh Ram (1858–97) joined the Peshawar Arya Samaj in 1880. Later he travelled to Ajmer, where Dayananda was residing, and was at his bedside when he died in 1883. He was firmly committed to the Arya Samaj and regarded Dayananda as his personal guru. In 1884 Lekh Ram resigned his job in order to devote himself fully to the Samaj.[15] Called Ārya

14 A place to perform a fire sacrifice according to Vedic rites.

15 For details about Lekh Ram's contributions to the Arya Samaj, see Jones (2006: 146–53) and Jones (1989: 101).

Musāfir (the Aryan traveller), Pandit Lekh Ram was one of the most important members of the śuddhi movement, a champion debater against Islam, and a leader of the militant āryas. His constant argument was that their ancestors had been pressured into accepting Islam, but now that Muslim rule had ended there was no reason to continue practising the religion. From the late 1880s onward he wrote extensively against Islam, most prominently the book *Risala-i-Jihād ya ya'nī Din-i-Muhammadī kī Bunyād* (Jihad, the basis of the Muhammadan religion).[16] Jones (1989: 101) notes: 'Lekh Ram portrayed Islam as a religion of murder, theft, slavery, and perverse sexual acts. Repeated writings by the Pandit angered Muslims who responded in kind.' Islamic leaders appealed to the courts, but they failed to silence Lekh Ram. The matter did not end there, and Lekh Ram was eventually murdered in March 1897. This murder was a warning to other Arya Samajists who were actively trying to convert Muslims. In Arya Samajist Sankrityayan's words, Lekh Ram was a *śahīd-e-dharm* (martyr for religion) (Sankrityayan 1998b [*MJY-1*]: 177). Lala Munshi Ram (Swami Shraddhananda) would later start a newspaper called *Ārya Musāfir* in his memory (Jones 2006: 329).

Ārya Musāfir Vidyālaya was a decisive institution in Sankrityayan's life, for it was there that his nationalist sentiment was first nurtured. His participation in the Arya Samaj's socio-religious activities, including regular discussions of the country's

[16] Sankrityayan later (1922) himself wrote a book on Islam, in Hindi: *Islām dharm kī rūprekhā* (An outline of the Islamic religion), published in 1923. The aim of it, as stated in the foreword, was 'हिंदुओं को अपने पड़ोसी मुसलमान भाइयों के धर्म की जानकारी कराना' [to inform Hindus about their neighbouring Muslim brothers' religion]. He notes in particular that there were as many different sects and opinions to be found within Islam as within Hinduism. Regarding relations between Indian Muslims and Muslims outside India, he compared the situation to that of Buddhists: '... as Buddhists all over the world have a special love for India, Bodh Gaya, and Indian Hindus and Buddhists, because they live in the land where Gautam Buddha was born and whence Buddhism spread throughout the world, similarly Muslims respect and love Arabs' (Sankrityayan 2005a: 48).

cultural and political situation in the school, along with his extensive reading of contemporary literature and newspapers, instilled a new sense of community in him. The schooling that he received there introduced him to the notion of the supremacy of Eastern culture, and of the Vedic religion in particular. Although he would soon come to moderate this view, this period was significant as the start of his nationalist education.

Sankrityayan himself assesses the importance of Ārya Musāfir Vidyālaya for himself in the following way:

> मुसाफ़िर विद्यालय धार्मिक नहीं राष्ट्रीयता का विद्यालय था।
>
> Musāfir Vidyālaya was not a religious school but a school of nationalist sentiment. (Sankrityayan 1957b: 94)

The normal course in Ārya Musāfir Vidyālaya lasted for two years. It was not an ordinary school, inasmuch as it focused on producing propagandists for the Arya Samaj, that is to say, on producing devotees competent in doing the work of śuddhi and śāstrārth. Sankrityayan underwent thorough training, and subsequently participated wholeheartedly in the Arya Samaj movement. Indeed, one condition of his admission to the school was that he would serve the organization after completing his education. Students who passed middle-school level (taught in Urdu) were admitted to the course of study, where they were taught Sanskrit, Arabic, and the primary cults, rituals, and other practices of both Hindus and Muslims. They were taught why the Arya Samaj was superior and why other religions had drawbacks to them. The Vedic religion, they were told, is the oldest religion in the world and the main source of every other religion. Only one Supreme Being was to be worshipped, for *bahudevvād* (polytheism), it was asserted, went against the Veda. This Supreme Being, who is called Īśvara (Lord) or Paramātma (Supreme Self), is not born, and the incarnation of what is unborn is not possible, they argued. This and the doctrine of *punarjanm*, or the rebirth and *karm* of individual souls, is what gives the Vedic religion its pre-eminent status among all religions. *Śrāddha*, a Hindu ritual commemorating death anniversaries, was explained as a ruse used by Brahmins to obtain food.[17] And as for caste, it is not something a person is born into; rather, humans should have the freedom to choose a profession of their own liking.[18]

Śuddhi

Śuddhi was the purification ritual meant to reclaim Hindus who had converted to Islam or Christianity; that is, it was a ritual of reconversion. Concerning it Jones (1989) writes:

> During the 1880s and early 1890s, Aryas conducted individual reconversions; however, considerable opposition existed to this practice and it was often difficult for a reconvert to find admission to Hindu society. In the wake of the 1891 census that reported an increase in Christian converts [...], Aryas and their Sikh allies in the Singh Sabhas[19] began to expand the use of *shuddhi*. [...] During the 1890s larger and larger groups were purified. [...] soon it was performed for anyone whose ancestors had once been Hindus. Aryas also used *shuddhi* to purify untouchables and transform them into members of the clean castes. (Jones 1989:101)

Students of the school practised the śuddhi ritual, adopting the role of a *purohit* (priest). Sankrityayan recalls in *MJY* that even though Muslims and Christians were less than willing to undergo the rite, many untouchables did so, thereby increasing the ranks of the *śuddhi-śudās* (purified people). He said that it was more in the way of being an *achūtoddhār*, a reformation of untouchables. The untouchables did indeed account for a large number of śuddhi-śudās. They mainly came from the local group of Camārs, the caste engaged in working with leather. Educated untouchables, who enjoyed a better economic

[17] 'Funeral practice and śrāddha inevitably attracted the hostility of the Aryan reformers. No trace of elaborate funerary forms can be found in the first book of Vedas; worse, the practice itself helped to confirm the dominance of the Brahmins and the perversion of true religion. Dayananda and his followers mounted a straightforward campaign to reinstitute the simple methods of burning enjoined in the ancient texts' (Bayly 1998: 158).

[18] This summary of Arya Samaj teaching is based on Sankrityayan's own in *MJY-1* (1998b [*MJY-1*]: 177).

[19] The Singh Sabha (Singh Assembly) was founded in Amritsar in 1872 with the aim of protecting Sikhism from outside interests.

situation, were especially keen on becoming respected members of society, and for this reason felt drawn to the ritual.

Śuddhi was one of the main preoccupations of the founder of Ārya Musāfir Vidyālaya, Pandit Bhoj Datt, who also happened to be the founder and president of the Akhil Bhārtīya Śuddhi Sabhā (All-India Purification Assembly).[20] The śuddhi ritual, as described by Sankrityayan in *MJY*, called for the following procedure: A day was to be set aside for the purpose. The family wishing to undergo śuddhi had first to fast for the entire day to demonstrate the seriousness with which they approached the *saṃskār* (ritual). In the evening the student–priests visited the host family's house. They prepared a *havan-kuṇḍ*[21] and performed a fire offering while chanting holy mantras in the presence of the head of the family, the *yajmān* (ritual client). Afterwards *prasād* (blessed food remnants) was distributed to the priests for immediate consumption.

Śāstrārth and *Vyākhyān*

The students of Ārya Musāfir Vidyālaya were all trained to be spokespersons of the Arya Samaj, that is, they were schooled in *śāstrārth* and *vyākhyān* (lecturing). This training provided Sankrityayan with notable skills as an effective speaker.

Every evening a period was set aside in the school for śāstrārth. There was an additional class during the evening to teach vyākhyān, the elements of effective delivery being expounded by seniors. Issues were announced for debate, and students randomly assigned to speak either in favour or against. Sankrityayan excelled in this activity. His strategy was not to spend time staving off attacks but to attack his opponents' defending arguments, thereby taking the initiative away from them.

On most days of the week students would be sent to the city markets to hold forth individually. They stood along the streets, and pedestrians would stop for a while to listen to them. The declamations were kept

[20] During Sankrityayan's stay at Agra, Pandit Bhoj Datt was suffering from tuberculosis and therefore barely saw his students.

[21] *Havan-kuṇḍ* is a square pit used for performing *havan*, a Hindu rite in which oblations are made to the god of fire, Agni.

short—approximately five to ten minutes. In Sankrityayan's opinion, this lecturing tradition was borrowed from the Christian missionaries (1998b [*MJY-1*]: 177). After some months in the school, Sankrityayan was sent to places outside Agra to deliver lectures and perform śuddhi, wherein he made rapid progress (Sankrityayan 1998b [*MJY-1*]: 179).[22]

The protection of cows was another of the Arya Samaj's major concerns, but Sankrityayan did not actively participate in this movement. As an Arya Samajist, however, sacrificing animals and eating meat were both unacceptable to him.

We now turn to the question: How did Ārya Musāfir Vidyālaya become for Sankrityayan a 'school of nationalism'?

Discovery of a New Light in the Arya Samaj

> राजनीति और देशभक्ति के विचारों से १९१४ तक मैं बिल्कुल अपरिचित था।
>
> Up to 1914 I was oblivious of politics and patriotism.
> (Sankrityayan 1957b: 93)

The chapter in *MJY-1* dealing with Sankrityayan's life between 1915 and 1922 is entitled '*nav prakāś*' (new light). It was during this period that he became involved in Arya Samaj activities and turned gradually to politics, and quite naturally to the Congress party in particular, since it was the only effective party in northern India at the time.

Sankrityayan was a Vaishnava sadhu when he entered the Arya Samaj in 1915, but his just concluded stay at a monastery had left him with a critical attitude towards the ascetic way of life. He had accepted ordination as a sadhu for the free education, travel, and freedom from home life it entailed, but in the end he judged that the drawbacks of asceticism outweighed the benefits. He was attracted to the Arya Samaj because it seemed to offer something more productive:

[22] Dayananda was indeed obviously influenced by the activities of missionaries, particularly ones involving lecturing and printing. For Dayananda's attraction to printing, see Section 'Sankrityayan and the Printed Word in Hindi' in the Introduction.

वैष्णवधर्म-वैरागी सम्प्रदाय-से मैं उदासीन हो गया था। धर्म का आकर्षण नहीं बल्कि घूमने-पढ़ने का आकर्षण, तथा घर से मुक्ति का ख्याल मुझे वहाँ ले गया था। वहाँ मेरे विचार वन्ध्या के समान थे, किन्तु यहाँ आर्यसमाज में अपनी बुद्धि को ज्यादा स्वच्छन्द, ज्यादा अनुकूल परिस्थितियों में पा रहा था।

I had become indifferent to the ascetic tradition of the Vaishnava religion. It was not the religion but the attraction of studies and travel, and the idea of freedom from home that had led me there. There my mind was unproductive; here in Arya Samaj, however, I found my mind more free, in more favourable circumstances.
(Sankrityayan 1998b [*MJY-1*]: 178)

The Arya Samaj represented a nationalist institution more than a socio-religious reform one for Sankrityayan. The presentation and description of it in his writings tends to be related in some way with his own nationalist sentiment. He notes that Dayananda's books insistently appeal to readers' *deś-bhakti* (devotion to country, patriotism) and raise the call for *svatantratā* (independence). He notes, too, that the British government was suspicious of the Arya Samaj's nationalist agenda and therefore kept close tabs on its members (see Fischer-Tiné 2004: 229–47). It was, he points out, natural to be a nationalist in those days and claimed that this was the only reason why he was one himself:

आर्यसमाज के राष्ट्रीय भावों की भनक अंग्रेजी अधिकारियों को लग गयी थी, इसलिए वह आर्यसमाज और उसके उपदेशकों को सन्देह की दृष्टि से देखते थे। इस वातावरण में आकर्षण राष्ट्रीयता की ओर होना स्वाभाविक था।

The British administrators had gotten wind of the Arya Samaj's nationalist sentiment, and therefore cast suspicious eyes on the Arya Samaj and those who promoted it. In this situation it was natural that one should be attracted towards nationalism. (Sankrityayan 1957b: 93)

Further,

राष्ट्रीय स्वातन्त्र्य का जोश अपने जैसे लाखों भारतीय नौजवानों की भाँति मेरे हृदय में भी भरा हुआ था।

My heart, like those of hundreds of thousands of other Indian youths, was filled with fervour for national sovereignty.
(Sankrityayan 1998b [*MJY-1*]: 182)

In 1915, the year Sankrityayan entered the Arya Samaj, Bhāī Parmānand (1876–1947), an Arya Samaj activist, was arrested in connection with the First Lahore Conspiracy Case and sentenced to death.[23] He had written a book on India's history which was banned by the government. Sankrityayan, who had read the book, said that he was ready to resort to any means, including armed action, to free Bhāī Parmānand or any other arrested comrade:

> प्राण देने वाले स्वेच्छा सेवकों की जरूरत पड़ती, तो मैं उनमें पहिले नाम लिखाता।
>
> If there was a need for volunteers willing to sacrifice their lives, I would have registered my name at the top of the list. (Sankrityayan 1998b [*MJY-1*]: 182)

Sankrityayan credited one teacher of the Ārya Musāfir Vidyālaya in particular, Maulvi Mahesh Prasad, for rousing the embers within him to flame. He wrote:

> भाई साहब ने हमें आँख दी, देश-पुकार सुनने के कान दिये, प्राणदान करने वाले हुतात्माओं के अनुकरण करने की प्रवृत्ति दी।
>
> Bhāī Sāhab gave us eyes, gave us ears to hear the nation's distress call, gave us the temper to follow in the footsteps of those who had sacrificed their lives. (Sankrityayan 1957b: 93)

This teacher is referred to by Sankrityayan in his writings as Bhāī Sāhab[24] (Respected brother). He was from Allahabad and taught Arabic in the school, having previously passed up a job in the police force in order to work for the Arya Samaj. He is credited by Sankrityayan with having taught him the meaning of deś-bhakti.

> मेरी स्वाभाविक प्रवृत्ति किधर को है, इसका परिचय मुझे नहीं था। यहाँ आगरा में भाई साहेब के सम्पर्क में आने पर मालूम हुआ, जैसे आदमी अँधेरी कोठरी से

[23] The sentence was later commuted and he was exiled to the Andaman Islands, where he was subjected to hard labour. Bhāī Paramanand went on a hunger strike for two months against the harsh treatment meted out to political prisoners and was finally released in 1920 as the result of a general amnesty order. For further details of his life, see Brown 1975: 17.

[24] Sometimes Sankrityayan uses an alternative spelling, Saheb.

निकालकर सूरज की रोशनी में रख दिया जावे, जैसे दम घुटती काली कोठरी से निकाल शीतल मन्द सुगन्ध-वायु परिचालित बाग में ला रखा जाये। अब मुझे मालूम होने लगा, दुनिया में ऐसे भी काम हैं, जिनके लिए जीवन की आवश्यकता है, ऐसे भी आदर्श हैं, जिनके लिए मृत्यु मधुरतम वस्तु है।

I was unaware of my own natural tendencies. After getting to know Bhāī Sāheb in Agra, I felt like a person taken out of a dark cell into the sunlight, like one taken out of a black stifling cell to a garden where there was a fresh, mild, fragrant breeze blowing. Now I began to realize that there were activities in the world to which one's life can be committed, ideals which to die for was the sweetest thing [imaginable]. (Sankrityayan 1998b [*MJY-1*]: 176)

The Arya Samaj helped Sankrityayan to discover his own *svābhāvik pravṛtti* (natural tendencies). This discovery of something within him that recognized and responded to a calling was the 'new light', that which awakened in him the desire to dedicate his life to the national cause, and to sacrifice his life for the sake of it if the need arose.

Sankrityayan's *Rāṣṭrīyatā*

Indian nationalism had developed in such a way that religious faith and the idea of a nation were not regarded as wholly separate from one another. The Arya Samaj was a religious organization, yet its members were also eager for India to acquire *āzādī* (freedom). Many Arya Samajists contributed significantly to the independence movement. For many, religion and nationality were synonymous. Sankrityayan fitted into this mould, but with a difference: he, more than others, tended to view religion through the lens of his nationalist sentiment. The reason the Vedic dharma of the Arya Samaj appealed to him was because it, unlike other religions, held the claim to being *sanātan* (eternal), and thus, paradoxically, ever in step with the times, and with the early years of the 20th century in particular, when it appeared to him as if customized to meet India's national aspirations. He recalls:

राष्ट्रीय स्वतन्त्रता के लिए मुझमें इतनी बेकरारी थी किन्तु उस वक्त राष्ट्रीयता के बारे में मेरी क्या धारणा थी? राष्ट्रीयता और धर्म को मैं उस वक्त अलग नहीं समझता था। धर्म से मेरा मतलब आर्यसमाज और स्वामी दयानन्द के मान्य वैदिक धर्म से था। बाकी धर्मों–ईसाई, इस्लाम, यहूदी, बौद्ध ही नहीं हिन्दू धर्म के अनेक सम्प्रदायों को भी मैं झूठे धर्म और विज्ञान के प्रकाश में शीघ्र लुप्त हो जाने वाले धर्म समझता था।

> I was impatient for national sovereignty, but what was my opinion of nationalism during that time? During that time I did not differentiate between religion and nationalism. The religion that had meaning for me was the Arya Samaj and the Vedic religion espoused by Swami Dayananda. Other religions—not only Christianity, Islam, Judaism, and Buddhism but also the many different sects of Hinduism—I regarded as spurious religions and as religions that would soon vanish in the light of science. (Sankrityayan 1998b [*MJY-1*]: 182–3)

Desai notes:

> The national-chauvinist Arya Samaj idealized India's past even to the fantastic extent of claiming that all knowledge, scientific, social, and spiritual, was achieved by the Aryans and lay deposited in the immortal Vedas. The Arya Samaj claimed that all marvellous discoveries and inventions of modern times, all principles and conclusions of modern physics, chemistry, biology and engineering, were stated in the Vedas only if one knew how to interpret them appropriately. (Desai 1954: 117)

It is clear from Sankrityayan's quotation above, then, that he believed that the ārya dharm alone was an authentic religion, the only one capable of being tapped as a source of scientific knowledge, and that therefore all other religions would in the march of time fall along the wayside, while it strode confidently on.

For all its claims to uniqueness, the Arya Samaj can be accommodated under the wider umbrella of Indian Hindu nationalism. Indian nationalism was typically understood as Hindu nationalism, one strand of which was represented by the doctrines of the Arya Samaj.[25] Partha Chatterjee (2011b: 110) writes: 'The idea of "Indian nationalism" is synonymous with "Hindu nationalism" in an entirely modern, rationalist and historicist idea. The notion of "Hinduness" is not defined by religious criteria at all, but more on its historical origin. Buddhism or Jainism which are anti-Vedic and anti-Brahmanical are also Hindu because they originated in India, out of debates and critiques that are internal to Hinduism.' Strictly speaking, to be sure, as Jaffrelot (1999: 17) notes, the 'Arya Samaj of Dayananda was not ... a proponent of Hindu nationalism. Its members, up to the beginning

[25] For details, see Jaffrelot (1999); Gould (2005); and van der Veer (1994).

of the 20th century, preferred to stress their specificity with relation to Hinduism, which was described as degraded from the Vedic religion'. As an Arya Samajist, it was a matter of shame for Sankrityayan to be called a Hindu; it was only the badge of his own organization that he wore proudly. At this point it will perhaps be worthwhile to review Sankrityayan's opinion about Hinduism both during his involvement with the Arya Samaj and after leaving it.

Sankrityayan's Contrasting Notions of a Hindu Community

While in the Arya Samaj, Sankrityayan learned to differentiate between Hindus and Arya Samajists:

> उस समय मैं आर्यसमाज के गर्मदली विचारों का समर्थक था, इसके सिवाय वेद के ईश्वरीय होने में किसी की आपत्ति को मैं सहन करने के लिए तैयार न था। [...] आर्यसमाजी को अपने लिए हिन्दू कहना, मैं शर्म की बात समझता था। आर्य-धर्म हिन्दू-धर्म से उतना ही दूर है, जितना ईसाई और इस्लाम-धर्म, यह मैं बराबर कहा करता। भारत पर आर्य-धर्म का विशेष अधिकार है। उसकी उन्नति और स्वतन्त्रता आर्य-धर्म और एक जातीयता की स्थापना से ही हो सकती है।
>
> At that time I was a supporter of the Arya Samaj's extremist thinking. I was not ready to listen beyond it to any objections raised against the Veda as being *īśvarīya* [created by īsvara]. [...] As an Arya Samajist, I was ashamed to be called a Hindu. I repeatedly said that the ārya dharm is as far removed from Hindu religion as it is from Christianity and Islam. The ārya dharm has special authority in India. India's progress and sovereignty is only possible through the ārya dharm and *ek jātīyatā* [single caste]. (Sankrityayan 1998b [*MJY-1*]: 183)

Later, after he left the Arya Samaj, his definition of 'Hindu' changed. Hinduness ceased for him to be subject to religious criteria at all. Chatterjee's notion of Hinduness, referred to above, that defines it in terms of 'historical origin' is similar to what Sankrityayan's became. In Sankrityayan's revised opinion, 'Hindu' was not the name of a religious community but rather of the collective bearers of Indian culture:

> हिन्दू किसी धर्म विशेष का नाम नहीं, यह हमारे सारे देश और उसकी हजारों वर्ष-व्यापिनी संस्कृति का नाम है। [...] हिन्दू नाम या शब्द केवल ब्राह्मणशाही के लिए प्रयोग गलत है। उसे ब्राह्मणशाही का पर्याय नहीं होना चाहिए।

> [...] Hindu is not the name of a particular religion; it is the name of our whole country and its culture, which extends over thousands of years. [...] The use of the name or word Hindu for Brahmanism is wrong. It should not be used as a synonym of Brahmanism. (Sankrityayan December 2007–November 2008: 39)

Furthermore, remembering what the Russian scholar Scherbatsky said, he wrote:

> वह कहा करते थे, 'हिन्दू सबसे प्रतिभाशाली जाति है।' 'है' की जगह 'थे' कहना चाहिए। अपने पूर्वजों को योग्य सन्तान सिद्ध करने के लिए अभी हमने बहुत कम कर पाया है।
>
> He used to say, 'Hindus are a most intelligent race.' He should have said 'were' instead of 'are.' So far we have managed to do very little to prove worthy descendants of our ancestors. (Sankrityayan 1957b: 197)[26]

Sankrityayan's respect for and pride in his Hindu ancestors is clearly stated here. He was not satisfied with his or his fellow Indians' efforts to live up to the high standards set by their ancestors. Sankrityayan here uses the word jāti[27] in the sense not of 'caste' but of 'race', or to be more precise, a group that shares a common cultural identity, in this case what he calls the Hindus. The term 'Hindu jāti' came to be used by Sankrityayan to indicate every Indian and not only members of a particular religious group.

Sankrityayan had no sympathy at all for the religion-based politics that was brewing in India between Hindus and Muslims. This is clear from his refusal to accept a felicitation award in 1925 proposed by the newly established Hindū Sabhā (Hindu Assembly) headquartered in Bihar (Sankrityayan 1998b [*MJY-1*]: 283).

After his involvement with the Arya Samaj, Sankrityayan struck out on his own. The organization had laid the groundwork for him, acquainting him with the concepts of 'us' and 'them',

[26] The third sentence of this quotation literally reads: 'So far we have managed to do very little to prove our ancestors worthy descendants.' A slip of the pen or typographical error has obviously occurred, the postposition को having been printed for the postposition के.

[27] See Introduction to this volume.

'friends' and 'foes,' and 'Indians' and 'British'. During the years 1919 and 1920, he described his anti-British nationalist sentiment as follows:

> अब मैं सोलहों आने गरम राष्ट्रीयतावादी था, और इस प्रकार अंग्रेजों तथा उनके खुशामदियों से चिढ़-सी रखता था।
>
> Now I was a one hundred percent impassioned nationalist, and thus felt aversion towards the British and their adulators.
> (Sankrityayan 1998b [*MJY-1*]: 226)

Nationalism in India grew out of a sentiment that the country fostered of its spiritual peculiarity. This sentiment was eventually aroused into a spirit of rebellion. Sankrityayan describes the beginnings of nationalism at the village level as follows:

> उस समय अंग्रेजों के प्रति राजनीतिक वैमनस्य का कोई भाव उस समाज में नही देखा जाता था, जिसमें कि मैं घूमता था। हाँ, अंग्रेज विधर्मी, म्लेच्छ हैं, इस भाव से कोई मुक्त नहीं था।
>
> During the times I travelled around, no feeling of political animosity towards the British was visible in society. True, no one was free from the feeling that the British were outside the dharma, were *mlecch*.[28]
> (Sankrityayan 1998b [*MJY-1*]: 117)

Since his years in the Arya Samaj, Sankrityayan's notion of nationhood had been of a casteless independent people who followed the Vedic dharma. This ideal of ek jātīyatā would remain unchanged for the rest of his life.[29] Some changes to his vision, however, did occur. The first hazy features he had glimpsed during his dawn days in the Arya Samaj were now taking on clearer shapes as the morning advanced. The Russian Revolution would soon do its part to make his concept of nationhood still clearer.

[28] Non-Indians, aliens, or non-Aryans.

[29] 'जाति-पाँत के खिलाफ़ जो मनोभाव मुसाफ़िर विद्यालय में मेरे हृदय में पैदा हुआ, वह स्थायी हो गया था।' [The mental attitude opposed to the caste system that took birth in me in the Musāfir Vidyālaya became permanent.] (Sankrityayan 1998b [*MJY-1*]: 190)

THE PRINTED WORD, THE RUSSIAN REVOLUTION, AND THE NATIONALIST 'TURNING' TO POLITICS

Sankrityayan first heard about communism in 1917 when he was twenty-four. It was censored newspaper articles containing two or three sentences about the Russian Revolution (*lāl krānti*, the 'red revolution') that first awoke his interest in it. At the time, he was working in Agra on behalf of the Arya Samaj. Every day after lunch he would visit the *Ārya Musāfir* newspaper office and spend a few hours poring over the day's happenings. The office subscribed to many important national newspapers, and so Sankrityayan was able to keep abreast of what was going on both at home and abroad.

This newspaper reading provided Sankrityayan with what he called an *asphut jhā̃kī* (inarticulate glimpse) of the nation. As to the party of labourers and farmers in Russia, he surmised that its aim was to fight for equal rights and facilities for all:

> इन खबरों से मालूम होता था, कि वहाँ गरीबों-मजदूरों, किसानों-की भी एक पार्टी है, जो गरीबों के हक के लिए लड़ रही है, वह भोग और श्रम के समान विभाजन का प्रचार करती है। मुझे ये ख्याल अखबारों के बहुत से अंकों को पढ़ते हुए सिर्फ बीज रूप में मालूम हुए।
>
> I learned from these reports that there was a party there of indigent workers and peasants that was fighting for the rights of the poor. It promoted the equitable distribution of labour and the fruits of labour. It was only in a rudimentary way that I came to know of these ideas, by reading many issues of newspapers. (Sankrityayan 1998b [*MJY-1*]: 204)

Having pieced together the trend of communist thought from news reports, he began to compare its thought with the Arya Samaj's principles (Sankrityayan 1998b [*MJY-1*]: 204). The spirit propelling the drive for national sovereignty, Sankrityayan came to feel, was the same kind as that motivating the Russian revolutionaries. On the basis of this comparison, he attempted to sketch a picture of his own imagined ideal community. Later, in 1923–4, *Bāisvī̃ sadī* emerged as the product of such reflection.

Concerning his attraction towards communism and his vision of a *sāmyavādī duniyā* (egalitarian or communist world), Sankrityayan wrote in his *MJY*:

1918 के प्रथम पाद तक छन-छुनकर काफ़ी खबरें रूसी मजदूर क्रान्ति की मेरे कानों तक पहुँचती थीं। [...] तीन पंक्ति की रूस-सम्बन्धी खबर भी मुझे काफ़ी चिन्तन का मसाला दे देती। मैंने [*sic*] इन उड़ती खबरों, और जब-तब समाचारों से सुन लिए साम्यवाद के विकृत आकार को अपनी समझ से सुलझाकर एक साम्यवादी जगत् की कल्पना करने लगा। 1918 के आदिम महिनों में ही मैंने इस विषय पर एक पुस्तक लिखनी चाही थी, [...] ।

By the first quarter of 1918 much information about the Russian workers' revolution had filtered down to me.[30] [...] Three-line news items about Russia also gave me much to think about. I began to imagine a communist world with the help of that flitting information and those occasional news reports, having first reshaped the misshapen form of communism heard about in the news. Already at the beginning of 1918 I had a desire to write a book about it [...]. (Sankrityayan 1998b [*MJY-1*]: 208)

His Arya Samaj activities had not been enough to fulfil Sankrityayan's desire to serve the nation. The Russian Revolution lit the spark in him to engage in political activity:

धर्म प्रचार की भावना के साथ-साथ अब मेरी अन्तर्निहित राजनीतिक भावनाएँ बाहरी वायुमंडल की अनुकूलता पर उभड़ने लगीं।

Now, complementing the sentiment of religious proselytizing, subconscious political emotions started springing up in me, having found a favourable external environment. (Sankrityayan 1998b [*MJY-1*]: 252)

The Arya Samajists were trained in a way that the desire to devote themselves to propagating the Arya Samaj worldview seemed to come naturally. This had happened to Sankrityayan. He had shared the goal of propagating the Vedic religion and the other principles of the Arya Samaj—the message of Swami Dayanand—to the world, for which purpose the movement formally organized missionary travel.[31] But

[30] The conjunctive participle छन-छुनकर in the Hindi sentence above is not found in dictionaries, but I assume that it is an echo formation based on the verb छनना, 'to be filtered'.

[31] 'हम लोग वैदिक धर्म–आर्यसमाज के सिद्धान्तों–ऋषि दयानन्द के पैगाम–को सारी दुनिया में पहुँचाने के लिए मिश्नरी तैयार किए जा रहे थे।' (Sankrityayan 1998b [*MJY-1*]: 177)

Students dreamt of visiting foreign countries. Sankrityayan differed from the majority, however, in desiring to go not to the USA or Europe, but to other

by the time he actually did start travelling abroad, he had, as already noted, left the Arya Samaj. His first trip to Europe was undertaken to promote Buddhism.

Sunday, 6 April 1919, was proclaimed a day of national humiliation by Mahatma Gandhi to protest the enactment of the Rowlatt Act.[32] During the start of the satyagraha, Sankrityayan was busy taking exams at DAV College in Lahore. He took time off, though, to observe the hartal in Lahore against the Rowlatt Act. A huge number of students, shopkeepers, and members of the educated middle class were caught up in it, and Sankrityayan himself was swept along in the fervour, and thereby experienced for the first time a large outburst of nationalist sentiment:

> छः अप्रैल (1919 ई.) को रविवार था, इसी दिन सारे भारत में रोलट-एक्ट विरोधी दिवस मनाने की गाँधीजी ने घोषणा की थी। उस दिन लाहौर के नजारे के बारे में क्या कहना है। सारी अनारकली सड़क के ओर से छोर तक नंगे काले शिरों से

---

countries of Asia (the Arab world, Iran, China, and Japan). Furthermore, he was not in any hurry. In this he differed from his senior, Dharmavir, who, very anxious to travel abroad to promote religion, had stayed for many days in a mosque in Bombay with the intention of visiting the Arab world (Sankrityayan 1998b [*MJY-1*]: 178). Later he would become the son-in-law of Bhāi Parmānand and, in 1933, would visit London (Brown 1975: 254), during which time Sankrityayan was also in Europe, but with the objective of propagating Buddhism.

Apart from providing direction to educational activities, the DAV School Managing Committee also oversaw the work of *pracār* (propagation) other than that carried out by individual Samajists. From 1894 to 1914 the hiring, firing, and support of *upadeśak*s (teachers) was under the committee. The number on the payroll varied from year to year but seldom exceeded half a dozen. In 1905 the college dispatched its most famous missionary, Bhāi Paramāmand, M.A., (who was idolized by young Arya Samajists during Sankrityayan's involvement with the Arya Samaj) to Africa to popularize the work of the Samaj among Indian residents in the British colonies (Jones 2006: 229–30), and to London to propagate the Vedic dharma there.

32 The Rowlatt Act was passed by the Imperial Legislative Council in London on 10 March 1919. This act effectively authorized the government to imprison for up to two years, without trial, any person suspected of terrorism living in the Raj, and gave imperial authorities power to deal with revolutionary activities. The hartal on 6 April is also known as the Rowlatt satyagraha.

भरी हुई थी। लोग तरह-तरह के नारे लगा रहे थे। जुलूस घूमते-घूमते चार बजे के बाद ब्रेडला-हॉल पहुँचा। गर्मी काफ़ी थी। लोगों को पानी पिलाने के लिए बहुत-सी सबीलें लगी हुई थीं। वहाँ, हिन्दू-मुसलमान का कोई फ़र्क न था। एक ही गिलास से दोनों पानी पी रहे थे। राष्ट्रीयता की पहली बाढ़ ने छुआछूत को बहा फेंका–यद्यपि वह बहा फेंकना स्थायी नहीं था, तो भी उसमें, कितनी ताकत है, इसका तो पता लग सकता था।

The 6th of April (1919) was a Sunday. Gandhiji declared it a day to be observed in protest against the Rowlatt Act. The spectacle in Lahore was indescribable that day. Anārkalī Street[33] was filled to bursting with a sea of uncovered black hair. People were shouting assorted slogans. After 4 o'clock the procession reached Bredla Hall. It was considerably hot. There were many *sabīls*[34] providing water to the public. No distinction was made between Hindus and Muslims.[35] They were drinking water from the same glass. The first flood of national sentiment had flushed away *chūāchūt* [untouchability]—and though this flushing away was not permanent, one could realize its power. (Sankrityayan 1998b [*MJY-1*]: 215)

The next day Sankrityayan left Lahore, very much inspired by the events of 6 April. He had experienced *rāṣṭrīyatā kī pahlī bāḍh* (first flood of national sentiment). Here rāṣṭrīyatā for Sankrityayan obviously meant first and foremost a type of devotion to one's country that transcended all caste barriers. He had witnessed, first-hand, Hindus and Muslims united in a cause to achieve a single free nation. The idea of ek jatīyatā, a casteless society of equals, gained strength in him for his having experienced one instance of its *tākat* (power).[36]

33 The street where the Lahore office of the Arya Samaj was located (Sankrityayan 1998b [*MJY-1*]: 190).

34 A stall-like facility offering refreshments to pilgrims.

35 Gandhi was in Bombay that day and went to Chowpatty Beach to pray and fast, where he was surrounded by Hindus, whom he requested to make a satyagraha pledge to Rama on his upcoming birth anniversary three days hence. Afterwards he left with some disciples to attend a mass meeting of Muslims being held in front of a mosque on Grant Road (Wolpert 2002: 99–100).

36 The main plot of Sankrityayan's novel *Jīne ke liye* (In order to live) recounts the life-long struggles of its main male character, Devrāj. The novel was written in the Chapra jail between March and May 1939. The period described in

Sankrityayan was now in a transition phase. He was becoming increasingly interested in the country's political development but was still active in the Arya Samaj. He was looking for a formal opportunity to take the plunge into a life of political engagement. It was during this time that he received the news of his father's death, which offered him a convenient excuse to take leave of the Arya Samaj. This he did, and, instead of going to his father's funeral, decided to become politically active.

> पिताजी की मृत्यु सुन छुट्टी लेने का बहाना मिला, और मैंने राजनितिक जीवन में प्रवेश करने का निश्चय कर लिया।
>
> I got an excuse to take my leave upon hearing of the death of my father, and I decided to enter into a politically motivated life. (Sankrityayan 1998b [*MJY-1*]: 252)

It was the time when the non-cooperation movement was in full swing. Thousands of students had left school, many lawyers had

---

the novel covers from 1905 to 1939. Devrāj, who has made service to the country his *jīvan ādarś* (life's ideal), very much reflects Sankrityayan's own life and personal opinions. His job in Calcutta during his teenage years, his visits to Europe and elsewhere, his love for and marriage with a non-Indian woman, his involvement with the Congress party, his election to the post of district Congress secretary, his participation in the Gaya congress in 1922 and disagreement with the status-quoists, his selecting Chapra as the site for his political activity, his receiving the news of his son's birth in jail, and his participation in the peasant movement are all drawn from the author's own life up to the time of writing. The character's enthusiastic support of Swaraj and peasants' rights and his antagonism towards sectarian politics are masterfully described. Sankrityayan had been badly injured before he was arrested: the mahout of a zamindar had hit him with a cudgel when he found him cutting sugarcane in his employer's field (Sankrityayan 1998b [*MJY-2*]: 314). In the novel, Devrāj is badly injured by the wielders of cudgels who are working for a zamindar but in his case he dies on the spot.

Sankrityayan states in the preface to the work that he considers it his first attempt at writing a novel if *Bāisvī̃ sadī* is excluded. (This latter, a utopian fantasy, would have been difficult to place in the same category as the realistic novels of Premchand that defined the genre at the time.) Sankrityayan elsewhere describes his writing career as a novelist as follows:

closed their practice, and financial contributions were pouring in for Gandhi's Tilak Swaraj Fund. Although he had decided to become politically active, Sankrityayan was still not sure where and how to go about it. The places he was most familiar with were Chapra, where he had lived as a sadhu for some time, and his own hometown. This latter, though, was now off limits to him, following his vow not to set foot there until well into future (Sankrityayan 1998b [*MJY-1*]: 199).

After deciding to engage himself politically, he consulted the Congress office in Chapra about working with rescue teams for flood victims, encouraging the public to boycott foreign goods and to oppose foreign rule, propagating the use of the spinning-wheel, and getting people to abjure alcohol consumption.[37] Following his active participation in flood-rescue activities, the leaders of the Congress welcomed Sankrityayan into their group and he was given an organizational role (Chapra District Congress Minister) on 29 October 1922. He was also actively involved in a Gandhi school in Ekma, Bihar, as a teacher. Other responsibilities included travelling to many neighbouring villages with his co-workers to promote Gandhi's programme. He

---

> १९३८ में किसान आंदोलन के संबंध में फिर जेल जाना पड़ा, वहाँ मिले समय का इस्तेमाल करते हुए मैंने जीने के लिए नामक अपना पहला उपन्यास लिखा, जिसमें वर्तमान शताब्दी की राजनीतिक और सामाजिक पृष्ठिभूमि को लेते हुए एक संघर्षमय जीवन का चित्र खींचा गया है। इसके बाद उपन्यास लिखने की ओर रुचि बढ़ी, लेकिन जल्दी ही मुझे मालूम हो गया कि ऐतिहासिक उपन्यासों को लिखना ही मुझे अपने हाथों में लेना चाहिए।
>
> In 1938 I was again imprisoned for being involved in the peasants' movement. There, using the time on my hands, I wrote my first novel, *Jīne ke liye*, in which a picture is drawn of a life of struggle against the political and social background of the present century. After this my interest in writing novels grew, but I soon realized that it was the writing of historical novels that I should take up. (Sankrityayan and Anand 1982: 133)

37 'Rahul Sankrityayan narrated another incident of Chapra where there was a dharna in front of liquor shop. [He] was also standing in front of the shop and requesting the customers to give up drink. But one customer despite his request went inside. The next day that customer's house was drowned in a flood. People spread the rumour that his house was drowned in a flood. People spread the rumour that his house was drowned in a flood because he had incurred the wrath of the saint [...]' (Singh 2012: 133–4).

gave speeches, generally two (but sometimes three) a day. At such gatherings, his co-workers would sing songs exhorting the public to boycott foreign goods and oppose colonial rule. Sankrityayan's speeches focused on national unity and the agitation against foreign rule more than on (what Gandhi was simultaneously calling for) propagating the spinning-wheel and abjuring alcohol (Sankrityayan 1998b [*MJY-1*]: 260). He played an active role in the hartal when the Prince of Wales visited Bihar on 22 December 1922. Sankrityayan and his group protested against the reception of the prince and organized a big protest rally of volunteers in Sonpur (1998b [*MJY-1*]: 268). His outspoken speeches alarmed the government and he was arrested for the first time on 31 January 1922 at a meeting of a district Congress committee that he was chairing.

Sankrityayan's major endeavour during this time went into achieving full autonomy. Raising public awareness and organizing were the important needs of the day in the struggle against the British, and it was to these that Sankrityayan devoted his energies. He was not happy with Gandhi's decision regarding the suspension of civil resistance. When he was released after a six-month term of imprisonment in August 1922 he said:

> राजनितिक स्वतन्त्रता हमारा स्थायी ध्येय था, हम गाँधीजी के चले जाने पर भी उसे छोड़ नहीं सकते थे, इस ध्येय के लिए संघर्ष करना अनिवार्य था। संघर्ष जनजागृति तथा संगठन बिना हो नहीं सकता था, इसलिए हमने उधर ध्यान दिया।
>
> Political autonomy was our consistent aim, [something] we could not abandon even though Gandhi had left [for prison]; the struggle for it was compulsory. The struggle was not possible without public awareness and organizing; thus we concentrated on them.
> (Sankrityayan 1998b [*MJY-1*]: 267)[38]

Sankrityayan realized that many people were sympathetic with the independence movement but lacked the motivation to join it. He continued his extensive travels in the district, trying to convince people to do so. Slowly Sankrityayan established his

[38] Gandhi was sent to prison for six years after his arrest on 10 March 1922 but was released in February 1924 for an appendix operation.

credentials with the party and eventually became a Congress district committee official.

In 1922 the annual national meeting of the Congress party was planned to be held in Gaya. After much canvassing for support, Sankrityayan was able to table a proposal at the meeting on behalf of the regional committee that the Maha Bodhi Temple be handed over to the Buddhists.[39] The proposal floundered, though, over another issue that resulted in a schism within the Congress party, producing the two groups of the status quoists and what later became the Swarajists. This dissension arose over Gandhi's decision to suspend the satyagraha. Sankrityayan was interested in promoting both the party of change and the Bodh Gaya proposal at the meeting. The opportunity to work with Buddhist monks during the Gaya congress, in any event, brought him closer to Buddhism. After the congress, at the request of Rājendra Prasād and other leaders, he lectured at a public meeting in Patna. There, calling to mind those who had been sentenced to death for the Chauri Chaura incident, he said:

> देश की आजादी के लिये इस तरह के शहीदों का खून देश-माता के लिए चंदन होगा।
>
> The blood of such martyrs for the independence of the country will be *candan*[40] for Mother India. (Sankrityayan 1998b [*MJY-1*]: 271)

Sankrityayan was again arrested for delivering what was considered an inflammatory speech and spent the next two years in the Hazaribagh jail. There he had the leisure needed to give the asphut jhā̃ki of his 'imagined community' literary form. He let his imagination roam among his impressions of the Arya Samaj, his notion of the Russian Revolution, and his desire for his own and his country's independence. The result was his first work, *Bāisvī̃ sadī*, set, as the title suggests, in the 22nd century. This creative work inaugurated Sankrityayan's career as a writer, a career that was to last for the rest of his life. By now he was beginning to understand the power of the printed word.

[39] For further details about the Maha Bodhi Temple, see section 'Initial Endeavours Relating to Buddhism' in Chapter 3 of this volume.

[40] Sandalwood paste, used for puja by Hindus.

BĀISVĪ̃ SADĪ: AN IMAGINED COMMUNITY

Sankrityayan's writing career begins with the portrayal of, to borrow Anderson's term, an 'imagined community', which can best be described as what the author himself calls a communist utopia. But, it may be asked, if at the time of writing the author was not fully aware of what either communism or a utopia fully entailed (Sankrityayan 1998b [*MJY-1*]: 265), how could he possibly succeed in conceiving a combination of the two? *Bāisvī̃ sadī* is, in any event, an attempt to represent what an ideal nation meant for him at the time.

Sankrityayan had neither discussed communism at any length with anybody who had studied it extensively nor had he yet studied it extensively himself. He had, however, remembered reading in 1922, when he was in the Baksar jail, a book by Trotsky translated into English entitled *Bolshevism and World Peace* (Sankrityayan 1998b [*MJY-1*]: 261). He admitted that he was unable to formulate what he actually got out of it (Sankrityayan 1998b [*MJY-1*]: 265). In any case, the regular news that reached him about the Russian Revolution kept turning his thoughts towards an imagined ideal community. During his travels in India he was able to observe poverty at close hand. In his dealings with landlords in Parsa,[41] for example, he came to learn how poor people were being exploited. India's highly discriminatory caste system, the practice of child marriage, and the appalling situation of child widows all etched themselves into his mind. This stream of thought, that of the injustice in his own society, came together with the other main stream of thought preoccupying him, the injustice of foreign rule. The result is clearly reflected in the first novel he wrote, wherein he seeks to describe a just society that has gained independence from the British. Equality, social and economic justice, and the dignity of the individual that would result from the abandoning of casteism were certainly important aspects of literary and public discourse in the first half of the 20th century in India. Raghupati Sahay Firaq's short story '*Ab se sau sāl bād*' (A hundred years from now [1925]), published a year after *Bāisvī̃ sadī*, presents an imagined future society similar to the one in it (Orsini 2010: 236).

[41] As a sadhu, he found himself trying to solve problems related to the ownership of land that had been donated to the monastery but had not yet been fully handed over.

The Russian Revolution provided one powerful model and a new vision of future Indian society to some of the public and some of its writers. Dissatisfied with the British Raj, developments within the Congress party, and the Gandhian non-cooperation movement, they envisioned a society that came closer to the ideals of socialism. After his experience with the Congress party and the Arya Samaj, the Russian Revolution presented itself to Sankrityayan as a third force that he imagined might be able to create a society without any kind of discrimination to it. Whatever forces may have played into his imagined egalitarian society, the title of his first work suggests a realization on his part that the intended goal was not anything that would be achieved quickly. He doubtless knew that it would take time to convince and organize people and that the struggle against the British for independence was but the first step on the road towards his imagined community. This was indeed Sankrityayan's plan: first independence should be achieved and then, slowly, his other ideas could be turned to account. And although he was in no hurry to see his vision fulfilled, he did give thought to how to publicize it and gradually win over public support for it. This thinking was instrumental in his decision to name the book *Bāisvī̃ sadī*. Not seeing any immediate possibility of establishing his imagined new social order, he presents it as deferred to the 22nd century.

When he first took up the pen to write the novel, he was just beginning to become aware of communism. He had heard the news coming out of Russia in 1917 and started to make preliminary notes in 1918. The school[42] he was teaching in at the time, though, closed down, and his notes, which he had given to his cousin Yāgeś during the process, got lost (Sankrityayan 1998b [*MJY-1*]: 208).

He began writing again from scratch in 1922. By then he had thought more deeply about communes and intended to provide clear links between his imaginary society and the experiments going on in the society of his own time. He created the character of a young *tapasvī* (ascetic) named Viśvabandhu and sent him off to the Himalayas. This new version, composed in Sanskrit verse and divided into five or six chapters, he named *Viśvabandhu-pradīpa*

[42] He was in Kalpi, Uttar Pradesh, on a mission for the Arya Samaj, requiring teaching, studying, and propagating.

(Viśvabandhu's enlightenment). He soon realized, however, that the vast majority of people would not understand the language and the purpose of having written the work would go to nought (Sankrityayan 1998b [*MJY-1*]: 265).[43] Sankrityayan's third attempt to write a book about an imaginary 22nd-century community was made in the years 1923 and 1924 during his imprisonment in the Hazaribagh jail. He switched from Sanskrit to Hindi, and from metrical verse to prose, and he also changed the title. However, his basic aim and the name of his main character remained the same.

When, in 1935, Sankrityayan first set foot in Russia, he was excited to find indeed a new type of society. There he remembered all that he had written in *Bāisvī̃ sadī*, inspired by the news from communist Russia in 1917. The villages, cities, men, and women that had been entirely created in his imagination in the novel now took on a real shape (Sankrityayan 1998b [*MJY-1*]: 218). Sankrityayan suggests in a prefatory note to his subsequent book *Soviyat bhūmi* (1938), a travelogue about Russia, that it can be considered a sequel to the earlier fictional work.

The Plot

Bāisvī̃ sadī is written in the first person and divided into sixteen chapters over some one hundred pages. Sankrityayan was in Nepal in March and April of 1923. During that time he lived for fifteen days in a cave in Shikhar Narayan,[44] in the south-western part of the Kathmandu Valley. The story of Viśvabandhu in *Bāisvī̃ sadī* starts in this cave. Viśvabandhu is a teacher of Nalanda School (in Nalanda, Bihar) with some thirty years of experience, and now, in February 1924, is on a journey to a more northerly part of the subcontinent. After reaching the cave, he falls asleep and wakes up only two hundred years later, in 2124. Stepping out of the cave and exploring around, he is bit by bit confronted with all the changes that have come about in the world, which for him has all the trappings of an imaginary civilization. Viśvabandhu's travels in *Bāisvī̃ sadī* from the cave back down to Bihar mirror Sankrityayan's own

[43] He had yet to become a Hindi nationalist, but he still realized that a book in Hindi would attract more readers.

[44] Also known as Shekha Narayan.

wanderings. The journey from the Shikhar Narayan cave in Nepal (Nepal, be it noted, does not figure as an independent country in the narrative) to different parts of India, provides ample opportunity to catalogue the changes that have occurred over a period of two centuries.

People now work only four hours daily, after which they engage in study, entertainment, and a variety of other activities. The government has mandated seventeen years of compulsory education for all. Education and medical treatment are free of charge. No one need worry about their old age, for the state takes care of everyone. Thus nobody is compelled to reproduce in order to insure support during their twilight years. People do not need money, nor do individuals own property. The government arranges all essential requirements for everyone, providing each household with a three-room apartment containing a bedroom, a living room, and a bathroom. Houses need not be locked up. Factories are only kept locked to prevent accidents occurring. Everyone has a uniform for work. There is no defence ministry, given that war is a thing of the past and the world has become one family. Paan, tobacco, alcohol, tea, and coffee are no longer consumed, failing as they do to contribute anything positive to society. Animals are all but absent from towns or villages. Only a few are kept for purposes of education. Animal flesh is not consumed, having been replaced by artificial meat. Animal hides, which produce a bad odour, are nowhere to be found. Indeed, animals are somehow rooted out from human society. All this reflects the strong influence the Arya Samaj was then exercising over Sankrityayan. At the time of writing he was a strict vegetarian.[45] In the novel, too, Sankrityayan imagined

45 'मांस-भक्षण और बलिदान को एक कट्टर आर्यसमाजी के तौर पर बुरा समझता था।' [As a fervent Arya Samajist, I thought of as immoral the eating of meat and sacrificing of animals.] (Sankrityayan 1998b [*MJY-1*]: 195)

The fact that Sankrityayan wished to clear human settlements of animals may have been due to the plight of animals he witnessed rambling about the streets of India, or possibly to his having been inconvenienced by them on occasion. Furthermore, given present-day attempts to manufacture artificial meat, one must acknowledge Sankrityayan's prescience in this regard.

After leaving the Arya Samaj, be it noted, Sankrityayan reverted to eating meat.

a common language for the whole of India—*Bhārtī bhāṣā*—which was meant to be the mother tongue of all in Bhāratvarṣ[46] (Sankrityayan 2006a: 8–9).

The Imagery of an 'Indian Nation'

Bāisvī̃ sadī portrays an imagined time in humanity's future in which the whole world has become one community. The author confines his attention, however, to the social, economic, educational, and political situation in the northern part of the Indian subcontinent. A standard division of work and leisure is in force throughout the whole population. There is no discrimination on the basis of colour, caste, or religion. The *varṇāśram* system does not exist any longer. The world is a single *varṇ*: 'एकवर्णमिदं सर्वम्' (Sankrityayan 2006a: 22). Jāti, which began as a word denoting the subdivisions of varṇ, is now being used in Sankrityayan's work as a synonym of varṇ. From a historically localized caste and community it advanced to mean for him, in 20th-century India, 'jāti as a nation', and then he took it a step further, in the present work, by applying both varṇ and jāti to a global community. One may argue that his concept of ek jātīyatā is simply a mature form of the preliminary idea of ek varṇ, which emerged in *Bāisvī̃ sadī*. Varṇ conventionally signifies a division under the varna-system of social hierarchies, which was not sufficient to address the problem, but ek jātīyatā over ek varṇ was a proper term to correct the existing social division and address cultural identity. One can also argue that he also adopted the popular concept of jāti of his time into his emerging idea of ek varṇ. In terms of his whole corpus, ek jātīyatā seems to be the expression he favours, starting from an earlier period of his life (see the first quote

46 'उत्तरं यत् समुद्रस्य हिमाद्रेश्चवै दक्षिणम्। वर्षं तद् भारतं नाम भारती यत्र संततिः।। नवयोजनसाहस्त्रो विस्तारोऽस्य महामुने!' (*Viṣṇu-purāṇa* 2/3/1–2)

Exactly north of the sea [that is, the Indian Ocean] and south of the snowy mountain [that is, the Himalayas] [lies the] country named Bhārat, where [live] Bhāratī [that is, the personification of India, later identified with Saraswati, the goddess of speech] [and her] descendants. O Mahamuni, its territory spreads out over nine thousand *yojanas* [a measure of distance, to which differing meanings are attached; according to McGregor (2006: 845), it is between four and eighteen miles].

in the section titled 'Sankrityayan's Contrasting Notions of a Hindu Community' earlier in this chapter). In *Bāisvī̃ sadī* we have the portrait of a society in which no form of discrimination is practised. The conventional picture of jātis within the framework of Bhāratvarṣ's culture have undergone a radical transformation, resulting in ek jātīyatā in a place that in many respects no longer seems like India.

This new world order comes into being in 2024 as what Sankrityayan, in the novel, calls a *sārvbhaum rāṣṭra* (universal country). This sārvbhaum rāṣṭra develops gradually.[47] Sankrityayan envisioned a *sārvbhaumī sabhā* (universal assembly) as the supreme political governing body, made up of 300 members, of which India sends forty representatives on the basis of population. One might argue that if there is a single world government, then there ought no longer to be any place for nations. In fact, though, these continue to exist as regional entities. Thus there also exist *deś sabhā*s (country assemblies), which are responsible for single countries with the help of *prāntīya* (regional), *jilā* (district), and *grām* (village) sabhās. Though there is a *sārvbhaum bhāṣā* (universal language), namely Esperanto, countries do continue to make use of their own languages (that is, Bhāratvarṣ's Bhārtī bhāṣā) and to cultivate their own identity. From today's perspective, one can argue, the region described by Sankrityayan in the book that is living under this new world order is limited to what is today's South Asia.

Bāisvī̃ sadī achieved popularity in both India and Nepal. Although Nepal does not exist as a separate country in it, having at some point become a part of Bhāratvarṣ, it is the name of a place. Some Nepalese understandably had reservations regarding Sankrityayan's depiction. The reference to the presence of a king only in books was a matter of satisfaction for some readers, the monarchy having been terminated,

47 The stages of development are as follows:

British Rule in India up to 1940

1940 to 1990, United Asia (Saṃyukt Eśiyā Rāṣṭra)

1990 to 2000, United Asia, Africa, and Australia (Saṃyukt Eśiyā Afrīkā Aṣṭreliyā Rāṣṭra)

2000 to 2010, United Europe and America (Saṃyukt Yūrop Amerikā Rāṣṭra)

and in 2024, One Globe (Bhūmaṇḍal Ek Rāṣṭra)

while causing displeasure to others, particularly the government.[48] Not only the king but also the Nepali language was consigned to the libraries. Niranjan Govinda Vaidya, one Nepalese critic of the book, expressed his consternation in this way:

> राहुलजी में एक बहुत बडा दुर्गुण भी था, वह है, बहुत अधिक राष्ट्रवादी होना, इसका ज्वलन्त उदाहरण बाइसवीं सदी पुस्तक है। साथ ही बडा राष्ट्र अहंकारवादी के शिकार भी वह थे। खासकर नेपाल के बारे में उनकी धारणा संकुचित थी। इन्हीं बातों को लेकर राहुलजी के साथ कलकत्ता में का. पुष्पलाल श्रेष्ठ का काफी वादविवाद चला था।
>
> Rāhul-jī also had one great demerit, namely that of being an extreme nationalist. A searing example of this is the book *Bāisvī̃ sadī*. He was, in addition, the victim of national arrogance. His concept of Nepal was especially narrow. Comrade Pushpa Lal Shrestha[49] had a grand debate in Calcutta with Rāhul-jī regarding all these things. (Vaidya 2002: 39)

In the novel, Viśvabandhu meets an *ācāryā* (female professor) named Gārgī of Andhra University on a train, and she tells him about the development of Bhārtī bhāṣā. According to her, people had fought long ago in India over Hindi and Urdu, but this clash ended when Bhārtī bhāṣā was established as the representative of both Hindi and Urdu and became the national language. And again, after many complications, Devanagari was selected as the common script for all the regional languages in India. To be sure, regional languages do continue to exist in the different settings portrayed in the book (Sankrityayan 2006a: 59).

During working hours, people in *Bāisvī̃ sadī* wear trousers, while dhotis are reserved as formal dress. An Indian figures as the president of the world's government—Sridatta, educated in Takshashila—while Prime Minister Ohora is from Japan, Education Minister Monolin from Russia, and Health Minister David is from America.

Sankrityayan's growing attraction towards Buddhism is also reflected. His pride in the philosophy, his respect for the Buddha, and his interest in rebuilding former Buddhist institutions in India are all manifested in the book. His desire to re-establish Nalanda as a centre

48 Again, however, history seems to have borne him out.

49 The founder of Nepal's Communist Party.

of Buddhist studies is particularly in evidence, both it and Takshasila having been destroyed by Muslim invaders in the past. One character in the work, bearing the Muslim name of Ismail (born in Nalanda and a graduate of its university), had a grandfather who had devoted a great deal of energy to resurrecting Nalanda. The inference that the author doubtless wishes the reader to draw is that Muslims have now reached a stage where they regret their past destructiveness and wish to make amends. Sankrityayan, an ardent learner of languages, portrays Nalanda as a place where many tongues come together. Both it and Takshashila have now become the world's leading centres of higher learning.

Sankrityayan believed that a bachelor's life was good for personal development. He thought that he himself had achieved success in life because he had been on his own and free of marital responsibilities in his youth and during the early years of adulthood (1998b [*MJY-1*]: 247). Couples are not compelled to live together in *Bāisvī̃ sadī* if they have irreconcilable differences (Sankrityayan 2006a: 106). Boarding schools care for and educate children, so that parents are freed from the burden of having to do so. Travelling from one planet to another is possible, while video telephone links and digital books are also commonplace.

Sankrityayan himself translated some parts of *Bāisvī̃ sadī* into Urdu, which were published in the newspaper *Milāp*[50] over the course of several issues, and it was also translated by others later on into Guajarati, Marathi, Nepali, Malayalam, and Burmese. Despite being his first fictional work, it provides a good repository of Sankrityayan's lifelong principles. Many aspects of his own life's journey—his travels in Tibet and his interest in scholarly work, Hindi nationalism, communism, and socio-religious reform (particularly the abandoning of hereditary endogamous castes in favour of ek jātīyatā)—are all reflected in it. Indianness, whether in language, dress, education, culture, or food, is a prominent theme of the work. *Bāisvī̃ sadī*, then, is an excellent source of information for understanding Sankrityayan as a man and as a writer.

50 A popular daily newspaper of that time, founded in Lahore on 13 April 1923 by the journalist (and one of the main leaders of the Arya Samaj) Lālā Khuśālcand 'Khursand'. The translation of *Bāisvī̃ sadī* was published in it in 1926.

* * *

This chapter has attempted to show how the Arya Samaj and the Russian Revolution were instrumental in forming the ideas of Indian nationhood and ek jātīyatā in Sankrityayan's imagination. At different stages in Sankrityayan's life, the influence of the Arya Samaj was an important one. In his own words:

> आर्यसमाज को मैंने गम्भीरता से ग्रहण किया था, वैरागीपंथ की तरह उसे 'ग्रामं गच्छन् तृणान् स्पृशति' के हल्के हृदय से नहीं स्वीकार किया था, इसीलिए यथाशक्ति आर्यसामाजिक विचारों के अनुसार चलने की कोशिश करता था।
>
> I took the Arya Samaj seriously, not as I had the *vairāgīpanth* [life of a sadhu], which I had ventured on light-heartedly, like one who 'goes to a village and tastes its delights'. I tried my best, then, to follow its principles. (Sankrityayan 1998b [*MJY-1*]: 195)

The asphuṭ jhā̃kī of a nation that he caught in the Arya Samaj had been refined on the basis of the information, albeit sketchy, he had received about the Russian Revolution. The notion of ek varṇ that he conceived during this phase formed the foundation for his more advanced idea of ek jātīyatā. The concept of 'us and them', 'friends and foes', propagated in the Arya Samaj had made him a *garam rāṣṭrīyatāvādī* (fervent nationalist), while the Russian Revolution turned him into an internationalist. It was with the light that came from these two sources that his eyes were able to envision the world of *Bāisvī̃ sadī*.

Sankrityayan refers to his contribution to politics as *rāṣṭrīya kārya* (national work) and to himself as a *rāṣṭrīya karmī* (national worker) (1998b [*MJY-1*]: 268, 284). It is clear, then, that he left the Arya Samaj for much the same reason he had earlier left his childhood surroundings, namely in order to expand his horizons and to experience the freedom of what he felt was a higher calling. It is interesting to observe that even though Sankrityayan's own narration of his past in *MJY-1* was written at a time when he had become a committed communist, he is still able to recount events in the Arya Samaj and as a member of the Congress party as if they were being relived in that earlier frame of mind. The narrating I thus imbues the narrated I with the same sense of enthusiasm for his rāṣṭrīya kārya as Sankrityayan actually felt during that time.

The instruction Sankrityayan underwent in the Arya Samaj provided him, too, with an appreciation of and respect for Buddhism. This same inspiration would later result in his Tibet journeys and in his efforts to collect works of Buddhist literature, which stand as monuments to India's glorious ancestral traditions. His two-year imprisonment (1923–5) had rendered Sankrityayan largely passive with regard to the Arya Samaj and Congress politics, but had increased his interest in Buddhism. His encounters with Buddhist monks at the Gaya conference (1922) and on a visit to Ladakh (1926), during which he witnessed their zeal in spreading their religion, served to fortify his own growing commitment to it. Recalling the Arya Samaj teachings, he writes:

> बात-बात में हमारे सामने ईसाई मिश्नरियों के धर्म प्रचार के लिए के लिए किये गये स्वार्थ त्याग और साहस की मिसाल पेश की जाती थी, और उससे भी ज्यादा, जापान-चीन-तिब्बत-मध्य एशिया के दुरूह रास्तों से शताब्दियों पूर्व बौद्धभिक्षुओं की यात्राओं का उदाहरण पेश किया जाता था। हम अपने को दयानन्द के भिक्षु और अपने विद्यालय को एक छोटी-सी नालन्दा- यद्यपि बहुत त्रुटिपूर्ण समझते थे।
>
> From time to time the selfless and courageous example of Christian missionaries in spreading religion was explained to us, and even greater than it the case of the journeys of Buddhist monks centuries ago on difficult paths through Japan, China, Tibet, and Central Asia was explained. We saw ourselves as monks of Dayananda and our school as a small if imperfect Nalanda. (Sankrityayan 1998b [*MJY-1*]: 177)

In the end, then, rather than in the interests of the Arya Samaj, it was with a mission to study Buddhism and to bring India's heritage back to India that Sankrityayan went abroad, to Sri Lanka, Nepal, and Tibet. Thus he proved to be an Arya Samajist but with a difference, even as later he proved to be a Buddhist but with a difference. In the Arya Samaj, he had come to recognize the serious nature of religion, but in the end rejected the form it took in that organization in favour of the more universal form of Buddhism. After he had shifted his allegiance to the latter, though, he began increasingly to view religion through the lens of his own native culture. He continued to respect Buddhism as an important aspect of Indian culture, namely as a religion that practised no discrimination based on castes. Although he accepted the trappings of Buddhism for a short period, therefore, he was destined to eventually leave it. He became a Buddhist monk, one may argue, because he recognized in Buddhism a path that led to some other as yet un-envisioned goal. Later on, when he was engaged in preserving Buddhist texts, he formed a clearer idea of what that goal might be, and so abandoned the life of a monk and again became a lay person. The following chapter will focus on these issues by exploring Sankrityayan's efforts on behalf of Buddhism, the pride he felt in the Buddha, and the strengthening of his relationship with Nepal through a growing awareness of the cultural values he shared with it. How did he regard Nepal? Is his view of it in *Bāisvī̃ sadī*, not as an independent country but as an integral part of India, something that also underwent change later, as he himself did? These questions are all germane to this study.

Sankrityayan's decision not to write his first book in Sanskrit but in Hindi, as a more suitable means of eventually turning his 'imagined community' into reality, suggests that he had well understood the power of print and that he saw *Bāisvī̃ sadī* as only the start of his work. This study will also examine Sankrityayan's evolving view of the printed word in the upcoming chapter.

Evaluating his own life in 1957, he writes to his wife Kamala:

> तिब्बत का अनुसन्धान और साम्यवाद की सेवा मेरे जीवन के सबसे बड़े आदर्श रहे हैं।
>
> Tibetan research and service to communism have remained the greatest ideals of my life. (Sankrityayan 1998b [*MJY*-5]: 388)

It was not the Vedic religion, not Buddhism, and not even communism, then, that represented Sankrityayan's ultimate goal in life. It was a singular combination of these latter two that were more than the sum of their parts. The following chapters attempt to define more closely the uniqueness of the man and the uniqueness of his goal.

CHAPTER THREE

Buddhism

A Source of Indian Pride

There has been a war between two sentiments both in my own heart and in that of my monk friend's. Rahul is not only a son of Buddha, he is primarily a son of India. He regarded social and political work as of primary importance. He started writing on political subjects. He has a powerful pen as well as a powerful speech. I intervened and begged him to leave politics, and he agreed. Often I search my heart and my conscience wars with my prudence and my love of literature and history, and doubts arise. Have I stood between Rahulji and the changing destiny of my country? Have I done the right thing? Was I wrong?

(Jayasawal 1984: 17)

Sankrityayan's contributions to the field of Buddhist studies have been highly regarded virtually universally. During large parts of his active life he devoted himself to restoring Buddhist philosophical texts, lost following the decline of Buddhism in India, and as a writer of Hindi fiction he made Buddhist themes a central part of his narratives. I have been arguing here that for Sankrityayan the Buddha was first and foremost an Indian cultural hero, and the Buddhism that arose in his wake not so much a religion as the epitome of India's rich and civilized culture for the wider world to learn from. It is no cause for wonder, therefore, that the Buddhist pilgrimage sites in India (including the ancient Buddhist centres of learning at Nalanda and Takshashila) and old Buddhist manuscripts containing philosophical treatises and other scriptures should have been of singular interest to him.

While the preceding chapter explained how the Arya Samaj became a 'new light' for Sankrityayan, this chapter attempts to answer the question of what Buddhism meant to him. If he did not regard Buddhism primarily as a religion, what kind of Buddhist was he, or was he indeed ever a Buddhist? It discusses Buddhism as a source of Indian pride for Sankrityayan, his initial endeavours on behalf of it, the different aims of his visits to Tibet,[1] and the Buddhist themes in his Hindi writing.

Sankrityayan's relationship with Nepal has been explored in the second half of this chapter. His efforts to promote Buddhism, including his visits to Tibet, were supported by numerous Nepalese in many ways, and as a result he became well acquainted with the latter country's Buddhist community. The years during which Sankrityayan visited Nepal overlapped with the Theravada movement taking place there at the time; the present chapter thus explores his connection with prominent figures active in it. Finally, it analyses his relationship with Nepal from several other perspectives. Given the cultural similarity between India and Nepal, the Nepalese readily welcomed Sankrityayan into their cultural community, so that Sankrityayan never really felt as if he were in a foreign land. This relationship has been described within the framework of the concept of 'nationalist kinship' or 'brotherhood' between two countries and their people.

BUDDHISM AS A SOURCE OF NATIONAL PRIDE

> Buddhism fervently advocated the brotherhood of man without any distinction of race, country or caste. The principle of coexistence embodied in the panch shila was put into practice by Buddhism. And its missionaries in foreign lands never dreamt of destroying the culture of any nation. (Sankrityayan 1970: 3)

The previous chapter traced the change that Sankrityayan underwent from having originally accepted the religious superiority of the Arya

[1] This chapter will not deal with the details of the manuscripts Sankrityayan collected or with the editing and translation work he did on them, but will instead focus on some of the background to the visits to retrieve the 'lost heritage of India'—a topic addressed in Gerke's unpublished 1995 paper. For actual manuscripts and paintings that Sankrityayan collected, see: Michael Torsten Much (1988); Frank Bandurski (1994: 9–126); and Ewa Allinger (2001: 101–15).

Samaj to later coming to regard all religion as an obstacle to his concept of nationhood. In this new context, he understandably tended to view the Buddha less as a religious teacher than as an important contributor to the advancement of India and Indian culture.

> बुद्ध केवल धर्म संस्थापक नहीं थे। वह उच्चकोटि के विचारक होने के साथ-साथ हमारे देश और संस्कृति के महान उन्नायक थे।
>
> The Buddha was not only the founder of a religion. He was a thinker of the highest order and a great uplifter of our country and culture. (Sankrityayan December 2006–November 2007a: 39)

Sankrityayan's attraction to Buddhism as a force that served the ends of his own national sentiment was not formed only within the Indian context. Sri Lanka, too, at whose Vidyālaṅkāra Pariveṇa Sankrityayan was appointed a Sanskrit teacher and where he studied Pali and the Tripitaka (1927–8), gave him a first example of how Buddhism could serve as a source of national pride.

Vidyālaṅkāra Pariveṇa was founded by Dhammaloka Mahastavir in 1875 with the intention of promoting the Buddhist revival, and admitted both lay students and monks who wished to study Buddhist philosophy. It soon became a symbol of the religious and cultural renaissance taking place in Sri Lanka (Sankrityayan 1957b: 169). Grant (2009: 57) writes of the institution and of its influence, which has continued up to the present: '[It] especially was a seedbed for the nurturing of activist *bhikkhus*, whose "*Mahavamsa* mentality" led them to engage directly in political protest, the most extreme example being the assassination by a *bhikkhu* of Prime Minister S.W.R.D. Bandaranaike in 1959.'[2] There

[2] The *Mahavamsa* is a historical poem written in the Pali language in the 6th century, composed by bhikkhus to address and consolidate the relationship between the monarchy and the Buddhist monastic community. It is a document, then, with a pointed political message, one the Sinhalese majority often use to support their claim that Sri Lanka has been a Buddhist nation from early times. See Grant (2009: Chapter 3).

In 1928, during their common stay in Sri Lanka, Sankrityayan suggested to Bhadant Ānand Kauśalyāyan (who that same year had become the first of many others from the subcontinent to be initiated as a Buddhist monk in Sri Lanka ([Sankrityayan 1957b: 165–7]) that he translate the Pali *Mahavamsa* into Hindi.

were about 150 students in Vidyālaṅkāra Pariveṇa when Sankrityayan was there; 40 of these were residential students and the others came during the day for lessons.[3]

Coincidentally, Sankrityayan arrived in Sri Lanka on the day of Vaiśākh Purṇimā,[4] and so witnessed the decorations in front of every house for the celebration of the Buddha's birth, enlightenment, and *parinirvana* (complete extinction). Thus a first chord was struck, and the following chords only served to increase his respect for the religion and its founder. He writes:

> इतने दिनों से सुनते आते बुद्ध के नाम में अब एक विचित्र प्रकार का आकर्षण, एक अद्‌भुत माधुर्य, एक विशेष आत्मीयता मालूम होती थी।
>
> I started feeling the peculiar attraction—the amazing charm—of, and a special intimacy with, the name of the Buddha, which I had been hearing for so many days. (Sankrityayan 1998b [*MJY-2*]: 16)

The marks left by the *Mahavamsa* mentality, the cultural nationalism, and the Buddhist revival Sankrityayan experienced first-hand in Sri Lanka were long-lasting. The country played another important role in his future activity, for his first journey to Tibet was financed by Vidyālaṅkāra Pariveṇa.

The translation was duly undertaken, completed within the year, and given to Sankrityayan to proofread and annotate (Śākya 1992: 70).

[3] Sri Lanka educated many Indian and Nepalese Buddhists and nationalists. Studying there gave them a grounding in Buddhism and the Buddhist reform. The key figures were: Dharmananda Kosambi (India) starting in 1902 (educated at Vidyodaya Pariveṇa); Bhikkhu Amritananda (Nepal) in 1940; and Rahul Sankrityayan (India) in 1927. Ambedkar for his part decided to convert to Buddhism after a visit to Sri Lanka to attend a convention of Buddhist scholars in 1950. There are many other Indians and Nepalese who undertook studies in Sri Lanka and went on to devote their lives to promoting Buddhism. Indeed people from all over the world went there for similar purposes. Sankrityayan met, in particular, a number of German scholars at Vidyālaṅkāra Pariveṇa.

[4] This festival shows that Sri Lanka's history is 'inextricably entwined' with the 'Buddha Dharma' and recalls that the Buddha himself chose Sri Lanka 'for the preservation of his teaching.' See J.R. Jayewardene's address at a Buddha Jayanti celebration, as quoted in Grant (2009: 109).

Sankrityayan highly respected the Buddhist monks and scholars of the past who devoted their lives to propagating or promoting Buddhism as a great philosophy or religion:

> Political conquests are mainly responsible for the spread of the Spanish in South America and Mexico, of the English in India, of the French in Indo-China and of the Dutch in Indonesia. The spread of Indian culture and the Sanskrit language in South-east and Central Asia, Tibet, China, Korea and Japan seems to be an exception to the usual phenomenon. Princes spurned the prospects of royalty, donned yellow robes and went to unknown lands to preach the holy gospel. [...] About two in ten could reach the destination—the rest would become victims of pestilence and pirates, slippery passes and swift rivers, dacoits and famines. There were no public organizations to collect funds and support the missionary activities. It was the fervour of idealism, the spirit of self-sacrifice and defiance of death that were at the root of the spread of *Indian culture* [emphasis added] in these distant lands. Let us offer our homage to the memory of those selfless saintly scholars and pray that their spirit may once more animate the soul of modern India, so that *she may once more rise to a glorious place in the comity of nations* [emphasis added]. (Sankrityayan 1984: 215)

This quote points up particularly clearly the fact that Sankrityayan viewed Buddhism principally as a means of spreading Indian culture. It was the 'selfless saintly scholars' who served as models for his own later determination to search for original manuscripts that would contribute to India's rise to a justified place of its own in the community of nations. His Hindi writings with Buddhist themes, too, were inspired by the same sentiment.

In late 19th- and early 20th-century India, especially in its literature, which often features heroes of the past and present who were thought of as embodying Indianness to a high degree. This trait is quite obvious in Sankrityayan. He wrote many biographies of just such figures (see Chapter 1) and devoted his active years to searching for lost texts relating to the one figure whom he regarded as the Indian hero par excellence. In writing about a visit to Matha Kuar,[5] he reflects:

5 A place where the Buddha stopped to drink water before proceeding on to Kushinagara at the end of his life.

मैंने बुद्ध की जीवनियाँ पढ़ी थीं, यद्यपि मूल प्राचीन भाषा में नहीं। उस भूमि के भीतर प्रविष्ट होते वक्त मेरा हृदय ढाई-हजार वर्ष पहिले के उस महान भारतीय की ओर खिंचा हुआ था, जिसने अपनी जन्मभूमि का नाम संसार-भर में फैला दिया, और संसार के एक तृतीयांश के मनुष्यों के लिए भारत को पुण्य भूमि बना दिया।

I had studied the life story of the Buddha, although not in the original ancient language. When I entered upon that ground, my heart was attracted towards the great Indian who spread the name of his land of birth throughout the whole world and made India a holy place for one-third of the world's population. (Sankrityayan 1998b [*MJY-1*]: 229)

In Sankrityayan's opinion, the Buddha is the central figure in history:

बुद्ध का व्यक्तित्व सत भद्र सर्वतो भद्र है। इतिहास में ऐसा व्यक्ति मिलना दुर्लभ है, जो प्रतिभा में, मधुर बर्ताव में, दीन-हीनों के प्रति कार्यरूप में संवेदना दिखलाने में इतना ऊँचा हो, जितने कि भारत के सर्वश्रेष्ठ पुत्र और मानवता के सर्वोत्तम पथ प्रदर्शक बुद्ध थे।

The personality of the Buddha is one of fundamental goodness, of utter goodness. It is difficult to find another such person in history, one who stands out as the Buddha in virtue of his brilliance, of his mildness, and of his display of active compassion to the poor and downtrodden—India's first son and he who shows to humanity its highest path. (Sankrityayan December 2006–November 2007b: 27)

Sankrityayan's belief in the cultural superiority of India rests upon the attainments of Buddhist culture:

भारत को बौद्ध धर्म की आवश्यकता इसलिए भी ज्यादा है, क्योंकि बौद्ध धर्म ने कला दर्शन और साहित्य के क्षेत्र में इतनी बहुमूल्य देनें दी हैं, जिनका इससे मुकाबला करना कठिन है।

India's need for Buddhism is [... so] great because it has given so many valuable gifts [to it] in the fields of art, philosophy, and literature—ones it is difficult to find anything comparable to. (Sankrityayan December 2006–November 2007c: 32)

For his own part, Sankrityayan felt that, although he himself was not a conventionally religious person, his devotion to the Buddha was not less for that:

यद्यपि धर्म में मेरी आस्था नहीं, पर हमारी संस्कृति या दर्शन के लिए बुद्ध ने जो किया है, उसके कारण मेरी श्रद्धा उस महापुरुष के प्रति किसी भी श्रद्धालु बौद्ध से कम नहीं है।

> Even though I do not believe in [any] religion, still, given what the Buddha has done for our culture or philosophy, my respect for that great man is no less than that of any faithful Buddhist.
> (Sankrityayan 1998b [*MJY*-5]: 334)

This view was one expressed towards the end of Sankrityayan's active life, so that we may assume that his basic commitment to Buddhism remained largely unchanged from the time of his first encounter with it. But were there aspects of his stance towards it that did undergo modulation? It is now time to address how he compared the three major philosophies of the Arya Samaj, Buddhism, and communism one with the other as he turned from one to the next, in order to determine in what ways he was at any point ambivalent about any of them and whether he modified his view of one on the basis of that of another.

Ambivalence in the Interstices between the Arya Samaj, Buddhism, and Communism

As Sankrityayan came under the successive spell of the three main interests of his life—the Arya Samaj, Buddhism, and communism—he was anxious to define where the superiority of each of them lay in turn. As he shifted his allegiance from one to the other, he necessarily succumbed to feelings of ambivalence. His basic approach was first to compare two competing philosophies in an attempt to find similarities between them, and only then to seek out what divided them. If, in the end, he found certain superior qualities in the new candidate for his devotion, ones that lifted it above the old one, he would proceed to immerse himself in it. While in the Arya Samaj, Sankrityayan became aware of both communism and Buddhism. Even then he was in a position, therefore, to compare all three, but he did so from the platform of the Arya Samaj. His initial conclusion was that communism was more distant from, and Buddhism closer to, the Arya Samaj itself. As an Arya Samajist, it was more obvious that he should have been led to compare the Buddha and Dayananda, and so should have felt an urge to strike out on the path of Buddhism, since both paths were religious in nature. But later, as a self-declared Buddhist, he turned to comparing the Buddha with Marx, saw similarities between them, and set about strengthening this conviction.

The various sources of the dissatisfaction that emerged in Sankrityayan's life between his childhood and adulthood aided and prepared him for major shifts such as these. He continually strove to improve himself, and became rapidly adept at immersing himself in a new situation, place, or philosophy. He was keen to ferret out all incompleteness in his own life, and this meant in particular seeking out deficiencies in the philosophy he happened to be espousing. The best way to do this was to compare it with a newly encountered philosophy, work through both and then, if convinced of the superiority of the latter, embrace it. But even though he left behind the life of a Vaishnava sadhu, an Arya Samajist, and a Buddhist monk, he did not simply renounce them. Especially in the case of Buddhism, his admiration for it as an unparalleled vehicle of Indian culture never wavered throughout his life. The latent driving force of his life, Indian nationalism, implicit in all of Sankrityayan's thinking, ensured that it never would. Referring to his first phase of ambivalence with regard to the Arya Samaj and Buddhism, he wrote:

> बुद्ध के प्रति मेरी भक्ति दयानन्द से भी बढ़कर थी–हाँ, उस वक्त मैं यह समझने की भी गलती कर रहा था, कि बुद्ध दयानन्द ही की भांति वैदिक धर्म प्रचारक ईश्वरविश्वासी ऋषि थे।
>
> My devotion to the Buddha was greater than that to Dayananda. Yes, I had mistakenly thought at the time that the Buddha, like Dayananda, had been a propagator of the Vedic religion and atheist seer. (Sankrityayan 1998b [*MJY-1*]: 239)

Later, after he left the Arya Samaj and turned to Buddhism, he found himself in a similar situation, this time with regard to communism and Buddhism:

> मैं अब आर्य समाजी नहीं था, मेरा एक पैर था बौद्ध धर्म में और दूसरा साम्यवाद में।
>
> I was no more an Arya Samajist; one of my feet was in Buddhism and the other in communism. (Sankrityayan 1998b [*MJY-2*]: 28)

The comparative evaluation was again applied until a final judgement was reached in favour of communism:

मैं अभी धर्म की बहुत-सी बातों से दूर हो गया था, बुद्ध के निर्वाण को भी बेकार की चीज समझता था।

Now I had become detached from the many matters relating to religion, and thought the Buddha's nirvana, too, worthless.
(Sankrityayan 1998b [*MJY-2*]: 191)

Although Sankrityayan had first learnt about communism in his youth and had even written a book about his imagined ideal nation in 1923, with a nod to some of its principles, he did not become a communist overnight. The process had to take its normal course, and the first order of business was to research thoroughly the historical developments pointing towards the emergence of an Indian nation. For all the fervour of his desire for the independence, sovereignty, and development of his motherland, Sankrityayan tried to compare the principles of the Arya Samaj and communism with all due soberness. In the end, he concluded that communism was closer in spirit to Buddhism than the principles of the Arya Samaj were, and that both were better suited than it to lead to the desire goal:

आर्य समाज के स्वतन्त्र विचारों के बाद मैं बुद्ध के पास पहुँचा, और उनके अनीश्वरवाद, विचार स्वातंत्र्यवाद, आर्थिक समतावाद से बहुत प्रभावित हुआ। उसके बाद मार्क्स के विचारों को अपनाना मुझे बिल्कुल स्वाभाविक-सा मालूम हुआ। बुद्ध का दर्शन इसमें और भी सहायक सिद्ध हुआ। बुद्ध विश्व की हरेक वस्तु को अनित्य मानते हैं। हरेक चीज क्षण-क्षण बदल रही है, बल्कि यह कहना चाहिए कि जो चीज क्षण-क्षण बदल नहीं रही है, वह दुनिया में है ही नहीं। वह केवल कल्पना-मात्र मिथ्याभ्रम है। अनात्मवाद, अनीश्वरवाद, ग्रंथ-अप्रामाण्यवाद ये सभी आदमी के मानसिक बन्धन को खोल देते हैं। यह सब होते हुए भी बौद्ध-धर्म या दर्शन वह काम नहीं कर सकता था, जिसे मार्क्स की शिक्षा कर सकती है। मार्क्स को दुनिया और उसकी वस्तुओं की व्याख्या ही नहीं करनी थी, बल्कि उन्हें बदलना था। बदलना और क्षणिकवाद को बौद्ध भी मानते हैं, पर मनुष्य अपनी इच्छा से वस्तुस्थिति को अपने अनुकूल बदलने में समर्थ मार्क्स के बतलाए रास्ते से ही हो सका। [...] बुद्ध और मार्क्स ईश्वर को नहीं मानते थे, इसलिए वे भगवान के सन्देशवाहक नहीं हो सकते थे। पर, उन्होंने दुनिया को महान सन्देश दिया, इससे कौन इन्कार कर सकता है।

I arrived at the Buddha after the independent views of the Arya Samaj, and was very impressed by his [notions of] atheism, freedom of thought, and economic equality. Subsequently I adopted Marxism, I realized, virtually spontaneously. The Buddha's philosophy proved to be supportive of this [decision] as well. The Buddha regards everything in the world as impermanent. Things change every moment, or rather, whatever does not change every moment does not exist in the world. [The notion of permanence] is only a fantasy, a false view. Rejection of an eternal self,[6] atheism, and not recognizing the authority of the Vedic texts release all persons from mental bondage. Still, Buddhist religion or philosophy could not do what Marxism can. Marx felt the necessity not only to explain the world and its entities but also to change them. Buddhists, too, believe in change and impermanence, but humankind has only been able to change situations for its own ends, in accordance with its own desires, through the effective way enunciated by Marx. [...] The Buddha and Marx did not believe in a supreme being; therefore they could not be the bearers of such a being's message. Still, no one can deny, they did deliver a great message to the world. (Sankrityayan 1998b [*MJY-2*]: 229)

Elsewhere he defines the essential difference between Buddhist philosophy and Marxism as follows:

Buddhism has made original contributions in several fields but those in the field of philosophy are unique. Of course, it will be erroneous to say that it helped Marx's philosophy or [that] it ever came anywhere near the fundamentals of marxism. But an understanding of marxist philosophy is easier for students of Buddhist philosophy. [...] Hegel held that mind or idea was primary and real and matter a product thereof. Marx held matter to be primary and mind to be its highest development. Buddhism in its highest and final form is in a large measure similar to the idealism of Hegel. The idea (vijnana) [the nature of cognition or consciousness] of yogachara [an influential school of Buddhist philosophy and its primary interest is in vijnana] philosophy is dynamic and nonmaterial. Like Hegel, the yogachara school of Buddhism too considers idea or mind as the ultimate reality. (Sankrityayan 1970: 3)

It is clear, then, why Sankrityayan, given the centrality he accorded to nationalist sentiment in the scheme of things, should have ended

[6] Cf. R. Bhaṭṭācārya (1993: 105–12) who, in his brief review of Sankrityayan's views on communism and Marxism, cautions against taking *anātmavād* as meaning 'materialism'.

up embracing a combination of two seemingly irreconcilable strains of thought, for both offered a 'dynamic' view of how the world operates. Thus, even though Sankrityayan did not formally practise Buddhism for long, he always remained a Buddhist at heart in his own eyes, since for him a Buddhist was someone who followed the Buddha's command to put his teachings to a private test. This Sankrityayan did, and settled upon key aspects of Buddhist philosophy to be guided by:

> बौद्ध धर्म के साथ मेरा कच्चे धागे का ही संबन्ध था। हाँ, बुद्ध के प्रति तो मेरी श्रद्धा कभी कम नहीं हुई। मैं उन्हें भारत का सबसे बड़ा विचारक मानता रहा हूँ, और समझता हूँ कि जिस वक्त दुनिया के धर्म का नामोनिशान न रह जाएगा, उस वक्त भी लोग बड़े सम्मान के साथ बुद्ध का नाम लेंगे। मैंने उनके वचनों को पढ़ने बाद समझा, कि वह भी दुनिया के साम्यवादी बनने का सपना देखते थे।
>
> My connection with the Buddhist religion was by a flimsy string. Still, my respect for the Buddha has never lessened. I continue to regard him as India's greatest thinker, and recognized that when there is no longer any trace of religion in the world, even then people will remember the Buddha's name with respect. After reading his discourses, I realized that he, too, had dreamt of a *sāmyavādī duniyā* [communist world]. (Sankrityayan 1998b [*MJY-2*]: 105)

Sankrityayan's comparative evaluation of Buddhism and communism has been regarded as a new contribution to Marxist thinking. The eminent Indian critic Nāmvar Siṃh, giving a talk on the occasion of the centenary celebrations of Sankrityayan's birth in 1995, credits him with introducing Buddhism into Indian Marxist theory. He further credits Sankrityayan with gifting Buddha's *karuṇā* (compassion) for the human brotherhood to Indian communism:

> बुद्ध का यह करुणा संदेश मैं समझता हूँ कि शायद भारत के कम्युनिष्ट आंदोलन को अथवा अंतर्राष्ट्रीय कम्युनिष्ट आंदोलन को राहुल की देन है। बौद्ध दर्शन से श्रद्धा लेकर राहुल ने इसे क्रांतिकारी मार्क्सवाद को देने की कोशिश की है। किंतु इस देन की चर्चा बहुत कम की जाती है। प्राय: उन चीजों की चर्चा ज्यादा की जाती है जिसमें वर्ग संघर्ष आदि और धार्मिक रूढ़ियों का विरोध होता है। [...] उस मानवीय करुणा के बिना कोई भी परिवर्तनवादी दर्शन या सिद्धांत या व्यवहार जैसा मैंने कहा कि बंध्या है। राहुल की यह देन आज भी उल्लेखनीय है, रेखांकित करने योग्य है। मेरा ख्याल है कि १९वीं शताब्दी का भारतीय नवजागरण, जो राजा राममोहन राय

> से शुरु हुआ जिसमें रामकृष्ण, विवेकानन्द, लोकमान्य तिलक जैसे मनीषी हुए, उनमें अकेले राहुल थे, जिन्होंने १९वीं शताब्दी के इस नवजागरण में बौद्ध आयाम को जोड़ा। इसके पहले वह उपनिषद् और गीता पर ही निर्भर था।
>
> The Buddha's message of compassion, I believe, was perhaps Rahul's contribution to the Indian communist movement or to the international communist movement. Rahul borrowed the [concept of] *śraddhā* [faith] from Buddhism and tried to pass it on to revolutionary Marxism. But this contribution is hardly ever discussed. Usually it is such things as the class struggle or opposition to religious fundamentalism that are discussed. [...] Without human compassion, any transformational philosophy or theory or mode of action is, as I said, unproductive. Rahul's contribution is notable and is worth underscoring. I believe that the 19th-century Indian renaissance, which started with Raja Rammohan Roy and which produced such wise men as Ramakrishna, Vivekananda, and Lok Manya Tilak—that among these it was only Rahul who added the Buddhist dimension to the 19th-century renaissance. Before, it had been based only on the Upanishads and the Gita. (V. Siṃh 1995: 32)

Sankrityayan saw Buddhist culture, then, as the epitome of Indian's glorious past and communism as the only possible means of developing the country into something of comparable grandeur. Buddhism was important for defining Indian identity—the country's unique civilizational place in the world—and communism for guiding the development of the nation back to its rightful place. This is what first motivated Sankrityayan to fulfil what he felt to be a national responsibility: to collect, edit, and publish lost original Buddhist texts that had made their way to Tibet, and thereby to help raise India's status back to what it once was. Thereafter he devoted himself to politics, the next form of 'national responsibility' (rāṣṭrīya kārya).

Sankrityayan's first endeavours relating to Buddhism, though, were not his visits to Tibet. He had earlier, during the Gaya congress, presented a proposal for handing over the Maha Bodhi Temple to Buddhists, and this, it can be said, was the first instance of his introducing Buddhist themes into politics. Regarding his emergent admiration for Buddhism, Sankrityayan credits Bhadanta Bodhananda, a Bengalese who was dedicated to re-establishing Buddhism in India, with opening up the world of Buddhism to him for the first time in 1916, in Lucknow (1957b: 126). Indeed, he does not hesitate to credit this figure with reintroducing all Indians to Buddhism. He (1957b: 127) remembers that when, as a devotee of the Veda, Ishvara, the Arya Samaj, and Swami Dayananda, he met Bodhananda and mentioned his desire to learn about the Buddha and Buddhism, he received immediate encouragement. In particular, he was told how to acquire Buddhist literature, since at that time, except for the *Dhammapada*, canonical works were not available either in the original or in Hindi translation (1957b: 126).[7] Bodhananda's biography recounts this episode in Sankrityayan's life, although it should be remembered that the latter's respect for the Buddha and the work of Buddhist monks in propagating and preserving Buddhism had already taken root during his time in the Arya Samaj. The following pages will go back over Sankrityayan's initial work on behalf of Buddhism.

Initial Endeavours Relating to Buddhism

Sri Lanka, a Theravada Buddhist country, was where Sankrityayan first seriously studied Buddhism and was initiated as a Buddhist monk. Much earlier, Anagarika Dharmapala (whose worldly name was Don David Hewawitarana), a Sri Lankan, had set out on a pilgrimage to sacred Buddhist sites in northern India that took him, quite naturally, to Bodh Gaya. There he felt the power of the Bodhi tree, supposedly an offshoot of the one under which Prince Shakyamuni had gained enlightenment, so overwhelming that everything else that he had experienced up till then paled in comparison. After the destruction of the north-Indian Buddhist monasteries by Muslim invaders, the disappearance of Buddhism in India, and the occupation of the Maha Bodhi Temple by a Hindu Saiva mahant,[8] Bodh Gaya became a holy place exclusively for Hindus. A restoration of the temple in Bodh

7 Bodhananda was himself a convert to Buddhism. He had long argued against the caste system, and had become interested in the religion because he had heard about its stance on the issue.

8 The temple was abandoned by Buddhists after the eradication of Buddhism under the Muslim invaders sometime in the 14th century. In 1590 a Hindu Saiva mahant, Gosain Ghamandi Giri, stumbled upon it and decided that he would make the secluded and peaceful place his permanent abode. See Ahir (2010: 15–16) for detailed information.

Gaya was accomplished with the help of both the Burmese royal government (in 1877) and the British colonial government (in 1880[9]), although it remained in the hands of a Hindu mahant. Buddhist pilgrims started visiting it from as far away as Mongolia.

On his return to Colombo from Bodh Gaya, Dharmapala founded the Maha Bodhi Society. Its main objectives were getting the Maha Bodhi Temple restored to Buddhist control, reviving Buddhism in India, promoting Buddhism in Ceylon and in the rest of the world, establishing educational institutions, printing literature related to Buddhism, and training *dhammadūtas*—monks and lay workers—to propagate the Buddhist religion and culture.[10] In 1892 Dharmapala began to publish a journal entitled *The Maha-Bodhi and the United Buddhist World,* the front cover[11] of which carried a picture of the Maha Bodhi Temple. That same year Dharmapala moved the society's headquarters to Calcutta in order to further the campaign to return the temple from Hindu to Buddhist control (Levine and Gellner 2008: 5–7).

In 1922 Sankrityayan, having recently entered politics, prepared a proposal to restore the Maha Bodhi Temple[12] to Buddhist control for debate by the regional Congress committee of Chapra. After a heated discussion, the committee agreed to forward the proposal to the annual national meeting of the Congress party scheduled to be held in Gaya later that year. Anagarik Dharmapala sent Bhikshu Shri Nivasa and Bhikshu Dharmapala, joined by a number of Burmese bhikkhus,

[9] The restoration resulted in an almost perfect replica of the original shrine seen by the Chinese pilgrim Hiuen Tsang in AD 637. Concerning his description of it, see Ahir (2010: 14).

[10] Sankrityayan visited Europe as a dhammadūta of the Maha Bodhi Society in 1932–3.

[11] The cover addressed an invitation to the journal's subscribers as follows (cited in Levine and Gellner 2008: 7): 'To revive Buddhism in India, to disseminate Buddhist literature, to Publish Buddhist tracts in the Indian Vernaculars, to educate the illiterate millions of Indian people, to maintain Bhikkhus at Buddha Gaya, Benaras, Kusinārā, Sāvatthi and Calcutta, to build Dharmasalas at these places, to send Buddhist missionaries abroad, the Maha-Bodhi asks every Buddhist to contribute 1/20 of his daily expenses to the Maha-Bodhi Fund.'

[12] For details on the Maha Bodhi Temple, see Ahir (2010: 12–21).

to the congress. A large meeting was organized in the tent of the Arya Samaj, and Sankrityayan and many other Buddhists and Hindus spoke on the topic. Sankrityayan also translated many speeches by foreign Buddhist guests from English, Sanskrit, and Pali into Hindi. But the larger issues being thrashed out between the status-quoists and the party of change overshadowed the proposal regarding the Maha Bodhi Temple. Nonetheless, the whole affair brought Sankrityayan closer to Buddhism and the Buddhist community (Sankrityayan 1998b [*MJY-1*]: 269–70).

> गया कांग्रेस में परिवर्तनवाद और अपरिवर्तनवाद का झगड़ा जोरों से रहा। इसलिए बोध गया मन्दिर का प्रस्ताव आने ही नहीं पाया। उस सम्बन्ध में मुझे जो बौद्ध भिक्षुओं के साथ काम करने का मौका मिला, उससे मैंने अपने को बौद्ध धर्म के नजदीक पाया।
>
> During the Gaya congress those in favour of change and those against change remained locked in battle. Therefore, my recommendation for the Bodh Gaya temple made no headway. From the opportunity I had to work with Buddhist monks in this regard, I found myself drawing closer to Buddhism. (Sankrityayan 1998b [*MJY-1*]: 270)

The inability of the Gaya congress to decide and act on the temple issue, along with the friction between the two factions, diminished Sankrityayan's interest in Congress party politics. Nonetheless, his nationalist sentiment kept him from taking any drastic action.

> गया कांग्रेस के बाद परिवर्तनवादी होने से मैं जिला कांग्रेस कमेटी के मन्त्रित्व से इस्तीफ़ा देने वाला था, किन्तु काम तो मुझे वैसे ही करना था।
>
> After the Gaya congress I was on the point of resigning from the post of district Congress committee minister, having become a supporter of the party of change, but I [felt I] had to work anyway. (Sankrityayan 1998b [*MJY-1*]: 270)

Sankrityayan's opinion regarding the failure of the campaign to return the Maha Bodhi Temple to Buddhists was that it was due to outside interference: 'महाबोधि मन्दिर को बौद्धों के हाथ में न जाने देने में सबसे बड़ा हाथ अंग्रेजी सरकार का है।' [The British government had a hand—the biggest hand—in keeping the Maha Bodhi Temple from being restored to the Buddhists] (1998b [*MJY-1*]: 285). The reason for British opposition was, he thought, that if the Maha Bodhi Temple were to have become an officially recognized centre of Buddhist pilgrimage, many more foreigners would visit the place than already did, and this was seen as against British government interests, inasmuch as many Buddhist countries were independent and their citizens could be expected to sow the seeds of independence in India. Many of these countries had, to be sure, raised their voices against the British government's decision. Sankrityayan's anger towards the British government shows just how strong his nationalist sentiment was. The temple issue was again raised in the year 1925 during the Hindu Mahasabha[13] session in Muzaffarpur, in which Sankrityayan could not participate because he was in prison at the time. Regarding the formation of the restoration committee, Rājendra Prasād (2007: 340) writes that a delegation under the leadership of Cassius Pereira from Sri Lanka approached the Congress party about the issue. The delegation then met Mahatma Gandhi, who requested Prasād to form such a committee and draft a report. He further writes that, owing to the poor attendance in the two committee meetings convened by him in Patna, it was decided to join the Hindu Mahasabha session in Muzaffarpur. The Mahasabha and the Congress had each formed its own committees to press for the restoration of the temple—both containing seven members.[14] Rājendra Prasād was the president, and Sankrityayan, Brajakishor Prasad, and Kashi Prasad Jayasawal were members of the committee. Anagarika Dharmapala was one of the committee

[13] The Hindu Sabha was formed in Punjab in the early 20th century as a purely Hindu organization that sought to advance highly charged communal policies. Local Arya Samajists initiated the Hindu Sabha. In 1915 the All-India Hindu Sabha held its first session in Hardwar. Later, in April 1921, it re-christened itself as All-India Hindu Mahasabha. Its members patronized anti-Muslim movements such as the śuddhi (purity) and *saṅgathan* (unity) with the aim of terrorizing Muslims and reconverting them back to Hinduism. The Mahasabha considered that Sikhs, Jains, and Buddhists were Hindus by reason of their national and political identity, and believed in the primacy of Hindu culture. Among its top leaders were Lala Lajpat Rai, Madan Mohan Malaviya, Swami Shraddhananda, Bhāī Parmānand, Bharti Krishnatirth, and Vinayak Damodar Savarkar. For details on Hindu Mahasabha, see Bapu (2013: 11–25) and Jaffrelot (1999: 17–25).

[14] Sankrityayan's own account substantiates the number of members; see Sankrityayan (1998b [*MJY-1*]: 285) and Prasād (2007: 340–2).

members, but had sent Bhrahmachari Devapriya Valisimha to represent him.[15] In the winter of 1925 the committee held a meeting in Patna and drafted a report recommending that management of the temple should be handed over jointly to Hindus and Buddhists. While he respected this decision, Sankrityayan's personal opinion was that administration should be the sole responsibility of Buddhists.

In Sankrityayan's opinion, Bodh Gaya was as important a holy pilgrimage site for Buddhists as Mecca was for Muslims and Jerusalem was for Christians. The priest there, however, believed that 'our Śaṅkarācārya had removed Buddhists from India', and Sankrityayan was understandably disappointed to see this important Buddhist pilgrimage site in the hands of such a person (Sankrityayan 1998b [*MJY-1*]: 285–6).[16]

After his unsuccessful bid during the district board elections in 1929, Sankrityayan retired from Congress politics, feeling it had nothing new to attract him. He went to Sarnath and there met Bhikkhu Sri Nivasa, whom he knew from the Gaya congress and who had

[15] Later someone else and the mahant of the temple were also invited to be members, but neither of them participated in the proceedings (Prasād 2007: 341).

[16] India's president, Rājendra Prasād (and the then president of the temple restoration committee), handed over the Maha Bodhi Temple to the Buddhists on 6 May 1955, and in doing so recognized the contribution made by Dharmapala.

Earlier, when Rājendra Prasād visited Sri Lanka with his colleagues after attending the Madras session of the Congress party in 1927, he personally requested Sankrityayan to guide them around the island. One stop on the tour was Anuradhpura (the cradle of Sri Lankan Buddhism and civilization, as attested by the ruins found there), where the group saw the Bodhi tree that had been planted by Sanghamitra, the daughter of Ashoka, from a branch of the tree under which the Buddha had attained enlightenment. After Sankrityayan explained the importance of the tree for Sri Lankans, Rājendra Prasād spoke up, saying, 'A branch of the peepul tree is respected and cared for in this way here, but what is the respect for the main Bodhi tree at our place. We have really done an injustice by seizing the Bodh Gaya temple.' Sankrityayan came back: 'That is why I was saying that the temple should under all circumstances be handed over to the Buddhists' (Sankrityayan 1998b [*MJY-2*]: 21–2).

A branch of the Sri Lankan Bodhi tree was also brought to Kathmandu and was planted in Ānandakuṭī vihara (Śākya 2000: 176).

represented Anagarika Dharmapala in it. Bhikkhu Sri Nivasa[17] was impressed by Sankrityayan's interest in Buddhism and suggested that he go to Sri Lanka, since the Vidyālaṅkāra Pariveṇa was looking for a Sanskrit teacher (Sankrityayan 1998b [*MJY-1*]: 311). He went so far as to write a personal recommendation for him to Bhikshu Naravil Dharma Ratna in the Maha Bodhi Society headquarters in Calcutta. Bhikshu Naravil, who had been a student of Vidyālaṅkāra Pariveṇa and was now working for the re-establishment of Buddhism in India, sent off a telegram, and money to cover Sankrityayan's travel costs arrived within two or three days (Sankrityayan 1998b [*MJY-2*]: 15). Sankrityayan reached Vidyālaṅkāra Pariveṇa on 16 May 1927.

Sankrityayan's close affiliation to Buddhism starts from his years in Sri Lanka, where he learnt Pali and studied the Tripitaka, earning himself the title of *tripiṭakācārya*. Later he went to Tibet to do further research on Buddhism. He was also sent to Britain by the Maha Bodhi Society to propagate Buddhism there. Details are already known about his collection of Buddhist texts from Tibet, and his editorial and other contributions to the field of Buddhist studies. Therefore, the immediately following pages of this study will concentrate on Sankrityayan's assorted reasons for visiting Tibet, his relationships with foreign Buddhist scholars, and the inspiration they provided throughout the remainder of his life.

The Different Trips to Tibet and Their Different Aims[18]

During his studies in Sri Lanka, Sankrityayan determined to visit Tibet in the future to witness the practice of Buddhism in the most

[17] Bhikkhu Sri Nivasa (1894–1968) was born in Sri Lanka and went to India at the request of Anagarika Dharmapala, who later appointed him secretary of the Maha Bodhi Society, Sarnath branch. After residing for about fifteen years in Sarnath, Sri Nivasa built a *viśrāmaśālā* (rest-house) in Nautanva (on the Nepal–India border) for pilgrims visiting Lumbini in Nepal, the place of the Buddha's birth. Called the Lumbini viśrāmaśālā, it would later, in July 1944, provide shelter for five Buddhist monks exiled by the Rana government. (The viśrāmaśālā was sold in 1956.) Sri Nivasa visited Nepal many times and helped to promote Theravada Buddhism there (Śākya 2000).

[18] I am obliged to Birgit Kellner for her helpful suggestions regarding this section.

extreme form history had endowed it with. He realized that, as he had been involved in the non-cooperation movement and jailed twice, the English government would be unlikely to let him cross the Indian border. Furthermore, he knew that some Indians had misused the hospitality of Tibetans to the point where Tibetans tended to be suspicious of them. Thus, the only realistic way left to go to Tibet was via Nepal, as a Nepalese. But permission to enter Tibet via Nepal would not be easy to obtain from the Nepalese government either, because Sankrityayan was a foreigner, while his activities in the non-cooperation movement could again raise the suspicions of the Ranas. Moreover, entering the Kathmandu Valley (which was then still called Nepal) was not always possible for Indian citizens. A visa was only easily obtainable (for Indian Hindu pilgrims) during the Śivarātri festival. With this in mind, Sankrityayan successfully planned a trip to the Kathmandu Valley for Śivarātri in 1929, determined to travel on from there to Tibet (Sankrityayan 1957b: 137).

The very next day, after the high point of the festival, Sankrityayan went underground in Bauddha, hoping that the Dukpa Lama[19] would help him to gain access to Tibet. Afraid of being identified by anyone as an Indian, he did not go out frequently. He started studying Tibetan with the help of Henderson's *Tibetan Manual* and asked the Dukpa Lama to take him to Tibet as a member of his travelling party, saying he wished to go there because '[n]ot all books on Buddhism are available in Sri Lanka, and so I want to go to Tibet to study them. I want to propagate Buddhism in India.'[20] The Dukpa Lama agreed. Sankrityayan learned from other Buddhist scholars in Patan that indeed the easiest way to get into Tibet was with the help of the Dukpa Lama.

Newar Buddhists in Patan, hearing Sankrityayan talk of himself as a Buddhist, were surprised that a Brahmin should have abandoned his caste (Sankrityayan 1990 VS: 60).[21] As a consequence, many people started visiting him in Bauddha, wishing to meet the Brahmin from Banaras. This naturally caused him some nervousness. He did

[19] The highest lama of the Dukpa sect.

[20] 'बौद्धधर्म के सभी ग्रन्थ सिंहल में प्राप्य नहीं हैं, इसलिए उनके पढ़ने के लिए मैं तिब्बत जाना चाहता हूँ। भारत में बौद्धधर्म का प्रचार करना चाहता हूँ।' (Sankrityayan 1998b [*MJY-2*]: 32).

[21] Though the Buddha is revered by Hindus in Nepal, they generally do not renounce Hinduism for Buddhism.

not see any possibility of going to Tibet with the Dukpa Lama anytime soon, since the latter had no immediate plans to do so. Sankrityayan began looking around for other ways and eventually stumbled upon the Nepalese Buddhist merchant Dharmaman Sahu. Dharmaman Sahu introduced him to a fellow merchant, Dasharatan Sahu, who later became a Buddhist monk called Bhikkhu Dharmalok. This latter took Sankrityayan to a friend's residence in Helambu outside the valley, from where he was able to reach Tibet easily.

Sankrityayan was not the first person to enter Tibet disguised as a Nepalese (and later as a Tibetan with the name Khunnū Chevaṅ). A Japanese Buddhist monk, Ekai Kawaguchi, had easily crossed the border in the 1890s, since he resembled a Nepalese (Subedi 1999: 6).[22] Later, when Sankrityayan visited Tibet via India as an Indian with a permit, he took an Indian friend of his named Rajnath disguised as a Nepalese citizen. 'Short in stature, Rajnath wore a Nepalese topi and pyjamas, and that appearance served instead of a visa' (Sankrityayan 1998b [*MJY-2*]: 151). Sankrityayan wrote: 'Rajnath was going on ahead with the other Nepalese. No one had asked him anything, but as I passed through, the policeman ran after and shouted at me to show my pass. Doing so, I asked, "Why do you ask only me?" He replied, "We do not ask Nepalese for passes". I smiled within—Rajnath had become a perfect Nepalese' (1998b [*MJY-2*]: 152).

Although Nepalese law was very strict, then, it was possible for people to get around it. Many non-Nepalese, such as Kawaguchi,[23] Sankrityayan, or Rajnath, entered Tibet pretending to be Nepalese. Since Nepal is a land of many ethnic castes and cultures, its people display many different facial features, whether Mongolian, Dravidian,

[22] Sankrityayan had read Kawaguchi's and Alexandra David-Neel's accounts of their visits to Tibet and garnered useful information from them (Sankrityayan 1990 VS: 2–3).

[23] Ekai Kawaguchi had left Japan in 1897 in order '[...] to go in search of the authentic texts to Nepal and Tibet where they were taken by those fleeing the Muslim invasion in India, and preserved carefully' (Subedi 1999: 15). 'Kawaguchi read that manuscripts were safely preserved in Tibet. He also learned that Brian Hogdson, the British official in Nepal, had also collected Sanskrit texts in Nepal' (Subedi 1999: 17). Sankrityayan had the same purpose in mind as these predecessors when he travelled to Nepal and Tibet. Sankrityayan would later (1935) meet Kawaguchi in Tokyo (Sankrityayan 1998b [*MJY-2*]: 204).

or Aryan. Śivarātri was a particularly suitable occasion to enter Kathmandu incognito, not only for foreigners but also for exiled Nepalese. One exiled Buddhist monk, for instance, Prem Bahadur Shrestha, later known as Mahāprajñā, visited the Kathmandu Valley during Śivarātri in 1930 (Śākya 1993: 25).[24]

Sankrityayan's main aim in visiting Tibet in 1929 was to study Buddhist texts (Sankrityayan 1998b [*MJY-2*]: 55), but his limited knowledge of Tibetan was not sufficient for the purpose. He had imagined that his command of Sanskrit would help him as much as it had in Sri Lanka. In fact, the opposite was the case; his Sanskrit was of no use at all. Indeed, he came to realize that Sanskrit was a poor source in comparison to Tibetan, for, as he found out, of the approximately 10,000 Sanskrit texts that had been translated into Tibetan, only some 250 still existed in the original (Sankrityayan 1998b [*MJY-2*]: 63). He had trouble enough finding any of the remaining Sanskrit manuscripts. Faced with this bitter truth, he was forced to concentrate on studying Tibetan.

Sankrityayan was staying with Newar merchants in their *koṭhī* (business house). He asked them to lend him the nine Sanskrit grammars that were preserved in their *pālā* (temple)[25] and began studying them together with their Tibetan translations. In the process, he started compiling Tibetan words and their meanings in Sanskrit.[26] Later some texts from the Tenjur were made available to him from Muru monastery, so that he was able to improve his knowledge of Tibetan still further.

Sankrityayan spent fourteen months in Tibet during his first visit. He had planned to stay much longer[27] but did not have the financial

[24] Some years later, however, when Shrestha visited Bhojpur, he was arrested while lecturing (on 14 January 1937) and was imprisoned for four months (three months in Bhojpur and one month in Dhankuta) and again exiled back to India (Śākya 1993: 35).

[25] This is the definition Sankrityayan gives for the Newari word. It would appear to be, more properly, a type of religious trust or social organization.

[26] This compilation is the unpublished dictionary mentioned by Kamala Sankrityayan.

[27] 'वस्तुत: मैंने अपनी इस यात्रा का प्रोग्राम आठ-दस वर्ष का बनाया था। तिब्बत से चौदह मास बाद ही लौट आने का ज़रा भी विचार न था।' [Actually I had planned this visit for eight to ten years. I had not thought that I would be coming back after 14 months] (Sankrityayan 1990 VS: 47).

resources to do so. There were two possible scholarships that would have allowed him to stay in Tibet, one from Ācārya Narendra Dev of Kaśi Vidyāpīṭh in Banaras, and the other from Vidyālaṅkāra Pariveṇa in Sri Lanka. The former had sent some money at his request, but it was not enough for his planned long stay (which later he had reduced to three years [Sankrityayan 1998b [*MJY-2*]: 64]). Finally he got a telegram from Vidyālaṅkāra Pariveṇa with a suggestion that he buy the written material he had found and return to Sri Lanka. This was advice he was forced to take.

Sankrityayan thus started purchasing every manuscript or painting available. He visited Samye monastery with a sense of pride, since it had been established by an Indian Buddhist scholar from Nalanda, Ācārya Śāntarakṣita, in the 8th century. Besides the main temple, there were twelve other temples and residences, and the whole area in and around it was called Gya-gar, Gya-gar ling, or Bhāratdvīp (Indian isle). This was the place where so many Indian pandits had translated Sanskrit books into Tibetan, and during the 11th century it had Tibet's biggest collection of such books.[28] Yet when Sankrityayan arrived there, not a single one was to be found. He surmised that a big fire in the monastery during the 11th or 12th century had burnt them all to ashes. Sankrityayan's excitement about collecting Sanskrit manuscripts was dampened somewhat, but by the end of the journey, when he received the *Vajra-dāka-tantra* as a gift (from Shalu monastery's Risur Lama), he was back to his normal high spirits. He had collected the Kanjur, Tanjur,[29] and paintings—whatever was available. Altogether, seventeen or eighteen mules were needed to carry his luggage to Kalimpong. The *Vajra-dāka-tantra* was the only Sanskrit manuscript (palm-leaf) among its contents. Written in the Kutila script during the 10th or 11th century, it is now preserved in the

[28] Sankrityayan quotes Dipaṅkara Śrījñāna, who lived in the 11th century, as having said that Sanskrit books that were not available in Vikramshila were available there (Sankrityayan 1998b [*MJY–2*]: 69).

[29] The Tibetan Buddhist canon is composed of two major sections—the Kanjur and the Tanjur. The teaching of Buddha or his inspired followers preserved in Tibetan is called the Kanjur or Kangyur. The Tanjur or Tengyur is a miscellaneous collection of some 225 volumes, mostly translated, of various Buddhist commentaries from Sanskrit or Chinese into Tibetan.

Patna Museum. 'This was the second Sanskrit manuscript recovered from Tibet; the first was "*Saddharma-Pundarika*" taken to Japan by Kawaguchi (1900–3). Both were found in Shalu' (Jayaswal 1984: ix).

Among the Tibetan paintings collected, Sankrityayan took some particularly beautiful ones with him to Europe when he visited as a dhammadūta of the Maha Bodhi Society, and they were exhibited at the Musée Guimet in Paris. He had thought first to sell them and earn some money towards re-establishing Nalanda, but when he realized their cultural importance, he decided to preserve them in the Patna Museum.

During this visit Sankrityayan met a number of European scholars of Indian and Tibetan studies, among them Sylvain Lévi in France, to whom he gifted his book *Abhidharmakośa* (1930).[30] He also showed Lévi the English translation of two of his articles, 'The Origin of Mahayana' and 'The Origin of Vajrayana and Its Eighty-Four Mystics', which were later published in the *Journal Asiatique* at Lévi's initiative.[31] Lévi suggested that he should visit Gilgit and write about the manuscripts found there. Sankrityayan also met Alfred Fouché in Paris, and Rudolf Otto and Richard Fick in Marburg, Germany. Moreover, he came to learn more about Theodor Ippolitovich Stcherbatsky and his works from Lévi.

Sankrityayan was keen to visit Russia on his return trip to India, but it was not to be. Instead, once back in India, he made plans for a second visit to Tibet in 1934 to search for Sanskrit manuscripts:

30 The end matter of *Tibbat mẽ savā varṣ* contains an advertisement for Sankrityayan's other books relating to Buddhist studies, including Vasubandhu's *Abhidharmakośa*, stating that it represents a restoration of the Sanskrit based on the Tibetan version (Sankrityayan 1990 VS: 5). Law (1949: i) acknowledges Sankrityayan's work as follows: 'Prof. Louis de la Vallèe Poussin has made our task easy by his invaluable translation of Hiuen Tsang's commentary on the *Kośa*, and Rev. Sāṅkr̥tyāyana by publishing the text of the *Kośa* with valuable notes and tables.' This book is no longer readily available in the market. One gathers from Law's description of it that it was not a verse-by-verse commentary but rather a Sanskrit reconstruction of the *Kośa* with occasional explanations. Sankrityayan himself and others cite it as either the *Abhidharmakośa* or *Abhidharmakośa-tikā*.

31 The English translations of both articles appear in Sankrityayan (1984).

अब की बार मेरी यात्रा विशेषकर संस्कृत पुस्तकों की खोज के लिए हुई थी। 'तिब्बत में बौद्धधर्म' लिखते समय जब मैंने भोटिया ग्रंथों के पन्ने उलटे तो विश्वास हो गया, कि भारत से कई हजार ताल पोथियों में से वहाँ कुछ जरूर होनी चाहिए। [...] अब मेरे सामने सबसे प्रमुख काम संस्कृत पुस्तकों की खोज के लिए सहायता प्राप्त करना था।

This time my trip was to search for Sanskrit books. When, as I was writing *Tibbat mẽ bauddh dharm*, I turned the pages of Tibetan books, I was sure that there must be some manuscripts [still remaining] out of the thousands [that had been brought] there from India. [...] My main job now was to seek [financial] help to search for Sanskrit books. (Sankrityayan 1998b [*MJY-2*]: 156)

As Sankrityayan himself saw it, it was a lack of money, not any lack of skill or other considerations, that put him at a disadvantage compared with European scholars:

[...] काफी पैसा रहने पर मैं किसी भी यूरोपियन अनुसन्धानकर्ता से सौ गुना काम कर सकता था, मेरी स्थिति ऐसी थी, कि उनसे हजार गुना अधिक तथा बहुत ही महत्वपूर्ण चीजें जमा कर लेता।

[...] If I had had enough money I could have accomplished a hundred times more than any European scholar. My situation was such that I could have collected a thousand times more—and much more important—things. (Sankrityayan 1998b [*MJY-2*]: 167)

Now that he had met many European scholars, Sankrityayan's interest in collecting manuscripts and working on them increased. He became aware that European scholars were also working on them,[32] and that they were keen, in particular, on finding manuscripts of Dharmakirti's *Pramāṇavārttika*.[33] During his second visit

[32] जर्मनी के शिक्षित मध्यम-वर्ग में बुद्ध के प्रति अनुराग रखने वाले आदमियों की बहुत काफी तादाद थी। संस्कृत और पाली भाषाओं के बड़े-बड़े विद्वान जर्मनी में पैदा हुए। उन्होंने हजारों ग्रन्थों का सम्पादन और अनुवाद किया।' [There were many [in the] educated middle-class population in Germany who liked Buddha. Many great scholars of Sanskrit and Pali were also born in Germany. They edited and translated thousands of books] (Sankrityayan 1998b: [*MJY-2*]: 113).

[33] Sankrityayan says that his interest in the *Pramāṇavārttika* was sparked after his first visit to Tibet, presumably first and foremost during his conversations with European scholars.

to Tibet, then, he tried to locate a copy of it. He had heard that Hemraj Sharma had an old copy of it in Kathmandu, and so he returned via Kathmandu to meet him[34] to see if he could borrow it.[35] Although they had met before under other circumstances, this time he presented himself to Sharma as an Indian scholar.[36] Sankrityayan learned there that the Italian scholar Giuseppe Tucci had already taken the manuscript of the *Pramāṇavārttika*. Still, although the original was not available, he was able to obtain a photographic copy of it, of which ten pages were missing, presumably from the bound volume that was produced from the photos.

Sankrityayan's third visit[37] to Tibet in 1936 was aimed specifically at finding a complete Sanskrit manuscript of the *Pramāṇavārttika*, which he succeeded in doing. Remembering his sickness before the trip he wrote:

> मैं इस साल अभी मर के बचा हूँ। मुझे उस वक्त अफसोस सिर्फ इस बात का होता था, कि मैं धर्म कीर्ति के महान ग्रन्थ 'प्रमाणवार्तिक' को दुनिया के सामने रख नहीं पाया।

34 Not only Sankrityayan but also many other scholars, including Sylvain Lévi, Giuseppe Tucci, Jayachandra Vidyalankara, and Kashi Prasad Jayasawal, received help from him when doing research on manuscripts (Nepāl 2057 VS: 2).

35 Sankrityayan received this information from Jayacandra Vidyalankara. Vidyalankara had visited Nepal at the beginning of 1932 and met Hemraj Sharma (Nepāl 2057 VS: 219), whom he was introduced to by Krishna Prasad Koirala. During his 20–25 days in Kathmandu, he often visited Sharma, and became familiar with his collection, so that he was able to answer Sankrityayan's questions about it.

One may note here that *TMSV* was published by Sharada Mandir, headed by Jayacandra Vidyalankara. Later Sharma requested Sankrityayan to soften his statements about the Ranas in the book.

36 See the biographical sketch of Hemraj Sharma with a brief discussion on their relationship in Appendix 1.

37 This trip was again taken via Nepal and was also facilitated by Hemraj Sharma.

> [...] I was spared from death that year. I had only one regret at the time, and that was that I would not be able to present Dharmakīrti's great work, the *Pramāṇavārttika*, to the world. (Sankrityayan 1998b [*MJY-2*]: 247)

In comparison to his first and second trips, Sankrityayan had a clearer aim during the third trip, and was consequently more successful in his endeavours. In the meantime he had also established good contacts with Stcherbatsky in Russia, having sent him his *Abhidharmakośa-ṭīkā* in 1932, thereby establishing an 'unseen friendship' (*adṛṣṭa maitrī*) with him. Stcherbatsky, Lévi, Louis de La Vallée Poussin, and other scholars had all planned to edit and translate the *Abhidharmakośa* in 1912, but nothing came of this owing to the outbreak of World War I.[38] The editing and commentary in the book Sankrityayan gifted to Stcherbatsky and Lévi was based on the French translation Louis de La Vallée-Poussin (Sankrityayan 1990 VS: 29) later did on his own.[39]

Sankrityayan continuously corresponded with Stcherbatsky and informed him about the Buddhist texts he had been finding during his third visit to Tibet.[40] He told him about discovering the *Pramāṇavārttika* and other manuscripts (Sankrityayan 1957b: 196). Stcherbatsky and Sankrityayan later planned to work together on the *Pramāṇavārttika*,[41]

38 In December 1912 Stcherbatsky met Lévi in Paris, and after they consulted with de La Vallée-Poussin (Belgium), D. Ross (England), and U. Wogihara (Japan), a plan was developed to edit and translate the *Abhidharmakośa* based both on manuscripts containing its Tibetan, Sanskrit, Uigur, and Chinese translations and on some commentaries. Source: http://www.orientalstudies.ru/eng/index.php?option=com_personalities&Itemid=74&person=242 (accessed on 18 October 2012).

39 De La Vallée-Poussin's work was published in six volumes between 1923 and 1931.

40 In 1910–11 Stcherbatsky himself had visited Darjeeling (on a trip that took him also to Bombay, Pune, Banaras, and Calcutta) in search of Buddhist manuscripts and information about the Buddhist monasteries there. The Dalai Lama was at that time in Darjeeling. Stcherbatsky took the opportunity to meet him and entreated him to be allowed to visit Tibet, but political considerations arising from relations between China and Tibet stood in his way.

41 Stcherbatsky also planned to write a Tibetan grammar and compile a Russian–Tibetan dictionary with Sankrityayan's help (Sankrityayan 1998b [*MJY-2*]: 338).

and consequently Sankrityayan went to Russia for a second time[42] at Stcherbatsky's invitation. Sankrityayan explained the aim of his second visit to Russia as follows:

यहाँ मैं इस अभिप्राय से आया था कि डाक्टर श्चेर्वात्स्की के साथ रहकर बौद्ध-न्याय के कुछ ग्रन्थों का उद्धार किया जाय, कुछ का यूरोपीय भाषाओं में भी अनुवाद किया जाय।

I had come here with the intention, together with Dr. Stcherbatsky, of rescuing a number of books on Buddhist logic and of translating some of them into European languages. (Sankrityayan 1998b [*MJY-2*]: 281)

Further:

उनकी बड़ी इच्छा थी, धर्मकीर्ति के मुख्य ग्रन्थ 'प्रमाणवार्तिक' का अनुवाद करने की, और यह भी, कि हम दोनों मिलकर बौद्ध दर्शन ग्रन्थों पर काम करें। वह इसके लिए कोशिश कर ही रहे थे, कि महायुद्ध छिड़ गया। जब जर्मन-सेनाएँ लेनिनग्राद की तरफ बढ़ने लगीं और राष्ट्र की बहुमूल्य वस्तुओं को विमानों और दूसरे साधनों द्वारा हटाया जाने लगा, तो इन महान् विद्वान् को भी [...] पूर्व की तरफ उड़ना पड़ा। [...] शायद उनको अब भी आशा थी कि लौटकर फिर वहाँ अपने कार्य को करेंगे, लेकिन वह पूरी न हो सकी। [...] उन्होंने [...] निर्वाण लाभ किया।

He [Stcherbatsky] had a strong desire to translate the *Pramāṇavārttika*, Dharmakīrti's main opus, and also that both of us should work together on Buddhist philosophical texts. He had been trying to do that when the Great [Patriotic] War started. When the German army advanced towards Leningrad and valuable national treasures began to be removed by airplane and by other means, this great scholar, too, had to fly east. [...] Perhaps he still hoped to return and go about his work, but this did not come to pass. [...] He [...] obtained earthly release. (Sankrityayan 1957b: 199)

Stcherbatsky died in 1942, two years before Sankrityayan's third visit to Russia. As Chattopadhyaya (1975: xvi) notes, Stcherbatsky had kept in

[42] The purpose of his first visit to Russia in 1935 had entirely been to experience communism being put into practice, although he did also try but failed to meet Stcherbatsky. The next two visits were for scholarly purposes, with the third visit focused on teaching at the Oriental Institute of Leningrad University.

close touch with eminent Indians of his time and followed their progress in the rediscovery of India. Sankrityayan dedicated his commentary on the *Pramāṇavārttika* to the memory of Stcherbatsky, for whom he composed the following two verses at the beginning of the book:

आकर्णितं तव यशो बहुशः सुहृद्भ्यो,–
ऽधीताश्च विस्मिततया कृतयस्त्वदीयाः।
वैदुष्यमीक्षितमहो नितरां गभीरं
लोकोत्तरेव विदिता त्वयि का विभूतिः॥१॥
कीर्तिर्विवृत्तहृदया किल धर्मकीर्त्ते-
दौंहित्र आत्मसदृशोस्तु मनोरथो मे।
कुर्याव लेनिनपुरे सह शास्त्रचर्चा-
मित्यस्मरः किमु न लोकवियोगकाले॥२॥

I heard about your renown again and again from friends; / With great amazement I studied your works. / Oh, I saw your very profound knowledge! / I wondered what seemingly transcendent power was known within you. /

[Yours is] indeed the open-hearted fame of Dharmakīrti. / At the time of your departure from this world, did you not remember / My desire was that [your] grandson would become like me, / And that we had hoped to discuss the shastras together in Leningrad? (Sankrityayan 1943)

Sankrityayan had first heard about Stcherbatsky in 1929 from the Indologist Heinrich Lüders in Sri Lanka, who spoke of him as being the greatest contemporary scholar of Indian (and especially Buddhist) philosophy. After he heard even more about him from Lévi while in Europe, he sent him his *Abhidharmakośa-ṭīkā*. Apart from their scholarly ties, Sankrityayan was more intimately bound to Stcherbatsky through his marriage with Ellena Narvertovna Kozerovskaya, who considered Stcherbatsky her *vidyā guru* (academic guru). Stcherbatsky had wanted to teach their son, Igor Rahulovich Sankrityayan, philosophy (Sankrityayan 1998b [*MJY-2*]: 374). The reference to the 'grandson' in the above quotation is to Sankrityayan's son, who was like a grandson to Stcherbatsky. When Sankrityayan revisited Russia in 1944, it could no longer, as originally planned, be for joint scholarly work with Stcherbatsky; instead he focused on collecting material for his upcoming book on the history of Central Asia.

Before Sankrityayan's second visit to Russia in 1937, the Bihar government had already agreed to allocate six thousand rupees for his next visit to Tibet. Once he was in Russia, though, he was more interested in remaining there than going to Tibet, but the political situation in Russia at the time was troublesome and the decision to grant him a residence permit was postponed, so that he was forced to return to India, where he decided to engage in politics. Before doing this, however, he went to Tibet for a fourth and final time to collect more manuscripts and to take more photos. He was no longer living the life of a Buddhist monk, but now he donned the yellow robes of one to facilitate travel.

This visit to Tibet in 1938 was the most relaxed one of all, in that he faced no financial and administrative problems. It was paid for and promoted by both the Indian and Tibetan governments. The Tibetan government instructed officials to break seals in the old libraries so as to be able to show him manuscripts and other artefacts. It also provided three horses and three mules for transport.

To summarize, Sankrityayan's first visit to Tibet focused only on studying Buddhist texts. After studying the Tripitaka in Sri Lanka, and believing that he could continue his studies in Tibet, he had a rude awakening upon finding that hardly any Sanskrit books were available there. He thus decided to learn Tibetan first, planning to stay for a minimum of three years in Tibet in order to do so. When this plan fell through owing to financial problems, he had no choice but to collect all the materials he could and return to Sri Lanka. When Sankrityayan later went to Europe and met other scholars and became acquainted with their work, he gained a new perspective on things, and this was reflected when mapping out his second, third, and fourth visits to Tibet. He had come to understand the importance of old paintings, for which people were ready to pay high sums of money, and of the manuscripts, which were highly prized by European scholars. During those visits he set about collecting Sanskrit manuscripts and took photos (also of the manuscripts) from the start and was largely successful in this endeavour. His aim in travelling to Tibet took on a more concrete shape during his third visit, which was mainly targeted at finding the *Pramāṇavārttika*, but during which he also collected many other manuscripts. The three trips to Tibet were made with his own resources, but when he did eventually receive assistance from both Indian and

Tibetan authorities for a fourth trip, the results expected from this, his most ambitious undertaking, did not materialize (Sankrityayan 1998b [*MJY-2*]: 297). However, we could say that his ambitious aim of restoring the lost Indian heritage (related to Buddhism) from Tibet could not be a success as he desired. We can observe the strong nationalistic sentiment, which inspired him in visiting Tibet was alive until the end.[43] He was not satisfied till his final or fourth visit. I would rather say that in this case Sankrityayan was overly ambitious, that his aim was beyond the capacity of a single person's contribution.

Sankrityayan had long dreamt about re-establishing Nalanda. To collect money for the purpose, he had planned to sell the paintings that he collected on his first visit to Tibet. After they were displayed in an exhibition in Paris, he entered into correspondence with an American museum that was interested in acquiring them, but he eventually realized the importance of preserving them in the land where Buddhism arose. One may note that Sankrityayan's original concept of re-establishing Nalanda in the service of Indian culture underwent important changes. In the end he understood that Indian culture could better be served by discovering, editing, and translating historic Buddhist documents, as European scholars were doing.

Sankrityayan's contacts with scholars from foreign countries were not, we have seen, first made during his visit to Europe. He had already heard about many foreign scholars of Indian and Buddhist studies while he was in Sri Lanka in 1928–9. There he had met Rudolf Otto (Sankrityayan 1998b [*MJY-2*]: 19) and Heinrich Lüders (Sankrityayan 1957b: 195); later he would send to Otto in Marburg some Tibetan paintings collected during his first visit to Tibet. Stcherbatsky's scholarship was already known to him. He had read Kawaguchi's and Alexandra David-Néel's accounts of their visits to Tibet.[44] He had also read and used for his own work Louis de La Vallée-Poussin's study of the *Abhidharmakośa*. Most European scholars, though, he only came to know about or meet during his visits to England, France, and Germany, including Caroline Augusta

[43] 'The fifth journey to Tibet that Rahulji had wished for became impossible because of the political situation in 1958, when Rahulji was in China and had sought permission' (Gerke 1995).

[44] It is possible that he later named his own travelogue *Tibbat mẽ savā varṣ* (One and a quarter years in Tibet) in imitation of Kawaguchi's *Three Years in Tibet*.

Foley Rhys Davids, Paul Pelliot, Junyu Kitayama, Richard Fick, Junji Sakakibara (a Japanese Buddhist scholar), and the family of Paul Dahlke.[45] Sankrityayan also met many Japanese Buddhist scholars during his visit to Japan in 1935, including Daisetsu Teitaro Suzuki, Watanabe Kaikyoku, Dr Ogihara Unrai, and Ekai Kawaguchi.[46] All these contacts show that he was interested in maintaining friendships with foreign scholars working in his own chosen field.

Buddhist Themes in Hindi Publications

> In the wake of the modern Indian renaissance the intelligentsia of this country evinced a newly stirred interest in the study of their own ancient scriptures, philosophies, and religious teachings. [...] Several schools of religious thought also inspired modern Indian thinkers and writers, and in these Buddhism occupied a very important place. (Kuppusamy 1992: 111)

Sankrityayan's writings in Hindi with Buddhist themes can be divided into three categories: biographical, philosophical, and historical. We will briefly consider each of them.[47]

45 During his stay in Germany in December 1932, Sankrityayan travelled to Berlin, where he was received by Dahlke's sister (Bertha Dahlke) at the train station. During his time in the city he resided for the most part in the Buddhist monastery Das Buddhistische Haus in Frohnau that Dahlke had founded. There he was able to collect much information on him and his scholarship (Sankrityayan 1998b [*MJY-2*]: 111–14).

46 He recalls that Kawaguchi was still able to speak Tibetan, which suggests that they may have used that language to communicate with one another, for by then Sankrityayan had already made two trips to Tibet. Sankrityayan met other Buddhist scholars, but as he records only their family names in *MJY-2*, it is difficult to identify them: Professor Kimura at Risso University, Messrs Takeda and Nagai, and Professor Inoe (Sankrityayan 1998b [*MJY-2*]: 204). He also visited Otani University (Sankrityayan 1998b [*MJY-2*]: 201).

47 Apart from literary and political writings and edited and translated Tibetan manuscripts, Sankrityayan also compiled a Tibetan–Hindi dictionary, published by Sahitya Akademi in 1972. Moreover, he was the chief editor of *Śāsan śabdkoś* (An administrative dictionary), with some 16,000 entries, published in Allahabad by Hindi Sahitya Sammelan in 1948. A third dictionary he edited was *Saṅkṣipt rāṣṭra bhāṣā koś* (A compact national language dictionary), published in Vardha by Rastra Bhasha Prachar Samiti in 1953.

Biographical Works

Sankrityayan's first work with a Buddhist theme in Hindi was *Buddha caryā* (The Buddha's way of life). Started in 1930 in Sri Lanka, soon after he had been initiated as a Buddhist monk, it was published the following year in Banaras. It is a description of the Buddha's life based on the Tripitaka. In essence, it consists of a series of scattered passages translated from Pali to Hindi (Urmileś 1994: 148). Much later, in 1956, he wrote *Mahāmānav Buddha* (The great man [who was] the Buddha), which again presents the life of the Buddha, this time in the author's own words, while at the same time reviewing his philosophy and his importance for Indian society. The short biographies of five Buddhist philosophers in *Pāc bauddh dārśnik* (1994) also fall under this category.

Two works centre on Sri Lanka. One, *Siṃhal ghumakkaṛ Jayavardhan* (1960), is a biography of the Sri Lankan Jayavardhan, a Buddhist wandering monk, also known as Indra Suman, whom he first met in Tibet. The other is *Siṃhal ke vīr* (Sri Lankan heroes, 1961), containing sketches of seven Sri Lankan luminaries: Vijaya (the primary source concerning whom is the *Mahavamsa*), Mahendra or Mahinda (who brought Buddhism to Sri Lanka), Dusta-Gramani, Vijayabahu, Mahaparakrama Bahu, Tikiri Bandara, and S.W.R.D. Bandaranaike.

Philosophical Works

Sankrityayan's translations and editions of Buddhist philosophical texts from among his large collection of works brought from Tibet belong to this category. Apart from these he published two books on Buddhism. The first one is *Bauddh darśan* (Buddhist philosophy, 1943), in which he sets forth Buddhist philosophy, its various schools, and its historical development. Sankrityayan's outstanding contribution to the field of philosophy is his comparative study of world philosophies and Indian systems. *Darśan digdarśan* (Philosophical bearings, 1944), written in Hazaribagh jail in 1942, presents the essence of his philosophical approach to life and the world in general and to India in the 1940s in particular. Concerning it, Machwe (1978: 46) writes, 'In Hindi there is no other book which gives such graphic and detailed description of Buddhist thought (100 pages) and Islamic thought (125 pages) in one volume.'

Historical Works

Historical works with a Buddhist theme may be subdivided into two categories: works dealing with the history of Buddhism and historical novels with a Buddhist theme.

The history of Buddhism: Sankrityayan deals with the spread of Buddhism in Tibet and its widespread acceptance there in his book *Tibbat mẽ bauddh dharm* (Buddhism in Tibet, 1935). By delineating the social and cultural situation in the country during the emergence of Buddhism, he is able to offer plausible reasons for why it took firm root there. Buddhist monasteries, Buddhist literature, and broader aspects of Buddhist culture in Tibet receive detailed treatment. Another study, *Bauddha saṃskṛti* (Buddhist culture, 1952), is a collection of Sankrityayan's speeches and articles on Buddhism that explore the history of Buddhism within its cultural context in such Asian countries as India, Sri Lanka, Burma, Indonesia, Korea, Japan, Tibet, and Mongolia. One posthumously published book-length work is *Navdīkṣit bauddh* (Neo-Buddhists,[48] 1975). He also wrote many separate articles on Buddhism, some of them, as in the case of his books, published posthumously. Urmileś (1994: 74–152) briefly introduces Sankrityayan's book-length writings, while A. Bhaṭṭācārya (2005: 205–15) presents an updated list of both his books and articles.

Historical Novels:

> Buddha preferred the political system of the republics (ganas). In that age slavery was prevalent, and hence in the Lichchavi (Vaishali) republic, the most prosperous and powerful at that time, democracy existed only for those who belonged to the Lichhavi clan. The slaves were movable property and they were numerous. The non-Lichhavi Brahmin or grahapati (trader) caste though free had no right of vote for the senate (samsad). They were at the mercy of the Lichhavis. All the same these republics were evidently better than monarchy.
>
> For Buddha the origin of monarchy did not lie in any divine source but kingship was the product of the growth of private property. Private property led to inequality of class division among the people, who

[48] Neo-Buddhist is the name given to the followers of Ambedkar. Sankrityayan wrote an article on this subject: 'Ambedkar: Navdīkṣit bauddh.'

started quarrelling among themselves and (overtly or covertly) started trying to snatch each other's property, and therefore they selected one from among them as their judge, who by accumulating power for selfish ends developed into a king.

Buddha lived in the 6th–5th century BC [...]. At that time too economic and social discrimination was very sharp. For the eradication of economic inequality Buddha confined his efforts to the monastic communes alone, but the abolition of social inequality he attempted on a universal scale. [...] Buddhism fervently advocated the brotherhood of man without any distinction of race, country or caste. (Sankrityayan 1970: 2)

Sankrityayan's historical novels in Hindi with a Buddhist theme are regarded as his most important scholarly contribution to the field of Hindi literature. *Siṃh senāpati* is a story set in the ancient Indian republics of Gandhar (in present-day northern Pakistan) and that of the Licchavis (Vaishali; in present-day eastern Bihar) during the Buddha's era (500 BC). The author portrays life in those republics as being free, in that they embodied a form of Buddhist–communist philosophy and had strictly abjured monarchy.[49] Another historical novel, *Jay yaudheya*, is a story set in another republic, the Yaudheya, situated between the Indus and Ganges rivers, during the Gupta era (c. A.D. 350–500). Sankrityayan states in the foreword that his aim in writing the novel was 'to present the political and social context of India during [the years] 350–400'.[50] The main character of this novel, Jaya, is interested in Buddhism and Buddhist pilgrimage sites, and therefore travels to Sri Lanka and becomes a bhikkhu there. The Yaudheya republic offers equal rights to its citizens, including freedom of speech, and is an example of a classless social system where there are neither masters nor slaves. Yaudheyas respected the Buddha and his teachings; indeed, their republic resembled a bhikkhu *saṅgh* (Sankrityayan 2005b: 119–20), but they were eventually defeated in battle by the Gupta emperor King Candragupta Vikramaditya, the

49 Fischer's 1990 dissertation contains a good analysis of this novel from the perspective of an Arya Samajist and Buddhist, and particularly focuses on different aspects of the society depicted in the novel.

50 'इसमें ई. सन् 350-400 के भारत की राजनीतिक-सामाजिक अवस्था का चित्रण किया गया है।' (Sankrityayan 2005b: 3)

very personification of monarchy.[51] Of the two novels, then, the first one depicts the period of the Buddha, and the second one a later stage in the development of Buddhism. In both these novels, Sankrityayan extols the 'ancient Indian republic, as opposed to the kingdoms, run on socialistic principles' (Das 1995: 119). Another novel, *Vismṛt yātrī*, recreates a historical figure, Narendra Yash, a Buddhist monk who was born, as Sankrityayan notes in his foreword, in AD 518 in India (in Swat, in present-day Pakistan), travelled through India, Sri Lanka, Central Asia, and China, propagating Buddhism along the way, and translated many Buddhist texts into Chinese (Urmileś 1994: 79). Das (1995: 119) writes of the novel: 'The kind of historical novel that he wrote is a direct outcome of his approach to the history itself. For him the history of man is not confined to the achievements of few individuals: kings and soldiers; but it is a story of the men, the tiller of the soil and the hewer of the woods.'

When, since the 1940s, the conflict between Gandhism and Marxism became crucial in Indian politics, its effect were also seen in the literature. Among the very few writers on Buddhism from a Marxist perspective in Hindi literature, the most prominent are Sankrityayan, Yashpal, and Nāgārjun[52]. They also share an optimism and vision of the new society. A common thread runs through their work, as Kuppusamy (1992: 121) notes: there was an 'attempt to draw Marxist ideals from Buddhism. They support Buddhism to the extent that it strengthens the Marxist ideals of the basic equality of all human beings, helping the exploited and oppressed, equality of all before the law, and the democratic as against the monarchic form of government.'

Sankrityayan's historical novels were popular in both India and Nepal. There is an interesting sidelight to *Siṃh senāpati*. Sankrityayan writes in the introduction to this novel that he is only the editor and Hindi translator of the original work, an account of General

[51] Sankrityayan (2005b: 3) informs the reader in his foreword that he relied heavily on Rakhal Das Benerji's *The Age of the Imperial Guptas* (1933) and Ramchandra Narayan Dandekar's *A History of the Guptas*. He also made use, for his descriptions of society, of Kalidasa's writings and the travelogue of the 5th-century Chinese Buddhist monk Fa-hsien.

[52] Born Vaidya Nath Mishra, he is also known as Baba Nāgārjun.

Simha's[53] life story in Prakrit inscribed on bricks discovered by him while quarrying in Chapra, Bihar. At the end of the introduction, he challenges orthodox Hindu readers, who are perhaps dubious, to visit Patna Museum and view the bricks displayed there for themselves. After reading *Siṃh senāpati*, the Nepalese Dirgha Raj Koirala took up the challenge and went down to Patna, where he confirmed that the 1,600 bricks do indeed exist. But returning home, he complained angrily to Janaklāl Śarmā (a friend of Sankrityayan's): 'I went to Patna to see those bricks but everything was false. Therefore, I do not trust Rahul' (Pokhrel and Dhakāl 2060 VS: 73). When Sharma relayed this criticism to Sankrityayan, he replied, '*Siṃh senāpati* is not a work of scholarship; it is a novel. Having a novelistic foreword for a novel is natural' (Pokhrel and Dhakāl 2060 VS: 73).

All these different kinds of books by Sankrityayan were read in Nepal. Those with Buddhist themes were popular among scholars and Buddhists, while his political books were popular among Nepalese youth. We have now arrived at a suitable juncture to examine Sankrityayan's relationship with Nepal.

SANKRITYAYAN AND HIS RELATIONSHIP WITH NEPAL

नेपाल सचमुच ही घर-सा है।

Nepal is really like home. (Sankrityayan 1998b [*JY-6*]: 328)

The above citation was the reason for commencing this study. Why was Nepal like home for Sankrityayan? Why did he never feel that Nepal and the Nepalese were distant foreigners? Why did he feel love for Nepal and its citizens? The following pages will attempt to answer these questions.

Sankrityayan's relationship with Nepal and the Nepalese began at a very early age and continued until the end of his life. The first Nepalese person who made a lasting impression on him was Baba Paramhams,[54] whom he met at the age of seventeen or eighteen. His

53 'The protagonist, however, is Simha (a name that occurs in Buddhist texts) who is the *senāpati* (general) of the Licchivis' (Das 1995: 119).

54 A sadhu living near his parental village, Kanaila. See the biographical sketch of Baba Paramhams in Appendix 1.

most intimate connection with Nepal was through his third wife, Kamala Sankrityayan née Pariyar. Sankrityayan had three wives: the first was an Indian, with whom he never lived; the second was the Russian with whom he would have lived longer had circumstances allowed; the third was Kamala Sankrityayan, a woman of Nepalese origin who resided in Darjeeling, India, and with whom he led a long and successful married life.

Sankrityayan's connections with Nepalese from different walks of life—scholars, merchants, politicians, writers, and others—are portrayed in Appendix 1. The present subchapter will analyse his relationship with Nepal from different viewpoints. This analysis is based on Peter van der Veer's (1994) conceptual framework established to relate the female body, gender, and nation as indexes of religious nationalism in South Asia, especially in its Hindu and Muslim forms (see particularly the section titled 'Brotherhood: Sankrityayan's Relationship with Nepal' later). Such nationalism he terms a 'brotherhood'. To characterize the relationship between India and Nepal, and more specifically between Sankrityayan and Nepal, I shall coin the term 'one cultural soul' and attempt to justify it as the reason why Sankrityayan looked upon Nepal as a familiar foreign land and its people as *sahodar*s (siblings).

As a devoted Buddhist scholar, Sankrityayan naturally was able to enjoy good relations with many Nepalese Buddhists. The Theravada movement was on the rise in Nepal during the period in which he was most active, and it will first of all be fruitful to explore the extent to which Sankrityayan cultivated relations with this movement and its supporters.

Sankrityayan and the Theravada Movement in Nepal

Sarah Levine and David N. Gellner (2008) carried out a study dealing with the Theravada movement in 20th-century Nepal, resulting in their book, *Rebuilding Buddhism*. They do not record any active involvement on Sankrityayan's part in this movement, but it is worth discussing the significance of it for him and of him for it during the period of his visits to Tibet and Nepal, which took place at the time when the Theravada movement was at its peak in Nepal. It is surprising to discover that Sankrityayan was not actively involved in the movement, and this study has concluded that although he was not so, he must certainly have supported it morally. The following pages will attempt to define more precisely Sankrityayan's links to it.[55]

During the 20th century, the Ranas determined to seal off Nepal to block the infiltration of foreign influence into the country, but this did not come about as they had wished. Their desire to obtain Western luxuries required the development of trading networks with India. Furthermore, education stood in the way. The acknowledged need for well-trained bureaucrats in the government and Sanskrit-literate priests served to keep the door of the country somewhat open. A number of Newar merchants set up permanent establishments in Calcutta, which paved the way for contact with the Maha Bodhi Society. Students who went to study in India developed good relations with the freedom fighters and leaders there, thus heightening their own political awareness. Though Nepalese students were sent specifically to further their religious or administrative education, the more open print market and public sphere inevitably turned their thoughts in other directions.

Jagatman Vaidya (1902–63) was the son of an Ayurvedic *vaidya* (traditional physician), Vrishaman Vaidya, an employee at the palace of Juddha Shamsher Rana. He was sent to India for further studies on a scholarship from the Nepalese government. Sometime after reaching Calcutta in 1921, he met Anagarika Dharmapala and fell under his spell, seeing the reflection of the Buddha in him (Śākya 1994: 144–5). Dharmapala in turn saw in Vaidya a promising advocate of Theravada Buddhism in Nepal (Levine and Gellner 2008: 27). He suggested changing his name to Dharmaditya Dharmacharya (Śākya 1994: 146). In the summer break of 1923, the student returned to Nepal with some books published by the Maha Bodhi Society, along

55 'Unlike in India, the Theravaadin movement in Nepal is not advancing through proselytisation. In India, following the inspiration and lead given by B.R. Ambedkar, most Theravaadin adherents are new converts drawn from the Hindu scheduled castes [...]. But, [...] in Nepal Theravaada is not converting non-Buddhists. It is a movement which gets its strength and support overwhelmingly from those who are already Buddhists by tradition. It has assumed the role of giving novel and rational orientation to the established Buddhism. It aims to promote a renewed religious consciousness in a traditional Buddhist community' (Tewari 1983: 70).

with issues of the Society's journal, the *Maha-Bodhi*. He shared them with his friends in Kathmandu and told them of his desire to establish what he planned to call the Nepal Buddhopasak Sangh (Association of Nepalese Lay Buddhists) to propagate Theravada Buddhism in Nepal. At a meeting in the house of Dharma Narayan Tuladhar,[56] his efforts eventually bore fruition.[57] Members of the sangha translated Buddhist texts from English and Pali into Nepāl-bhāṣā (Newari) and made carbon copies of their results, which served as the basis for their later publication in Dharmapala's journal *Buddha-dharma* in Calcutta. *Buddha-dharma* was the first periodical ever brought out in Nepāl-bhāṣā (Levine and Gellner 2008: 28).

Though it was difficult during the Rana regime to do such things, three weeks after the male association was established, Dharmaditya Dharmacharya established the Nepal Buddhopasika Sangh (Association of Nepalese Female Lay Buddhists) in Patan under Hiramaya Upasika and Dhanamaya Upasika (Śākya 1994: 149).

Dharmaditya Dharmacharya also proposed, in 1923, that a renovation of Kindol Mahavihara in Swayambhu be undertaken. He discussed this with Dharmaman Sahu and wrote a request to the same effect to the Rana prime minister, Chandra Shamsher. Later, in the journal *Bauddha Bhārat*, he notes that 'one *śiṣya* [disciple] (Dharmaman Sahu) donated 1,500 Nepalese rupees and Prime Minister Chandra Shamsher Janga Bahadur Rana donated 1,500 Nepalese rupees' (cited in Śākya 1994: 150).

When Sankrityayan was hiding in Kathmandu in 1929, he met Dharmaman Sahu at the same house in Ason where the Nepal Buddhopasak Sangh had been established six years before. His

[56] He was also known as Dhamma Sahu, Dharmaman Sahu, or Dharma Sahu. Sankrityayan wrote a short biographical sketch of him under the title 'Dharmā sahū' in *JMK*.

[57] The executive committee of the Sangha was as follows:

1. The main propagator and manager: Dharmaditya Dharmacharya
2. Administrator: Khadga Raj Tuladhar
3. Treasurer: Triratna Man Tuladhar (son of Dharmaman Tuladhar)
4. Business co-coordinator: Chittadhar Tuladhar 'Hridaya'
5. Assistant for other works: Kuldip Upasak
6. Member: Buddhi Ratna

desire to visit Tibet to study Buddhist texts and, upon returning, promote Buddhism met with a promise to help him on the part of Dharmaman Sahu. Sankrityayan stayed at Dharmaman Sahu's house for two days. Sankrityayan was grateful to him for his help, since his political activities back home threatened to undermine his plans:

> उन्होंने बड़े आग्रह पूर्वक एक अप्रैल से दो अप्रैल तक अपने यहाँ मुझे रखा। यह बिचारे बड़े भोले-भाले थे, उन्हें इसमें भी डर नहीं होता था कि चाहे कितना ही मेरा काम और भाव शुद्ध हो, लेकिन मालूम हो जाने पर नेपाल सरकार मेरे लिए उनको भी तकलीफ पहुँचा सकती है।
>
> With great insistence he put me up in his house from 1 April to 2 April. The poor man was very simple. He was not even afraid that, no matter how pure my plans and motives were, the Nepalese government, were it to find out about them, could create trouble for him. (Sankrityayan 1990 VS: 69)

On 1 December 1934, during Sankrityayan's visit to Kathmandu on his way back to India from his second visit to Tibet, Dharmaman Sahu introduced him to General Mohan Shamsher, having been instructed to do the same with every Buddhist monk or guest who visited his house.[58] They had a short talk and Sankrityayan later wrote that Mohan Shamsher was surprised to learn that Buddhists were atheists (1998b [*MJY-2*]: 187).[59]

[58] The Rana government, wary of any major changes to the social fabric, had instituted a law according to which no conversion from one religion to another was permissible, and the instruction to Dharmaman Sahu shows to what lengths it was prepared to go to make sure that the law was observed.

[59] In Nepal, Newars practise both the Newar variant of Vajrayana Buddhism and Theravada Buddhism. Many Buddhist groups in Nepal are also influenced by Hinduism. Buddhists have long felt the strong influence of Hinduism owing to their close contacts with the Hindu castes and because they themselves were integrated into the caste system. Many of them eventually adopted Hinduism. What is called Newar Buddhism is the form of Mahayana–Vajrayana Buddhism (mainly) practised in the Newar ethnic community of the Kathmandu Valley. The intertwined-ness of Hinduism and Buddhism in Nepal resulted in the Buddha being declared the ninth avatar of Vishnu. Fisher (1997: 11) notes that '[a]ccording to Hindu discourse the king

After a few days he moved into the newly renovated Kindol Vihara.[60] The full renovation of Kindol Vihara was undertaken by friends of Dharmaditya Dharmacarya.[61] Sankrityayan did not feel safe there because the vihara was always crowded, and he asked Dasaratan Sahu,[62] one of the members of the vihara renovating group, to lodge him in a more secluded place. He was afraid that he might be identified because of his involvement in the Indian freedom movement and knew that if he were he would instantly become a persona non grata. Dasaratan Sahu took him to an uninhabited house out of public view.

---

is a re-incarnation of Vishnu, and to the annoyance of Buddhist minority, so was the Buddha'. The main focus of Fisher's book, Tanka Prasad Acharya, serves as a representative example of this belief. Acharya, an orthodox Hindu Brahmin, is quoted as saying (Fisher 1997: 212), 'I revere the Buddha as much as I do Vishnu.' Hindus often place a statue of the Buddha in their worship room, while many monasteries or Buddhist temples feature similar statues of Hindu gods and goddesses. As the king was regarded as an incarnate form of Vishnu, the Nepalese monarchy had the strong support of Hindus, while the status attributed to the Buddha at least served to keep Buddhists loyal to it. Nepal's rulers, in short, treated Buddhists and Hindus, who shared many festivals and much iconography, largely on equal terms.

But as Fisher observes, many Buddhists have strong reservations about this. Bhattachan (2005) rejects the Hindu appropriation of the Buddha as the ninth avatar of Vishnu. His article accuses Hindus of annexing Buddhism to Hinduism, mindless of the fact that Nepalese Buddhists hold many views diametrically opposed to their own. For example, he criticizes the Hindu worship of a supremely powerful deity while subordinating others, and their worship of certain animals while at the same time slaughtering others.

For details on Newar Buddhism, see D.N. Gellner (1992).

60 'किन्दू स्वयम्भू के पास ही है। अभी यहाँ नया विहार बनाया गया है।' [Kindū is close to Swayambhu. A new vihara has now been built here.] (Sankrityayan 1990 VS: 76).

61 These included Siddhi Ratna Tamrakar (Gvara Sahu), Buddha Ratna Sahu, Siddhiharsa (Babukaji Guruju), Bekharatna, Kulbahadur Manandhar, Lokratna Tuladhar (Upasak), Dasaratan Sahu (later Bhikṣu Dharmalok) and Lakshminani Tuladhar (laterAnagarika Dharmacari) (Śākya 1994: 150).

62 Dasaratan Sahu's son, too, would become an important bhikkhu, Anirudha, after he was sent to Sri Lanka to study Buddhism at the urging of Sankrityayan (Lewis and Tuladhar 2007: xliv).

In Sankrityayan's (1998b [*MJY*-2]: 34) words: 'Dasaratan Sahu was a great devotee [of Buddhism], and he also understood my problems well. He did not let anyone come to this house.'

Once Sankrityayan finally realized that there was not any possibility of entering Tibet with a Tibetan lama, he asked Dasaratan Sahu to take him to Yolmo (Helambu). Sahu agreed, and they both undertook the trek in Nepalese dress. Sankrityayan was now happy to be out of reach of the Nepalese government. Dasaratan Sahu took him to a friend's house, and from there Sankrityayan went to Tibet in Tibetan clothing. In Lhasa, he resided at Dharmaman Sahu's *kothi*.

The Ranas had prohibited the public use of non-Nepali languages and banned the printing of religious texts and literary works in them, and in Newari in particular. However, a strong feeling of ethnic identity persisted among most Newars, and this was channelled into cultural activity, including the establishment of organizations such as Cwasa Pasa (Friends of the pen)[63] and the Nepāl-bhāṣā Pariṣad (Newari language council).[64]

The Rana government of Nepal eventually made good on its threat, arresting a number of Newars who wrote in Newari, Chittadhar 'Hridaya' (born Tuladhar) (1906–82) being among the most prominent.[65] Fatte Bahadur Singh had compiled and published *Nepāli vihāra*, a collection of classical and modern poems in Newari in 1940 and was imprisoned for doing so. Chittadhar Hridaya was imprisoned alongside him because he had published a poem (whose title translates as 'Mother') in that collection (Lewis and Tuladhar 2007: xix). Whilst in prison, Chittadhar Hridaya wrote his best-known work, *Sugata saurabha*, a poetic retelling of the life of the Buddha. Sankrityayan's books on the Buddha and Buddhism were consulted as reference sources for it, Sankrityayan having made friends with the Tuladhar family while in Kathmandu. In the words of Hridaya (Lewis and Tuladhar 2007: xlv):

[63] Cwasa Pasa was established on Vaiśākh Purṇimā, VS 2007 in Calcutta (Śākya 1994: 156). See also Whelpton (2011: 182).

[64] The Nepāl bhāṣā Pariṣad was established on 3 March 1951 (Śākya 1994: 156).

[65] Sankrityayan describes the imprisonment of Chittadhar Hridaya and Dharmaratna Yami in his book *Dharmaratna 'Yami'* (1963).

> Sometime later, everyone had some religious books brought into the jail for them after we made a plea that we needed them for prayer. My sister first brought the *Dhammapada* for me, and this inspired me to start my own poem, a wish I could not suppress ... Later on, the *Buddhacarrya* by Mr. Rahul Sanskrityayana [*sic*] also came in as a prayer book. When this book came in, it helped me a lot. Or else I would have ... been dependent on what I had studied in my childhood from the *Lalitvistara*[66] by Shri Nishtānanda. (Hridaya, cited in Lewis and Tuladhar 2007: xlv)[67]

On 22, 23, and 24 January 1953, after the Ranas had ceded power, Cwasa Pasa organized a Virāṭ Nepāl-bhāṣā Sāhitya Sammelan (General Nepāl-bhāṣa literary festival) in a big courtyard of Hanumandhoka in Kathmandu. The first day of the festival was organized under the chairmanship of Siddhicharan Shrestha, the second day under Chittadhar Hridaya, and the third day under Fatte Bahadur Singh (Śākya 1994: 156–7). Sankrityayan participated in this festival and gives the following description of it:

> 22 जनवरी को नेपाल भाषा साहित्य-सम्मेलन का प्रथम अधिवेशन उसी हनुमानढोका के विशाल आँगन में हुआ, जिसमें आज से पौने दो सौ वर्ष पहिले वह राज भाषा

66 Bhikkhu Mahapragya (Prem Bahadur Shrestha) had translated Sankrityayan's *Buddha caryā* into Newari under the title *Lalitavistara* and published an edition of eighty copies in 1997 VS (Śākya 1993: 38). This, as we have seen, has nothing to do with the classical Sanskrit work of the same name upon which Nisthananda's Newari translation, published in 1914, is based. See Lewis and Tuladhar (2007: xliii). This latter translation was apparently well known. The Newar merchant Dalchini Manandhar had years earlier told Prem Bahadur Shrestha that 'bhajans are being sung only of Ram, Kriṣṇa, Hari, and Hara (i.e. Shiva) in our country; no one sings bhajans for the Buddha. You can compose bhajans and [other] songs, so please compose a couple of bhajans.' Manandhar gave him the *Lalitvistara* written by Pandit Niṣṭhānanda Bajrācārya. After reading it, Prem Bahadur Shrestha composed a collection of bhajans. He had worked in the palace of Kathmandu as a member of the entertainment group (acting in dramas, singing, playing musical instruments, and so on) for some time until 1982 VS (Śākya 1993: 2–5).

67 A separate study of the writings mentioned would be worthwhile to see exactly where the influence of Sankrityayan's work lay.

के तौर पर विराजमान थी। नेवार सरस्वती आज उस आँगन में मुखरित हो रही थीं। बाहर के आँगन के एक तरफ के फाटक से हम भीतर के एक छोटे आँगन में गए, जहाँ कोत-पर्व हुआ था—कान्छा महारानी के हुकुम से जंग बहादुर और उसके भाइयों ने निहत्थे आदमियों के साथ खून की होली यहीं खेली थी, उनका निर्मम बध किया था। वह झरोखा भी मौजूद था, जहाँ से उस निष्ठुर रानी ने हुकुम देकर इस वीभत्स दृश्य देखने का आनन्द प्राप्त किया था।

नेवार भाषा का यह पहिला अधिवेशन था, लेकिन देखने से साफ पता लगता था, कि नेवार भाषियों में सांस्कृतिक परिपक्वता है।

The first sitting of the Nepāl-bhāṣā Sāhitya Sammelan was organized in a big courtyard of Hanumandhoka, where the language was regarded as the kingdom's language two hundred years ago. The Newar Sarasvati was today intoning her voice there. We went through one of the gates of the outside courtyard into the small courtyard where the Kot massacre had occurred—[when,] on orders from the younger queen, Janga Bahadur and his younger brothers had played Holi with the blood of unarmed men and ruthlessly killed them. The window from which the merciless queen had enjoyed the cruel scene after issuing her orders was still in place.

This was the first festival of the Newar language; it was clear, however, that the Newari-speaking people had [already attained] cultural maturity. (Sankrityayan 1998b [*MJY-2*]: 108)

One of the main exponents of Theravada Buddhism in Nepal, Amritananda Mahanayaka[68] Thera (Lal Kaji Shakya), was also particularly influenced by the books of Sankrityayan (Ahir 1993: 190–5). Amritananda, along with four other monks, was expelled from Nepal in 1924 for having converted to Buddhism. The Rana prime minister at the time, Chandra Shamsher, had invoked the previously mentioned law according to which no conversion from one religion to another was permissible. The overthrow of the Rana regime in 1950–1 was understandably most welcomed by Nepalese Buddhists, and also because the previously self-exiled and now newly reinstated King Tribhuvan took a keen interest in Buddhism and the affairs of his

68 This title (great leader) was given to him in Sri Lanka in 1984. Source: http://anandakutivihar.com.np/big1.html (accessed 24 December 2012).

Buddhist subjects. In November 1956, Nepal hosted the Fourth General Conference of the World Fellowship of Buddhists (WFB) organized by the Dharmodaya Sabha (Council for the Advancement of the Dharma, also known as the Buddhist Society of Nepal) under the presidency of Amritananda.[69] The conference, in which Sankrityayan also participated, received generous financial assistance from the government of Nepal. One of the participants, Bhadanta Ānand Kauśalyāyan, later wrote that 'the two personalities, Ambedkar and Sankrityayan, were the cynosure in the conference' (Kauśalyāyan 1992: 4).

Thus it is clear that Sankrityayan had close relations with many members of the Theravada movement in Nepal. He himself, though, was neither active in it nor did he ever write anything relating to it directly or on its behalf. Two causes may be supposed for this. The first reason Sankrityayan did not accept Anagarika Dharmapala's request to engage in promoting Theravada Buddhism may have been because his own priorities lay in researching Buddhist texts and pursuing other scholarly activities. Second, he wanted to keep on good terms with the government of Nepal lest they stood in his way to visiting Tibet. He had already refused to propagate Buddhism as a religion in India and other parts of the world, and he had all the more reason not do so in Nepal, where the Theravada movement was illegal. The main persons behind the Theravada movement (Dharmaman Sahu, Bhikkhu Amritananda, Chittadhar Hridaya, and Bhikkhu Dharmalok) were all Sankrityayan's good friends, and had he written in support of the movement, it would only have created problems for them. Furthermore, his own Buddhist writings would have stood no chance of being sanctioned in Nepal, his political works having already been banned by the Rana government. Still, even though he kept to the background, he followed events closely and offered encouragement where he could, for he realized that Nepal had played a key role in the history of Buddhism:

69 The Dharmodaya Sabha had been founded in Sarnath by Amritananda and his fellow monks on 30 November 1944 while in exile. Sankrityayan's friend Ānand Kauśalyāyan was the first vice-president, and Amritananda the first secretary. The Dharmodaya Sabha's first order of business was to appeal to Buddhists in India and in other countries to protest against the government of Nepal regarding the expulsion of the monks.

> *Nepal:* At a very early time Buddhism was introduced into Nepal. When after the Mohamadan conquest of India, Buddhism disappeared from there; it still prevailed in that country. Most of the Buddhist canonical works on philosophy and written in Sanskrit were found there, though the whole of the last century was a period of slothfulness and inactivities on the part of the Buddhism there, that state has now changed and the young Buddhist Nepalese are awakening. (Sankrityayan 1984: 134)

Brotherhood: Sankrityayan's Relationship with Nepal

This subchapter attempts to define Sankrityayan's relationship with Nepal in terms of Peter van der Veer's (1994: xiv) concept of 'brotherhood'. His work examines the roles in which the ritual construction of gender is reshaped and adopted in the context of nation-building so as to yield a nationalist 'brotherhood'. The three main elements of his schema are 'body, gender and nation'. Applying this to South Asia, he observes that countries there are regarded as a mother, while relationships between male nationals tend towards a form of brotherhood (van der Veer 1994: 85): 'The nation is often imagined as a brotherhood of men protecting their womenfolk. Men are portrayed as strong and powerful; women as weak and powerless.' The country as a whole, then, is understood as a female, while governing authority is invested in groups of males acting in the guise of a collective confraternity of the nation. I shall first present some examples of various ways in which Nepalese visualize their country as a mother. These will be followed by an inquiry into the extent to which the relationship between Sankrityayan and his Nepalese friends can be defined as a 'brotherhood' in van der Veer's sense. Sankrityayan's wider relationship with Nepal will also be observed, from two different angles: culture and religion. We will see how Sankrityayan conceived of the Nepalese as being members of his imagined cultural community and how the Nepalese in turn imagined his place within their religious community. In the end it will be concluded that Sankrityayan and his Nepalese friends shared 'one cultural soul'.[70]

[70] The expression 'cultural soul' was used during the *ekātmatāyajña* (translated by van der Veer as 'sacrifice for unity'), a large-scale ritual procession in 1983 organized by the Vishwa Hindu Parishad (World Hindu Council), to

Motherhood and Brotherhood

In the South Asian (textual) imagination, both the earth and the nations on it are represented as being female. Women are able to generate other bodies, to give birth, which nature also does. They then go on to breastfeed their children, just as the earth is the living force that supports life, even as it is the source from which all life arises. This productive character or role of women (that is, motherhood) lies behind imagining the earth as a female and a mother.

A woman is described in the *Manusmr̥ti* as someone who by right deserves to be protected by men. The Hindu or South Asian notion of a nation as being a mother or a female, therefore, placed responsibility for guardianship of it upon males.[71] *Rāṣṭrabhūmi* (nation) and *mātr̥bhūmi* (motherland) are interchangeable terms in Sanskrit-rooted languages such as Hindi and Nepali. The expressions Bhārat *mātā* (Mother India) in India and Nepāl *āmā* (Mother Nepal) in Nepal continue to be widely used.[72] In the famous nationalist novel *Ānand maṭh*[73] by Baṅkimcandra Caṭṭopādhyāya, rebel sannyasis revolt in the name of a Hindu mother-nation to unseat Muslims from power. His song *Vande Mātaram* (Worship the mother[land]), the national song of India, is an expression of Hindu nationalism (Gopal 2009: 33).

---

play up the cultural similarities shared by Nepal, Bhutan, Burma, and India. For details, see van der Veer (1984: 124–6). The sentence from the statement issued on that occasion, as quoted by him (van der Veer 1984: 126), reads: 'It proved that Nepal, Bhutan and Burma may be politically separate from Bharat [India] but the cultural soul of all these countries is one within.' From this I have developed the expression to read 'one cultural soul' so as to better convey the underlying idea.

[71] बाल्ये पितुर्वशे तिष्ठेत् पाणिग्राहस्य यौवने।
पुत्राणां भर्तरि प्रेते नभजेत् स्त्री स्वतन्त्रताम्।। (*Manusmr̥ti* Chapter 5, Verse 148)
In childhood [a female] should be subject to her father, in youth to her husband, / [And] when her husband has died to her sons; women should not enjoy independence.

[72] '*Mātā bhūmiḥ putro'haṃ pr̥thivyāḥ*' [My mother is the land and I am a son of the earth] (*Atharvaveda*, Pr̥thvīsūkta).

[73] Chatterjee (2011a: 54) notes that Bankimchandra Chattopadhyaya was one of the first systematic expounders in India of the principles of nationalism.

Viewing the country reverently as a mother has also been the traditional outlook in Nepal. Bālkr̥ṣṇa Sama (2054 VS: 388) claimed that he was the first one to address the country as Nepal āmā in his poem *Bhūkampa jvar* (Earthquake fever) in 1990 VS, written shortly after the big tremor of that year.[74] He goes on to acknowledge, though, that a similar expression, Nepāl mātā, was current 400 years earlier in the country (Sama 2054 VS), citing as evidence a text inscribed on a sculpted representation of the Aṣṭamātrikās (Eight Mother Goddesses) from the time of Pratap Malla.

Gopal Prasād Rimāl's most famous poem, *Āmāko sapanā* (A mother's dream), written on the eve of democracy in 1951, has two characters in it: Nepal as āmā and her *chorā* (son), representing the Nepalese people. Analysing Rimāl's poem, Michael J. Hutt (1993: 74) points out the symbolism: the mother standing for Nepal, and her son for the forces that would eventually inaugurate a new dispensation—a theme that recurs in many subsequent poems in Nepali literature.[75]

In contexts beyond the family hearth, then, the mother surrenders her authority. When it comes to relations between countries or competing political systems, the family turns into a bastion in which virility prevails. The relation between two countries is not seen as one between two motherly (or sisterly) figures but between two brothers. The motherland is vulnerable and needs the protection of her brave sons. Men stand guard at the door and parlay with their equals beyond the gate. This notion of their brotherhood is what harmonious rela-

74 The line in question reads: 'नेपाल आमा, तँ धैर्यले बस् हिमालमा सूर्य हे उँदायो' [O Mother Nepal, remain calm; see, the sun has risen over the Himalaya!]

75 Another famous poet, Mādhav Ghimire, composed a poem about Nepāl āmā titled 'Parantu euṭai mūrtimā virāṭ' (But on one grand statue), collected in *Kinnar Kinnarī* (Ghimire 2060 VS: 3), reads:

नेपाल आमा कहीं छौ घाम, कहीं छौ छाया हे,
परन्तु सारा सन्तानमाथि एउटै माया हे,

[O Mother Nepal, you are in places sunlight and in places shadow, / But you have equal love for all your children.]

Another Nepalese poet, Bhikhāri Mansur, has written a similar poem in Hindi titled 'Mā̃' (Mother) about Nepal:

ऐ माँ नेपाल तेरा
गिरते आँसू रोक डालेंगे। [O Mother Nepal, we will stop your flowing tears.]

tions between two countries rest upon. The sons of the motherland are called upon to be ever vigilant and, when necessary, brave and warrior-like; when conflict arises, the mother worries and sheds tears.

Sankrityayan (1998b [*MJY-1*]: 271) likewise refers to India as his *deś mātā* (mother country), but when he talks about the Nepal–India relationship it is one between brothers. He had always respected Nepal as an independent nation, but its people belonged to one family that in his imagination transcended borders. In a speech given on 23 March 1958 in Kathmandu, he said: 'Nepal is not small. It can develop greatly, and India will always regard the progress of Nepal as the development of a younger brother.'[76] Moreover, Sankrityayan imagined the bond of brotherhood that existed between India and Nepal as being stronger than similar bonds between other countries. The difference can be understood in terms of a distinction made in South Asian culture: cousins are regarded as brothers and sisters, and are addressed as such, but there is another, rarely used term, 'sahodar' (born from the same womb), for siblings. Sankrityayan used this latter to define the relationship between India and Nepal:

> नेपाल भारत का सहोदर है।
>
> Nepal is India's sibling. (quoted in Miśrā 1993: 4)

One Cultural Soul

The central idea underlying Sankrityayan's (and, in his eyes, India's) relationship with Nepal—that of brotherhood—is what I term the 'one cultural soul' shared by both parties. Sankrityayan repeatedly presents himself as being areligious. Even as he regarded Buddhism

76 नेपाल सानो छैन। यसले धेरै उन्नति गर्न सक्तछ नेपालको उन्नतिलाई भारत सानु भाईको उन्नति संझन्छ।' (as reported in *Gorkhapatra*, 24 March 1958).

Many Nepalese writers, too, used the term *bhāi* (younger brother) for Indian nationals. One such writer, Shambhu Prasad Dhungyal (1946–86), states in the foreword to his Hindi novel *Prem kāntā* (cited in Rākeś 2003: 26):

'मैं अपनी नेपाली भाषा में छोटा-मोटा लेख तो लिखता ही रहता था परन्तु हिन्दुस्तानी भाइयों से मेरा परिचय बहुत कम था।'

I was continually writing short articles in my own language of Nepali, but my acquaintanceship with [my] Indian brothers was very small.

in terms of the wider Indian culture, so too his relationship with Nepal, while outwardly tied to religion, had, according to him, a wider cultural foundation. Though he never professed a conventional faith in any religion, his relationship with Nepal was based in part on the conventional trappings of religion: the ritual, the beliefs, and the cultural accessories. He had visited Nepal as a sadhu during Śivrātri and participated in Nepal's grandest religious festival;[77] however, this was not the main aim of his visit. Whether he assumed the robes of a sadhu or of a Buddhist monk, or enrolled as a Brahmin in the study of Buddhism mattered less to him than the fact than that he was thereby granted membership in a brotherhood. Nepal and India share many cultural roots that go back far in time, and these still serve to make both peoples feel at home in the other's country.

As noted by van der Veer (1994: 84), religions and the particular ways of practising them each gives rise to particular ways of imagining the world. He argues that ritual takes pride of place when it comes to communicating most compellingly such imaginative ideas of religious community. Hindu and Buddhist religious customs, both of which Sankrityayan had at one time or another followed, created a sense of fellowship. His pilgrimage as a sadhu during Śivarātri, the hospitality he received at the house of a Nepalese Buddhist family, his visits to Tibet in the robes of a Buddhist monk, and his time spent searching for, studying, and editing Buddhist texts there are examples of activities that bonded the areligious Sankrityayan with Buddhist believers beyond India's borders. Sankrityayan's relationship with Hemraj Sharma tells the same story in Hindu terms. Sharma was the *rājguru* (royal priest) to Nepal's governing family, the Ranas. He was a Brahmin Sanskrit scholar looked upon as one of the most senior religious authorities in Nepal, and exercised temporal power through his association with the ministerial court. Sankrityayan visited his house as a guest and received gifts,[78] as if from a fellow 'twice-born one'.

77 'A remarkable number of sadhus visit Pashupatinath every year from different parts of India. The Pashupati Area Development Trust and Guthi Sansthan arrange food and accommodation for sadhus in Kathmandu. In 2011, 705,000 devotees visited the temple and among these 15% are Indian pilgrims every year'—(*Kantipur*, 3 March 2011).

78 For details, see the sketch of Sharma's life in Appendix 1.

Sharma, an orthodox Hindu, would not have cultivated such close relations with Sankrityayan had he thought of him as an areligious person, that is, as someone other than a Hindu Brahmin or a Buddhist. The normal way he treated others has been described as follows:

> [...] his [that is, Sharma's] house in Dhoka Tole—called Bharati Bhavan,[79] the 'House of Learning'—in the heart of Kathmandu [...]
>
> In the first quarter of the century, not only Nepal but also Hem Raj's house was closed to foreigners. Lévi wrote in 1925 that twice a week he had an academic meeting with Hem Raj at the Government Library, but he would have not been allowed to enter the Raj Guru's house since people would have been scandalized to see a *mleccha* (barbarian) profane the residence of such a sacred person. (Garzilli 2001: 118–20)

But the door of Bharati Bhavan was always open for Sankrityayan, because in the eyes of the Nepalese he was either an Indian Hindu or Buddhist and born into a Brahmin family.

Similarly, Sahu Dharmaman would not have let Sankrityayan come to or stay at his house in Kathmandu and Lhasa, or have helped him journey to Tibet, if he did not have what seemed to be genuine Buddhist credentials. The fact that Dharmaman and others were already secretly active in the Theravada movement only meant that they even more open-heartedly welcomed Sankrityayan, someone who was devoted to the same cause in India as they were in Nepal (see the section titled 'Sankrityayan and the Theravada Movement in Nepal' earlier). Both Sharma and Dharmaman, then, viewed Sankrityayan as belonging to their community.

Pilgrimage Centres

Van der Veer (1994: 120–1) highlights pilgrimages as one key component of the glue that holds imagined communities together. He sees pilgrimages as being rituals that take place over a wider expanse of the community of believers, linking people from at least two different places under one umbrella of discourse, thus serving to cement the

[79] Nepāl (2057 VS: 1) has written that Bharati Bhavan was actually Sharma's library.

bonds of religious nationalism. The Hindu religion boasts of a large number of major pilgrimage sites in both Nepal and India, though to be sure, given their difference in size, there are fewer in the former. They are typically located where two rivers meet or at strategic river crossings, or else in places associated with great religious icons, be they the main Hindu deities, mythological figures, or historical saints (for example, places of birth, visitation, residence, or miracles, as recorded in religious books or oral tradition). The places in India most visited by Nepalese Hindus have always been Gaya and Banaras,[80] while Janakpur (the birthplace of Sita), Pashupatinath in Kathmandu, Lumbini (the birthplace of Buddha), and Muktinath are the main pilgrimage centres in Nepal that are visited by Indian Hindus and Buddhists. Gaya,[81] which is regarded as the preferred pilgrimage destination for the performance of the first-year śrāddha for one's parents among Hindus, is also a pilgrimage centre for Buddhists—the place where the Buddha attained enlightenment. Banaras, too, is an important pilgrimage site for both Hindus and Buddhists, because Sarnath, where the Buddha first taught the dharma and where the sangha came into existence, lies just 13 kilometres to the north-east. The major religions of Nepal and India, then, Hinduism and Buddhism, have common pilgrimage centres on each other's territory, which serve to bind the people of both countries closer to one another.

Banaras has not only been a religious but also an educational centre. The main Indian centres for Nepalese education at that time were Calcutta and Banaras.[82] In addition to being a centre of religion

[80] One traditional saying recommends that seven cities be visited in order to ensure salvation: अयोध्या, मथुरा, माया, काशी, कांची, अवन्तिका। पुरी, द्वारावती चैव सप्तैते मोक्षदायका:।। [Ayodhya, Mathura, Maya (that is, Haridvar), Kashi, Kanchi, Avantika (or, Ujjain), Puri, and Dvaravati (that is, Dvaraka) are (the cities) that provide salvation.]

[81] There is a trend among Nepalese Hindus to complete the first-year śrāddha of one's parents in Gaya, and since Banaras is nearby, it too is visited on the same occasion.

[82] Generally, students opting for an English-language education went to Calcutta, while those who desired a Sanskrit-based one went to Banaras. The latter played a major role in Sankrityayan's life in this regard. He studied and later attended literary gatherings there, and in the end it was the place that

and education, Banaras was also noted for its publishing houses.[83] A famous Nepali proverb acknowledges the latter city's long history of erudition: *vidyā harāe kāśī jānu, nyāya napāe gorkhā jānu* (If knowledge is lost, go to Banaras; if justice is not obtained, go to Gorkha[84]). Banaras was *the* holy pilgrimage centre (*tīrtha*) for Nepalese Hindus. Many Hindu Nepalese spent the last years of their lives in Banaras, wishing to die there and to be cremated at the Manikarnika Ghat on the banks of the Ganga—a custom known as *kāśīvās* or *kalpavās*[85] (dwelling in Kashi until death).[86] Martin Gaenszle (2002 and 2006) presents an array of evidence—including the temples and *dharmaśālās* (rest-houses) they built—confirming Kashi's status as a

---

awarded him the title of mahāpaṇḍit. Virtually every Nepalese who was studying in Banaras (or even elsewhere in India) at the time knew or knew of him, his scholarly work, his books, and his travels; the writings of his that deal with Nepal only added to his recognizability.

[83] As Chalmers (2002: 35) details, Banaras was the furnace in which the Nepali-language print industry was forged, and which continued to dominate it for decades.

[84] A saying that goes back to King Prithvi Narayan Shah.

[85] Hemraj Sharma was among those who, in 1953, went to Banaras to end out their days—the same year that Sankrityayan met him in Nepal during his visit to the country in preparation for writing a book on it. Sharma's last letter to his grandson, written on 19 November 1953 (published in Raj 2003: 31), explains his daily routine: because of bad health he did not go to the Ganga every day to bathe, and only occasionally, in the evening, did he walk to Dashashwamedh Ghat or to the Chowk. The rest of the time he spent reading and worshipping.

As the royal priest of the Ranas, he had been gifted a house by the youngest *mahārānī* of Prime Minister Chandra Shamsher during a *kotihom* (ten million oblations in fire) in 1939. The house was at Rathyatra Chaumuhani near Mahmoorganj. Neither of his two sons was present at his death. The last rites were performed by Iswari Raj who came from Bombay to Varanasi after hearing the news of his coronary thrombosis. (Information about the house and the final rites is from an email correspondence with Prakash A. Raj on 17 March 2011.)

[86] This practice has receded now that India is increasingly perceived as a foreign country. The pilgrimage site of Devghat in Nepal (at the confluence of the Gandaki and Trishuli rivers) has now largely usurped this role. Many

place of pilgrimage for Nepalese from all walks of life.[87] He also notes the importance this city has had for Nepal's recent political history.[88]

In short, it is not hard to see why Banaras played such a vital role in awakening in Sankrityayan's imagination the picture of tight-knit Nepalese Hindu and Buddhist communities of which he felt a fellow member.

One crucial factor explaining the unique place Sankrityayan occupies within Nepal's modern cultural landscape was his Sanskrit education and his scholarly relationship with the rājguru Hemraj Sharma. Under the strict Rana rule, no one besides the Ranas or their favoured ones were allowed to study modern academic subjects; Sanskrit education, to be sure, was permitted in the case of Brahmins, most of whom went to Banaras for this purpose. The Ranas were Hindus and believed in the efficacy of rituals, and it was for this purpose that they loosened their control, for they needed Brahmins to perform the rituals, make astrological predictions, and help them beyond religious impasses. Even though there were some Sanskrit schools in the country, students had to go to Banaras for their final university exams. Given the smallness of the educated population in Nepal at that time, Sankrityayan was able, as an educated person himself, to establish good relations with members of the intelligentsia, including such scholars and literary figures as Janaklāl Śarmā, Lakshmi Prasad Devkota, Bālkr̥ṣṇa Sama, Chittadhar Hridaya, and Kedarman Vyathit; and such politically engaged persons as Dharmaratna Yami and Pushpa Lal Shrestha (see section titled 'Sankrityayan's Banned Books in Nepal' in Chapter 4); and, most significantly, Hemraj Sharma, who was both a Sanskrit scholar and someone with clout within the ruling clique.[89] Sankrityayan therefore had many channels through which his own concerns could gain a wider audience and turn him, too, into a celebrated figure for the public at large.

Nepalese have built small houses or have donated money in return for living quarters in Devghat; see Gaenszle 2006: 308.

87 See also Chalmers (2003).

88 Though Nepal's first political party, the Nepali Rashtriya Congress, was established in Calcutta (on 26 January 1947), the central office was located at 65, Dudhvinayak in Banaras.

89 See Appendix 1 for brief biographical sketches of the persons listed.

* * *

This chapter has sought to explore what Buddhism and the journeys to Tibet and Nepal meant for Sankrityayan. The question raised at the beginning of this chapter may be answered by saying that Sankrityayan was a Buddhist but that his Buddhism was different from that of conventionally religious Buddhists. Although he was ordained as a monk in Sri Lanka, his objective in life was not mainly to propagate and practise Buddhism as the religion leading to nirvana. Apart from donning monastic robes off and on (especially when travelling in Tibet), he temporarily cultivated the habit, as mentioned in his autobiography, of eating once a day, as a practising monk normally would. The devotion he demonstrated in such activity was rather for purposes of reviving Buddhism and keeping it alive as a pivotal aspect of Indian cultural identity and as a source of Indian pride within the community of nations. Indeed, he had taken the personal step of embracing it as a means of expressing through it his own pride in his nation.

This study has observed, then, that Sankrityayan's initial attraction to Buddhism was due to the Buddha's role in enriching Indian culture and spreading it around the world. After studying and working in Sri Lanka, meeting Buddhist scholars there from abroad, and experiencing Sri Lankans' devotion to Buddhism, he was inspired to contribute to the study of Buddhism himself, and this entailed delving more deeply into Indian religions and cultures, for which reason he went to Tibet in search of original Buddhist manuscripts. Faced with financial problems, he had to curtail his visit and go back to Sri Lanka with what he had managed to collect. After his visit to Europe, he realized the importance of this collection of Tibetan material, and of the Buddhist manuscripts in particular. His commentary on the *Abhidharmakoṣa*, completed before going to Europe, shows that already early on, his interests extended beyond simply collecting. Indeed, his activities display a constant expansion of interest in Buddhism from the point that this study identifies as his first active endeavour on its behalf (before his trips to Sri Lanka and Tibet), namely his proposal during the Gaya congress of 1922 to hand over control of the Maha Bodhi Temple to Buddhists. This early encounter with the sangha would later be reflected in the admiration he expresses in his Hindi novels for the early republics (*gaṇtantra*) that arose under Buddhist influence in ancient India.

Was Sankrityayan a Buddhist? This chapter has made clear that he was never a Buddhist in the normal sense of the term; rather, he was what could be called a fervent admirer of the Buddha and Buddhism. He did not see Buddhism as embodying his own personal religious goals, but he was proud to claim it as an essential part of Indian culture and to see its message spread throughout the world. He was proud in particular to recall the periods during the ancient past in which various republics had existed as systems with communistic features inspired by the Buddhist sangha.

During the course of this study, it has been interesting to see how Sankrityayan expresses his admiration for the Buddha as a great world figure. One way he does this is by comparing other persons he admired to him—for instance, Dayananda, Marx, and Gandhi. It is the Buddha who stands as the touchstone for all who come after him. After Gandhi's assassination, for example, he writes the following:

> गाँधीजी अजातशत्रु थे, वह किसी का अनिष्ट नहीं चाहते थे। उनके भी शत्रु पैदा हो सकते हैं? और सो भी हिन्दू सभ्यता और संस्कृति के अभिमान करने वाले लोगों में? [...] बुद्ध के बाद क्या भारत में कोई इतना महान् व्यक्ति पैदा हुआ? हमारे देश की परम्परा ने हमे शाविचार-सहिष्णुता को जगा कर रखा। बुद्ध अनीश्वरवादी थे, जात-पात और कितनी ही दूसरी रूढ़ियों के जबर्दस्त शत्रु थे, स्पष्ट वक्ता, थे और गाँधी की तरह प्रिय भाषी भी।
>
> Gandhi did not look upon anyone as an enemy; he never wished anyone ill. Could then enemies have risen against him? And among persons proud of Hindu civilization and culture at that? [...] Has ever such a great person [as he] been born since the Buddha in India? Our country's tradition has always been to be tolerant of [others'] beliefs. The Buddha was an atheist, he was a sworn enemy of the caste system and a host of other forms of conservatism; he was plain-speaking but also, in the way Gandhi was, soft-spoken. (Sankrityayan 1998b [*MJY-4*]: 267).

Sankrityayan felt Nepal to be his second home, a view grounded in the notions of 'one cultural soul' and 'brotherhood'. He developed intimate ties with Nepal and the Nepalese through his devotion to Buddhism and Buddhist studies. In the context of this study's examination of Sankrityayan's relationship with Nepal, his speech at the Fourth World Buddhist Conference held in Kathmandu in December 1956 is worth quoting from. In front of a large gathering on the parade grounds of Tundikhel, where all the guests and King Mahendra Shah were assembled, he gave a spontaneous response in Hindi to the welcoming speech:

> मुझे नहीं लगता हम विदेश में आए हैं। नेपाल और भारत की संस्कृति एक है। ... ये जो विश्व के दूर देशों से मेहमान आये हैं, हमारे और आपके साझा मेहमान हैं। इनको बुद्ध की जन्मभूमि और कर्मभूमि का सही परिचय मिले ऐसा हम लोगों को मिलकर करना चाहिए।
>
> I do not think that we have arrived in a foreign land. Nepal and India have one culture.... The guests who have come here from faraway countries are our common guests. We need to act in concert so that they will truly become acquainted with the *janmbhūmi* [birthplace, that is, Nepal] and *karmbhūmi* [field of action, that is, India] of the Buddha. (Sankrityayan, cited in Miśrā 1993: 2)

This statement is clearly emblematic of Sankrityayan's vision of India–Nepal relations and why he regarded both countries as historically bound one to the other. In his opinion, their common culture (their one cultural soul) had united both countries into a brotherhood that would not have been possible with other countries, even when they shared a common religion, such as Japan, China, or Thailand.[90] The common link between India and Nepal through Buddhism goes deeper, in that they witnessed the birth of the religion, but their links go far beyond even Buddhism.

This was a state of affairs that Sankrityayan believed transcended even the politics of the day. The Rana government may have expelled Buddhist monks newly converted to Theravada, but Sankrityayan, who was himself a relatively new convert to Buddhism, was able to enter and sojourn in Nepal with apparent ease. One obvious reason for this, this study has shown, was his seemingly chameleon-like identity, his ability to shift from political activist, to Buddhist, to Brahmin, to communist, to scholar, to sadhu, to Arya Samajist—something that could easily have thrown anyone with suspicions off their guard. On his early visits to Nepal, Sankrityayan travelled without official

90 'The guests participating in the Fourth World Buddhist Conference came from China, Burma, Ceylon, Japan, etc.' (*Gorkhapatra*, 21 November 1956).

permission, incognito. Later he re-emerged as a scholar of Buddhism of such obvious talent as to impress other serious scholars working in the field, especially the rājguru Hemraj Sharma, and this made entry into Nepal easier. But just when Sankrityayan was beginning to enjoy this new-found freedom, a number of his books were banned in Nepal. His books on the Buddha and Buddhism, to be sure, were still available there, but readers no longer had ready access to his political writings. The following chapter will turn its attention to these banned books. By very reason of their illegal status, his communist-inspired literature enjoyed great popularity in Nepal, which became an important print-market for all his works. The next chapter will again take up the thread of his literary contributions to the Hindi language and its literature and to the reception they enjoyed in Nepal.

CHAPTER FOUR

Hindi

An Indian Voice

This study has identified the final transformation in Sankrityayan's intellectual journey towards what may be called Hindi nationalism, the foundation of what he thought would be a nation comprising Indians proudly sharing a common Indian culture and officially recognizing Hindi as their *sammilit bhāṣā* (common language). Sankrityayan's final incarnation is generally taken to be that of a communist,[1] but there are good reasons for seeing it rather as a proponent of Hindi nationalism. Towards the end of his life, his wish to make Hindi the only national language of India and what others took to be an overweening pride in Indian culture and history led to his dismissal from the Communist Party of India. Although he had been ready to renounce his party membership, it had never been his intention to do so, and after his dismissal from the party he both remained a convinced communist and continued to argue in favour of making Hindi the national language. In other words, his nationalist sentiment had driven a wedge between him and his fellow communists. Furthermore, as he himself stated, he was not by nature a political activist; his instincts lay rather in imaginative thought and writing. He wrote extensively and chose Hindi as the language best suited to him for propagating his ideas, which included, prominently, the advocacy of *premāspad Hindī* (the beloved Hindi language). He realized the power of the printed word and indeed saw it as the best medium for spreading ideas, given the wider audience it could reach at the time than could speech. Furthermore, the readership of his

[1] See, for example, A. Bhaṭṭācārya (2005: 135–71).

books was not limited to India, but extended to the neighbouring country of Nepal, where Hindi was also understood.

This chapter will explore the new turning in Sankrityayan's life as a member of the Communist Party of India, the form of Hindi nationalism he propounded, and the importance he ascribed to the print medium (one indicator of which was the smuggling of his books into Nepal). In the context in which he found himself, then, it was not just the printed word but the printed word in Hindi that he saw as the chief means of both exercising responsibility and achieving progress (through the propagation of ideas) on a national level, and both bringing pleasure and providing an income on a personal one. This chapter will devote special attention to his works that propagate communism and to the mixed response they received in Nepal.

After Sankrityayan returned from his fourth journey to Tibet, his intention was to enter into the political fray. He had already experienced, as he stated, the Arya Samaj as 'a new light' in his life, and now he hoped that his becoming a member of the Communist Party of India would similarly represent 'the beginning of a new life' for him. He was later disabused of this belief. He did not prove to be a successful political activist and to be able to totally revamp his life as a Communist Party member as he had hoped. One sign of this failure was his inability to secure any high post in the party, and this may have been one reason why he increasingly turned his attention to writing and publishing, and to campaigning on behalf of Hindi nationalism instead. This chapter explores how Sankrityayan's later political life as a member of the Communist Party of India started and how he then switched lanes and devoted himself fully to *sāhitya sevā* (the literary pursuit).

BEGINNING A NEW LIFE

Sankrityayan's political activities as narrated in his autobiography are seen to be divided between almost equal periods under the banners of the Congress party and the Communist Party of India. He was imprisoned for two-and-a-half years (first for six months and later for two years) as a Congress political activist, and again for almost the same period and under similar circumstances as a peasant leader and a communist. Of his five years of active political involvement as a declared communist after 1939, then, he spent half the time behind bars, but his pen was unflaggingly engaged throughout in producing communist literature, so that his activism never really ebbed. His scholarly contributions as an intellectual to the communist cause through the written word in Hindi outshone his more mundane political activities (see section titled 'Print: Progress, Pleasure, Profit, and Propagation' later in this chapter).

The year 1920 was a watershed in the history of the communist movement in India, and it was M.N. Roy who played the major role in it. From outside India, he and other communists made vigorous attempts to get the movement off the ground.[2] Roy saw the 37th annual session of the National Congress at Gaya as the moment he was waiting for to come out in the open with his ideas. He sent off an article in absentia stating them.[3] When, after the Chauri Chaura incident, Gandhi urged the Congress party to boycott the upcoming elections and called off the non-cooperation campaign, unsatisfied groups within the party coalesced under the leadership of Chittaranjan Das (C.R. Das). The proper response became a major discussion point on the agenda during the convention, and as a result the group, unsatisfied with Gandhi's recommendations, formed the Swaraj Party. The communists, Roy in particular, viewed this situation as an opportunity, hoping that Das would lead their combined forces. Many communist leaders from both within India and abroad

[2] For detailed studies of Roy and his place in history, see Overstreet and Windmiller (1959), Haithcox (1971), and Manjapra (2010).

[3] '[J]ust before the Gaya session Roy offered, through the pages of *Advance Guard*, a wide-ranging program that, if accepted, would align the Congress with the "exploited workers and peasants." The "Program" was a comprehensive document which called for complete national independence, universal suffrage, abolition of landlordism, nationalization of public utilities, full rights for labor to organize, minimum wages in all industries, an eight-hour day, profit-sharing in industry, free compulsory education, the abolition of the standing army, and "arming of the entire people to defend the National Freedom".[...] Hundreds of copies of this issue of *Advance Guard* were sent to India for distribution among the delegates at Gaya. The British authorities intercepted 540 of them, but admitted that a large number got through' (Overstreet and Windmiller 1959: 49).

were present at the congress, but the result was not as fruitful as had been anticipated.[4]

This was exactly the time that Sankrityayan was entering politics. His major aims during the Gaya congress were handing over the Maha Bodhi Temple to the Buddhists and drumming up support for the Swaraj Party (see Chapter 3 of this volume). It is clear from Sankrityayan's autobiography that he neither got to read Roy's article that was distributed during the congress nor met any of the communist leaders in attendance or was even aware of them. He later wrote (1998b [*MJY-1*]: 268): 'If any ism was dear to me, it was communism, but I still had [only] a vague knowledge if it.'[5] Even in the early days of his political involvement he considered poverty and humiliation humanity's greatest curses, and so dreamt of a Raj of empowered farmers and workers. During the conference, Sankrityayan was urged to meet Das. He went to the latter's bungalow, but tired of having to wait for the introduction and so returned. One can only speculate what course Sankrityayan's life would have taken had communist leaders in search of dedicated cadre met him on that occasion and realized his genuine commitment. His aggressive speech on the Chauri Chaura incident would soon land him in prison for two years. After his release, and now the author of *Bāisvī̃ sadī*, he did not see any rewarding future with the Congress party. Instead he would swerve away from politics towards Buddhism and sojourns in Sri Lanka and Tibet.

While Sankrityayan was in Europe during 1932–3, he tried to meet Indian and German communists there and desired to go to Russia, but all this proved impossible at the time. He had no problem meeting or learning about many foreign scholars in the fields of Buddhist and Indic studies, however, and they guided him onward in his scholarly pursuits.

When Sankrityayan appointed himself to the task of collecting manuscripts from Tibet, this meant interrupting his political activities. After returning to India from his third journey to Tibet in 1936, he confessed that this lull had served to stimulate his desire to work for the poor:

4 For details, see Overstreet and Windmiller (1959: 14–58).

5 'मुझे यदि कोई वाद पसन्द था, तो वह साम्यवाद, किन्तु अभी तक मुझे उसका बिल्कुल अस्पष्ट-सा ज्ञान था।'

जिन हृदयोद्गारों को मैं 'बाईसवीं सदी' और 'साम्यवाद ही क्यों?' में प्रकट कर चुका हूँ, वह दिल में अब भी मौजूद है। अभी मैंने बहुत जोर देकर अपने को गरीबों के लिए लड़ने के क्षेत्र से अलग कर रखा था, शायद ज्यादा दिनों तक मैं वैसा न कर सकता था।

The deep feelings which I have previously expressed in *Bāisvī̃ sadī* and *Sāmyavād hī kyõ?* are still with me. With great strain I had for the time being withdrawn myself from the field of fighting for the poor, but I could not do so for long. (Sankrityayan 1998b [*MJY-2*]: 260)

One aim of Sankrityayan's socialist agenda was to free the country from poverty in hopes of reaching the third position in the list of the world's powerful nations. This shows a sense of sober realism on his part. He was not confident that India would ever attain the first position, at least not in the short run.

गरीबी दूर करके हिन्दुस्तान को एक बलवान देश बनाना है। रूस और अमेरिका के बाद तीसरी जगह अपने देश को लेनी है।

India needs to be turned into a powerful country by removing poverty. Our country needs to assume the third position after Russia and America. (Sankrityayan 2004a: vii)

As Sankrityayan experienced life in Russia at close hand, he felt increasingly motivated to join in liberation movements. At times, for instance, he thought of going to Spain or China to participate in revolutionary activities there, but his 'Indianness' got the better of him:

मैंने अब सोवियत के जीवन को नजदीक से देखा। कितने संघर्षों, कितनी कुरबानियों के बाद उन्हें यह जीवन प्राप्त हुआ है। स्पेन में उस वक्त फासिस्तों के साथ संघर्ष चल रहा था। चीनी कम्युनिष्ट भी पीसे जा रहे थे। अपने देश में हम भारतीय भी गुलाम थे। इन बातों को ख्याल करके मेरे मन में होता था, मुझे अब युद्धक्षेत्र में कूदना चाहिए। स्पेन या चीन में भी चला जाता, लेकिन जानता था, मैं वहाँ उतना उपयोगी नहीं हो सकूँगा। मेरे लिए सबसे अच्छा क्षेत्र अपना ही देश है। मैंने तय किया कि भारत जा के स्वराज्य-संघर्ष में सक्रिय भाग लेना चाहिये।

I observed Soviet life closely. How many struggles and how many sacrifices it had taken to attain this way of life! During that time Spain[6] was

6 Sankrityayan's desire to go to Spain and join the revolution was fulfilled in a literary sense in the novel *Jīne ke liye*, in which Jenny, the wife of Devrāj (see n39 in Chapter 2 of this study), takes part (and later dies) in the war in Spain.

> struggling with the Fascists. The Chinese communists, too, were being oppressed. We Indians were also slaves in our own land. Thinking over these things in my mind, I had the feeling that I should now rush to the battlefield. I could have gone to Spain or China, but I knew that I could not be useful there. For me the best field of action was my own country. I decided that I should go to India and take part in the Swaraj struggle. (Sankrityayan 1998b [*MJY-2*]: 281–2)

Of the time after his fourth visit to Tibet he wrote:

> तिब्बत फिर आने की मुझे बहुत कम आशा रह गई थी, क्योंकि एक तो अब मैं लौटकर राजनीति में प्रवेश करने वाला था, जिसके कारण भारत में अंग्रेजी शासन के रहते मुझे इधर आने की कौन अनुमति देता, दूसरे मैं अपने साथ इतनी पुस्तकों के फोटो ले जा रहा था, जिनके सम्पादन और प्रकाशन के लिए दस-पन्द्रह वर्षों की जरूरत थी।
>
> I had very little hope of coming back to Tibet once more, because firstly, after returning [to India] I would be politically active, and who under British rule would have given me permission to come? Secondly, I had been photographing so many books that ten to fifteen years would be needed for editing and publication. (Sankrityayan 1998b [*MJY-2*]: 300)

Sankrityayan's first entry into and involvement in politics fell between the years 1921–7. He had worked with the Congress party in Bihar and had also been imprisoned for more than two and a half years. But when in 1938 he decided to engage himself again politically, India's political situation had changed, and Congress was now part of the Bihar ministerial government (Mule 1998: 84). The Congress party had done extremely well in the 1937 elections, Bihar being one of the five provinces in which it had won an absolute majority (Sarkar 1984: 349). However, Sankrityayan was distressed by the situation facing farmers in Bihar. Indeed, this had been his motivation for returning to politics in the first place:

> मैं पहले भी राजनीति में अपने हृदय की पीडा को दूर करने आया था–गरीबी और अपमान को मैंने [*sic*] भारी अभिशाप समझता था। असहयोग के समय भी मैं जिस स्वराज की कल्पना करता था, वह काले सेठों और बाबुओं का राज नहीं था, वह राज था किसानों और मजदूरों का, क्योंकि तभी गरीबी और अपमान से जनता मुक्त हो सकती थी। अब तो देश-विदेश देखने के बाद और भी पीडा को अनुभव करता था।

मैंने भारत जैसी गरीबी कहीं नहीं देखी। मार्क्सवाद के अध्ययन ने मुझे बतला दिया, कि क्रान्ति करने वाले हाथ हैं, यही मजदूर किसान; क्योंकि उन्हीं को सारी यातनाएँ सहनी पड़ती हैं, और उन्हीं के पास लड़ाई में हारने के लिए सम्पत्ति नहीं है। लेकिन यह सब रहते हुए जब तक वह अपना मजबूत संगठन तैयार नहीं करते तब तक क्रान्ति करने की शक्ति उनमें नहीं आ सकती। उनका संगठन तभी मजबूत हो सकता है, जबकि रोज-ब-रोज के कष्टों को हटाने के लिए संघर्ष करें।

I came to politics to relieve the pain of my own heart—I considered poverty and humiliation a curse. The Swaraj I had imagined during the non-cooperation movement was not a Raj of black seths and babus[7]; it was a Raj of farmers and workers, because only by it could people's poverty and humiliation be relieved. Now, after travelling in- and outside the country, I felt all the more grief. I had not seen poverty like that in India anywhere else. The studies of Marxism had already told me that the hands that fight the revolution are these same workers and farmers, for it is they who have to endure all the torture; moreover, they do not have any property to lose. But be that as it may, until they have a strong organization in place, they will not have the strength to revolt. And their organization can only be strong when they struggle to rid themselves of day-to-day grievances. (Sankrityayan 1998b [*MJY-2*]: 303)

The desire to rid his country of poverty was thus the main aim of Sankrityayan's political involvement, which was strengthened and provided with a theoretical basis by his study of Marxism. Sankrityayan viewed Marxism as a method to eradicate poverty. For all his admiration of communism, however, he again, as with previous belief systems, made it serve his own ends, in this case adapting it specifically to the Indian context:

मार्क्सवाद का प्रयोग (व्यवहार) हरेक देश में उसकी परिस्थिति के अनुसार करना पड़ता है, जो सबसे मुश्किल काम है।

Marxism needs to be applied [put into practice] in every country according to the local situation, which is a most difficult task. (Sankrityayan, cited in Mācve 2005: 32)

Sankrityayan proposed the ambitious idea of *pañcāytī khetī* (council farming) for improving the situation of Indian peasants and

7 The white seths and babus were British, and the black ones were Indians.

developing the country. He contended that by implementing it, India would never suffer food shortages. All land and cattle would come under the control of the councils, which would arrange for reliable irrigation, modern farming machinery, suitable composting, and better flood-prevention measures. Indian farmers were too poor to afford such facilities on their own, whence both they and their families suffered. All of this, of course, is based on the ideal he cites: the Russian system of collective farming.[8]

The Communist Party of India faced daunting problems in gaining a foothold in India. By 1934, when it was declared illegal, it had attracted only 150 members (Overstreet and Windmiller 1959: 155). After the Congress Socialist Party was formed that same year, the Communist Party established contact with it. Two years later the Congress Socialist Party adopted a secret resolution in its Meerut meeting to admit communists into the party. In December 1938, during a meeting of a regional branch of the Congress Socialist Party in Muzaffarpur, Sankrityayan was offered membership in it by Jayaprakash Narayan (J.P. Narayan).[9] Sankrityayan at first refused, objecting to the presence of such members as M.R. Misani, who were against the Soviet Union's policy.[10] In the end, though, Sankrityayan relented, having been reassured by Narayan that such were personal opinions and not the party's (Sankrityayan 1998b [*MJY-2*]: 305). Post-revolution Russia was a pilgrimage destination for communists from around the world, and from the start Sankrityayan had been much impressed with the country's political development as a model of the Marxist programme. That he had in addition both intellectual and family ties there only served to solidify his attachment to the country. Criticizing Misani, Sankrityayan writes:

[8] For details, see Sankrityayan (2004a: 245–55).

[9] The party's foremost leader, Jayaprakash Narayan, had been a communist during his student days in America and aspired to unify all Marxist groups under the banner of the Congress Socialist Party. See Overstreet and Windmiller (1959: 156).

[10] 'Early in 1936 Minoo R. Masani, joint-secretary of the CSP and by this time a most bitter opponent of the Communists, got possession of another confidential CPI document that described appropriate methods for capturing CSP units. Masani published this document, and pressed for action against Communists' (Overstreet and Windmiller 1959: 166).

सोवियत मेरे लिए साम्यवाद का साकार रूप था, सोवियत की बुराई करके जो अपने को साम्यवादी या समाजवादी कहे, उसे मैं बंचक या बेवकूफ छोड़कर और कुछ नहीं समझ सकता था।

The Soviet Union was for me a clear-cut form of communism. Anyone who criticized the Soviet Union and still called themselves communists or socialists I regarded only as deceitful or stupid and nothing else. (Sankrityayan 1998b [*MJY-2*]: 303–4)

Sankrityayan's political re-engagement in 1938 after returning to India from his last journey to Tibet centred on participating in the peasants' resistance movement. During this period he was able to witness the new formation of a communist party in India. The Communist Party was still illegal at the time, and Sankrityayan at first had only heard about it. He was able to see it in action first-hand in Wardha, in October 1939, when he was a participant of an All-India Congress Committee meeting.[11] Later he himself became involved in the establishment of the Bihar Communist Party in Munger, and finally became a party member on 19 October 1939. In 1940 he was elected president of both the Prāntīya Kisān Sabhā (Regional Peasants' Union) and Akhil Bhārtīya Kisān Sabhā (All-India Peasants' Union) and designated chairman for the upcoming annual session of the All-India Peasants' Union's congress to be held in Palasa, Andhra Pradesh that same year.[12] These events of 1939 and 1940 are described

[11] The supporters of communism collaborated with the socialist wing of the Congress party before establishing an official party of their own. Sankrityayan writes that the group of supporters who attended the committee meeting consisted of thirty people from various parts of India (1998b [*MJY-2*]: 329). Later, though, he mentions (1998b [*MJY-2*]: 335) that in a meeting of the socialist wing of the Congress party on 14 February 1940 the leaders were flustered over whether to exclude the communists from the party. As Overstreet and Windmiller (1959: 179) note, they eventually did: 'At its Ramgarh meeting in March, 1940, the CSP National Executive [...] decided to expel all communist members.' Gupta (2008) provides a good running commentary on the conflict between the right and left wings of the Congress party after the outbreak of the Second World War and the consequent development of the Communist Party in India.

[12] According to Overstreet and Windmiller (1959: 384), it was N.G. Ranga, a member of a wealthy landholding family of Guntur district (Andhra

in his autobiography under the chapter title 'Ek aur naye jīvan kā ārambh' (The beginning of one more new life).

In early 1939, when Sankrityayan questioned farmers about their problems in Chapra, he was told how zamindars, fearing that the government might expropriate their leased fields in the case of tenants of long standing, had reclaimed them and otherwise troubled them when they went on farming. He took these complaints to administrative officers but this had no impact, since both the state administration and the Congress leaders backed the zamindars. Following this, Sankrityayan visited several villages in an effort to unite the farmers, with the result that a satyagraha was organized (Mule 1998: 85). He had planned to start the satyagraha from Hathua but was forced to switch to the village of Amvāri instead.

An incident on 24 February 1939 added fuel to the fire. Sankrityayan personally participated in the Amvāri satyagraha, which involved cutting sugarcane in the reclaimed field of a tenant farmer. The zamindar had posted mahouts—armed with cudgels and accompanied by two elephants that had been drugged with alcohol—ready to attack the farmers. Sankrityayan had heard rumours that the zamindars were planning to kill him and that the police, though aware of this, felt no need to be on hand.[13] The mahouts, seeing that Sankrityayan was dressed in the robes of a Buddhist monk, hesitated

Pradesh), who started organizing the peasant movement. The All-India Peasants' Union was formed on 11 April 1936 at the Lucknow session of the Indian National Congress under the leadership of its first president, Swami Sahajanand Saraswati, a peasant leader from Bihar. In its second congress, held in Faizapur in December 1936, Ranga was elected president. Overstreet and Windmiller (1959: 385–6) note: 'The non-Communist nationalists, like Ranga and Saraswathi, saw the Kisan Congress as a sort of auxiliary of the nationalist movement. However, their organizational work among the peasants was not fully appreciated by some leaders of the Indian National Congress [...]. [...] [T]he Communists increasingly tended to regard the organization as subsidiary of the CPI.' In 1942 it came under the control of the Communist Party after the latter was legally recognized in India. See also Overstreet and Windmiller (1959: 182), containing a brief outline of the annual session of the Union in Palasa, in March 1940.

13 'मृत्यु से भय खाना मेरे मरने से भी बदतर है।' [Fear of death was worse for me than death itself] (Sankrityayan 1998b [*MJY-2*]: 314). The zamindars had

to attack him.[14] Sankrityayan moved forward with ten other unarmed non-cooperators and, after only two sugarcanes were cut, received a cudgel blow to his head.

Following this incident Sankrityayan was kept under arrest for six months. There were public demonstrations against his detention, with newspapers publishing extensive reports and updates on the story. The Kisān Sabhā called a strike for 1 April 1939 and named it 'Rāhul par prahār virodhī divas' (Protest-the-attack-on-Rāhul day) (Urmileś 1994: 63). Sankrityayan had first been sent to the jail in Sivan but later was transferred to the Chapra prison. During the transfer he and his friends shouted the following slogans:

> 'इन्क्लाब ज़िन्दाबाद', 'किसान राज कायम हो', 'मजदूर राज कायम हो, जमींदारी प्रथा नाश हो', 'कमाने वाला खायेगा, इसके चलते (लिए) जो कुछ हो।'
>
> '*Inklāb zindābād*!'[15] 'Let peasant rule be established!', 'Let labour rule be established [and] the zamindar system abolished!' 'The one who does the work will reap the benefit, no matter what it takes!' (Sankrityayan 1998b [*MJY-2*]: 315)

During Sankrityayan's active involvement in the Communist Party, the party was banned in India and its leaders were arrested and imprisoned by the government. Sankrityayan again found himself behind bars, for two years starting in 1940.[16] Looking back later on this period, he realized that his enthusiasm for political activity was dampened

---

good reason themselves to fear Sankrityayan, for he was by now a well-known figure, particularly in Bihar, renowned for his zeal and efficiency in uniting people around a cause.

14 These were the same yellow robes he had donned before going to Tibet to make the journey easier; he had continued to wear them after his return.

15 This is a Persian phrase, which translates as 'Long live the revolution!' Commonly used by revolutionaries during British rule in India, it was first recorded in prose by Maulavi Hasrat Mohani following a workers' strike in Calcutta. Information accessed (19 December 2011) from http://dictionary.sensagent.com/inquilab+zindabad/en-en/.

16 He was arrested from a house of a fellow comrade in Allahabad, pursuant to the Bhārat Rakṣā Kānūn (Defence of India Act) on 15 March 1940, as he was busy preparing a conference speech for the Akhil Bhārtīya Kisān Sabhā's annual session to be held in Palasa, Andhra Pradesh (Sankrityayan 1998b

considerably during it.[17] However, he did use the time in prison for creative writing, producing his autobiography and six other books[18].

In *Communism in India*, Overstreet and Windmiller (1959: 183–6) discuss the repression of the Communist Party of India under colonial rule and the arrest of party leaders in 1940 under the Defence of India Act. There, surprisingly, Sankrityayan is listed as a non-communist (Overstreet and Windmiller 1959: 183): 'The arrest also extended to such non-Communists as J. P. Narayan, N. G. Ranga, Rahul Sankrityayana, and Swami Sahajanand Saraswati.' Later, however, in presenting biographical data on some leading Indian communists, they (Overstreet and Windmiller 1959: 572) do mention his joining the CPI in 1939 and rejoining it in 1955. Sankrityayan's many masks may have been one source of confusion; it is hard to keep track of the various times when he was a member of the CPI, a peasant leader, a president of the Akhil Bhārtīya Kisān Sabhā (regarded as a subsidiary organ of the CPI before its legalization), and a non-communist. We will come back to this point in more detail in the concluding chapter.

[*MJY*-2]: 337). Overstreet and Windmiller (1959: 183) note concerning the imprisonment of Indian communists in early March of 1940, immediately after the start of the textile strike:

> The official British response to these CPI pronouncements and actions was exceedingly drastic. It amounted to the most effective repression yet undertaken against the Communist movement in India [...] On March 15 [...] the press [they quote *The Hindu* (Madras), 15 March 1940, p. 9] published a note in which the central government announced that it had determined to 'pass orders for the detention of the main Communist leaders under the Defence of India rules.' The Communists, the note declared, 'by means of subversive propaganda and in other, organized ways, have attempted to prejudice the internal peace of India and to interfere with the efficient prosecution of the war by impeding the supply of men and material.' [...] [B]y February, 1941, the home minister could report that the government had detained 480 persons who were 'acknowledged Communists or else active supporters of the communist program of violent mass revolution'.

[17] See the section titled 'A Freethinking Cultural Nationalist' in the Afterword for further background on the reasons for his waning political activities.

[18] *Viśva kī rūprekhā* (1942), *Mānav-samāj* (1942), *Darśan-digdarśan* (1942), *Vaijñānik bhautik'vād* (1942), *Volgā se Gaṅgā* (1942), and *Siṃh senāpati* (1944). The years are the publication dates.

After his release Sankrityayan did, to be sure, again engage in political activities, alongside writing and travelling to many places in India. When, however, he received an invitation to teach at Leningrad University, he was quick to accept, mindful of his family in Russia that wanted to be with him. His two-year sojourn in Russia beginning in October 1944 marked the end of his active involvement in politics.

In the end, though, Sankrityayan returned to India two days after India gained its independence in August 1947, still in time to share in the exhilaration of the moment.[19] He no longer had it in him to engage actively in politics as he had before, nor did he wish to. He showed his dissatisfaction on disunity among left-wing politicians (Sankrityayan 1998b [*MJY-4*]: 228). The political situation had completely changed, and his health was no longer the best. However, he still had his pen, and he continued writing in an effort to sway people's minds in favour of communism and to advocate the use of Hindi as the national language. This indeed was the future he had mapped out for himself while still in Russia:

> हमारे सामने अब प्रश्न था–क्या यहाँ रहकर आराम का जीवन बिताएँ, या भारत लौटकर अपने साहित्यिक काम को जारी करें। पहिला रास्ता मुझे जीवन-मृत्यु जैसा मालूम होता था। ऐसी आराम की जिन्दगी लेकर क्या करना था, जब कि वास्तविक काम को मैं यहाँ रहकर ठीक तरह से कर नहीं सकता था।
>
> Now the question arose before me: should I lead a comfortable life here [in Russia] or should I return to India and continue my literary work. The first option seemed to me a living death. What was I to do with such a life of comfort when I would not be able to perform my real duty properly by remaining here. (Sankrityayan 1998b [*MJY-3*]: 182)

Sankrityayan's plan to devote himself to literature bore the hoped-for fruit. It was, he felt, his *jīvan-kartavya* (life's duty), one that overrode even *māyā-moh* (family attachments) (1998b [*MJY-3*] 192). He had been brought to the realization that he was not made for day-to-day politics (Sankrityayan 1998b [*MJY-2*]: 136). His field of action would no longer be party debates or demonstrations but pen being put to paper and seeing works that advocated communism into

19 'मुझे [...] नये भारत में लौट आने का बड़ा आनन्द हुआ।' [I was [...] extremely happy to be back in New India.] (Sankrityayan 1998b [*MJY-3*]: 221).

publication. His language of choice would be Hindi, which he felt to be the best and most effective vehicle of communication for India. His love for Hindi and his ideal of ek jātīyatā would result in his dismissal from the Communist Party, but he remained true to what he felt was his calling. The following pages will now proceed to consider Sankrityayan's 'Hindi nationalism'.

HINDI NATIONALISM

> राहुल जी ने राष्ट्रीयता की आत्मा के रूप में हिन्दी भाषा को ही स्वीकार किया था।
>
> It was Hindi that Rāhuljī had accepted as the soul of nationalism. (Śukl December 2006–November 2007: 194)

'Language was one of the essential concerns of the Indian reformers in the nineteenth century, a basic constituent of their discourse of progress and reform' (Orsini 2010: 18). The question of a national language (and in particular whether to crown Hindi in preference to Urdu) inevitably found its way onto the agenda of the Indian freedom movement.[20] Hindi became an important symbol of nationalism in India's Hindi-speaking belt during the 19th and the 20th centuries, and the move to establish it as a national language was a product of this early momentum it had acquired. Dayananda Saraswati was one of the more important figures to tout Hindi in the 19th century, calling it the Ārya *bhāṣā* (language of the Aryans). Indeed he was the first one to propagate the official use of Hindi at an organizational level. His Arya Samaj was also very active in promoting, from the end of the 19th century on, the use of the Nagari script. Hindi and Sanskrit were chosen as the languages best suited to furthering the movement's vision of a reformed Hindu society.[21]

[20] Urdu (or more generally, Hindustani), written in the Arabic–Persian script, had been the official language of British India since 1835, but Hindi replaced it in post-1947 India after partition. For more details, see Khan (2006: 13).

[21] As explained by Swami Shraddhanand, Dayananda searched for the reason for Mother India's *duḥkha* (misfortune) and found the answer in the rhetorical question of how a mother could be happy if her children followed

Sankrityayan defines the exceptional status he himself ascribes to Hindi in the following words:

> मैंने भोजन, वस्त्र एवं धर्म को कई बार बदला, किन्तु यदि मुझमें कोई वस्तु अपरिवर्तनशील है तो वह है राष्ट्र-भाषा के प्रति मेरी दृढ़ आस्था।
>
> I have changed my diet, attire, and religion any number of times, but if there is something unchangeable in me, it is the strong devotion to the national language. (Cited in U. Tivārī 1971: 215)

Sankrityayan's Hindi nationalism quite naturally took root in the Arya Samaj, and throughout the remainder of his life he passionately advocated Devanagari as the *rāṣṭra lipi* (national script)[22] and

---

different religions and spoke different languages at home. Dayananda proposed two remedies. The first was that there should be a single religion in the world, and that this could only be the *vaidik dharm* (Vedic religion). The second was that the *Ārya bhāṣā*, Hindi, should be the country's official language. The reason for this is that 'Vedic religion is based on Sanskrit. With this as its support, the *Ārya bhāsā* (Hindi) has been spreading among the public, and it is it that should become the official language of India. Then the oneness in conduct and way of life of all India's offspring will be achieved with ease.' [वैदिक धर्म की नींव देववाणी संस्कृत पर है। इसका आश्रय लेकर आर्यभाषा सर्वसाधारण में फैल रही है। वही सारे देश की भाषा होनी चाहिए। तब बडी (हिन्दी) सरलता से सारी 'भारत सन्तान' के आचार व्यवहार एक हो जावेंगे।] (Bhārtīya 1987a: 67). Shraddhanand further notes: 'The day Dayananda began to write his *Satyārthprakāś* in Hindi, leaving his mother tongue Gujrati behind, was the day on which the second instrument for the rescue of India was given concrete shape.' [अपनी मातृभाषा गुजराती पर आर्यभाषा को प्राथमिकता देकर जिस दिन ऋषि दयानन्द ने अपना ग्रन्थ 'सत्यार्थप्रकाश' इस भाषा में लिखना आरम्भ किया, वही दिन भारतवर्ष के उद्धार के द्वितीय साधन को मूर्त्तरूप में लाने का था।] (Bhārtīya 1987a: 69).

[22] Addressing a group who favoured the Roman script, while accepting Hindi as the national language, Sankrityayan said that the Roman script was not suitable because its twenty-six letters could not represent all the sounds of Hindi. Moreover, he believed that the Devanagari script was better suited than the Roman script to transliterating the world's languages (Sankrityayan 2004d: 30).

Describing the situation in India at that time, R.D. King (1998: 86) writes: 'Muslims would hate a Devanagari script, Hindus would hate a Perso-Arabic script; everybody would hate a Roman script.'

Hindi as the national language of India. Moreover, he suggested that the Devanagari script be used for Urdu (Sankrityayan 2004d: 31). Alok Rai (2007: 67), citing Krishna Kumar, notes that the initial impetus for founding the Nāgarī Pracāriṇī Sabhā (Society for the Promotion of the Nagari Script) apparently came from the Arya Samaj. In any case, the efforts of the Samaj on behalf of Hindi as the official language of instruction, publication, and government transactions was highly significant. Rai (2007: 67) goes on to note that even though the social reforms aimed at by the organization did not materialize, Hindi certainly did advance to the status of a (if not *the*) national language. Since extensive research has already been done on language issues in 19th- and 20th-century India (and particularly the active movement in support of Hindi),[23] I will focus now specifically on Sankrityayan's key opinions and arguments within this context.

Sankrityayan strongly advocated making Hindi the national language in conference speeches starting from 1932 (Śāstrī 1971: 84).[24] In 1947, Sankrityayan faced dismissal from the Communist Party of India following his speech at the 35th Akhil Bhārtiya Hindi Sāhitya Sammelan (All-India Hindi Literary Conference) in

[23] For comprehensive accounts of various aspects of the Hindi language issue in India, see: C. Shackle and R. Snell (1990); Paul Brass (1974); Amrit Rai (1991); Christopher R. King (1995); Robert D. King (1998); Vasudha Dalmia (1997); Alok Rai 2007); Francesca Orsini (2010); Abdul Jamil Khan (2006); and Tariq Rahman (2011).

[24] Some of the formal programmes before 1947 in which Sankrityayan spoke on behalf of this campaign were the Bihār Prāntīya Sāhitya Sammelan (Bihar Regional Literary Conference) in Ranchi (1932); Hindī Sāhitya Sammelan (Hindi Literary Conference) in Saran, Bihar (1932); Indian Oriental Conference in Badauda (1933); Hindī Sāhitya Goṣṭhī (Hindi Literary Meeting) in Rangoon (1935); Jilā Sāhitya Sammelan (District Literary Conference) in Munger, Bihar (1936); the 13th annual conference of the Baliā Hindi Pracāriṇī Sabhā's (Balia Hindi Promotion Union) (date unknown; Sankrityayan spoke as chairman of the conference), Akhil Bhārtīya Pragatiśīl Sammelan (All-India Progressive Conference) in Allahabad (1947; see Śāstrī 1971: 84–8); and Hindi Sahitya Sammelan (Hindi Literary Conference) in Banaras (1939).

Bombay on 27 December of that same year.[25] He refused a demand to recant and continued to call for the adoption of Hindi and the Devanagari script. Dr Ram Vilas Sharma (1912–2000), a renowned progressive literary critic, linguist, poet, and thinker, then suggested that the secretary of the Indian Communist Party, P.C. Joshi, strip Sankrityayan of his party membership, saying:

> हिंदी भाषी जनता की एकता की तरफ राहुल जी का दृष्टिकोण मुख्यत: विघटनकारी रहा है। इसका पहला कारण यह है कि वह हिंदू संस्कृति और मुस्लिम संस्कृति की धारणाओं से अपने को मुक्त न कर सके। हिंदी को वह हिंदुओं की भाषा और उर्दू को मुसलमानों की भाषा मानते रहे हैं। पाकिस्तान के सवाल पर उनका कहना था कि जिन प्रदेशों की भाषा में मुसलमानों का बहुमत है, अगर वे अलगाव की मांग करते हैं तो उसे हिन्दुओं को मान लेना चाहिए।
>
> Rahul-ji's opinion regarding the unity of Hindi-speaking people is on the whole destructive. The first reason is that he has not been able to free himself from the notions of Hindu culture and Muslim culture. He has always thought of Hindi as the language of Hindus and Urdu as that of Muslims. What he has said on the question of Pakistan is that if Muslims wish to secede in the states where they make up the majority of the population, Hindus should agree to this. (cited in Gautam December 2007–November 2008: 239)

[25] Sankrityayan made the following points during his speech at the conference (summarized from Sankrityayan 2004d: 24–56):

1. Hindi should be the only national language of India.
   A country should have only one official language. Switzerland's multi-linguistic solution is not suitable for India. Rather, the example afforded by Russia, where there are sixty-six spoken and written languages but only one official language, should be followed. In the case of India, Hindi is the best candidate for the official language, given that it is the most widely spoken, new Indo-Aryan language and the fact of Sanskrit's strong influence on the Dravidian (60 per cent of the vocabulary) as well as the Indo-Aryan languages.
3. Urdu and Hindi have developed from the same roots and have the same grammatical structure but they developed in two different directions into two distinct languages.
4. Hindi should be written in a very simple way that is easily understood by all.
5. Accepting English as an official language of India would be a sure sign that it is not yet independent.

Sankrityayan writes that he himself had written to party authorities about his pending dismissal in an effort to stave it off.[26] About his speech in Hindi in Bombay he writes:

> हिंदी-उर्दू के बारे में जो मत मैंने उसमें प्रकट किया था, और मुसलमानों को शताब्दियों की सांस्कृतिक बायकाट छोड़कर सांस्कृतिक एकता को स्थापित करने में आगे बढ़ने के लिए कहा था, उस पर मेरे साथियों को विरोध था। वह चाहते थे, मैं इस अंश को अपने भाषण में से निकाल दूँ।
>
> The opinion I expressed in that [speech] about Hindi–Urdu, and my request to Muslims to abandon their centuries-long cultural boycott and to create cultural unity, met with the opposition of my friends. They wanted me to remove this part from the speech. (Sankrityayan 1998b [*MJY-4*]: 252)

The Hindi–Urdu controversy that troubled 19th- and 20th-century India kept simmering because the difference between Hindi and Urdu was also viewed in religious terms. As we have seen, though, Sankrityayan's understanding of Hindu culture was not based on any religious concept (see section titled 'The Imagery of an "Indian Nation"' in Chapter 2 of this volume). He envisioned not only Muslims but the followers of every religion becoming Indianized. He mentions in his Bombay speech that 'none of the religions could bear fruit in new India without accepting Indianness completely'.[27] The activities of missionaries that led people to convert to Christianity in colonial

---

6. Hindi is suitable for every field: administrative, scientific, and so on.
7. Primary education should be provided in the mother tongue, and further education in Hindi together with additional foreign languages.
8. Devanagari is the only option for Hindi as a script.
9. Urdu and Hindi can be written in a similar Devanagari script:
   - 9.1 Persian script is not suitable for Hindi.
   - 9.2 The Devanagari script will ensure Urdu literature a larger readership, because many more people can read and write Devanagari than its current script.
10. Islam should become Indianized.

[26] Cf. the passage in *MJY-4* cited at the end of the section titled 'Hindi as the Symbol of Nationalism and English that of Slavery' in this chapter.

[27] '[...] नवीन भारत में कोई भी धर्म भारतीयता को पूर्णतया स्वीकार किए बिना फल-फूल नहीं सकता।' (Sankrityayan 2004d: 31).

India produced only a religious shift but not a cultural one, in his opinion. A people's ancestry, culture, and reputation left an indelible *saṃskār* (impression) upon their collective character.

> आइजक महाशय मेरे सामने एक आदर्श भारतीय का उदाहरण पेश कर रहे थे। धर्म बदलने से संस्कृति नहीं बदलती, अपने पूर्वजों के यश-अपयश की जिम्मेवारी से आदमी मुक्त नहीं हो जाता। आज भारतीय संस्कृति में डूबे कितने ही ईसाई मिलते हैं।
>
> Mr. Āijak represented an example of the Indian ideal for me. Culture cannot be changed by changing religions; a person cannot free himself from what was either the reputable or disreputable responsibility of his ancestors. Today we can find hosts of Christians [still] deeply embedded in the Indian culture. (Sankrityayan 1957b: 104–5)[28]

Indianness for Sankrityayan was not a religion but something beyond it, namely culture. In his opinion, Islam and Christianity were adopted religions, not products of the Indian soil. Adopting them or another foreign religion did not mean abandoning Indianness. Both Islam and Christianity could be adapted to the Indian context, and any true Indian Muslim or Christian would still retain respect for India and its culture. He saw Indianness as comprising Indian civilization, history, sentiments, food, and dress (Sankrityayan 2004d: 31–2). What his idea of Indianness was in the case of dress,[29] for instance, comes out in the following quote:

> महमूद दूध पीते समय अँग्रेजी बोलने वाली आया की गोद में पले। फिर नैनीताल के एक यूरोपियन स्कूल में पढ़े। अन्त में वर्षों के लिए वह पढ़ने के वास्ते इंगलैंड भेज दिये गये। इस प्रकार अँग्रेजी उनकी मातृभाषा हो गई थी, पर वह अँग्रेज कभी नहीं बने। वह पक्के हिन्दुस्तानी और केवल हिन्दुस्तानी थे। आक्सफोर्ड की डिग्री लेकर देश की सेवा करने का संकल्प करके वह बम्बई उतरे। वहीं उन्होंने विलायती पोशाक उतारी और खद्दर का कुर्ता-धोती पहन लिया। इसी पोशाक में जब वह अपने घर में पहुँचे, तो बेगमों में कुहराम मच गया। [...] धोती-कुर्ता हिन्दुओं की पोशाक थी। [...]

[28] Semuel Aijak was an Indian whose father, a Brahmin, had converted to Christianity.

[29] Sankrityayan was not happy with Nehru's preference for *servānī* as the national dress, because it was Asian-European, having been adopted by Muslims who believed it to be Turkish (1998b [*MJY-3*]: 116). In *Bāisvī̃ sadī* he again identifies the dhoti as the national dress.

> धोती-कुर्ते से बढकर राष्ट्रीयता पोशाक एक भारतीय की क्या हो सकती है? इस घटना से मालूम होगा कि महमूद भारतीय रंग से कितने रंगे हुए थे।
>
> Mahmud[30] grew up suckling on the lap of an English-speaking nanny. Then he studied at a European school in Nainital. In the end he was sent to England for years of study. Thus English had become his mother tongue, but he never became English. He was a pukka Indian and only an Indian. He arrived in Bombay with a degree from Oxford aiming to serve the nation. He gave up British dress and wore a khaddar kurta and dhoti. This caused a furore among the ladies of the family when he reached home [...]. Dhotis and kurtas were the attire of Hindus. [...] What else could the national dress for an Indian be other than dhoti and kurta? This incident doubtless shows how deeply dyed Mahmud was with Indian dye. (Sankrityayan 1957b: 235)

Sankrityayan the Hindi nationalist regarded Hindi as a badge of bhārtiyatā (Indianness), but one without any religious overtones to it. Like every Hindi nationalist of his time, he saw it more particularly as a replacement for the badge of slavery that people wore whenever they spoke English—a perspective that will be discussed in the following section.

HINDI AS THE SYMBOL OF NATIONALISM AND ENGLISH AS THAT OF SLAVERY

> अंग्रेज़ हमारी उग्र राष्ट्रीयता का प्रतीक समझ उसे (हिंदी को) फूटी आँखों देखना नहीं चाहते थे।
>
> The British with their poor eyesight never liked seeing Hindi [being used], because for them it was a symbol of our extreme nationalism. (Sankrityayan 2004d: 57)

Hindu revivalist leaders and Hindu politicians demanded that any social and economic progress should be accompanied by a return to cultural roots, and among other things this meant that Hindi and the Devanagari script should become the medium of instruction in public schools and the working language of courts and government offices. For Sankrityayan, no religion (Hinduism or any other) merited being

30 Full name: Mahmudujjafar, Sankrityayan's friend and freedom fighter.

the showcase of national pride; only to Indian culture as a whole did this honour fall. And language for Sankrityayan was the very essence of culture:

अपनी भाषा के साथ जिस व्यक्ति का प्रेम नहीं, वह संस्कृति विहीन है। भाषा केवल शौक की चीज नहीं, वह एक बड़ी शक्ति है।

He who does not love his language is *saṃskṛti-vihīn* [uncultured]. Language is not only something [one approaches] as a *śauk* [hobby]; it is a great source of power. (Sankrityayan 1998b [*MJY-5*]: 262)

In the first half of the 20th century, the English language had come to be associated with the shackles of colonialism. By very reason of its prominence and status as the established language in India during that time, it was unacceptable to Indian nationalists that any official role should be assigned to it in an independent India.

The language issue was not settled with India's independence in 1947. A single national language of India had not yet been confirmed, and English was still one of the country's official languages. Before 1947 English was the language of those from whom Indians had been trying all along to gain independence, and after 1947 it was the language of those from whom they had just achieved independence. Sankrityayan's efforts to make Hindi the sole national language of India were more energetic after independence, since, as he believed, continuing to use English as the national language would, in contrast to Hindi, leave an indelible mark of enslavement that would frustrate attempts to achieve Indian unity:

[...] हमारे संघ की राष्ट्र स्वदेशी होनी चाहिए या विदेशी, यानि अंग्रेज़ी होनी चाहिए या भारतीय?

आश्चर्य करने की बात नहीं है कि यदि अब भी कुछ दिमाग यह सोचने का कष्ट नहीं उठाते और अब भी अंग्रेज़ी को राष्ट्रभाषा बनाए रखने का आग्रह करते हैं। यह भी दासता के अभिशाप का अवशेष है।

[...] should the national language of our federation be native or foreign? That is, should it be English or Indian?

It is not surprising that there are still some brains that do not bother to think about this question and still urge that English be retained as the national language. This is a relic of slavery's curse. (Sankrityayan 2004d: 25–6)

It offended Sankrityayan's nationalist sentiment to see the continuing hold of the English language upon India's elite after independence:

अंग्रेज़ गए लेकिन वह अपने धर्म पुत्रों को देश में छोड़ गए हैं, जो इस बात को सहन नहीं कर सकते, कि अंग्रेज़ी अपने स्थान से जरा भी च्युत हो।

The English have gone but they have left back in the country their godsons, who cannot bear the thought that English should lose its status. (Sankrityayan 2004d: 62)

Sankrityayan was not only against the language but also the left-hand traffic system of the British, when right-hand traffic was the world norm. This was something he also desired to change after independence. He wrote:

इंग्लैंड और इंग्लैण्ड के साम्राज्य को छोड़कर सारी दुनिया में लोग सड़कों और रास्तों पर दाहिने चलते हैं, लेकिन अंग्रेज बाएँ चलो की बात को मानते हैं। जिस वक्त भारत गणराज्य घोषित होने जा रहा था, उसके एक ही दो दिन पहले मैंने नवनिर्वाचित राष्ट्रपति से कहा, कि अंग्रेजों के रख छोड़े कम-से-कम इस बड़े कलंक को तो दूर कर दीजिए और 26 जनवरी (1950) को गणराज्य घोषणा के साथ-साथ यह भी घोषित कर दीजिए-आज से हमारे यहाँ चलना दाहिनी ओर होगा। [...] फिर भारत क्यों अंग्रेजों के पीछी [*sic*] वाममार्गी बना रहे।

Apart from England and its colonies, all other countries in the world observe right-hand traffic; yet the English believe in left-hand traffic. Two days before India was to be declared a federation, I called on the newly-elected president to at least remove the blot the English have left us and to announce on 26 January [1950], together with the declaration of the federation, that from that day on driving would be on the right-hand side. [...] why should India remain on the left side of the road, in tow to the English? (Sankrityayan 1998b [*MJY-3*]: 91)

The British Raj had been a bitter experience for Sankrityayan, in reaction to which he had developed both his nationalist sentiments (in the Arya Samaj) and then, gradually, his communist loyalties. On his last journey to Tibet in 1938, he met an old Finnish woman who told him of the Russian invasion of Finland and her happiness after its independence. Sankrityayan responded to her:

> हम हिंन्दुस्तानी उसे अच्छी तरह समझ सकते हैं, क्योंकि गुलामी कितनी कड़वी होती है, इसे हम जानते हैं।
>
> We Indians can well understand this, because we know how bitter slavery is. (Sankrityayan 1998b [*MJY-2*]: 302)

Neither Urdu nor Hindustani

Sankrityayan held that Hindustani was a second, more recent name for Urdu. The reason for the distinction between Hindi and Urdu in Sankrityayan's opinion was the divide-and-rule policy of rulers in the past, which could be corrected by using Devanagari as the common script:

> उर्दू के लिए अच्छा यही है कि वह अरबी अक्षरों का मोह छोड़कर नागरी को अपना ले, ताकि अधिक-से-अधिक लोग उसे पढ़ सकें। पुराने समय में शासकों की सांस्कृतिक पृथक्करण की नीति ने उर्दू (अरबी-फ़ारसी-मिश्रित हिन्दी) को जन्म दिया। आज पृथक्करण नहीं, सांस्कृतिक समन्वय हमारे देश और दूसरे देशों में भी ध्येय माना जाता है, नागरी लिपि को अपनाकर हम उसमें एक कदम आगे बढ़ते हैं।
>
> It would be well for Urdu to abandon its fondness for Arabic letters and to adopt Devanagari, so that more and more people could read it. The strategy of cultural division practised by rulers in the past created Urdu (Hindi mixed with Arabic and Persian [vocabulary]). Today the major goal is not separation but *cultural unity* [emphasis added] in our country, and in other countries too; by accepting the Nagari script we can move one step ahead. (Sankrityayan 2004d: 11)

Sankrityayan had always been against Hindu and Muslim sectarianism, wishing for unity rather than friction between the two communities. He was saddened, in particular, by the lack of intermarriage between Hindus and Muslims[31] and saw the same challenge

[31] An interesting incident in Sankrityayan's life is worth mentioning. In December 1951 a friend of Sankrityayan's, one Mr Chauhan, visited him with a young Muslim friend, to whom Sankrityayan gifted a copy of the Urdu translation of his most popular book, *Volgā se Gaṅgā*. The following year

facing the language barrier. The sentence 'उर्दू भाषा और लिपि के लिए वहाँ कोई स्थान नहीं है।' [There is no place for the Urdu language and its script there] (Sankrityayan 2004d: 31) in his Bombay speech contained words that the Communist Party found intolerable. Yet one can argue that this sentence was not intended as an insult to the speakers of Urdu as a language of Muslims but rather to point out that it could not serve as a vehicle for the unifying concept of Indianness. His argument was based on the premise that Urdu speakers had, up to then, not been willing to accept Indian culture. Sankrityayan knew that many, if not most, Indian languages contained a large stock of Sanskrit words, in either a genetically modified or directly borrowed form, which would make Hindi, the most widely spoken of them, easily acquirable as a national language. Urdu, whose grammar is basically the same as Hindi's, had developed in a direction of its own by enriching its vocabulary with Arabic and Persian loan words, and it was this that stood in the way of accepting it on the same level as Hindi (Sankrityayan 2004d: 10).[32] His solution was to make Urdu a state language, if needed. However, if

---

Sankrityayan found out that the recipient had been so angered when reading the story 'Suraiya', about the marriage of a Muslim girl with a Hindu man, that he had torn the book into pieces. Sankrityayan maintains in his autobiography that he had not written the story to insult Muslims. The long tradition of Muslim men marrying Hindu women was only half the solution, which would only come about when marriage was also possible between Hindu men and Muslim women. Muslims, he felt, should grant freedom of religion to their spouses, as the emperor Akbar had to his wife.

[32] Criticizing Sankrityayan's 1947 speech, Sardar Jafri wrote in his essay 'On the Formation of the Hindustani Nation and the Problem of Its National Language':

> In December 1947, the annual session of [the] Hindi Sahitya Sammelan was held with Mahapandit Rahul as its president. The Tandon leadership had been discredited in the eyes of democratic Hindi writers. The big bourgeoisie and the feudalists needed someone with 'progressive' views to put across their communal poison[.] They found a ready servant in Rahul for this. He said things in the Sammelan which no communist had dared utter even on the Sammelan platform. His communist frenzy did not abate but increased as time passed. In 1950, his book *Aj ki Rajniti* was published where he made his dramatic characters talk about teaching a lesson to Pakistan through war. In his own person, he put forth the most virulent communal propaganda

Urdu were made the official language of a state the majority of whose population did not accept it as their language, this would be unfair:

> उर्दू भाषा-भाषियों को उर्दू के माध्यम से शिक्षा प्राप्त करने का अधिकार होना चाहिए, और यदि कोई छोटा-से-छोटा भी क्षेत्र ऐसा मिले, जहाँ के अधिकांश लोगों की भाषा उर्दू है, वहाँ उर्दू को राज्य भाषा-बनाया जाना चाहिए। लेकिन हिन्दी-क्षेत्र के ऊपर परिगणित भाषाओं के प्रदेश में ऐसा कोई क्षेत्र नहीं है, जहाँ के बहुसंख्यक लोग अपनी भाषा उर्दू मानते है, इसलिए उर्दू को राज्य-भाषा बनाने का प्रयत्न बहुसंख्यक जनता की इच्छा के विरुद्ध होगा।
>
> Urdu speakers should have the right to receive an education in Urdu, and if there is any small area in which the majority of people speak Urdu, it should be made a state language. But there is no place in which the majority of the population speaks Urdu in the region in which scheduled languages overlie Hindi-speaking areas, [so that] making Urdu the state language would be against the wish of the majority population. (Sankrityayan 2004d: 11)

The Congress party also aimed to propagate Hindustani (in the sense of the form of Hindi spoken around Delhi, which contains many Urdu words). Guru Lal (1944: 25) names two factors decisive in popularizing Hindustani all over India: firstly, the Indian National Congress's decision to use Hindustani in meetings and speeches, and making

---

> ever known in India—all in the name of the language question! 'Was it Urdu after all?' he thundered; 'Is it not the Indian pillar of victory of the Arab *jehadis*? Was not filling the language with Arabic words in place of national vocabulary the so wing of the seeds of *durrastriyate* [*sic*] (approximately something anti-national)? We accept that this was nothing new for them in Bharat. Whatever Islam might have said, the Mussalmans have refused to be a part of the country's stream of life.... It would be beneficial to nationalize Islam. If the outlook of Maulana Azad persists in Indian Muslims, their loyalty and sympathy will always remain with Pakistan in comparison to Bharat. This feeling will end by turning Indian Muslims into hidden fifth-columnists...."'
>
> It cannot be denied that such propaganda did succeed in misleading a good many writers in Hindi. With the aid of such propagandists the Congress governments, particularly in UP, were able to present their policy of suppressing Urdu as a policy of upholding national culture. (Jafri, quoted in Pradhan 1985: 187–8)

Hindustani compulsory in schools as one of its first acts after forming the ministries in 1937. The second factor was Hindi cinema, a popular form of entertainment, which in fact used Hindustani to make films more widely understandable. Sankrityayan expresses his dissatisfaction regarding Hindustani in a diary entry written in 1955 in Bombay:

> आजकल बम्बई प्रदेश की सरकार ने हिन्दी के सम्बन्ध में एक नया गुल खिलाया है। पहिले हिन्दुस्तानी के नाम से हिन्दी के मुकाबले में उर्दू को खड़ा किया जाता था। उसमें सफलता नहीं हुई तो अब हिन्दुस्तानी को दरवाजे से नहीं तो खिड़की से लाना चाहते हैं। यहाँ के कुछ लोगों की खोपड़ी में समाया था कि संघ की भाषा के तौर पर जो हिन्दी स्वीकृत की गई है, वह वह हिन्दी नहीं है, जिसका व्यवहार हिन्दी प्रान्त वाले करते हैं। अर्थात् इस प्रकार नई हिन्दी गढ़ने का मौका मिल जाये, और हिन्दुस्तानी को लाकर सिंहासन पर बैठा दिया जाए। हिन्दी का रास्ता अब भी साफ नहीं है, यह तो इन लोगों की चालों से मालूम ही हो रहा है, लेकिन दुनिया में कहीं भी फरमाइश पर भाषा नहीं गढ़ी गई, बल्कि सिद्ध समामनाय (प्रयोग में आता व्यवहार) है, उसी को लोग मानते हैं।
>
> The Bombay government is now muddying the waters anew concerning Hindi. In the beginning they supported Urdu under the name Hindustani against Hindi. They did not succeed in this, and having been unable to bring Hindustani in through the door, they now wish to bring it in through the window. It has dawned on some people here that the Hindi which has been accepted as the language of the federation is not the Hindi current in the Hindi[-speaking] states. The idea thereby is to concoct a new [form of] Hindi and set Hindustani on the throne. The road ahead for Hindi is not yet clear, which is obvious from these people's ploys. However, nowhere in the world are languages made to order. Rather, people accept what has been proven by custom (practices that are in use). (Sankrityayan 1998b [*MJY*-5]: 198)

There is a passage of dialogue in *Bhāgo nahī̃ (duniyā ko) badlo* (Do not run away; change the world) that suggests that Hindi and Urdu cannot be brought back together, because they have grown so far apart despite going back to the same root:

> सोहनलाल: तो भैया तुम हिन्दी-उर्दू को मिला के एक भाषा नहीं करना चाहते?
>
> भैया: मिलाना हमारे बस की बात नहीं है, [...] हिन्दी-उर्दू बनाने में सैकड़ों बरस न जाने कितनी पीढ़ियों ने काम किया है। मैं जानता हूँ कि हिन्दी और उर्दू भाषा मूल में

एक ही भाषा हैं। 'का, में, पर, से, इस, उस, जिस, तिस, ना, ता, आ, गा,' दोनों ही में एक से हैं, खाली झगड़ा है उधार लिए सबदों का। हिन्दी ने संसकीरत से सबदों को उधार लिया है और उर्दू ने अरबी और कुछ-कुछ फारसी से भी; लेकिन दोनों ने इतना अधिक उधार लिया है, कि अकबाल की कविता समझने वाला सुमित्रानन्दन पंत की कविता को बिल्कुल नहीं समझ सकता और सुमित्रानन्दन पन्त की कविता जानने वाले अकबाल को बिल्कुल नहीं समझ सकता।

Sohanlal: So brother, why don't you want to merge Urdu and Hindi together and make them one language?

Bhaiya: Merging them is not something in our power to do. [...] Hundreds of years and countless generations have worked to create Hindi and Urdu. I know that Hindi and Urdu are basically one language. [The basic functional forms] *kā, mẽ, par, se, is, us, jis, tis, nā, tā, ā, gā,* are common to both. The quarrel is only about loan words: Hindi has borrowed words from Sanskrit; Urdu, from Arabic and also some from Persian. But both have borrowed so much that a person who understands a poem by Akbal cannot at all understand a poem by Sumitranandan Pant, and one who understands a poem by Sumitranandan Pant cannot at all understand Akbal. (Sankrityayan 2004a: 225)

Still, Sankrityayan was constantly at pains to make it clear that he was not against Urdu per se:

किसी ने झूठ ही कहा है, कि मैं उर्दू का विरोधी हूँ। मैं हिन्दी-उर्दू दोनों को एक ही भाषा मानता हूँ और दोनों की शैली में लिखे साहित्य को चिरस्थायी देखना चाहता हूँ।

Someone has spoken the untruth that I am against Urdu. I believe that Hindi and Urdu are one language and I wish a long life for the literature written in the style of both. (Sankrityayan 1957b: 236)

It is clear from the above citations that Sankrityayan's reason for wanting to make Hindi the national language was simply that it was the language of the people. Failing to see the difference between Urdu and Hindustani, he was unwilling to accord any special status to the latter beyond the regional language that he took Urdu to be. Sankrityayan had studied and felt great devotion for Sanskrit, and had promised many times in his student life to speak only in it. Yet he was consistently against the idea of making Sanskrit the national language,[33] again because it was not the language of the people. He further wrote regarding the language issue that was discussed during the Hindi Sahitya Sammelan (Hindi Literary Conference) organized in Varanasi in 1939:

> हिन्दी-हिन्दुस्तानी का झगड़ा खड़ा था। लोग हिन्दुस्तानी का विरोध कर रहे थे, मैं भी विरोधी था, लेकिन हिन्दू संस्कृति और हिन्दू नाम के धर्म पर नहीं, बल्कि दो विस्तृत और सुविकसित साहित्यों को एक नकली भाषा के द्वारा एक करने का प्रयत्न मुझे बिल्कुल लड़कपन मालूम होता था।
>
> There was a conflict between Hindi and Hindustani. People were against Hindustani; I, too, was opposed to it, but not in the name of Hindu culture or Hindu religion. Rather, I felt the attempt to merge two vast and fully developed literatures into one through a bogus language childish. (Sankrityayan 1998b [*MJY-2*]: 330)

The Indianness of Hindi in Sankrityayan's opinion was based on the fact that it was the language most widely understood in India, being closely related to most of the other major languages in northern India. While not related to the Dravidian languages in the south, it was, given the strong Sanskrit influence on them, not a foreign language to the same extent that English was, and indeed it was understood by many of their speakers. Thus Hindi would not be entirely unfamiliar to southerners, for they too shared 'our literature and culture' (*hamāre sāhitya aur saṃskṛti*):

> सारे देश की सम्मिलित भाषा होने और हमारे साहित्य और संस्कृति के वाहन बनने के कारण हिन्दी हमारी प्रेमास्पद है।
>
> Hindi, being a common language and vehicle of our literature and culture, is an object of our love. (Sankrityayan 1998b [*MJY-5*]: 189)

Sankrityayan conducted historical research into Hindi as a language, collecting folktales and folksongs, publishing them under the title *Ādi Hindī kī kahāniyā̃ aur gītẽ* (Stories and songs in old

[33] One member of Parliament, Pan. Lakshmikant Maitra, suggested making Sanskrit the national language and wished to relegate Hindi to the status of a state language.

Hindi, 1950),[34] and editing a large volume, the *Comprehensive History of Hindi Literature*[35] (sponsored by the Hindi Sahitya Sammelan, Allahabad). He also went back to the earlier languages out of which Hindi emerged, compiling Saraha's songs of realization from around the 8th century into *Sarahapā dohā koś* (Sarahapa's collected dohas, 1957) from material acquired in Tibet and bringing out *Hindī kāvya dhārā* (A collection of Hindi poetry, 1945), containing material dating from between AD 760 and 1300 that illustrates the modification the proto-language was undergoing during that period. In *Dakkhinī Hindī kāvya dhārā* (A collection of Dakkhini Hindi poetry, 1950), Sankrityayan discusses the contribution of Dakkhini[36] to the development of Hindi literature.

To conclude, there was widespread support for the idea of a single national language during the independence movement (Rai 2007: 106), and after independence was won Hindi speakers continued to push for it to become the only national language, within a given timeframe of fifteen years. Their efforts came to nought when English was finally recognized as an 'associate additional official language'.

Sankrityayan was a polyglot. Machwe has counted thirty-three languages that Sankrityayan knew (1978: 9). But among these many languages, including his mother tongue, Bhojpuri, he accepted only Hindi as his *apnī bhāṣā* (own language) (Sankrityayan 1998b [*MJY-4*]: 248). After he lost his memory, the only language he spoke and understood was Hindi. When he went to Russia for treatment in 1962,

[34] 'He believed that the language spoken in Meerut and Agra was the original mother of modern Khari Boli Hindi (that is, the vernacular form underlying the standard literary form of Hindi); he called it Kauravi. These folksongs and folktales have Haryan and Braj influences and contain a lot of Urdu-isms too' (Machwe 1978: 35).

[35] This work is entirely devoted to what Machwe (1978: 36) calls sub-languages (*upbhāṣā*) of Hindi (such as Braj, Avadhi, Bundelkhandi, Rajasthani, and Malvi).

[36] The common language spoken in the Deccan plateau. Closely related to Urdu, it developed as an independent language during a large migration of Muslims southward in the 15th century. The forms Dakhani, Dekani, Dakhini, and Deccani are used interchangeably.

his son, Igor Rahulovich Sankrityayan, and wife, Ellena Narvertovna Kozerovskaya, tried to speak to him in Russian, but he showed no signs of understanding. Yet Sankrityayan's pro-Hindi activities had already had repercussions for his family. They were the reason for all contact ceasing between Sankrityayan and his Russian wife after 1948, following his expulsion from the Communist Party. His wife, the secretary of the Indo-Tibetan department at Leningrad University, was fired from her job for refusing to divorce her non-communist Indian husband after he was expelled from the Communist Party of India.[37] Still, Sankrityayan's determination to fight for the cause was undimmed:

> नागरी लिपि में लिखी संस्कृतनिष्ठ हिन्दी ही भारत संघ की एक मात्र भाषा हो सकती है और होकर रहेगी।
>
> Sanskritic Hindi written in Nagari script can alone become the national language of India, and of this there is no doubt. (Sankrityayan, cited in Sankrityayan and Anand 1982: 31)

On the very day of his speech at the Akhil Bhārtīya Hindi Sāhitya Sammelan, Sankrityayan wrote to Communist Party authorities to tender his resignation from the party, since he could not support its language policy. This was a watershed moment in his life and, from then on, all his effort went into Hindi nationalism. He writes:

> पार्टी की इस नीति के साथ न होने के कारण मैं अपने को पार्टी में रहने लायक नहीं समझता, पर मैं सदा पार्टी के साथ रहूँगा। एक तरह से इतने बड़े निर्णय को मैंने उतावलेपन से किया। लेकिन, अब उस निर्णय को बदलने में वर्षों की जरूरत थी। उस समय मैं समझता था, पार्टी वाले राष्ट्रीयता के बारे में हल्के दिल से सोचते हैं, और मतवाद की संकीर्णता को प्रश्रय देते, दूर भविष्य में होने वाले प्रभावों को नहीं समझ पाते। पर ऐसा समझने में यदि त्रुटियाँ थीं, तो वह एक नहीं, बहुत-से मस्तिष्कों के सोचने के परिणाम थीं। यदि गलती हो रही थी, तो पार्टी अपने तौर से उसे आगे सुधार लेगी।
>
> As I do not go along with this [language] policy of the party, I do not feel it suitable for me to remain in the party, even if I will always be

37 This information is based on an article by Igor Rahulovich Sankrityayan (December 2006–November 2007: 301).

> with it. In a way I have taken such a momentous decision in haste. But many years were needed to change my mind. In my opinion, party members were not serious on the matter of nationalism; they support a narrowness of ideology and are not able to understand its impact on the future. But if there were mistakes in their thinking, it was the result of the thinking of not only one but of many brains. If an error occurred, the party will correct it in its own way in the future. (Sankrityayan 1998b [*MJY-4*]: 253)

Sankrityayan's major contribution to Hindi lay in his numerous printed books in the language. The following section will focus on what the printed word and service to Hindi meant to him.

PRINT: PROGRESS, PLEASURE, PROFIT, AND PROPAGATION

Sankrityayan mainly used the space offered by print to reach out to the public masses and share his ideas with them. In his opinion, print was the medium best suited to his own ends. For someone as articulate as he was, making writing his main occupation in life was an obvious choice. Print was not only a means of propagating ideas for him; it was a source of income and pleasure as well. The main importance of the printed word, though, and particularly of literature, was to serve as an agent of progress and as a generator of national pride. The following pages will review Sankrityayan's opinions of the print world in terms of progress, pleasure, pecuniary benefits, and propagation. Why did Sankrityayan write? More particularly, what did the printed word in Hindi mean to him?

Print and Progress: *Sāhitya-sevīs* and Their Dāyitva

The traditional Hindu concept of communal life lays great stress on the notion of 'service' (*sevā*). Any kind of work may be defined as *sevā*, which can be more accurately translated as 'selfless service'. This concept continued to be popular among Indians in the 20th century, when the country was in conflict with its colonial rulers. Any contribution to the welfare of society and its people was then termed *deś-sevā* (service to the country) or *mātṛbhūmi kī sevā* (service to the motherland). Literary activity, including the reading and propagating of Hindi, was regarded as one form of deś-sevā.[38] The progress of one's language was understood as a source of all further forms of progress.[39] Sankrityayan, a self-proclaimed *sāhitya-sevī* (servant of literature), took up writing as a solemn duty, one that would only be fulfilled if he could create literary works capable of reviving India's reputation in the eyes of the world. In Sankrityayan's opinion, creating such literature was a *parīkṣā* (test) every writer faced:

> हमारे साहित्य सेवियों को अपने दायित्व को अच्छी तरह समझना चाहिए और ऐसे साहित्य का निर्माण करना चाहिए जो भारत के दूसरे प्रदेशों तथा विश्व में हमारे मस्तिष्क को ऊँचा रख सके। हमें विश्वास है कि हम इस परीक्षा में उत्तीर्ण होंगे।
>
> *Sāhitya sevī*s need to understand their duty well and create a literature that lets us [that is, speakers of Hindi] hold our heads high in other states of India and in the world. I believe that we will pass this test. (Sankrityayan 2004d: 15)

Already in the 19th century, Hindi journalism had been playing an important role in initiating discussion of matters relating to social and cultural reform, colonialism, and agenda in support of Indian patriotism. Journals or newspapers were seen as powerful tools for increasing public awareness. The publication, starting in 1826, of *Udant Mārtaṇḍ* (Harvest sun) as a weekly Hindi newspaper based in Calcutta first provided Hindi speakers with an effective forum for public communication. Although it was not the first newspaper published in India, it was considered to be the first published *hindustāniyõ ke hit hetu* (for the sake of Hindi speakers' welfare).[40] By the beginning of the 20th century Hindi journalism had reached a point where it could be said to be flourishing, and almost every Hindi literary writer was affiliated to one or another of the newspapers.

[38] Orsini (2010) discusses the concept of sevā as it relates to Hindi literature.

[39] This is a key point made by Bhāratendu Hariścandra in a speech he gave in Balia in 1884; see Dalmia (1997: 21–7) and Orsini (2010: 18–19). More generally, see also Pāṭhak (2005) for a study of the Hindi renaissance before 1947.

[40] An article by the editor of the newspaper, Pundit Jugal Kishor, expresses the purpose of the weekly in precisely these terms. The quote from this article is taken from Pāṭhak (2005: 164).

It is no exaggeration to say that Hindi newspapers played a vital role in creating Hindi literary writers in the first place. All print media were thus engaged in collaboratively widening the public platform for the speakers of Hindi in India.[41]

Sankrityayan's own introduction to the Russian Revolution and the ideals of deś-sevā and sāhitya-sevā came about by way of newspapers. He started reading newspapers in 1915, and his first Hindi article appeared that same year in *Bhāskar* (published from Meerut), and was directed against bogus sadhus.[42] The main newspapers he read during this period were *Āryagajaṭ, Prakāś, Hindustān, Deś, Saddharmpracārak, Satyavādī* (Sankrityayan 1998b [*MJY-1*]: 176), *Pratāp, Buleṭin, Pais Akhbār, Milāp,* the *Tribune* (in English), the *Leader* (in English) (Sankrityayan 1998b [*MJY-1*]: 188), and Gandhi's *Navjivan*. Apart from these, he was also a regular reader of the well-known Hindi journal *Sarasvatī*. By the 20th century, Hindi periodicals had become divided between the political and literary categories. Although *Sarasvatī* is considered a mixture of both, the other periodicals read by Sankrityayan were mainly political.

After Sankrityayan's writing career began in 1915, it took him eight years to get his first book, *Bāisvī̃ sadī*, published. His writing in Hindi in the beginning was not centred on the ideal of sevā, but rather on presenting the wide range of his early interests to the general public in an understandable language. That his main concern was simply to get his ideas across is reflected in the fact that his first book had been begun in Sanskrit and later changed to Hindi (see section titled '*Bāisvī̃ sadī*: An Imagined Community' in Chapter 2). After writing *Bāisvī̃ sadī*, he translated a number of English novels into Hindi. These were obviously not motivated by any sense of Hindi nationalism, but rather undertaken 'in order to pass the time' (*samaya kātne ke lie*) while in jail (Sankrityayan 1998b [*MJY-1*]: 281).

His affiliation to the Arya Samaj and his reading of newspapers were the two main breeding grounds of Sankrityayan's political consciousness. The present study suggests that Sankrityayan first became

[41] For detailed information on the Hindi public sphere, see Orsini (2010).

[42] A. Bhaṭṭācārya (2005: 212) states that the title of this article is unknown but that the article itself was about the so-called 'sadhus'. Sankrityayan (1998b [*MJY-1*]: 177) relates how happy he was to see his first article published over two issues of *Bhāskar*.

attuned to deś-sevā in the Arya Samaj as a universal ideal, and later he settled upon sāhitya-sevā as his own personal means of serving that larger ideal. This is indeed the track that his life history follows: in the earlier days and up until 1944 his political activities, including his journeys to Tibet, Russia, and other places in search of material to highlight India's past, were carried out on an equal footing with his parallel contributions to Hindi literature, but after 1947, when he returned from Russia, he began devoting himself fully to the latter. In March 1951 he wrote concerning the post-1947 years:

> हिन्दी का लेखक ठहरा, और उसी के लिए एक तरह से अपना समय दे रहा था।
>
> I was established as a Hindi writer, and in a way I was devoting all my time to it. (Sankrityayan 1998b [*MJY*-5]: 48)

Because the struggle for Hindi did not end with the gaining of independence in 1947, the challenges of sāhitya-sevīs were not yet over, and indeed were only now beginning in earnest. Sankrityayan's main contributions to resolving the language question were thus products of his own carefully crafted products of language, no matter whether they appeared in the press or in bound form. He counted upon the wide circulation of ideas to bring about any country's development and foster its sense of national awareness. In the context of Nepal, for instance, he blamed the 'limited circulation of newspapers' (*akhabārharūko kam pracār*) as one reason for that country's backwardness.[43]

Print and Pleasure

A list of Sankrityayan's writings provided by Mācve (2005: 57–63) shows that his literary output in Hindi between 1923 and 1940 is less than that after 1940. Still, it was astonishingly large. Besides numerous newspaper articles, *Bāisvī̃ sadī*, an introductory book on Islam (*Islām dharm kī rūprekhā*), and four novels translated from English

43 'यहाँ अखबारहरूको कम प्रचार छ। साधारण दुनियाँ आँखा अगाडि कुनै कामलाई नदेखी शासन सुधारमा पत्यार गर्दैन।' [Newspapers do not circulate much here. Common people do not believe in administrative improvement if they do not witness it firsthand.] From a speech of Sankrityayan's as reported in the *Gorkhapatra*, 12 January 1953, p. 1.

into Hindi, he wrote eight travelogues[44] and a number of political (communist) works. During this time he was also engaged in translating and editing many Buddhist texts. How was it possible for him to be so prolific given his tireless political activities and travels? The answer can only be that one will find time to devote to what gives one the most pleasure. Sankrityayan always found time for writing, which, along with travelling, was his favourite occupation, and concerning which matters he never listened to others' advice:

> पुस्तकों को लिखने में मुझे जितना आनंद आता है, उससे कही अधिक आनंद उनके प्रूफ देखने में आता है। पुस्तकों का लिखना मानों उनका गर्भ में आना है, और प्रकाशित होना जन्म लेना। आदमी इससे अपने परिश्रम को समझता है।
>
> The pleasure I get in proofreading [my books] is somewhat greater than what I get in writing books. Writing books is like conceiving, while publishing is to give birth. One can appreciate one's labours from this [result]. (Sankrityayan 1998b [*MJY-5*]: 84)

Sankrityayan's inspiration found expression in almost every literary prose genre, be it autobiography, biography, newspaper articles, short stories, novels, plays, memoirs, travelogues, or translations, yet he wrote virtually no poetry in Hindi.[45] Concerning this dearth of verse he writes:

> कविता-सुन्दरी को मेरी सेवाएँ पसन्द नहीं है। एक समझदार आदमी की तरह मैंने फिर उस रास्ते में पैर बढ़ाने का ख्याल नहीं किया।
>
> Lovely Lady Poetry does not like my services. Being a sensible man, I for my part gave up all thought of striking out on that path. (Sankrityayan 1998b [*MJY-2*]: 257)

44 *Merī Laddākh yātrā* (My journey to Ladakh; 1926), *Laṅkā* (Sri Lanka; 1926–7), *Merī Yūrop yātrā* (My journey to Europe; 1932), *Merī Tibbat yātrā* (My journey to Tibet; 1937), *Yātrā ke panne* (Pages of a journey; 1934–6), *Jāpān* (Japan; 1935), *Īrān* (Iran; 1935–6), *Tibbat mẽ savā varṣ* (One and a quarter years in Tibet; 1931).

45 A few poems he wrote during his imprisonment in 1922 are collected in Appendix 1 of *MJY-1*. They are in Sanskrit, Hindi, and Urdu (in Devanagari script). One example of his Sanskrit poetry, dedicating one of his books to Stcherbatsky, is quoted in Chapter 3 of this work. Kamala Sankrityayan (1995: 65) says that this stanza was his final verse composition.

Print and Profit

In a discussion about remuneration for published writings in Hindi, Orsini (2010: 60–3) has remarked that there was a tendency to view all such payment for sāhitya-sevā as improper, a case in point being Jaya Shankar Prasad, who considered that any payment for his writings would have been a blemish on his worship of Sarasvati, the goddess of learning. Sankrityayan, however, having no other major source of income, was happy to receive royalties for his published books. For example, he mentions that his payment from the publisher Kitab Mahal in 1951 was 4,327 Indian rupees (1998b [*MJY*-5]: 48). From the end of 1955, Kitab Mahal switched to paying a fixed sum of 500 rupees every month (on the basis of 15 per cent in aggregate) instead of the 20 per cent royalty. Since regularity of payment was important to Sankrityayan's day-to-day existence, he agreed to the provision, even though it potentially earned him a lower amount in the long run (1998b [*MJY*-5]: 227). Sankrityayan notes in *MJY*-2 that most of the journeys he undertook were made possible thanks to his income from royalties:

> शायद पाठकों को यह जानने की इच्छा होगी, कि आखिर दुनिया में इतनी-इतनी जगह मैं घूमा और सब जगह पैसों की जरूरत होती ही है; फिर यह पैसे कहाँ से आते थे? इसके बारे में इतना ही कहना है, कि यूरोप-यात्रा में महाबोधि सभा जैसे धनिक संस्था ने मुझे भेजा था, वह अमेरिका भी भेजना चाहती थी, लेकिन मैंने स्वयं जाना पसंद नहीं किया। बस वही यात्रा थी, जिसमें पैसे की ओर से कुछ निश्चिन्त था। बाँकी यात्राओं के लिए पैसे कुछ तो अपनी लेखनी से मिले–सबसे अधिक पैसा एक अमेरिकन पत्रिका ने मेरे लेख के लिए दिया था, और यह बड़े अच्छे मौके पर जापान में मिला था, जिसकी वजह से मैं रूस, ईरान भी हो आ सका था।
>
> Perhaps readers wish to know how I visited so many places in the world when money is needed everywhere; where did this money come from? I have only this to say: a rich institution of the likes of the Maha Bodhi Sabha sent me to visit Europe, and it also wanted to send me to America, but I did not want to go. This was the only trip where I was at ease from financial worries. For the other trips I earned some money from my pen—the biggest amount ever given for one of my articles coming from an American magazine, and I by great good fortune received it in Japan, so that I could also go to Russia and Iran. (Sankrityayan 1998b [*MJY*-2]: 166)

Though his royalties were Sankrityayan's major source of income, he was not happy with the price his books sold for, as he expresses in the case of his travelogue *Rūs mẽ paccīs mās*:

मेरी पुस्तकों से [*sic*] अधिक दाम होने की शिकायत अनेक पाठकों को है। लेकिन, बीकानेर के प्रकाशन ने दाम रखने की हद कर दी। पुस्तक का दाम पाँच रुपये से अधिक हर्गिज नहीं होना चाहिए था, लेकिन उन्होंने आठ रुपये रखा। बेबस लेखक बेचारा क्या करे।

Many readers have complained about the high price of my books. But Bikaner Publishers has gone to the limit in setting the price. The price of the book should in no way have exceeded five rupees, but they decided on eight rupees. What can a helpless writer do? (Sankrityayan 1998b [*MJY*-5]: 68)

Still, as with other decisions in his life, Sankrityayan never wrote any book against his own wishes, so that the content can be assumed to faithfully reflect his personal views:

मैं कभी किसी की फर्माइस पर पुस्तक लिखने का आदी नहीं हूँ।

I am not used to writing books at someone else's request. (Sankrityayan 1998b [*MJY*-5]: 82)

One case may serve as a representative example. One Shyamlal Pahadiya urged Sankrityayan not to publish *R̥gvaidik ārya*, because it presented Aryans as consumers of horse and ox meat. He was even ready to pay Sankrityayan the amount that he expected to earn from the book, but Sankrityayan did not agree to this:

उन्होंने बहुत चिरौरी-विनती की-इस पुस्तक को न छपवाएँ। शायद समझते थे कि पुस्तकों के लिखने में प्रेरणा मुझे पैसा ही देता है, इसलिए कहने लगे—इससे जितना पैसा मिलने वाला हो उतना मैं दूँगा। मैं उन्हें क्या समझाता?

He implored me not to release this book for publication. Perhaps he thought that money was the only motivation for writing books, for he started saying that he would give me the amount I would earn from the book. What could I have done to explain things to him? (Sankrityayan 1998b [*MJY*-5]: 303)[46]

46 Mentioned in the diary entry of 10 June 1956.

Sankrityayan, then, could be counted on to remain true to his own principles. For a while, in 1942, he was the editor of a weekly newspaper, *Huṅkār* (War cry), but he soon resigned the post, because of an advertisement the British government had sent to be published in the newspaper. The caption of the advertisement, *guṇḍõ se laṛiye* (fight against hooligans), was accompanied by a picture of a person holding a burning piece of wood dressed in a Gandhian topi and Jawahar[47] jacket. Sankrityayan decided that this advertisement should not be published, in deference to Congress party political activists. But because the advertisement could bring in a large sum of money, other executive members were willing to accept it, and Sankrityayan thereupon resigned from his post (cf. Urmileś 1994: 66–7). Later, in 1948, the post of editor for the daily newspaper *Navjīvan* from Lucknow was offered to him, but he turned it down because by then it would have cut into his travelling and personal writing, and because the newspaper was associated with groups like the Hindu Mahasabhaists (Sankrityayan 1998b [*MJY-4*]: 258).

Sankrityayan's own opinion about print capitalism is discussed in *Bhāgo nahī̃ (duniyā ko) badlo*. There he explains print media as the business of profit-making capitalists who invest big money in the expectation that they will earn handsomely from doing so. At the same time, though, he concedes that it is an important weapon in the battle for people's hearts and minds, comparing it to cannons, tanks, and fighter aircraft. He moves on by saying that such Indian newspapers are circulated in a big number; and they publish everything that supports capitalists' interest:

> अखबार तोप, टंक और हवाई जहाज से भी बढ़कर हथियार है। बिडला के अखबार तो अभी तीस-तीस, चालीस-चालीस हजार तक छपते हैं, लेकिन बिलायती करोड़पतियों के अखबार पन्द्रह-पन्द्रह सोलह-सोलह लाख रोजाना छपते हैं। उनमें जो कुछ लिखा जाता है, वह अपने मतलब का ख्याल करके।
>
> Newspapers are more lethal weapons than even cannons, tanks or aircraft. Birla's[48] newspapers now have a circulation of thirty or forty

[47] The fashion of wearing a half jacket of the type Jawaharlal Nehru customarily wore was quick to catch on, and the piece of apparel was named accordingly.

[48] A Marwari clan that became the largest industrial house in India in the 20th century and also supported independence movement. Sankrityayan (2004a: 206) notes that the Birlas invested capital in such daily newspapers

thousand, while British millionaires print fifteen or sixteen lakh of theirs every day. Whatever is written in them is done with their own interest in mind. (Sankrityayan 2004a: 206)

लाखों रुपया लगाते और लाखों रुपया पैदा करते हैं।

[Capitalists] invest lakhs of rupees and make lakhs of rupees. (Sankrityayan (2004a: 206)

It is not the case, in any event, that Sankrityayan got his books easily published; he had to work very hard towards that end, and was not always successful. One significant example, a book on Nepal, ended with his wife Kamala bringing back the rejected manuscript from the press. With this bitter experience behind him, he had thought of publishing his books in magazine instalments, but in the end gave up the idea. In addition, he tried publishing three books on his own, but soon realized that this required both capital and time that he as a writer was short of (Sankrityayan 1998b [*MJY-4*]: 345).

Most of Sankrityayan's literary works were published in Allahabad. Kitab Mahal was his major patron, bringing out thirty-five of his Hindi volumes. Other publishers in Allahabad were the Law General Press, Indian Press, Nav Bharti Prakashan, New Book Syndicate, Hindi Sahitya Sammelan, Sahitya Niketan, Indian Publishers, and Vidyarthi Granthagar. After Allahabad, the second most important publishing centre for him was Delhi, home to Rajkamal Prakashan and Peoples Publishing. Beside these publishers, others were located in Banaras, Calcutta, and Patna. Although most of his books that relate to Buddhism were published either by the Maha Bodhi Society or other such organizations and persons, his major popular works in Hindi were published by Kitab Mahal.[49]

Sankrityayan's autobiography also makes it clear that publishing books in Sanskrit was even more difficult than publishing in Hindi. He writes in January 1948 of the difficulties he faced in finding a publisher for his edition of the *Pramāṇavārttikabhāṣya*:

---

as *Hindustan Times* (Delhi), *Search Light* (Patna), *Leader* (Allahabad), and *Hindustan* (Delhi).

49 This information is based on the publication list provided in an appendix to A. Bhaṭṭācārya (2005).

> चौदह वर्ष से प्रमाणवार्तिकभाष्य छपने की प्रतीक्षा कर रहा था। तिब्बत से कितने परिश्रम और प्रेम से उतारकर लाया था। कई दरवाजों को देखा, आशा हो-हो करके भी वह प्रेस का मुँह न देख सका। [...] और अन्त में सात वर्ष बाद जायसवाल-संस्थान ने उसे प्रकाशित करने का पुण्य कार्य किया।
>
> *Pramāṇavārttikabhāṣya* had been waiting fourteen years to get printed. I had copied it with great difficulty and as a labour of love. It saw many doors, but for all the hope invested in it it was unable to find a press. [...] Finally, after seven years, the Jaysawal Institute undertook the meritorious job of printing it. (Sankrityayan 1998b [*MJY-4*]: 271)[50]

Print and Propagation

Hindi writers in 20th-century India contributed prominently to the liberation of their country. As Orsini (2010: 309) notes: 'Writers [...] believed that they were serving the movement, by fighting with their pens. Literature, the press and politics were seen as a continuum, a joint effort to liberate the country.' Sankrityayan embodies in his own person the reciprocal support those engaged in politics and literature were offering to each other during those years:

> मैं भड़ामशाही मार्क्सवादी प्रचारक नहीं था, कि हरेक को कन्वर्ट (मत-परिवर्तन) करने के नशे में 24 घंटे चूर रहूँ। अपने जीवन में मुझे ऐसा करने की आवश्यकता इसलिए भी नहीं थी, कि मौके-बेमौके बोलने से जो काम नहीं हो सकता था, उतना मेरी किताबें कर रही थीं।
>
> I was not a raucous propagandist of Marxism obsessed with converting everyone 24 hours a day. I did not need to do so, because what could not be done by speaking, whether in appropriate or inappropriate situations, was being done through my books. (Sankrityayan 1998b [*MJY-3*]: 220)

Sankrityayan was confident on the basis of his own personal experience that his books would inspire people more effectively than speeches or any oral tour de force. He had seen the powers of speech being put to use to enlist people to a cause while in the Arya Samaj and later during the satyagraha campaign, and as a result had devoted his life instead to writing, in order to propagate both com-

50 The *Pramāṇavārttikabhāṣya* was published in 1948 by the Jaysawal Research Institute, Patna (A. Bhaṭṭācārya 2005: 210).

munist thought and nationalist ideals. As to the former, he was a self-taught communist, first through his reading of newspapers and books, and second through his experience of Russian life. His works on communism itself may be divided into three kinds: (*a*) explanations of communism, (*b*) future visions of a communist India, and (*c*) biographies of communist leaders.

When Sankrityayan was writing about communism and communist leaders, there were very few materials available in South Asia on the leaders and their thought. Writing about or propagating communism was rare in those days, out of fear of reprisal from the authorities. Indeed, people were not even comfortable reading communist literature. P.C. Joshi, a writer on the history of communism in India, notes that an article written by Har Dayal in 1912 under the title 'Karl Marx: A Modern Rishi' was the first such ever penned by an Indian on either the man or his ideas (Brown 1975: 99). In this context, Urmileś assesses Sankrityayan's contribution in this field as follows:

> एक लेखक के रूप में मार्क्सवादी सिध्दान्तकारों की जीवनियों को लिखने में राहुल को काफी मेहनत करनी पड़ी। उस वक्त मार्क्स, लेनिन, स्टालिन और माओ के जीवन और कृतित्व के बारे में भारतीय उपमहाद्वीप में काफी कम सामग्री उपलब्ध थी। तथ्यों और सूचनाओं के संकलन का यह चुनौतीपूर्ण काम राहुल जैसा कोई महापंडित और प्रतिबद्ध लेखक ही कर सकता था। उस वक्त मिडियाकर और औसत दर्जे के लेखक बुद्धिजीवी 'कम्युनिष्ट' घोषित किए जाने के भय से 'मर्क्सवादी [*sic*] साहित्य' के पठन-पाठन से भी बचते थे।
>
> As a writer, Sankrityayan had to struggle considerably to write the biographies of Marxist theorists. Very little material was available on the Indian subcontinent about the lives and activities of Marx, Lenin, Stalin, and Mao. Only a scholarly and committed writer like Rahul was able to do the challenging work of collecting the facts and information. At that time many mediocre and run-of-the-mill writers and intellectuals did not read 'Marxist literature' out of fear that they would be branded as 'communists'. (Urmileś December 2007–November 2008: 49)

Most of Sankrityayan's Hindi literary writings are seen to have been written after 1937, and they came, as the progressive writer Nāgārjun has noted, at a time when they were bound to be most effective:

दूसरी बार (1937 ई.) जब रूस से लौटे तब से उन्होंने वही लिखा है, जनता को जिसकी आवश्यकता थी। लोकचेतना को अकलुष और स्फूर्तिमय बनाने वाला उनका यह साहित्य देश के कोने-कोने में पहुँचा है।

After returning from his second visit to Russia he wrote what the people needed [to know]. This literature of his, which purified and roused people's consciousness, reached every corner of the country. (Nāgārjun 1983: 96)

Progressive writers believed that historical writing was a particularly great need of the moment. To meet this need, Sankrityayan wrote many historical novels, and visited Tibet to obtain lost historical Buddhist texts. S.A. Dange, a Marathi progressive writer,[51] hoped to see Indian/Hindi literature supplied with such works as Kenneth Roberts's *The Rabble in Arms,* set during the American War of Independence. He praises Sankrityayan for writing along these lines:

> We want the *Historical Novel* [emphasis in the original] to be faithful to real history wherein the people and their heroes have moved in unison against oppression wherein not the heroes are everything [...]. We want the epochs of social changes done in his 'Volga to Ganges', the most outstanding piece of literature of the present times. It has no equal in any Indian language. Rahulji, the learned, the historian, the Buddhist scholar, the communist has come before us as artist interpreter of the soul of the oppressed and exploited through ages. (Dange 1985: 29)

Sankrityayan always kept both his readership and the larger public clearly in mind when writing. The Hindi language in *Bhāgo nahī̃ (duniyā ko) badlo* is a striking example of this. The language he uses in it is neither standardized nor Sanskritized literary Hindi nor any other language spoken in Indian villages of the Hindi-speaking belt. Sankrityayan said that the language of this book is aimed at those who have only a primary level of Hindi education. Sankrityayan devoted his life to writing; he wrote extensively. He wrote on topics which he thought useful to readers. The most prominent such topics were communism, Buddhist studies, travels, historical novels, biographies,

[51] Addressing the Fourth All-India Progressive Conference on 7 June 1943 in Bombay.

and his autobiography. His purpose in writing the work, consisting of a series of dialogues divided into chapters, was to raise awareness in the broader public. It was his opinion that merely providing citizenry with the right to vote was not enough; people should be made cognizant of the both the good and bad aspects of society and also of the complexity of politics. He states expressly in *MJY-2* that the work was not written to promote Hindi but rather to bring its activist theme home to *majdūr*s (labourers) and *kisān*s (farmers).

Sankrityayan's interest in the print medium and his championing of Devanagari and Hindi were not limited to the Indian context. He was aware of how his books were being received in Nepal. He suggested to Newars in Nepal that they use the Devanagari script in print to enable the Newari language to reach a wider public. Recalling Sankrityayan's suggestion, Dharmaratna Yami wrote:

> खासकर हम नेवारी भाषियों को भी देवनागरी अक्षर अपनाकर अपनी विशिष्ट संस्कृति और साहित्य को नागरी के विशाल पाठक वर्ग तक पहुँचाने की प्रेरणा देने वाले महापण्डित वही थे।
>
> It was mainly he, the *mahāpaṇḍit,* who prompted us to appropriate the Devanagari script in order to put our own special culture and literature into the hands of the broad masses of Devanagari readers. (Yami 1993: *ka*)

It is obvious that Sankrityayan's idea in pushing for a common script was to expand the reach of the Hindi print market as far as possible. The positive response in Nepal to his books that advocated communism, however clandestine their circulation was, only strengthened his belief in the power of print. The following pages will discuss in more detail the reception of his books in that country.

SANKRITYAYAN'S BANNED BOOKS IN NEPAL

Printed material in Hindi has not only been the main means of supporting currents of political and national consciousness in north India but also of shaping political and literary (or intellectual) consciousness in Nepal. Nepali and Hindi, being members of the same language family and both borrowing heavily from Sanskrit, have grown up together, as it were. Since Sanskrit has been the vehicle for transmitting Hindu religious and philosophical tradition, it has imposed undeniable similarities upon the cultures of the speakers of both the modern languages, and it has been the Sanskrit-educated population that has dominated writing and publishing activities in both India and Nepal. Yet while Hindi books have attracted many Nepali readers, Nepali books have tended to be read by very few speakers of Hindi, for there is a great disparity in the areas covered by the two languages.

The political and literary influences that spread out from the Hindi-speaking region of northern India spilled over into the neighbouring country of Nepal, the movement between whose two peoples to engage in shared religious practices and to seek education had long been considerable. Now the works of northern Indian Hindi writers and the public debate there influenced Nepali writers increasingly fired by the anti-Rana movement in Nepal. The poet Motiram Bhatta, who was inspired by Bharatendu Harishchandra during his time in Banaras, is one important example of this (see Chalmers 2002: 37).

In the context of popular Hindi books in Nepal, Sankrityayan's occupied a space of their own, given their unique character, and indeed they attracted a unique readership. The language Sankrityayan used in print was a very simple form of Hindi geared to the common reader. Therefore, his writings were easily understood by the Nepalese public. Though Sankrityayan did not speak Nepali, he communicated adeptly with Nepalese and understood them very well. He recognized Nepali's place as one of the modern Indo-Aryan Himalayan languages spoken within and on the border of the Hindi-speaking territory (Sankrityayan 1998b [*MJY*-5]: 104–5). His written correspondence[52] with Hemraj Sharma may have been conducted in Sanskrit, a language that could function as a common vehicle only for scholars, in this case between one who was devoted to the monarchy and the other against it. In the end, though, it was Hindi that Sankrityayan was counting on to unite the peoples of the two countries.

Hindi, then, was one of the things Sankrityayan had going for him in Nepal. The other thing in his favour was his communism. During the agitation in Nepal against the Ranas the young generation there

[52] Letters written to Sharma by foreign scholars such as Sankrityayan, Tucci, and Lévi are printed in Nepāl (2057 VS).

was drawn to Marxist ideology. They represented a readership that Sankrityayan's works, rare purveyors of the communist doctrine in Hindi, seemed tailor-made for. Another reason Sankrityayan's books were so popular was because they were cheap to come by.

Though Sankrityayan's books on Buddhism were readily available in the market, his political books and works with comments on the Rana government were banned in Nepal. Evidence of this can be seen in Rājguru Sharma's request to Sankrityayan in 1936 to excise a section of the book *Tibbat mẽ savā varṣ* in which he comments on the Rana rulers:

> राजगुरु ने एक दिन कहा–'तिब्बत में सवा वर्ष में यहाँ के शासक-वर्ग के बारे में आपने जो टिप्पणी की है, उससे वह बड़े असंतुष्ट हैं। इसकी वजह से आपकी दूसरी किताबों के आने में बड़ी रुकावट हो रही है, इसलिए उसे आप हटा दें, तो अच्छा है।' इस असन्तोष का एक और पता २४ मार्च को लगा। अपनी पुस्तक 'जापान' और 'खुद्दक नियाय' (पालि) के प्रूफों को डाक से भेजने के लिए जाने पर कस्टम अफसर (भँसारवाले) अफसर ने उन्हें रख लिया और कहा, कि हम इन्हें तब तक नहीं देंगे, जब तक कि 'तिब्बत में सवा वर्ष' की एक कापी नहीं मिल जाती। हमारे पास पुस्तक कहाँ थी और वह तो सरकार द्वारा जब्त थी। गुरूजी ने बहुत कोशिश की, तब जाकर प्रूफ भेजे जा सके। राजगुरु के सुझाव पर मैंने 'तिब्बत में सवा वर्ष' के प्रथम संस्करण के ३३ से ३६ पृष्ठों को नरम करके दुबारा लिख दिया।
>
> One day the Rājguru said, 'In *Tibbat mẽ savā varṣ,* where you have commented on the rulers here—they are very unhappy with it. For this reason there is a great obstacle to your other books coming here. So it will be good if you take that [part] out.' On 24 March I came to learn more about this dissatisfaction. When I went to send proofs of my books *Jāpān* and *Khuddaka nikāya* (in Pali) by post, the customs officer took them and said that they would not give them back until I gave them a [revised] copy of *Tibbat mẽ savā varṣ.* I did not have [a copy] of the book, and [so] they were seized by the government [from the market]. After great efforts on the part of Gurujī the proofs could be sent. At the Rājguru's recommendation, I toned down pages 33 to 36 of the first edition of *Tibbat mẽ savā varṣ.* (Sankrityayan 1957b: 139–40)

Despite the government's strict controls, Sankrityayan's political books were smuggled into Nepal and widely read there. These books were very effective in propagating communist philosophy. Govinda Bhatta, Basanta Kumar Sharma, Shyamdas Vaishnav, Shyam Prasad

Sharma, Modanath Prashrit,[53] Aravinda Rimāl,[54] and Mohan Bikram Siṃh are prominent Nepalese who in their youth were inspired to become communists by Sankrityayan's writings. Mohan Bikram Siṃh[55] said during an interview:

> किताब अध्ययन तथा जीवन व्यवहार को सिलसिलामा मैले सबैभन्दा आदर्श देखेका तीन जना व्यक्ति छन्, लेनिन, राहुल सांकृत्यायन र म्याक्सिम गोर्की। लेनिनको सम्पूर्ण सैद्धान्तिक र राजनीतिक व्यक्तित्वबाट म प्रभावित छु। सांकृत्यायनको दूरदृष्टि, ज्ञान, भ्रमण र अनुसन्धान कार्यको व्यापकताले मलाई धेरै प्रभाव पारेको छ। सुरूमा म उनक किताब पढेर कम्युनिस्ट पार्टीको नजिक आएको हुँ। २००९ सालमा काठमाडौंमा राहुलसँग मेरो भेट भएको थियो। मैले उनका धेरै राजनीतिक किताब पढें। यी तीन व्यक्तिले मेरो जीवनमा धेरै प्रभाव पारेका छन् र मेरो प्रेरणाको स्रोत पनि यिनै हुन्। [...] मैले पढेका र धेरै नै रुचाएका अरू किताबमा [...] राहुल सांकृत्यायनका 'वैज्ञानिक साम्यवाद' [*sic*], 'तुम्हारी क्षय', 'भागो नहीं दुनियाँ [*sic*] को बदलो', 'दर्शन दिग्दर्शन' आदि हुन्। यी किताब अहिलेका युवा पुस्ताले पनि पढ्नु जरूरी छ।
>
> As for reading books and living my life, I have regarded three persons as my greatest ideals: Lenin, Rahul Sankrityayan, and Maxim Gorki. I am impressed by Lenin's entire theoretical and political individuality. The comprehensiveness of Sankrityayan's foresight, knowledge, travels, and research work have made a great impression on me. In the beginning, reading his books brought me closer to the Communist Party. I met him in Kathmandu in 2009 [VS]. I have read many of his political books. These three persons have had a great influence on me and they are the source of my inspiration. [...] Among the books that I have read and liked a lot are [...] Rahul Sankrityayan's *Vaijñānik sāmyavād* [*sic*], *Tumhārī kṣaya*, *Bhāgo nahī̃ duniyā̃* [*sic*] *ko badlo*, and *Darśan digdarśan*. Today's younger generation, too, should read these books. (M.B. Siṃh 13 October 2012)

Nirañjan Govinda Vaidya (2002: 37) is another well-known communist leader who credits Sankrityayan's writings with successfully

[53] Based on personal communications with Bhatta, Basanta Kumar Sharma, Vaishnav, Shyam Prasad Sharma, and Prashrit during the field trip to Nepal in 2008.

[54] Rimāl (2062 VS: 148).

[55] At present Mohan Bikram Siṃh is the general secretary of the Communist Party of Nepal (Masal).

propagating communism in Nepal: 'Before establishing the Communist Party of Nepal in 1949, Comrade Pushpa Lal Shrestha had suggested to me to read Sankrityayan's books. This implies that he had read them [himself]. When I read his books, I began to become a most [diligent] disseminator of them. Before the Communist Party was established in Calcutta, [...] I had secretly visited Nepal and had brought Sankrityayan's books with me and distributed them to friends to read.'[56]

Later Vaidya established a bookshop in Kathmandu. He wrote about selling Sankrityayan's books there:

> [...] राहुल जी की पुस्तकों की काठमाण्डू के 'मानदास-सुगतदास' फार्म द्वारा बिक्री का प्रबन्ध होता रहा। उसके बाद आज से 32 साल पहले से प्रगतिशील पुस्तक भण्डार, के नाम से प्रगतिशील साहित्य बिक्री करने का काम मैंने आरम्भ किया जिसमें अधिकतर पुस्तकें राहुलजी की होती थीं, [...]
>
> The sale of Rahul's books in Kathmandu was continuously managed by Mandas–Sugatdas Forum. Afterwards, 32 years ago, I started selling progressive books in the [shop] named Pragatiśīl Pustak Bhaṇḍār (Progressive bookstore), most of whose books were Rahul's. (Vaidya 2002: 38–9)

The Nepali poet and playwright Shyamdas Vaishnav recalls what reading Sankrityayan's books meant to him thus:

> Mahāpaṇḍit Rahul Sankrityayan appeared on the scene as a bugle of revolution for Nepal. We read many of his books before the revolution: *Bhāgo nahī̃ (duniyā ko) badlo, Viśva kī rūprekhā, Mānav-samāj, Sāmyavād hī kyõ?* For those who did not read English and strove after awareness through Hindi, these were like the four Vedas. [People] read his books, were spurred on, and reaped awareness. No one was able to rise up against the Ranas. There was a tradition of reading books.

56 '[...] 1949 में कम्युनिस्ट पार्टी की स्थापना से पहले कामरेड पुष्पलाल श्रेष्ठ राहुलजी की पुस्तकें पढ़ने के लिए मुझे समय-समय पर सलाह देते थे। इसका अर्थ है उन्होंने राहुलजी की पुस्तकें पढ़ ली थीं। जब मैंने उनकी कुछ पुस्तकें पढ़ डालीं तो मैं उन रचनाओं का अधिक से अधिक प्रचारक बनने लगा। कलकत्ता में [...] कम्युनिस्ट पार्टी की स्थापना करने से पहले मैं भूमिगत रूप से काठमाण्डू आया था तो साथ में कुछ राहुल साहित्य भी छिपाकर ले आया और दोस्तों को पढ़ने के लिए दे दिया।'

> [People] read books. Rahul played a progressive role. [...] There was the impulse to buy Hindi books and spread awareness. Rahul's books added radiant power to this.[57]

A *Khatarnāk Badmash*

Because of his political writings, Sankrityayan became a person most disliked by the Ranas. That, however, made him all the more esteemed, visited, and read by young communists and members of the Theravada movement. Another basis for official reproach was the fact that he had given up the religion of his birth and converted to Buddhism. Conversion was prohibited in Nepal at that time, for which reason Theravada Buddhist monks often faced exile. Sankrityayan, therefore, to use a common Hindi word, was a *badmash* (dishonest) in the eyes of the Ranas. This comes out in a conversation among Dharmaratna Yami, Keshar Shamsher, and Padma Shamsher (the latter two are Ranas):

> केशर शमशेर ने धर्मरत्न से पूछा–'तुम्हारा सम्बन्ध राहुल से भी तो है?'
> 'वह बौद्ध धर्म के मेरे गुरू हैं।'
> इस पर पद्मशमशेर ने कहा कि दोनों बदमाश हैं।
>
> Keshar Shamsher asked Dharmaratna Yami, 'Do you also have relations with Rahul?'
> 'He is my guru of Buddhist philosophy.'
> Thereupon Padma Shamsher said, 'Both [Sankrityayan and Yami] are badmashes.'(Sankrityayan 1963: 19)

Many adventurous young persons, in any event, continued to secretly visit Sankrityayan in Kathmandu. Basanta Kumar Sharma, a Nepali literary writer and lexicographer, remembered

57 'महापण्डित राहुल सांकृत्यायन नेपालका लागि क्रान्तिको बिगुल भएर उदाए। क्रान्ति पूर्व उहाँको धेरै किताब हामीले पढयौं। 'भागो नहीं (दुनिया को) बदलो', 'विश्व की रूपरेखा', 'मानव समाज', 'साम्यवाद ही क्यों?' ती बेलाका अंग्रेजी नपढ्ने हिन्दी भाषाबाट जागृतिलाई आत्मसात गर्नेलाई चार वेद जस्तै थिए। राहुलको किताबबाट प्रेरणा प्राप्त गरेर जागृति ल्याए। राणाको विरोधमा कोही उभिन सक्दैनथे। किताब पढ्ने चलन थियो। किताब पढ्थे। राहुलले अग्रगामी भूमिका निभाउनुभएको थियो। [...] हिन्दी किताब किनेर जागृति फैलाउने लहर चलेको थियो। त्यसमा उज्यालो थप्रे काम राहुलको किताबले गरे।' Taken from a personal recorded interview in Kathmandu, 12 August 2008.

meeting Sankrityayan under such circumstances during the latter's Kathmandu visits.[58] Sankrityayan himself recalled these occasions:

नेपाल में मेरी पुस्तकें पढ़ी जाती हैं। मैं खतरनाक आदमी था, तब भी छिप कर यहाँ के जो तरुण मेरे पास पहुँचते थे, अब वह प्रौढ़ हो चुके थे।

My books are read in Nepal. I was a dangerous person. The youths there who came to meet me secretly at that time are now adults. (Sankrityayan 1998b [*MJY-5*]: 103)

Sankrityayan also met some underground communist leaders during his trips to Nepal, but he does not mention their names or the circumstances of their meetings in his writings. Some Nepalese writers, however, have shed light on them. One such is Krishnaman Shrestha:

त्यसताका यहाँ हिन्दी साहित्यका अग्रणी राहुल सांकृत्यायनको नाम खुबै चलेको थियो। उनका पुस्तकहरू निकै लोकप्रिय थिए। [...] राहुलजीलाई पुष्पलाल बसेको ठाउँमा लगी दिएँ। उहाँहरूको करीब दुई घण्टाको कुराकानी भयो। त्यसपछि राहुलजीलाई फेरि यमिजी कहाँ नै लगिदिएँ। [...] राहुलजी जस्ता प्रख्यात व्यक्तिलाई भेट्न पाएको [...] उहाँ र भूमिगत पुष्पलालजी को बीचमा भेट गराउनु [*sic*] पाएकोले म त्यसबेला असाध्यै गौरवान्वित भएको थिएँ। मलाई अति नै ठूलो उपलब्धी [*sic*] हासिल गरेको जस्तो अनुभव भएको थियो। [...] फलस्वरूप त्यसै बेलादेखि ममा एउटा नयाँ भावना जागृति भयो—राजनीतिमा आफूले पनि केही गरेर देखाउने।

During that time a leading light of Hindi literature, Rahul Sankrityayan, was on everyone's lips. His books were very popular. [...] I took him to where Pushpa Lal was staying. They talked for about two hours. Then I took him back to Yamiji. [...] I was very proud to have had the opportunity to meet a famous person like Rahul and to have been able to arrange a meeting between him and Pushpa Lalji,[59] [then] underground. I felt that I had achieved something very great. [...] [A]s a result a new feeling arose in [and stayed with] me from that time on— that I, too, should do something in politics [worth] showing. (Kṛṣṇamān Śreṣṭha 2046 VS: 75)

[58] Personal communication in Kathmandu in 2008.

[59] This took place during Sankrityayan's 1953 visit to Nepal. The Nepal Communist Party was banned, even after democratic reforms had earlier been instituted, from 24 January 1952 to April 1956 (K.C. 2065 VS).

Sankrityayan met Pushpa Lal Shrestha in 1956 in Kathmandu, but he had also encountered him earlier in Calcutta, where, as Vaidya (2002) recalls, the two discussed *Bāisvī̃ sadī* (see section titled 'The Imagery of an "Indian Nation"' in Chapter 2 of this work).

Our review of Sankrityayan's reception in Nepal has confirmed that he was treated by the public as a celebrated Hindi writer during his time there, and that his books, banned or otherwise, were not only celebrated but ardently read. Dharmaratna Yami (1993: *ka*) credits him and his books with acquainting Nepalese citizenry to what was going on around them in the world beyond their borders.[60] He echoes Vaishnav's judgement above that Sankrityayan's books were valuable precisely because they were able to explain such things to a population largely unversed in English.[61] This is not to say, though, that everything he wrote about Nepal and the Nepalese passed muster even among the wider public. The description of Nepal and the Nepali language in *Bāisvī̃ sadī* (see Chapter 2.), his article on Lakshmi Prasad Devkota (see Appendix 3), and Muralidhar Bhattarai's dissatisfaction with parts of his biography of Dharmaratna Yami (Appendix 2) are examples of this. Still, the overall positive reception of Sankrityayan's writings is a remarkable and undeniable fact.

60 'बार-बार नेपाल आकर उन्होंने नेपालियों को सचेत किया। [...] जो हमारे राष्ट्रभाषा की निकटतम भाषा है, मैं [*sic*] अनगिनत किताबें लिखकर हमें जगाते रहे। राजनीति और ज्ञान विज्ञान के साहित्य लेखन के माध्यम से भी वे नेपालियों में नयी चेतना फूंकते रहे। राहुल की हिन्दी रचनायें नेपाल में जितनी लोकप्रिय हुईं उतनी और किसी की नहीं। यह कोई अत्युक्ति नहीं–हाँ अंग्रेजी भाषा पर विशेषाधिकार रखने वाले विशिष्ट वर्ग की तो बात ही और है।' [He visited Nepal time and again and raised awareness among Nepalese. [...] He wrote in the language which is closest to our national language. He wrote countless books and awakened us. He breathed new awareness into Nepalese by writing political and scientific literature. No Hindi literature was as popular as Sankrityayan's. This is no exaggeration. Of course, that special class of persons who accord a special right to the English language is another matter.]

61 It may be noted that owing to the strict limitations in access to education during the Rana rule, very few people could understand English in Nepal.

* * *

For Sankrityayan nationalism and communism were neither one and the same thing, nor were they ideals that could be treated independently of each other; they were inextricably linked, with the latter being, he felt, an inalienable part of the former. His focus, unmistakably, was upon nationalism (which for him in his own time and place meant Indianness), and during his life he used different lenses—be they culture, language, or Marxism—to sharpen that focus. His ideal seemed to many communists to be merely a private vision and thus by definition a falsification of history. Siṃh has provided a good explanation of why, for example, other Indian communists took exception to this vision:

> जैसा कि हम सभी यह जानते हैं कि राहुलजी सोवियत संघ की साम्यवादी व्यवस्था के शुरू से ही समर्थक रहे हैं और अपने देश में भी वे वैसी ही व्यवस्था चाहते थे जिसके लिए उन्होंने–कर्म और–विचार–दोनों दृष्टियों से लगातार प्रयत्न किया। इस स्वप्न के पीछे उनके मन में यह कहीं गहरी इच्छा थी कि प्राचीन भारत के सांस्कृतिक केन्द्रों–नालंदा और तक्षशिला–की तरह की पुनर्स्थापना हो; इसी कारण कुछ मार्क्सवादी आलोचकों ने उनको पुनरुत्थानवादी ही कह डाला। असल में, राहुलजी की व्यवस्था में इन सांस्कृतिक केन्द्रों के प्रति आग्रह कोई पुरातनवादी धारणा नहीं थी। वरन् इसके पीछे उनकी वह विवेकपूर्ण दृष्टि थी जो गतिशील परम्परा से उन तत्वों को ले रहे थे जो 'भारतीय' हैं। इसी साम्यवादी व्यवस्था के तहत वे फासीवाद एवं साम्राज्यवाद का विरोध कर रहे थे, सामाजिक रूढ़ियों और अन्धविश्वासों पर आघात कर रहे थे तथा जन-आन्दोलनों में भाग ले रहे थे।
>
> As we all know, from the beginning Rahul-ji was a supporter of the communist system of the Soviet Union, and he wanted the same system for his own country, towards which end he constantly exerted himself in thought and deed. Somewhere behind this dream lay a deep desire [to see] such ancient Indian cultural centres as Nalanda and Takshashila restored; therefore, some Marxists accused him of being a revisionist. In reality, the urging on behalf of these cultural centres in Rahul-ji's plan was not a conservative idea; the perceptive view behind it, rather, was to take those elements of an ever-changing tradition which were 'Indian'. It was on the authority of this same communism that he opposed fascism and imperialism, dealt blows to conservative views and superstitions, and took part in popular movements. (V. Siṃh 1995: 119–20)

Sankrityayan's turning to communism has been called by those who have studied his life and works one of the most important such events, and so it is; but this study has not devoted a separate chapter to it. The first and obvious reason for this would be that, though his contributions to the communist cause were outstanding and though he viewed himself as a true communist, he had to face dismissal from the party over the issue of his Hindi nationalism. This study has found it justifiable, therefore, to merge the discussion of Sankrityayan's communist and nationalist leanings into one chapter. Second, his contributions to the communist cause took the specific form of awakening India's peoples to it through the Hindi print medium, whose influence was felt not only in the Hindi heartland but also beyond it, in Nepal. In sum, then, when one talks of his contributions as a Hindi progressive writer, one must realize that for him Hindi itself was a crucial tool for achieving social progress along the path of communism. The pleasure and pecuniary benefits that propagating his ideas through Hindi brought him personally may also be seen as the fruition of his own activity within the communist movement. All of these things were cut from the same cloth and had meaning for him only in their interdependence, not separately. They offer, then, new coigns of vantage within Sankrityayan studies from which to gain a better understanding of their subject.

This chapter started with Sankrityayan beginning a new life as a member of the Bihar Communist Party and gradually shifted to observing him from various angles as a Hindi literary writer. The idea of making Hindi the sole national language of India was a reflection not merely of Sankrityayan's national sentiment but also of the hopes he had pinned on the use of Hindi as a print language. When he realized that he was not made for politics, he concentrated on literary endeavour instead, in the language he knew most people in the country would understand. The same motive fuelled his campaign for the use of Devanagari, for if the script had been accepted by the many language communities in the Indian subcontinent, Hindi would have been understood by many more Indians, most of whose languages were strongly influenced by Sanskrit, and to this extent mutually comprehensible. This was proved in the case of Nepal. There he would not have been able to engage in politics openly, that is, through the oral transmission of ideas. Still, he was able to propagate communism there through his writing and the power of print. His political literature considerably influenced the Nepalese youth of that time. The same applies to his influence in India. The importance of print in gaining acceptance for Sankrityayan's ideas was far greater than any other means available. His success can be attributed to the fact that he regarded writing as both a solemn social duty and as a stimulating personal pleasure, and this success led to his being able to live off the fruits of his labour.

For all the sense of fulfilment that Sankrityayan achieved through writing, it was won only at great cost, principally in the form of the criticism he faced largely for the thoughts embedded in his writing. In India, he was criticized for being a revisionist or a nonconformist, and in Nepal for being a communist writer and a strong Indian nationalist. Although Sankrityayan's Nepalese readership has dwindled over the years, two of his books have recently been translated into Nepali: *Viśva kī rūprekhā* (1942) was translated by Nārāyan Giri as *Viśva ko rūprekhā* (2066 VS), and *Bāisvī̃ sadī* (1923) was translated by Dhir Kumār Śreṣṭha as *Bāisaũ śatābdī* (2067 VS).[62]

This final chapter points up that Sankrityayan understood the print medium to be a commodity which capitalists have used to generate profit for themselves. However, he knew they could do so only if they supplied the public with material it was willing to read. They were, therefore, dependent on writers even like him who opposed capitalism and imagined a future India under communism and were able to capture a wide audience eager to imbibe their views. That Sankrityayan's main occupation and only source of income was writing is surely one reason why he was so productive as a writer. In the context of 20th-century India, earning a living from writing, even with Hindi as the vehicle, can be considered to have been exceptional. In his case, too, he had to put up with the fact that writers were

[62] Dhir Kumār Śreṣṭha wrote to me in an email (29 May 2012) about what led him to translate *Bāisvī̃ sadī*. Having originally started without reflecting why he was doing so, he now assumes in retrospect that the description of Nepal contained in the work, its easily understandable language, the interesting narrative, and its foretelling the end of the monarchy and the coming electricity shortage in Nepal were probably the main motivating factors. For details concerning *Bāisvī̃ sadī*, see Chapter 2.

often treated by publishers as exploitable labourers. His wife Kamala (Sankrityayan 1995: 14) writes that Sankrityayan upon occasion gave his manuscripts to publishers on the basis of verbal agreements and ended up being cheated. Sankrityayan himself considered writers to be the most suppressed of all labourers:

> लेखक आज हमारे सबसे अधिक शोषित कमकर हैं। उनके परिश्रम को कौड़ी के मोल खरीदा जा रहा है। उनका 'करतल भिक्षा तरुतल बास' किसको नहीं विदित है? जीवन भर घुट-घुटकर परिश्रम करना, बीमारी और बुढ़ापे में असहाय हो भूखे मरना; ये ही मानों उनके भाग्य में लिखा हुआ है। इससे छुटकारा पाने का एक ही मार्ग है, लेखकों का संगठन।
>
> At present writers are our most suppressed workers. Their hard labour is being bought at a very cheap price. Who does not know of their 'shelter under a tree and the alms on their palms of their hands.' Doing suffocatingly hard labour their whole life and helplessly starving to death in sickness and old age is written into their fate. There is only one way to gain relief: establishing a writers' association. (Sankrityayan, cited in Sankrityayan and Anand 1982: 33)[63]

The form of communism which Sankrityayan adopted and was intent on propagating was one he felt needed to be Indianized. His first step towards that end involved setting it beside Buddhism and considering how the latter might fructify it. This was the tack taken in the domains of religion (such as Islam or Christianity) and language (Urdu in Devanagari script) as well. The Communist Party revoked his party membership for such deviation. Still, Sankrityayan remained a passionate devotee of communism, with the same order passion as he felt for Indianness or Hindi. His dismissal from the Communist Party did not leave him in peace, and in February 1955 he returned to Delhi, filled in an application form for membership, and re-obtained it. He later wrote about this incident: 'I was very happy that day. I was afraid of dying outside the Party.'[64]

63 Quoted from Sankrityayan's speech as chairman of the Akhil Bhārtīya (Hindī) Pragatiśīl Lekhak Sammelan (All-India [Hindi] Progressive Writers Conference) in Allahabad, September 1947.

64 'मुझे उस दिन बड़ी प्रसन्नता हुई। मैं डरता था, पार्टी मेंबर न रहते कहीं महाप्रयाण न करना पड़े।' (cited in Mule 1998: 155).

AFTERWORD

Rahul Sankrityayan

A Freethinking Cultural Nationalist

The quest to draw a link between Rahul Sankrityayan's multiple identities has now reached the concluding stage within this study. The problem we formulated at the beginning concerned the mutability of his personality, his transformed identities, and the apparent absence of a link between these. Despite the high regard with which his contributions to political, literary, social, and scholarly pursuits have been held, it was never particularly clear why he had undertaken to make them all. It could be argued today that this problem has stood in the way of a sober evaluation of these contributions within the context of Indian history and that as a consequence he still remains a conundrum, a disparate personality whose motivations and inspirations are unclear. Indeed it is the complexity of the problem he poses—the large volume of his written work over many genres and fields, and the mutable authorial presence behind them—that has attracted the attention of modern researchers, and in some cases distracted them to the point of them flinging their hands up in despair. He veritably invites every newcomer to study his life history within the historical context of India in the first half of the 20th century and attempt to identify whatever thread there may be that held together the different beads of his personality in a cohesive way. The present research has taken up this challenge to consider Sankrityayan once again during the important period of historical transformation in which he lived, which saw the development of the Indian independence movement and later forms of Indian nationalism, and it has done so through the somewhat unconventional prism of a person-centred ethnography. This approach called for peeling away the multiple masks he variously wore to reveal what, if anything, underlay them. It can arguably be claimed that what emerges is Sankrityayan as a freethinking cultural nationalist.

This study, having reviewed the main features of the place and time in which Sankrityayan lived, revalidates them as constituting the age of nationalism in India. Sankrityayan himself, as a nationalist, we have come to understand, in one way fit that mould, but we have also come to realize that his own ambitions were greater, namely to determine more precisely the shape that he felt that mould ought to take, not only for himself but for the nation as a whole, and this involved for him an exploration of different fields and the assumption of multiple identities. We have observed that Sankrityayan maintained his distance from the mainstream of the Indian nationalist movement in that, despite his involvement in the popular movement, he did not permanently remain associated with any particular party, organization, or group. If his sometime affiliation to major political and religious organizations of the time and his active contributions to them (such as the Arya Samaj, Indian National Congress, Maha Bodhi Society, and Communist Party of India) can be summed up, he seems to have belonged both everywhere and nowhere at the same time. I suggest that this is also the reason why Sankrityayan has become such a complicated subject to understand. From his own perspective on nationalist sentiment, we may conclude that he saw his life's work as coming down to honing the concept of Indianness into ever finer shape. Such a form of rāṣṭrīya kārya was what drove him from one key turning point to the next in his life.

Geertz's notion of culture as being foundational in the making of a person into a 'particular kind of man' is singularly applicable in the case of Sankrityayan. The more complex the culture, the more paths it offers its members for the shaping of a self. Sankrityayan trod various religious paths, principally Sanātanism, Vaishnavism, the Arya Samaj, and Buddhism. The beliefs and practices of sanātanī Brahmanism, into which he was born, were inculcated upon Sankrityayan during his childhood and teenage years, but he remained largely indifferent to it as a philosophy and way of life. Later, upon his own initiative, he experimented with Vaishnavism, the Arya Samaj, and Buddhism. He soon gave up the first of these, but eagerly participated in the Arya Samaj for a limited time during his youth before turning to

Buddhism, which he finally settled upon as the cultural or religious path of choice, the one to which he would remain true on his own terms throughout the remainder of his life. Cutting across these religious paths was the broader path of Hindi nationalism—the one that Sankrityayan in the end seemed most intent on following, as if it were the one destined to lead to the desired goal. All the forms of cultural or religious affiliation and activity were at the same time, and for him more importantly, socio-political in nature, in that they stoked his own creative imagination of what a true Indian community ought to look like.

CHAPTER REVIEW

Of the various transformations in Sankrityayan's life (Chapter 1), three major turning points stand out as defining periods in it (discussed from various angles in Chapters 2, 3, and 4). Nationalist sentiment first emerged as a driving force in Sankrityayan's life through his involvement with the Arya Samaj, and it is this that marks the first major turning point in his life. The analysis of his affiliation to the Arya Samaj in the second chapter makes clear that during the time that he was a member of the Samaj he identified with its aims completely. He seems to have always had an innate sense of the superiority of the culture into which he was born (one reflex of which was his denying his grandfather's request to pursue an English education). This sense sparked his interest in Sanskrit studies and Vedanta (see Chapters 1 and 2)—nothing that would have been uncommon in India at that time—and they were perhaps what most instigated him to join the Arya Samaj. He had not given any serious thought to the notion of nationhood before doing so. The Arya Samaj provided the fertile ground in which nationalist sentiment could grow and provided him with a strong vision of what it meant to be an Indian. Although his own concept of nationhood may not have differed from that of his fellow Arya Samajists, he most assuredly stoked the fires of his own nationalist sentiment more enthusiastically than the average member was likely to have done. He called himself a garam rāṣṭrīyatāvādī and declared himself ready to follow other freedom fighters and sacrifice his life for the nation, if called upon. In the Arya Samaj, then, he came to realize that there were activities in the world to which one's life could be committed, ideals for which to die was the sweetest thing imaginable. This realization set the course for the rest of his life, although the precise nature of the ideal and of his contribution to it kept on changing. His limited early understanding of nationhood expanded after he left the Arya Samaj and decided to become involved in politics.

Sankrityayan's second major turning point, discussed in Chapter 3, concerns his relationship with Buddhism as a source of Indian pride. The Buddha's life can be divided into two parts: a retreat from the world in search of truth and, having found it, a return to the world to live that truth out. Sankrityayan's four visits to Tibet can be seen, perhaps somewhat analogously, as a retreat from his own society in search of lost truths, hidden away in manuscripts that India no longer possessed, and, once he had found them, returning with them to make their content known by editing and publishing them. But his own goal was no longer individual in nature but a national one: a reclaiming of India's rightful place in history and a reaffirmation of its cultural superiority. The wish for a rāṣṭrīya kārya and a renewed sense of cultural superiority and pride in the country's history, all of which had been implanted in Sankrityayan during his involvement with the Arya Samaj, became even stronger after he left it. He lived during an age when almost all Indian intellectuals and political leaders looked back upon Indian history as a source of identity sorely lacking in the current context. Sankrityayan found his own beacon in the Buddha and Buddhist culture, and the many instances of Buddhist monks wandering far and wide on behalf of the dharma motivated him to undertake his own hazardous journeys to Tibet. What sorts of changes can be observed during this stage in Sankrityayan's life? What happened when he left the Arya Samaj, entered politics, and then converted to Buddhism? The narrow boundaries of Vedic communal life had collapsed for him, but the central anti-British nationalist sentiment, the sense of cultural superiority, the pride in Indian history, and the desire to sacrifice his life for the nation remained unchanged. What did change was his understanding of what sacrificing one's life for the nation might mean in practice. The results of this new insight were the many years devoted to politics, to the search for manuscripts in Tibet, and to his publishing activities. In any case, sufficient proof that he would not have been afraid to die while fighting during the independence movement against the British[1] is offered by the journeys to Tibet.[2]

His rāṣṭrīya kārya continued to occupy him beyond his journeys to Tibet and India's independence in 1947. He became active in Bihar in the establishment of the Communist Party of India and participated in the peasant movement there, which once again (after his incarceration for Congress-related activities in the 1930s) led to prison. We also observed in Chapter 4 how he finally came to view his rāṣṭrīya kārya as having shifted from that of a political activist to the pursuits of a writer. His sense of cultural identity had solidified to the point that he now saw nationalism almost wholly in terms of such identity, whence the importance he attached to Hindi and the Devanagari script. His national duty, as he conceived it, was to instil that identity in others by writing in this language, which was understood by the majority of the people. We observed in Chapter 4, too, the measures that he took to get Hindi recognized as India's only national language and on behalf of its rich literary tradition. He wrote extensively for the general public to inform them about the world, history, religions, philosophies, languages, politics, places, and peoples. He believed the printed word to be the best medium for communicating with the public and raising awareness, and so for inculcating nationalist sentiment. By writing himself, he was also simultaneously enriching Hindi and its literature towards gaining recognition as the national language.

Sankrityayan did not limit himself to any particular theme while writing. The popularity of his books in Nepal had encouraged him, and he saw that they were furthering his aims. His notion of what the Indian nation was meant to be remained strong until the end of his life. To be sure, his contributions were not always highly regarded. His almost nostalgic look back upon Indian history in search of

[1] His friend Udayanārāyaṇ Tivārī quotes from Sankrityayan's letters written to him from prison during the years 1940–2 that his supreme desire was to die during the independence movement against the British (1971: 214).

[2] If collecting important manuscripts meant going to Tibet, that was something Sankrityayan was willing to stake his life on. He realized, though, that death is not confined to any single place. At one point, one of his Sinhalese friends wrote a letter to him requesting him to return from Tibet immediately, and looking back on that episode in his autobiography, he

paradigms to apply, if possible, to his own period was criticized by several modernists.[3] It is clear that his motives were not purely academic, and that academia was simply another of those institutions he was involved with for his own ends. What he finally merits attention for most is the seriousness of his lifelong nationalist sentiment based on a conviction of Indian cultural superiority, which he sought to underpin by reasoned arguments retracing the steps of Indian history. Thus I believe that any evaluation of Sankrityayan's contributions to literature, history, and society must be undertaken in full cognizance of the nationalist sentiment that underlies them.

Sankrityayan's relationship with Nepal and his readership there (see 'Sankrityayan and His Relationship with Nepal' in Chapter 3 and 'Sankrityayan's Banned Books in Nepal' in Chapter 4), two further aspects of this study, casts additional light on our understanding of the man, providing as it does an outside perspective onto his work and ideals. This relationship points up the importance of cultural ties that, he felt, enable two peoples to imagine a religious or cultural community that transcends geographic, linguistic, and ethnic boundaries.

A FREETHINKING CULTURAL NATIONALIST

In retracing Sankrityayan's life history in the chapters above, we witnessed that the pride in the Vedic golden age—and more generally the Brahmanic cultural nationalism—that he embraced during his

---

muses: 'Were death itself to have issued an invitation to me, [do you think that] I would have come, leaving my work here?' [मौत भी निमन्त्रण देती, तो भी क्या वहाँ का काम छोड़कर मैं चला आता?] (Sankrityayan 1998b [*MJY-2*]: 159). Of course, he was not unmindful of the perils that his stay in Tibet posed: 'If I had taken this fear [of death] into consideration, I would not have been able to come to Tibet. I am fully satisfied with the work I have been able to accomplish by accepting this risk' [अगर इस डर का ख्याल करता तो, मैं तिब्बत में नहीं आ सकता था। मैंने खतरे को उठाकर जो काम कर पाया है, उससे मुझे पूरा सन्तोष है।] (Sankrityayan 1998b [*MJY-2*]: 247).

[3] 'Mahapandit Rahul has been trying to trace the old tribes and tribal confederacies in Hindustan and to divide them according to the pattern that prevailed in the good old days of Lord Buddha. [...] For Rahul there was little difference between the Hindustan of 1943 and the Janapads of 600 B.C' (Sardar Jafri, cited in Pradhan 1985: 191).

involvement with the Arya Samaj shifted to a pride in Buddhism, which in turn helped to give final shape to a pride in Indian history and culture as a whole. It was this, a powerful cultivation of bhārtīyatā, that was required for producing the social solidarity needed for any future return to glory. During each of his turnings, there were figures he could look up to and attempt to emulate. While he was in the Arya Samaj, it was Dayananda. As a Buddhist, he naturally gravitated towards the Buddha, but since the latter had passed into history, it was a greater challenge to discover what his true teachings were. Whole sects had arisen over this very question. Sankrityayan took the Buddha's admonition to be a light unto oneself seriously. It had been a message to all Indians to stand on their own two feet. In the modern context this meant freeing themselves from foreign domination. For Sankrityayan personally, it meant going back to Buddhist source texts, and using his own two feet to travel to Tibet, Sri Lanka, Nepal, and Russia in the search for or in the study of them. His studies and his travels allowed him to transform his sense of national pride in the Buddha and Buddhism into an international form of social solidarity, namely Marxism, which he viewed as a modern philosophy with aims similar to those of Buddhism, and which he therefore thought could play a useful role in the development of modern India. He dreamt of introducing pañcāytī khetī, based on Marxist theory but adapted specifically to the Indian context. This idea underlay the final stage of his political activity including the literary forms it took in the effort to gain acceptance of it among the general public. In his final major turning, he broadened this idea into that of ek jātīyatā as the full expression of his intellectual maturation. By then, though, he had realized that he was not made for politics; he spent out the rest of his days devoted to scholarly pursuits.

The concepts of bhārtīyatā and ek jātīyatā, which formed the basis of Sankrityayan's imagined community, underwent a process of broadening after first being cultivated while writing *Bāisvī̃ sadī* in 1923, but they were never abandoned. The culture of Bhāratvarṣ was the spirit that he felt suffused his nation's whole territorial expanse—a conviction that was not compromised on. Thus when he became a communist, he still imagined a community based on this concept. The cultural artefacts that underpinned Sankrityayan's imagined nation were first and foremost the Hindi language together with other key elements of Indian culture. For Sankrityayan, Indian culture was a fusion of *Hindustān kī sabhyatā* (Indian civilization), *gauravpūrṇ itihās* (glorious history), *manobhāv* (sentiment), *khān-pān* (food), and *veś-bhūṣā* (dress) (Sankrityayan 2004d: 31–2).

For Sankrityayan, however, the glorious past was marred by the institution of monarchy, the Muslim interlude, and the British Raj. These shortcomings, he felt, could be overcome in the future. The Indian nation that he imagined was a casteless and secular community with a rich cultural, literary, and philosophical history, proud of its great ancestors, and having Hindi as an officially recognized language that united its citizens despite their different mother tongues into a nation state, in which poverty would be eradicated through communism and which would come to rank third among the countries in the world in strength.

Language and religion have in modern times provided the cohesive force of nationalism in South Asia, and in India in particular. Although religion is the dominant factor in determining identity in India, it has also been, in Sankrityayan's opinion, the cause in times past of disunity. He was fervently against all forms of bigotry. His free thinking and sense of individuality were not always welcome, either in his own family or in the literary or political circles in which he moved. His family was not happy with his decision to study Sanskrit, and when he portrayed Aryans as consumers of beef,[4] he was criticized by Hindus. When he presented his idea for Indianizing Islam and making Hindi the national language, he was criticized by Muslims and his fellow members of the Communist Party. And when he presented religion as an obstacle to national unity, he was criticized by virtually everyone.

The fact that Sankrityayan was so quick to point out what he felt were social blemishes all but ensured that he would not, in the long run, remain a member in good standing of any organization, be it political, religious, or otherwise (the Arya Samaj, the Maha Bodhi Society, the Indian National Congress, and the Communist Party of India being the most prominent). He dreamt of an India free from

[4] In, among other works, *Rgvaidik ārya*, *Siṃh senāpati*, *Volgā se Gaṅgā*, and *Bhāgo nahī̃ (duniyā ko) badlo*. He made public pronouncements to this effect when Hindu organizations supported the movement to protect cows. Sankrityayan reported having eaten yak meat himself during his stay in Tibet. His dining with Muslim hosts was also unacceptable for Hindus.

the British Raj, but he was never against the Muslims or their culture, including the Urdu language. Rather, he was convinced that Indian culture, the culture which had developed into Bhāratvarṣ, could accommodate Islam, assuming that it in turn developed a certain quality of bhārtiyatā. He respected Akbar for his religious and cultural tolerance and argued (Sankrityayan 1998b [*MJY-1*]: 284) for *Hindu Musalmānõ kī ek roṭi-beṭi, ek jātīyatā* (commensality and marriage between Hindus and Muslims and [the acceptance] of a shared caste [that is, cultural identity]). Sankrityayan's concepts of ek jātīyatā and bhārtiyatā posed a challenge within the Indian context of his time, during which religion was the most powerful determinant of identity. Addressing the problem of disunity regarding divided Hindustan (Pakistan and India), he said:

> एकता तभी होगी, जब कि दोनों भागों में धर्मान्धता का स्थान राष्ट्रीयता और वैयक्तिक स्वार्थ का स्थान-समाज स्वार्थ लेगा।
>
> Unity will only be possible when nationalism replaces bigotry and social interest replaces personal interest in both regions. (Sankrityayan 2004d: 33)

Despite all the years of his activity in politics, Sankrityayan was too much of an outsider ever to be able to gain a secure foothold in it. It took him some time to realize this. Perhaps it finally dawned on him when he failed to be offered any political or administrative post after India's independence, despite his contribution to the independence movement.[5] Sankrityayan himself offers the following explanation of why he was not a successful politician:

5 Sankrityayan's nomination as editor-in-chief of a projected compilation of the *Hindi viśvakoś* (Hindi Encyclopedia) by the Nāgarī Pracāriṇī Sabhā was rejected due to political manoeuvring in 1957. The appointment committee had approved him in 1955, and he had already started research for the project. Instead, in the end, Hazari Prasad Dwivedi was appointed to the post. Kamala Sankrityayan tells of how after this episode, which she regards as a slap in the face to her husband from the collectivity of Indian scholars, Sankrityayan's mental and physical health deteriorated to the point of depression. He made plans to settle in Russia or China (Sankrityayan 1998b [*JY-6*]: 391–4), but in the event went to Sri Lanka instead to chair the department of philosophy at Vidyālaṅkāra University.

> मैं प्रकृत्या राजनीति के लिए नहीं बनाया गया। 16 अक्टूबर को मैंने दैनन्दिनी में लिखा भी था–(1) 'अत्यन्त आदर्शवाद, [...] (2) इतिहास की खोज की ओर उत्कट रुचि' [...]। मेरे राजनैतिक सहकारी जैसी बयार बहती थी। वैसे बन जाते थे–कहीं जाति-पाँति की भावना के सहारे काम निकालना चाहते थे और कभी निजी स्वार्थ के फेर में पड़ जाते थे। मैं इस पैंतरेबाजी में कितनी बार अकेला रह जाता था। दूसरी ओर विद्यासंबन्धी कार्यों का आकर्षण था ही। तो भी वर्तमान सामाजिक और राजनीतिक विधान से मैं सन्तुष्ट नहीं था, इसलिए समय-समय पर अपने को काबू में नहीं रख पाता था।
>
> I was not made for politics. I wrote in the diary on 16 October [1933]—(1) 'extreme idealism, [...] (2) strong desire towards historical investigation'.... My political colleagues followed the whims of the time—sometimes they achieved their ends with the aid of caste-bound sentiments and sometimes they very much pursued their own self-interest. Many times I was left to my own devices during this manoeuvring. On the other hand, there was the attraction of scholarly work. Still, I was not satisfied with the social situation, and therefore at times I was unable to control myself. (Sankrityayan 1998b [*MJY-2*]: 136)

This quotation contains a frank assessment of the dilemma that Sankrityayan found himself facing. His strongest desire was to render service to his nation by engaging in politics, but the ethos of political life was not to his liking. He was, though, a scholar at heart, who in the end consigned himself to fulfilling what he felt to be his rāṣṭrīya kārya through literary activity.

The quote also makes clear that he thought of himself as a free-thinker. What he refers to as his 'extreme idealism' was nothing else than the strong idiosyncratic sense of Indianness that left him unfit for long-term membership in any group. He did, though, have certain more permanent ties, and these were the ones with Russia, Tibet, Nepal, and Sri Lanka—centres of his scholarly pursuits. There would have been no way that he could have realized his political ambitions in any of them; they represented, rather, retreats from the rough and tumble of public life in India. But it was to India that he always returned.

What kind of nationalist was Sankrityayan? This is a question that the preceding pages have been devoted to answering. To sum up: Although Sankrityayan was linked to various religions and his national sentiment took hold in the Arya Samaj, religion in the end did not form the basis for his eventual concept of nationalism. He could not identify himself wholly with such Arya Samajists of his time as Lala Lajpat Rai or Swami Shraddhanand. Nor did he rise to become an influential peasant leader or a true-blue member of the Communist Party of India, his own personal commitments in the end putting him beyond the pale, as far as his comrades were concerned.[6] For all that, one thing bound them together: opposition to making religious criteria a factor in politics. He regarded religion as hindering the development of the country and the unity of its people. Still, he was a religious person for a period in his life, but unlike his friend and colleague Bhikkhu Ānand Kauśalyāyan, he was not a lifelong Buddhist monk. And while he was a progressive writer, he was not one pure and simple. Further, he was not a university graduate, but still he managed, as a self-made intellectual, to rise to the rank of an academic. His study of Buddhism and his contributions to this field were no less than those of any university-educated scholar of Buddhism, as is proven by his teaching assignment at Leningrad University and later as chair of the department of philosophy at Vidyālaṅkāra University in Sri Lanka. It is clear that what Sankrityayan consistently conceived himself as was a nationalist, in that he identified himself with the nation. Both he and India found themselves confronted with the challenge of defining themselves, their futures, and their place in the world. This meant coming to terms with the past and deciding which parts of it deserved to be held on to and which needed to be discarded.

Sankrityayan's concept of nationhood did not hinge on the language question, and it would do him an injustice to depict nationalism as he understood it in solely those terms. To be sure, according to John Hutchinson, language issues, while not central to cultural nationalism, do partially define a distinctive and historically rooted way of life.[7] As we have seen, though, Sankrityayan saw the determinant

[6] See 'Hindi Nationalism' in Chapter 4 of this volume.

[7] '[A nation] is a quasi-natural institution like the family which is composed of distinctive individuals united by love. This love is expressed through a participation in the way of life of the national community. The nation is a source of unique charisma or creative energy, expressed in its origin, myths,

factors as spanning the entire range of Indian culture (history, civilization, sentiment, food, and dress).

Hutchinson goes on to note (1999: 402) that cultural nationalists are often highly educated individuals from widely varying social strata and, as intellectuals, able to provide new direction in times of social crisis, primarily by acting as moral innovators. One can reasonably apply this insight to Sankrityayan by arguing that he viewed India's unity as a moral issue and was chiefly concerned with providing Indians (a people following a host of different religions and speaking dozens of different languages) the wherewithal to achieving it, namely by demonstrating to them what Indianness was and why it could, if embraced, bring about unity. His programme represented one possible solution to the social crisis which arose along the fault line between the major religions in India before and after 1947. Social solidarity, in his opinion, was only possible through acceptance of ek jātīyatā, meaning a strong sense of what bound Indians together despite all their diversity. Virtually all of his prodigious literary output was aimed at bringing the public to an awareness of the unifying factors.

Here we must again note, though, that the elements constituting Sankrityayan's national sentiment failed to gain wide acceptance. Each of the organizations he had been affiliated to found individual parts of it unacceptable. The fact that he refused to make religion, which he saw as a cause of disunity among the peoples of India, a mark of identity could only alienate a large number of faithful believers, be they Hindus, Muslims, or Arya Samajists. Again, his touting of Hindi as the country's official language sparked opposition among still other groups whether they were speakers of other languages or communists. As a freethinker, then, Sankrityayan was at odds with

history, culture and landscape. [...] [C]ultural nationalists argue that a strong sense of history allows for social solidarity to be combined with a powerful cultivation of individuality. [...] [H]istorians, philologists, artists of all kinds [...] are the primary leaders of cultural nationalism. What triggers them into collective action is evidence of social demoralization and conflict which they believe results from a loss of continuity with the national heritage and a subsequent adaptation of foreign values' (Hutchinson 1999: 399–400).

just about everyone over important issues relating to what form the Indian nation of his time should take, and his proposals remained all but unheeded. People, cognizant of the multiple stances he had taken over the course of his life, remained puzzled about precisely what he stood for.

One might wonder why it is that Sankrityayan remains so much less known than Gandhi, Ambedkar, Savarkar, or Premchand in the West. The answer would be, as suggested above, that the different strands of his personality made him a complex subject to understand. One might go so far as to compare the difficulties he posed to those of the proverbial Indian elephant being examined by three blind men. His way of engaging in his chosen fields of activity and the philosophical stances he embraced were not as eye-catching or straightforward as in the case of the above-mentioned figures. Nor did he consistently and doggedly follow his pursuits, and this meant risking perplexing sympathizers. Indeed, he is as complex and multifaceted as South Asian culture itself. But we have seen that many people in Nepal who came from a similar cultural background understood him very well. They had no problem accepting Sankrityayan as both a politically active communist and a Buddhist. Concerning this seeming contradiction, we can say that as a product of Indian culture, Sankrityayan was well placed to cast insightful light on communism through his understanding of Buddhism. Indian or Nepalese communists may express open opposition to religion on principle, but in practice they are customarily unable to abandon it completely. Being an outspoken atheist made it hard for Sankrityayan to gain acceptance in the context of his age, but this was offset by his being a Buddhist with strong links to the religious life of South Asia. In this respect he resembles Ambedkar.[8] Ambedkar could have campaigned for Dalits'

[8] Dr B.R. Ambedkar delivered a speech on 'The Buddha and Karl Marx' during the Fourth General Conference of the World Fellowship of Buddhists held in 1956 in Nepal. A similar article had appeared much earlier, in 1912, under the title 'Karl Marx: A Modern Rishi', written by Har Dayal (see section titled 'Print and Propagation' in Chapter 4 of this work). In all these cases, the form of religion serving as the basis for comparison is that of the founding periods, not to the decadence that inevitably set in afterwards.

rights under a secular banner; instead he chose to adopt Buddhism and to attempt to create a respected religious space for them under its umbrella.

Concerning the relevance of this study for the present, I would suggest that Sankrityayan's life is an open textbook that can be read for a better understanding of India of the first half of the 20th century and beyond. To recur to Geertz's notion of culture being the foundation in the making of a person, this is true of Sankrityayan to such an exceptional extent that his own complexity and flexibility mirror more clearly than normal that of the Indian culture of his age. He was a true product of the Indian soil, but one who at an early age pulled up his stakes and left in search of what his country had to teach him. Without the advantages of the wealth or a foreign education enjoyed by the previously mentioned luminaries, he nevertheless obtained a strong grounding in politics, research, and literary writing. What he did have was the ability to tap into India's rich cultural and religious traditions and, having adopted them, adapt them to a world view of his own making, which was again complex in being indebted in part, too, to influences beyond India's borders.

I have not attempted to present Sankrityayan as a great man and do not suggest that all of Sankrityayan's proposals deserved to be taken more seriously than they actually were, but I do argue that his wish to replace bigotry by nationalism and personal interest by social interest could have served to better ensure harmony among Indians. His notion of ek jātīyatā, in particular, had it been taken seriously, could have been an important principle for unifying people of different religions, creeds, and castes.

The time during which Sankrityayan lived was a period of nation building, and not conducive to focusing on individual careers. It was a time during which many men and women left their studies, jobs, and businesses to join the independence movement, Gandhi being the paradigmatic example. Sankrityayan, too, found himself swept along by the rush of events. This fact is perhaps what most unites him with those of his time and place, but more than others he gravitated to the cross-currents to guide him through the distinct phases of his life. Sankrityayan's multifaceted career should therefore not be viewed as something pre-planned, but nor was it something he had no control over. Rather, he worked his way conscientiously through each of his major turnings to arrive at a considered understanding of the basic need of the historical moment. In this sense, it may be argued, Sankrityayan's life story is a reflection of (the first half of) 20th-century Indian history. His life history presents us with a multifaceted picture of India itself, covering many important aspects of its rich past and its struggle to make the transition to a future worthy of that past. Both he and the country as a whole charted out what they thought would be the proper route. Their roadmaps differed, and both came to grief over them. The long-enduring troubles since then suggest that the India of 1947 would perhaps have done well to take Sankrityayan's proposals more seriously.

This study concludes with a quote from Sankrityayan himself, in which he identifies what he calls *viśvās* (idea or belief) as the true lodestar of his life. He changed his identity many times in an attempt to remain true to this elusive fixture—elusive because, as an ultimate idea, it could only be approached through conventional concepts. His life story reveals that it was this viśvās that guided his endeavours and was the only thing that gave him real satisfaction. Given that nationalist sentiment was what he most insistently saw as the truest expression of viśvās, and that this was what he himself remained true to throughout, all his multiple identities fade away, leaving a single identity, that of a freethinking cultural nationalist:

> अपने जिस विश्वास के लिए मैं सनातन धर्मी से आर्यसमाजी बना, आर्य समाज छोड़कर बौद्ध बना, बौद्ध छोड़कर कम्युनिस्ट बना और यदि मेरे उस विश्वास को धक्का लगता है, तो मैं कम्युनिस्ट पार्टी को भी छोड़ सकता हूँ।
>
> For belief's sake, from a *sanātandharmī* I became an Arya Samajist, from an Arya Samajist I became a Buddhist, and from a Buddhist I became a communist, and if that belief suffers injury, I can also leave the Communist Party. (Sankrityayan, cited in A. Bhaṭṭācārya 2005: 193)

APPENDIX 1

Rahul Sankrityayan's Relationship with Nepal

> [...] यहाँ अपना घर-सा अनुभव करते थे। यहाँ के मित्रों-परिचितों से जो स्नेह उनको मिला, वह उनके जीवन में मूल्यवान रहा।

> [...] He felt at home here. The love he received from friends and acquaintances remained valuable throughout his life. (Kamala Sankrityayan in Sankrityayan 1998b [*JY-6*]: 412)

Sankrityayan enjoyed very good relations with many Nepalese. Biographical sketches of the main Nepalese personalities who formed ties with Sankrityayan, and of other Nepalese mentioned in this study, are presented on the following pages. This information was collected from a variety of bibliographical sources. The subjects selected are mainly persons who turn up on sundry occasions in Sankrityayan's own writings. I have tried to define their relationship with Sankrityayan as concisely as possible, on the basis of the sources, and I was particularly interested in trying to pinpoint what first brought them into contact with Sankrityayan. The personalities include religious sadhus, Nepalese Buddhists, businessmen, scholars, literary writers, and Ranas.

The biographical entries are for the following persons, given in alphabetical order (by first name/title):

1. Baba Paramhams
2. Balkr̥ṣṇa Sama
3. Bhikku Mahanam
4. Bhikku Dharmalok

5. Chittadhar Hridaya
6. Dharmaman Sahu
7. DharmaratnaYami
8. General Keshar Shamsher
9. Janaklāl Śarmā
10. Kamala Sankrityayan
11. Lakshmi Prasad Devkota
12. Mandas Sahu
13. Padma Shamsher
14. Rājguru Pandit Hemraj Sharma
15. Svami Purnanand

Baba Paramhams (Shaligram)

Sankrityayan was early on drawn to the sadhu's way of life as a solution to the need he felt not to be tied down to a single place and its social norms while at the same time as a simple means of meeting his simple needs of accommodation and food. The first impulse to engage in *sanyās* (the ascetic way of life) had come in around 1909/10, at the still young age of seventeen–eighteen, from a Nepalese sadhu.

Baba Paramhams (his given name: Shaligram) was born in Pokhara at the beginning of the 19th century (VS). He studied Sanskrit in Pokhara and then went to Banaras for further studies. There he became a sadhu, staying near Rajghat. But after the bridge was built over the river Ganga, there was little peace left for a person who wanted to attain samadhi, and he started looking for another, quieter place, and eventually found his way to Umarpur in India, near Sankrityayan's parental village, Kanaila. When Sankrityayan met him in 1909–10 villagers told him that he was 120 years old. On one occasion the king of Nepal sent envoys to try, unsuccessfully, to lure Paramhams Baba back to Nepal (Sankrityayan 1957b: 37).

Baba achieved great renown but was reserved, not seeking contact with the outside world. There was a disciple of his named Harikarandas at his hermitage with whom Sankrityayan established a good friendship and whom he often visited. It was through him that his own wandering way of life, which had started a few years earlier during the journeys to Banaras and Calcutta, would come into its stride.

Baba Paramhams and his disciple Harikarandas were Sankrityayan's main role models during his teens.[1] Remembering his youth, Sankrityayan wrote: 'I was not calm or satisfied after my six/seven-month-long Kolkata sojourn. I wanted to fly off on the next long journey in the winter of 1909–1910. Baba Paramhams's life and the words of his disciple Harikarandas were my only ideals' (Sankrityayan 1957b: 28). His introduction to both turned Sankrityayan into an ardent believer. He became interested in Vedanta after his first few visits to the hermitage. He began to recite a *śloka* regularly: का चिन्ता मम जीवने यदि हरिर्विश्वम्भरो गीयते (There is no need to worry in life if [the name] Hari Viśvambhara is intoned) (Sankrityayan 1998b [*MJY-1*]: 81). After his initiation as a sadhu he started performing *sandhyā* (the morning, noon, and even prayers of a Brahmin), ate once a day food that he cooked himself, and became very quiet and introspective. This raised suspicions among his family, culminating when he disregarded his grandfather's request to study English. Finally, following Harikarandas's suggestion, Sankrityayan fled home to undertake a Himalayan pilgrimage, and afterwards went to Banaras for further studies. While there, he planned first to study Sanskrit and Vedanta, and then to become a sanyasi. His plan fell through, however, and he returned to the life of a sadhu in Chapra without having completed his education as he had wished.

Sources: Sankrityayan (1957b; 1998b [*MJY-1*].

Bālkṛṣṇa Sama (1903–81)

Bālkṛṣṇa Shamsher Janga Bahadur Rana was born into the aristocratic Rana family. Taking exception to his status, at the age of 45 (in 1948) he shortened his family name-cum-title, Shamsher Jangabahadur Rana, to Sama, meaning 'equal' after spending several months in prison for his association with political forces inimical to his family's regime. His immense contribution to Nepali literature earned him a title of his own: *nāṭya samrāṭ* (king of drama). He contributed to virtually every genre of Nepali literature, including drama, poetry, short stories, biographies, autobiography, essays, and epics.

[1] Paramhams Baba was one of only two sadhus who had a truly seminal influence on Sankrityayan's life, the other being Brahmachari Manganiram in Banaras (Sankrityayan 1957b: 56).

Sankrityayan met Bālkr̥ṣṇa Sama in 1953 while attending various literary meetings in Kathmandu. Later, having been invited to his house for tea,[2] Sankrityayan also met his family (Sankrityayan 1998b [*MJY*-5]: 106–7). He writes (1998b [*MJY*-5]: 106): 'None of the Ranas have made any progress recently by introducing education to the family line. Sama was an exception to this. His entire family are admirers of literature and art. He himself is a great dramatist.'

Sources: Sankrityayan (1998b [*MJY*-5]); Bhattarāī (2051 VS); Hutt (1993); Sama (2054 VS).

Bhikkhu Mahanam

The Nepalese Newar monk Mahanam visited Darjeeling on 6 April 1963 to attend Sankrityayan's 70th birthday, and also participated in his funeral after he died on 14 April. On the day of the obsequies, 15 April, a question arose as to which ritual to follow. Sankrityayan's youngest brother, Shyamlal, wished to follow the Hindu ritual, whereas Bhikkhu Mahanam favoured the Buddhist one, reasoning that Sankrityayan had never renounced Buddhism after taking vows. The dispute was finally resolved with the decision to perform both. The news of Sankrityayan's death spread very fast in and outside India. The Nepali national daily *Gorkhapatra*[3] published the news on its front page.

Sources: Sankrityayan (1998b [*JY*-6]); Śākya (1992).

Bhikkhu Dharmalok (also known as Dhammālok) (1891–1977)

Born in the Ason quarter of Kathmandu, Dasharatan Tuladhar grew up to become a tradesman who did business in Lhasa and taught Buddhism on the side as a layman. He sent his son Anirudha to Sri Lanka to study Buddhism at Sankrityayan's recommendation. He helped Sankrityayan remain incognito in Kathmandu in 1929 and took him safely to Yolmo (Helambu), from where Sankrityayan went on to Tibet. They met again by chance in Kalimpong when Sankrityayan was going to Tibet for the second time in March 1934, but by this time

[2] Sama had sent his car to bring Sankrityayan to his house (Sankrityayan 1998b [*MJY*-5]: 106).

[3] *Gorkhapatra*, 15 April 1963.

the latter had become Bhikkhu Dharmalok, a Buddhist monk, and they proceeded together towards Tibet.

Sources: Sankrityayan (1995; 1998b [*MJY-2*]; 1990 VS).

Chittadhar Hridaya (1906–82)

Chittadhar Tuladhar 'Hridaya' was one of Nepal's most eminent 20th-century writers. He wrote in the Newari language (Nepāl bhāṣā) and is regarded as the pre-eminent Newar poet of that century. Most importantly, he wrote *Sugata Saurabha*, with the help of Sankrityayan's *Buddha caryā*. He was imprisoned by the Ranas for publishing in his mother tongue.

Sources: Lewis and Tuladhar (2007); Sankrityayan (1963).

Dharmaman Sahu (1861–1937)

During Sankrityayan's underground period in Kathmandu, his aim of visiting Tibet was widely known among the Buddhist community there. Within it Dharmaman Sahu was the person who most helped him to achieve that aim. Besides being the richest and best-known Nepalese Newar merchant in Lhasa, with a *koṭhī* (business house) of his own, he was a devout Buddhist and committed to helping Buddhist monks. When Dharmaman learned about Sankrityayan, he invited him to his house at Ason, Kathmandu, and introduced him to Dasharatan Sahu, whom he requested to do what he could for his guest. He also wrote a letter to his sons in Lhasa asking them to accommodate Sankrityayan there. Sankrityayan stayed in Dharmaman's own house in Ason during his visits in 1929, 1934, and 1936—hospitality acknowledged in the following words: '*sāhū-jī* arranged my stay in his five-storey house. The house of Sahu Dharmaman was always open for guests. Every time I visited the house, there was always a lama or other sojourners' (Sankrityayan 1995: 11).

The close relations with Dharmaman and his three sons, Triratnaman,[4] Gyanaman, and Purnaman, shielded Sankrityayan from suspicion that he might be a spy of the English in Tibet rather

[4] Tirthaman Tuladhar was the treasurer of the Nepal Buddhopasak Sangh (Association of Nepalese Lay Buddhists) (see note 57 in section titled 'Sankrityayan and the Theravada Movement in Nepal' in Chapter 3).

than a Buddhist scholar (Sankrityayan 1957b: 187). His last meeting with Dharmaman Sahu was in 1936, before he left the Ason house after staying there for two months for his third journey to Tibet with Gyanaman. Dharmaman was 74 at that time and was suffering from asthma.

Dharmaman Sahu and his sons had several branch offices, in India, Nepal, and Tibet. Sankrityayan wrote: 'The Nepalese were the Marvāḍīs (that is, a particularly business-savvy caste of Jain traders) of Lhasa. Every *koṭhi* (business house) has millions in wealth' (Sankrityayan 1998b [*MJY-2*]: 59). He tells of what happened when he visited Ladakh in 1933 after coming back from his journey to Europe: 'I was running out of money, but a branch of the Nepalese merchant Dharmaman had already been established there. Mahila Sahu [the second son of Dharmaman, Gyanaman] was there; therefore, there was no problem in getting money' (Sankrityayan 1998b [*MJY-2*]: 127).

The Nepalese koṭhī also provided accommodation during Sankrityayan's second and third visits to Tibet. The business houses of Dharmaman Sahu in Gyantse and Lhasa were home to him, and Sahu's family provided most of the help he received during his visits to Tibet (Sankrityayan 1995: 11). Sankrityayan expresses his gratitude to the Newar and his sons in many places in his Tibet travelogue.

Sources: Sankrityayan (1995; 1957b; 1998b [*MJY-2* and *MJY-5*]; 1984); Śākya (1994).

Dharmaratna Yami (1915–75)

DharmaratnaYami (born Dharmaratna Tuladhar) was a Nepalese freedom fighter and a writer. A Newar Buddhist and a communist, he became a supporter of the monarchy, after the Panchayat system was institutionalized,[5] and is remembered for his individualistic views. In 1951 he became a deputy minister in the Nepali Congress government led by Matrika Prasad Koirala, and in 1962 was nominated to the national legislature, the Rastriya Panchayat.

Sankrityayan first met Dharmaratna Yami in 1934 during his second visit to Tibet while staying in the business house of Dharmaman

[5] The panchayat system of Nepal was in effect from 1962 to 1990, having been set up by King Mahendra after he had disbanded the democratically elected government and dissolved the parliament in 1960.

Sahu in Lhasa, where Yami was employed. Later Yami returned to Kathmandu and got involved in politics and actively participated in the anti-Rana movement. Sankrityayan wrote about Yami's struggles in three articles in 1953, which were later published as a book in 1954 under the name *Dharmaratna Yamī: āj ke nepāl kā rājnītik sipāhi* (Dharmaratna Yami: A political soldier of modern Nepal).

In 1953, Janaklāl Śarmā arranged for Sankrityayan, at the latter's request, to stay at B.P. Koirala's bungalow in Putali Sadak (a main artery of Kathmandu) during a visit to Nepal. However, transportation was not easy in Kathmandu in 1953, and back then the house in Putali Sadak was outside the inner city area. Sankrityayan thus preferred Dharmaratna Yami's house and shifted there, since it, too, had a bathroom[6] and was conveniently situated inside the old city.

This was Sankrityayan's first visit to Nepal with his wife Kamala following the advent of democracy, and the situation was far more favourable than before. Although previous journeys had not been particularly private affairs, this time the visit was much more devoted to such activities as attending public meetings and seminars and delivering speeches. Of all his trips to Nepal, the one in 1953 can be regarded as the most important in terms of public relations. However, Sankrityayan was rather troubled by the fact that meeting people in this way distracted him from working on a projected book to be titled *Nepal*. He wrote: 'Together with other things, I was again and again on the point of collecting new data for my book, but Yamijī's house had become a venue for the non-stop meeting of poets' (1998b [*MJY*-4]: 105).

His book *Nepal* was never published. In 1955, Sankrityayan visited Mohan Press, Patna, which had been given the manuscript well before, in January of that year, and was not happy with developments. He wrote: 'Mohan Press was publishing *Saraha[pa] ke dohākoś* and

[6] Sankrityayan needed a room with a bath attached on account of his diabetes. Around 2008 VS, King Tribhuvan gifted Yami with one lakh Indian rupees to buy a house and with that amount he had acquired a huge house in Bhurungkhel, in which he lived with his first wife, Hiradevi Kansakar (2002–25 VS), who had also actively participated in the anti-Rana movement. In 2026 VS, a year after her death, Yami married Savitri Devi Dahal. Later he built a new and smaller house beside the older one and moved into it with his new wife, leaving, according to his son, Bidhanratna Yami, the old one for him and his fellow siblings from the first marriage.

was also making a mess out of *Nepal*. *Nepal* has been in press for three years. Four hundred pages have already been printed. I said, "Print a further two hundred pages and make the first part ready, and after that you will start getting returns." He replied, "Yes, yes." Mohan Babu of Mohan Press is very good at being humble. I do not believe that *Nepal* will come out of the swamp any more' (Sankrityayan 1998b [*MJY*-5]: 250). Sankrityayan's fears were proven true. Later the manuscript and the printed sections were brought back home from the press by Kamala Sankrityayan.[7]

During Sankrityayan's visit to Nepal from 13 to 21 November 1956 to attend the World Buddhist Conference, he resided at Dharmaratna Yami's new house, built next to the old one. Yami arrived two days after Sankrityayan. Janaklāl Śarmā always accompanied Sankrityayan and helped him with his insulin injections. Along with attending the conference, he continued to meet with his old friends. His health problems meant that he could not enjoy this stay as he had others. He wrote to his wife Kamala in a letter: 'What a difference it is if a man is healthy, [for] then he likes to do every work. The beautiful mountains and green valley were so much more attractive before, but now I do not even like to look at them. I have brought many films, but now I have no interest in taking pictures. My weight is 159 pounds. People here complain about my weight. Some suspect that I am sick. How many should I explain things to?' (Sankrityayan 1998b [*JY*-6]: 326).

Sources: Sankrityayan (1963; 1998b [*MJY*-2, *MJY*-4, and *MJY*-5]); *Dharma Ratna 'Yami' smrti grantha* (2046 VS).

General Keshar Shamsher Rana (1875–1952)

Keshar Shamsher Rana was the son of the Rana prime minister, Chandra Shamsher Rana. During his lifetime he occupied various posts in the civil and military administration. He fought hard to preserve the Rana regime, but after 1951 cooperated loyally with King Tribhuvan, his brother-in-law. Sankrityayan first met Keshar Shamsher in 1934 at his palace, Keshar Mahal, on which occasion he

7 Based on a personal interview with Kamala Sankrityayan in Vienna, December 2007. She was planning to edit and publish the work but died in October 2009.

was able to inspect the latter's personal library, and in 1953 he again visited him to renew his relationship. Shamsher had a number of Sankrityayan's books in his library[8] and in 1934 asked him to sign his copy of *Buddha caryā*. While Sankrityayan made clear his respect for his host's scholarship, Keshar Shamsher was not happy with his guest's political leanings, and more particularly with his hostile relations with members of the anti-Rana movement (see Sankrityayan's Banned Books in Nepal' in Chapter 4 of this study). Keshar Shamsher was an avid book collector with a large personal library in his house, which is now open to the public at Keshar Mahal.

Sources: Sankrityayan (1998b [*MJY-2* and *MJY-5*]); Whelpton (2011).

Janaklāl Śarmā (1978–2056 VS)

Janaklāl Śarmā was a well-known writer and researcher. Impressed by Sankrityayan's description of Nepal in *Bāisvī̃ sadī*, he was formally introduced to its author in 1934 in Gangtok, Sikkim. They met again in Wardha in 1948–9, whereupon they became close friends. Śarmā was an active supporter of Sankrityayan during his visit to Nepal in 1953. Before coming to Nepal in 1953, Sankrityayan wrote a letter to Śarmā about his planned visit to collect material for a book on Nepal (as opposed to just passing through, as on earlier trips) and asked for help in arranging a place to live. Śarmā organized two rooms in the same house in which he was staying but then received another letter[9] from Sankrityayan stating: 'I am suffering from diabetes, so a room with an attached toilet is necessary.' At that time it was difficult to obtain such rooms except in modern bungalows (which were very rare), Rana palaces, and government guest houses. Eventually Sankrityayan was accommodated first in the bungalow of B.P. Koirala in Putali Sadak, which had every modern facility and included the services of a cook (Pokhrel and Dhakal 2060 VS: 66–7), and then in Dharmaratna Yami's house. He had previously always stayed in the house of Dharmaman Sahu, but this time he visited there just once. He wrote: 'The daughter-in-law of Gyanman Sahu complained very unhappily: "You always

[8] My first contact with *MJY-1* was this library's copy.

[9] Some of Sankrityayan's letters to Janaklāl Śarmā are preserved in the National Archives, Kathmandu, Nepal.

visited us [before] so why didn't you come this time?" I accepted my mistake. I replied in turn, "I knew that Triratnaman and his brothers were not here so I did not come"' (Sankrityayan 1998b [*MJY-4*]: 112).

On previous journeys he had made his way to the Kathmandu Valley on foot, disguising himself as a sadhu or a Buddhist monk, but this time he arrived by plane. His ties with Nepal had become stronger, particularly through his marriage to a woman of Nepalese origin. There were many people to welcome him at the airport, including Janaklāl Śarmā, Dharmaratna Yami, and Yami's uncle, Mandas Tuladhar. Sankrityayan wrote in his diary of this journey: 'Entering Nepal before was very difficult. The borders were opened only a week before Śivarātri in order [to allow persons] to enter the Valley; otherwise the Ranas had made it highly complicated for any Indian to enter. Yes, but it was not so for the English; a mere note was enough for them. This [easy entry] was a good sign that the Rana regime had indeed ended' (Sankrityayan 1998b [*MJY-4*]: 101).

In 1954, Janaklāl Śarmā accompanied Sankrityayan on a field trip to Kumaon and Gadhwal for research and to collect material for what would be published in 1956 as the latter's *Kumāū̃*.[10] During Sankrityayan's 1953 visit to Nepal, a committee was formed at Sankrityayan's recommendation to search for old poetry in the Nepali language in Kumaon and Gadhwal.[11] Although Keshar Shamsher donated one lakh Indian rupees for this project, for several reasons it never materialized. As Śarmā was himself keen to visit Kumaon and Gadhwal, he decided to accompany Sankrityayan on this journey, during which he began his later intermittent practice of giving Sankrityayan insulin injections for the latter's now acute diabetes (Pokhrel and Dhakāl 2060 VS: 46–59).[12]

Sources: Sankrityayan 1998b; Pokhrel and Dhakāl (2060 VS); J. Śarmā (2052 VS).

10 Sankrityayan returned the favour by writing a foreword to Śarmā's book on fine art and literature in which he called on the people of independent Nepal to continue their efforts to keep traditional art alive (J. Śarmā 2023 VS: *gha*).

11 The two neighbouring areas are believed to be the cradle of the Nepali language.

12 Kamala Sankrityayan had been giving insulin to Sankrityayan but could not go with him on this trip owing to the birth of their daughter.

Kamala Sankrityayan née Pariyar (1920–2009)

Kamala Sankrityayan née Pariyar was Sankrityayan's third wife. A Hindi literary writer and a scholar in the fields of Hindi and Nepali literature, she was an Indian of Nepalese origin whose parents had moved to Darjeeling from Okhaldhunga district in Nepal.[13] Rahul Sankrityayan and Kumari Kamala Pariyar were married on 23 December 1950 and lived together up to the end of Sankrityayan's life. The couple had a daughter, Jaya, and a son, Jeta.

Sources: Sankrityayan (1998b [*MJY-4*, *MJY-5*, and *JY-6*]); Prasāī (2007).

Lakshmi Prasad Devkota (1909–59)

Lakshmi Prasad Devkota was the leading poet of the Romantic era of Nepali literature and is known as that era's *mahākavi* (great poet). Sankrityayan first met him in 1953 when he went with B.P. Koirala to meet him at his house in the Maitidevi quarter of Kathmandu. After his visit to Kathmandu that year, Sankrityayan wrote an article about the poet where he linked his output with that of three celebrated Hindi writers, Jaya Shankar Prasad, Sumitranandan Pant, and Suryakant Tripathi Nirala.[14] Devkota misunderstood the article, and on the same night that he read it, wrote an angry reply in the form of a poem titled 'Pāgal' (A mad man), which became one of his best-known works (see Appendix 3).

Sources: Ātreya (2066a VS) and (2066b VS); Hutt (1993); Sankrityayan (1998b [*MJY-5*]); J. Śarmā (2052 VS).

Mandas Tuladhar (Sahu) (1900–75)

Mandas Tuladhar was a Newar businessman and the owner of a bookshop that served as an outlet for Sankrityayan's books. The bookshop was the joint enterprise of Mandas Tuladhar and Chittadhar Tuladhar 'Hridaya'. Tuladhar was Dharmaratna Yami's uncle and was also related to Hridaya. During the Rana period, Sankrityayan's political volumes were secretly acquired in the bookshop and supplied to

[13] Based on a conversation with Kamala Sankrityayan in Vienna in December 2007.

[14] *Ājkal*, New Delhi, May 1953, p. 87.

readers. There was, however, no restriction on the buying or selling of his books on Buddhism.

Mandas Tuladhar also established a library named Bodhi Gyān Pustakālaya in Swayambhu. The library remains and has many books and photos of Sankrityayan. The bookshop, however, no longer exists.[15]

Tuladhar's relations with Sankrityayan have been described as follows (I am obliged to Gehini Joshi for her help in translating this Newari passage):

> मानदासया भारतया प्रकाण्ड विद्वान राहुल सांकृत्यायननाप सन् १९५३ स्वयां न्ह्यःनिसें स्वापू दु। वयकःपिनि दथुइ खासयाना स्वापू शैक्षिक जगत व उकिया कारोवार, बौद्ध धर्म अले नेपाःया लोकसाहित्यया माध्यम धायेमाः।
>
> Mandas had a very good relationship with the prominent Indian scholar Rahul Sankrityayan even before 1953. The points of contact between them were the educational world, business, Buddhism, and folk literature. (Bajrācārya 1989: 86)

Sources: Bajrācārya (1989); Sankrityayan (1998b [*MJY*-5]).

Padma Shamsher Rana (1883–1960/1)

Padma Shamsher succeeded Juddha Shamsher Rana as prime minister in 1945. He favoured political reform, and in 1948 with Indian assistance adopted a constitution. But his steps were not acceptable to conservative Ranas, and he was forced to resign in 1948 and go into self-imposed exile in India.

Sankrityayan first met Commander-in-Chief Padma Shamsher on 6 March 1936. The latter had read his *Tibbat mẽ savā vaṛs*, and on that occasion commented on it by saying that 'the truth is mainly bitter'. He also praised him for his adventurous journeys (Sankrityayan 1995: 16). The reference to the bitter truth concerned the far from positive information Sankrityayan had supplied about the Rana regime.

This meeting came two years after the earthquake of 15 January 1934 had struck Nepal with a magnitude of 8.4, leaving many people dead or homeless. The Nepalese were stunned, and astrologists had

[15] Based on a personal conversation with Mandas's son Sugatdas in Kathmandu and a follow-up visit to the library in August 2008.

further terrified them by forecasting another earthquake, impelling many to leave their homes for more secure shelter. The palace of Padma Shamsher had been among those destroyed by the quake, and it had still not been repaired, meaning that he was staying in a simple temporary house when Sankrityayan went to see him (Sankrityayan 1998b [*MJY-2*]: 240). Sankrityayan mentions that Padma Shamsher was appreciated by the people for his contribution to the rescue efforts and aid given to them after the earthquake.

Sources: Sankrityayan (1998b [*MJY-2*]; 1995); Whelpton (2011).

Rājguru Pandit Hemraj Sharma (1935–2010 VS)

Hemraj Sharma[16] (1935–2010 VS) was the chief royal priest and an advisor to the Rana family as well as a scholar, bibliophile, and a collector of manuscripts. Indeed, he was famous in India and the wider world for his scholarship and manuscript collection. His most important learned contributions are his edition and detailed introduction to the *Kāśyapasaṃhitā*,[17] an article in Sanskrit entitled *Mahābhāratasambandhe kaścana vicāraḥ* (An examination of the Mahabharata),[18] and his own *Candrikāvyākaraṇ*,[19] which is the first published Nepali grammar book. Sanskrit poems by him were also

[16] Garzilli (2001) contains a short account of Sharma's life in English. Sankrityayan's article on him published in *JMK* and the book by Nepāl (2057 VS) are the key sources of information about Sharma available to Hindi and Nepali readers. Two works by Sharma's grandson Prakash A. Raj—*Vidvacchiromaṇi Hemrāj Śarmā jīvanī* (Kathmandu: self-published, 2035 VS; and *Portraits & Photographs from Nepal* (Kathmandu: Nabeen Publications, 1994)—are accompanied by photographs of Sharma. Nepāl (2057 VS) has diary entries by Sharma from 23 March 1906 to 16 February 1953. The diary entries are important historical sources of information that not only relate to Sharma's life but also more generally to the history of 20th-century Nepal.

[17] Published in Bombay by the Nirnaya Sagar Press, 1995 VS.

[18] Referring to an article by A.D. Pusalker, Garzilli (2001: 118) notes that this article of Sharma's, based on the oldest Nepali manuscript of the *Ādiparvan*, discusses some important problems connected with the history of the epic Mahabharata. Nepāl (2057 VS: 183–98) has translated it into Nepali.

[19] This grammar was printed in 1969 VS on his own press, which was installed on the ground floor of his house in Kathmandu.

published in 1935 in *Amarabhāratī*, the journal of Banāras Sanskrit Mahāvidyālaya.[20]

Sharma was fluent in Hindi, Nepali, and Sanskrit, was conversant in Bengali, and spoke some Marathi and a little English. He was crowned with the title Vidvacchiromaṇi [Crown jewel of scholars] by King Tribhuvan in 1992 VS. He had his own library in his house, which he named Bhāratī Bhavan. Garzilli (2001: 119) notes in her article that he owned over 6,000 Sanskrit manuscripts and almost 25,000 books in Sanskrit, Pali, Bengali, Tibetan, Hindi, Chinese, Persian, Marathi, Gujarati, ancient Greek, and English. He printed and reprinted many rare texts on his press in his house. After his death the library was sold to the government, and now the collection is kept in the National Library of Nepal, in Lalitpur.[21] The family informed Garzilli that Sharma was not able to manage his money, spending too much of it on books and too much time gambling.

Sankrityayan and Sharma As early as 1920, when Sankrityayan was still in the Arya Samaj and not yet involved in politics or practising Buddhism, his thoughts turned to Nepal and Tibet. In that year, as planned, he did indeed enter the Terai, Nepal's plains, on the other side of the Nepal–India border and there visited Lumbini (the birthplace of the Buddha) and Kapilavastu (the capital of King Shuddhodana). He ventured further north, but became afraid of being caught by the police, and so cut short the journey. His disguise as a sadhu had helped him to gain accommodation, food, and transportation. Back on the border, in the neighbouring towns of Raxaul (India) and Birgunj (Nepal), he tried to obtain permission to visit Nepal (Kathmandu) but without success, and thus had to wait for a later Śivarātri festival to obtain one.

[20] Nepāl (2057 VS) has included them in his book together with a Nepali translation by Bharat Raj Pant. Six *samasyā-pūrtis* (poetic riddles) in praise of the Sanskrit language are among them, along with a seventh one extending good wishes to the journal.

[21] I visited the library in 2008, and found some books by Sankrityayan in the collection. His political works were not represented there, however.

Again disguised as a sadhu, Sankrityayan visited Kathmandu Valley in February 1923 during the festival. On that occasion, visas[22] were easily granted to Indian sadhus and pilgrims to visit the Paśupatināth temple. Sadhus were provided with accommodation and food by the government according to their status. Food, tobacco, and firewood were obtained free of cost from the Mahārājā (the Rana prime minister) (Sankrityayan 1990 VS: 56).

The visits to Nepal in 1920 and 1923 do not really reveal any clear aims other than the journey itself. Later, however, it would be his interest in Buddhism and Buddhist studies that drew Sankrityayan back. He wrote of his first Kathmandu visit in 1923 that it was meant as 'a rest from the pressure of political work' and in fulfilment of a long cherished desire (1957b: 136).

Whatever else Sankrityayan gained from his 1923 visit, it did pave the way for his excellent working relationship with Sharma. He stayed in a math in the Thapathali quarter of Kathmandu, and it was there, in the evening of 15 February, that he first met the royal priest of the Ranas. He was immediately impressed with Sharma's scholarship but had no idea how much wealth he had and how much power he wielded in Nepalese politics (Sankrityayan 1998b [*MJY-1*]: 272). On the very day of Śivarātri, Mahārājā Chandra Shamsher visited the Thapathali math and was curious to learn what Sankrityayan had to say about the political situation in India. The latter proved rather incommunicative, wishing to hide his identity as a political activist (Sankrityayan 1998b [*MJY-1*]: 273). One of the religious fraternities of the Thapathali

[22] As described by Rimāl (2062 VS: 15), the Ranas employed the strategy of divide and rule. They had always tried to create distance between the people, and therefore divided the country into three parts and gave each a name: the Kathmandu Valley was called Nepal; the hill region, Pahāḍ; and the plains, Madheś. They made visas compulsory for their own people in order to enter or leave the Kathmandu Valley. Any kind of political activity was banned, and political science was not taught as a subject at the only institution of higher learning, Tri Chandra College, the closest subjects being foreign history and geography. The main aim of studies was to learn the virtue of nunko sojho ([being] true to one's salt), that is, earning a normal living and displaying fidelity to the rulers. But times were changing, since it was students of Sanskrit who had demanded instruction in history and geography—a campaign known as the Jayatu Saṃskr̥tam Āndolan (Long live the Sanskrit movement) (Nepāl 2057 VS: 5–8).

math had known Sankrityayan as an Arya Samajist speaker (having seen him at the Gaya congress when he translated the speeches of Buddhist monks in the Arya Samaj tent) and as a student of many languages (see the section 'Initial Endeavours Relating to Buddhism' in Chapter 3). This information, passed on, made access to rations easy: instead of having to stand in a queue, Sankrityayan now found his rations being directly delivered to his room, and in larger than normal quantities (Sankrityayan 1998b [*MJY-1*]: 272).

The police in Nepal were preparing to send pilgrims back after the festival, but Sankrityayan wanted to stay in Kathmandu for several more days, so he went to a village, Shikhar Narayan, in the south of the Valley near the Dakṣiṇkālī temple. There he remained for two weeks, reading Sanskrit and English books. Then he turned his attention to searching for Buddhist texts, and towards this end visited some Buddhists in Patan. There he found out about the existence of some valuable Buddhist texts in the library of Hemraj Sharma, to whose house he directed himself. When he arrived, Sharma was busy with colleagues preparing for an upcoming debate on animal sacrifice with the famous Indian swami Saccidananda. Sharma, being a *śākta*, believed in animal sacrifice. After Sankrityayan had given him some ideas about how to present the argument in favour of animal sacrifice, he was impressed and asked him to speak against the swami. Sankrityayan refused to participate because he was still a supporter of the Arya Samaj,[23] and was in fact still a supporter of the swami's position (Sankrityayan 1957b: 137).[24]

Hemraj Sharma later forgot about having met Sankrityayan at his home, but Sankrityayan never did, having been very much impressed

[23] Sankrityayan's involvement with the Arya Samaj or Congress would have created difficulties for his further stay had this fact become known to the government. The Ranas were always wary of any kind of political or social agitation in India. This was what Chandra Shamsher had asked Sankrityayan about. Shukra Raj Shastri would later be arrested, and on 24 January 1941 hung, for simply preaching a discourse on the Bhagavad Gita, because the Ranas were suspicious of him for having travelled to India to see Gandhi and having associated with the Arya Samaj.

[24] This scholarly debate was organized in Singha Darbar (the palace of Chandra Shamsher Rana) for twelve hours over two days. Many of the members were in favour of animal sacrifice, but the debate ended with neither side

with his scholarship and personality. During the stopover when returning from Tibet in 1934, he went on to develop a very good personal relationship with the man. Sankrityayan would meet Rājguru Sharma every time he visited Kathmandu thereafter.

During his visit to Tibet in 1934, Sankrityayan had been looking for a copy of the *Pramāṇavārttika*, and unable to find one, had decided to return via Kathmandu. This time he let himself be introduced to Sharma as an Indian intellectual. The Italian scholar Guiseppe Tucci, it turned out, had already taken a manuscript copy of the text Sharma had in his possession, but even though the original was not available, he was given copies of photographic prints, of which ten pages were missing.

Nepāl (2057 VS: 233) has mentioned that Sharma had borrowed the *Pramāṇavārttika* from a *gubhāju*[25] of the Ghantaghar quarter but never returned it. The reason he could not was because Tucci never returned it to him. He was later criticized in Nepal for having made gifts of the country's treasures to foreigners.

For his third journey to Tibet, in 1936, in search of still other manuscript copies of the *Pramāṇavārttika*, Sankrityayan again chose to travel via Nepal. During this stay his friendship with Rājguru Sharma remained very close, with the latter providing him the use of his own car, horses, and porters. By travelling in such style, Sankrityayan was able to receive special courtesies at the customs offices along the way (Sankrityayan 1995: 21). In an article titled 'On the Way to Tibet' (1984: 83), he wrote about the help Rājguru Sharma had given him for his 1936 journey to Tibet:

> The great Sanskritist and royal preceptor Pandit Hemraja Sharman has always taken a paternal interest in my journeys. This time also I received many a valuable advice and much material assistance in my undertaking. He not only gave me a dozen film packets, but also told me that I should not worry about the expenses, and use the services of photographer if available [...].

---

convincing the other. Prime Minister Chandra Shamsher, trying to smooth things over, told the swami, 'I am satisfied with your logic; however, stopping animal sacrifice in the country is beyond my power. But I swear I myself will not sacrifice animals anymore' (Sama 2026 VS).

25 A Newar Buddhist chief priest.

> 15th April was the date fixed for our departure from Nepal. The three porters engaged to carry our luggage up to Nenum had left Kathmandu early in [the] morning. Two ponies which Guruji (Pandit Hemraj Sharman) gave us with the permission that we could take them as far as we liked were also sent ahead. [...] After taking leave of our kind host Sahu Dharmaman and his family, whose hospitality we had enjoyed for the last two months and to whose generosity all of my Tibetan journeys are due, we went to say good bye to Gurujī, the scholar and patron saint of learning in Nepal. Already suffering from chronic gout, just one day before we started, he got several bruises by falling from the stair-case. At the age of sixty, this is a serious mishap, but with his smiling face covered with grey hair, like a snow-capped Himalayan peak, he was ready to bid us farewell with kind words. With a thankful heart, but without its outward expression lest it might be disagreeable to our venerable friend we took leave; he filled our hands with fruits, suggesting that our venture would be as fruitful. (Sankrityayan 1984: 82–3)

The correspondence between Sharma and Sankrityayan shows Sharma's own great interest in collecting books and manuscripts. It also shows that Sankrityayan sent copies of his printed books to Sharma, or else handwritten drafts of works in progress. The letters tell us, for instance, that Chitta Harsha Bajracharya[26] copied Sankrityayan's Tibetan–Sanskrit dictionary (compiled in 1930, unpublished) for Sharma.

During the 1953 visit, Sankrityayan renewed his old friendship with Sharma in what was to be his last meeting with him:

> Strolling along, we reached the house of Māhilā Gurū.[27] He knew that I was a communist and I also knew that he was a supporter of autocratic feudalism. In spite of this, Sanskrit, Indian culture, and research

[26] I was able to meet Chitta Harsha Bajracharya's son Purna Harsha Bajracharya (82) in Kathmandu in 2008. He said that his father had been a teacher to children who had difficulty in getting admission to Darbar High School and that Sankrityayan had visited their house in the Ghantaghar quarter. The government financed this teaching, and people believed that their children were getting an education equivalent to that on offer at Darbar High School. Chitta Harsha Bajracharya's father, Siddha Harsha Bajracharya, also helped in teaching occasionally.

[27] Hemraj Sharma was at times called Māhilā Guru, being his parents' second son (*māhilā*).

> relating to it were [sufficient] reasons to keep our friendship alive for nineteen years. When I first met him, he was a strong pillar of the government and its influential royal priest. Now the Ranas were gone, so he was like a fish out of water. Age was taking its toll on him. But he met me just as before: openheartedly and with affection. We had a talk for two or three hours that roamed over literature and research. (Sankrityayan 1998b [*MJY*-5]: 102)

Hemraj Sharma noted salient parts of Sankrityayan's visit to Nepal in 1953 in his diary.[28] At one gathering, for example, where Sankrityayan argued strongly for the non-existence of God, Sharma spoke against this, but the entry bears no sign of hostility. Indeed, both often expressed in writing their appreciation for the other (Nepāl 2057 VS: 238). Sankrityayan described Pandit Sharma as follows: 'The personality of Rājguru Pandit Hemraj Sharma was the beautiful combination of scholarship, love for knowledge, tenderness, awareness of art and politics [...]. He was an encyclopaedia of Nepal' (1957b: 140–1). It may be noted that Sankrityayan and Hemraj Sharma shared their family name, Paṇḍe, although neither used it publicly.[29]

Sources: Garzilli (2001); Nepāl (2057 VS); Sankrityayan (1957b; 1998b [*MJY*]; 1995).

[28] Not all of Sharma's diaries are available. Those that are available have been edited and published by Jñānmaṇi Nepāl (2057 VS). Prakash A. Raj, Sharma's grandson, kindly provided me copies of the original diaries along with a diary of his own, written when he was nine years old, in which he tells of Sankrityayan's visit to his home. This entry latter shows that by that time Sankrityayan was a household name in Nepal. Similarly, I have come across another diary entry—made by Rochak Ghimire on 13 March 1958, during Sankrityayan's visit to Nepal with his family—which describes a lecture of his in the Nepal–Bharat Cultural Centre, Kathmandu, during which Sankrityayan expressed his sorrow at not being able to meet the great poet Lakshmi Prasad Devkota because of his cancer. On 22 March 1958 Ghimire wrote about another lecture of Sankrityayan's in which he expressed gratitude for the scholarly information he had received in Nepal and from the Nepalese, which he hoped to repay by sharing the fruits of his research in the future. (Both diaries were made available to me in August 2008 by the writers Prakash A. Raj and Rocak Ghimire.)

[29] Though they had one family name, their gotras were different: Sankrityayan's was Sāṅkṛtya, whereas Sharma's was Kashyap. The Pāṇḍes

Swami Purnananda

During the time Sankrityayan was studying in Banaras following his arrival there in 1912, his convictions underwent a shift from theism towards atheism. Another Nepalese, Swami Purnananda, played an important, if indirect, role in this. They first met in the Indian town of Bareli in 1910, during Sankrityayan's first Himalayan pilgrimage. Sankrityayan had stopped for the night in a pilgrimage shelter (dharmaśālā), as had a caravan of Nepalese sadhus. One of the members of the caravan was Purnananda, who provided Sankrityayan information about Nepal's natural features and religious life. This aroused a desire in the latter to see Nepal with his own eyes (a desire that would take thirteen years to be fulfilled). Swami Purnananda spent part of his time in Banaras (Sankrityayan 1998b [*MJY-1*]: 102); Sankrityayan obtained his address and later looked him up when he went for studies there.

Sankrityayan was much impressed by Purnananda's imperturbability and hoped to learn, through him, more about the Nepalese character. In addition, his new interest in Tantrism was another drawing point. Purnananda was a tantric, and Sankrityayan was well aware that there were many others like him in Nepal. He obtained a number of related Sanskrit texts from Purnananda and started studying them in private, which helped him to improve his Sanskrit, if not to turn him into a tantric master himself overnight (Sankrityayan 1998b [*MJY-1*]: 111). In his desire to become a tantric master, though, Sankrityayan did perform many experiments with the help of the texts. These included, for example, trying to make gold from copper and aromatic oil. For all the time and money spent on this endeavour, he was not, unsurprisingly, successful, but he nevertheless became well known among

---

in Nepal belong to one of six gotras, namely Kaśyap, Gautam, Batsa, Parāśar, Upamanyu, and Bhāradvāj, but never to the Sāṅkṛtya gotra. Sharma was a Kumai Brahmin, whereas the family of Sankrityayan were Saryūpārin Brahmins. The Saryū is a river which flows through northern India, and the Brahmins who lived across it to the south are called Saryūparins, even as those who lived west of the Seti River are called Kumai Brahmins. Saryūpārin Brahmins are found in northern India and in the western Tarai area. For detailed information on the Brahmins of Nepal, see Raj (1996).

his friends as a tantric master, to the point where he was once asked by a couple to cure their infertility. He continued meeting Swami Purnananda and finally requested him to teach him how to perform *devatā siddhi* (direct communication with a deity). The latter was first unwilling but eventually he gave in to the repeated requests. In the end Sankrityayan decided to practise the *navrātra* (nine nights [of the Dashain[30] festival]) sadhana. He had first wanted to perform the sadhana associated with one or the other god or goddess, but Swami Purnananda convinced him to worship Durga in her nine forms instead, telling him that after nine hundred thousand *jāp*s (recitation of a mantra) the goddess would appear and offer to grant a boon.

Convinced of this, Sankrityayan began his sadhana, as instructed by Purnananda, in a room of his teacher Mukhram-ji, who had gone home on holiday. He drank a glass of milk in the evening and otherwise strictly fasted the whole day. Early every morning he took a bath in the Ganga, before anyone could see him. By the eighth day he had become a little frustrated and started wondering why the goddess Durga was showing no signs of appearing. The next day he admitted failure and became so depressed that he wrote two suicide notes and then consumed some poisonous, white thorn apple seeds that he had brought to offer to Durga. Fortunately, his friend Yagesh visited his room that evening and saved his life. Sankrityayan took a long time to recuperate and could not even read books for several weeks. This incident marked his turn towards atheism and towards materialist thought. In the future he would live more for the world and, sloughing off Kedarnath Pandey, procreate Rahul Sankrityayan.

Source: Sankrityayan (1998b [*MJY-1*], 1957b).

Sankrityayan developed social contacts with other prominent Nepalese besides the above-mentioned persons. They included such literary personalities as Balchandra Sharma, Bhimnidhi Tivari, Kedarman Vyathit, Siddhicharan Shrestha, Mahananda Sapkota, and Chitradhar Upasak; and such political personalities as B.P. Koirala, Pushpa Lal Shrestha, Ganeshman Simha, and Dilliraman Regmi. Their meetings and friendship are known of only from scattered sources, not from the interlocutors themselves.

30 *Daśahrā* in Hindi.

APPENDIX 2

Muralidhar Bhattarai's Challenge and Rahul Sankrityayan's Response to It

Sankrityayan stayed at Dharmaratna Yami's house in Kathmandu for a month with his wife Kamala during his visit to Nepal in 1953 (Sankrityayan 1998b (*JY-6*): 411). After his return to India, he wrote three articles about Dharmaratna Yami for the year's May, June, and July issues of a monthly magazine, *Jīvan sāhitya*, to show his admiration for his friend and gratitude for his hospitality. Those three articles were published the following year as a book by Shankar Bahadur K.C. in Kathmandu. A reprint of it was published in 1963. The second edition has thirty-six pages, which not only present Yami's life story but also sketch the political and social situation in Nepal before and after the coming of democracy in 1950. Dharmaratna Yami was one of the country's freedom fighters; the book thus contains important source material relating to Nepalese history.

The account, however, stirred up animosities among some, among whom Muralidhar Bhattarai was the most outspoken. So unhappy was he with Sankrityayan's narration that he challenged the writer to a debate during the latter's next visit to Nepal in 1956.

On 14 November 1956 Sankrityayan wrote regarding this incident in his diary:

> यमि ने मेरे द्वारा लिखित जीवन साहित्य में दिल्ली में छपी अपनी जीवनी को पुस्तकाकार छपवा दिया था। इसमें श्री मुरलीधर और श्रीरामजी उपाध्याय को राजाओं का चापलूस लिखा है, अब दु:ख होना ही चाहिए। बात चाहे सच्ची हो, पर दूसरे के कलेजे को छेदना बहुत बुरा है। मुझे बहुत दु:ख हुआ। तबसे वे मिले नहीं। सभ्यता की रक्षा करते हुए कुछ करना ही होगा।

> Yami-ji has published the biography of him that I wrote and had published in *Jīvansāhitya* in Delhi. It is written therein that Mr Muralidhar and Mr Ramji Upadhyaya fawn on kings; now there has had to be some unpleasantness. This [accusation] may be true, but piercing someone's heart is very bad. It has caused me much pain. I have not met him since then. I shall have to do something in the interest of civility. (Sankrityayan 1998b (*JY-6*): 326)

Muralidhar Bhattarai's Challenge[31]

ऊँ

हूँकार

CHALLENGE

राहुल सांकृत्यायन को ललकार

राहुल जी,

1] "धर्मरत्न 'यमि'" नाम की आप की दृष्टि में सर्व श्रेष्ठ पुस्तिका में आपने जो झूट-मूट, अन्ट-सन्ट बातें लिखी हैं उसके प्रमाणभूत कागजात आप के साथ हों तो जनता के सामने पेश करने का साहस कीजिए। कोई माई का लाल केवल तर्क से भी उन आक्षेपों को सिद्धकर सकने का साहस करता हो तो सामने खड़ा कीजिए। या तो इस महान् भूल के लिए माफी मांग कर मानवता का परिचय दीजिए।

2] आप कहेंगे लोग ऐसा कहते हैं तो उन लोगों को और आप को भी लोग विकृत मस्तिष्क तथा विक्रीत-आत्मा कहते हैं, क्या मैं इन बातों पर विश्वास करूँ?

3] मैं पूर्ण आस्तिक, आप भयंकर नास्तिक! आइए मैदान में इस शर्त पर शास्त्रार्थ करें कि विजित को विजयी के आजन्म विस्तर उठाए चलना होगा।

4] माध्यम संस्कृत, हिन्दी, नेपाली जो आप चाहें।

आपका प्रतिद्वन्द्वी:
प्रतिवादिध्वान्त विध्वंसक
पं मुरलीधर भट्टराई

भगवती प्रेस, ठहिटी, नेपाल

[31] Courtesy of Ghimire (2056 VS). These pamphlets were made available to me by Rochak Ghimire in 2008.

English Translation of Muralidhar Bhattarai's Challenge

OM

Hũkār

CHALLENGE

A Challenge to Rahul Sankrityayan

Rahul-ji,

1. In your booklet titled *Dharma Ratna 'Yami'*, which is a jolly fine booklet in your opinion, you have written a tissue of lies and utter nonsense. If you have written proof [of your claims], then have the courage to present it in front of the public. If there is some person bold enough to prove these charges, then bring him forward. Otherwise show some humanity by apologizing for this great mistake.
2. You may say that when persons utter such [confessions], then people say about them—and will say about you—that they are sick in mind or have sold their souls. Should I believe such things?
3. I am fully a believer and you are an utter atheist. Come let us engage in public scholarly debate on the condition: whoever loses will carry the winner's bedding [for him] for the rest of his life.
4. The medium will be Sanskrit, Hindi, or Nepali, as you wish.

Your rival, destroyer of darkness in adversaries,
Pandit Muralidhar Bhattarai

Sankrityayan's Answer to the Challenge and Muralidhar Bhattarai's Response to It

महापंडित राहुल सांकृत्यायन ने पं मुरलीधर से क्षमा माँगी

"मेरे चैलेञ्ज" के उत्तर में राहुल जी ने यह पत्र लिखकर मानवता और विद्याविनयसम्पन्नता का परिचय दिया है जिससे मैं अत्यन्त प्रभावित हुआ।" —पं॰ मुरलीधर

राहुल सांकृत्यायन
काठमांडू २०।११।५६

पंडित श्री मुरलीधर भट्टराई के प्रति मेरी लेखनी से अन्याय हुआ है। मैंने अपने 'नेपाल' में उनके नाम से जो लिखा है वह उनके लिए दुःखप्रद है। मैंने सुनी-सुनाई बातें लिखीं। जिनके बारे में मैं जाँच नहीं कर सकता हूँ। उनके दुःख के लिए मुझे बहुत पश्चाताप है। मैं उनसे क्षमा माँगता हूँ।

उनकी विद्वता से मैं प्रभावित हूँ। नेपाल के स्वतन्त्रता आन्दोलन में जो उनका काम है, जो उन्होंने कष्ट सहन किया है उसका मैं प्रशंसक हूँ।

—राहुल सांकृत्यायन

भगवती प्रेस, ठहिटी।

Mahapandit Rahul Sankrityayan's Apology to Pandit Muralidhar

'Rahul-ji has shown his humanity and a true sense of scholarly humility by writing the following letter in response to 'my challenge', and I am very much impressed by this.'—Pandit Murali Dhar

Rahul Sankrityayan
Kathmandu 20.11.56

My pen has done an injustice to Pandit Sri Muralidhar Bhattarai. What I wrote in my [book] *Nepal*[32] in connection with his name has caused him pain. I wrote what I had heard by word of mouth. I have not been able to investigate [the truth of] the matter. I greatly regret the pain caused to him. I beg his forgiveness.

I am impressed by his scholarship. I praise his work on behalf of Nepal's freedom movement, which he undertook at the cost of [great] suffering.

—Rahul Sankrityayan

32 Sankrityayan's book on Nepal never got published, as noted in the biographical sketch of Dharmaratna Yami in Appendix 1. Sankrityayan's quote from *JY-6* above makes it clear that the work in question was the booklet *Dharma Ratna 'Yami'*.

APPENDIX 3

Lakshmi Prasad Devkota's 'Pāgal' and Rahul Sankrityayan

Lakshmi Prasad Devkota's well-known poem, 'Pāgal' (The madman) is a masterpiece of Nepali poetic literature. It has been described as reflecting his own experiences during his time in the Indian mental hospital in Ranchi and at the same time as delivering a revolutionary political message (Hutt 1993: 43). However, the initial incitement to write the poem was an article by Sankrityayan that appeared in the Delhi-based Hindi monthly journal *Ājkal* (1953). Indeed, the poem was an immediate response to it. It was published that same year.[33]

The background to the poem is as follows: There was a 'tea shop'—Laptan Hotel—in the Dillibazar quarter of Kathmandu, which was a gathering spot for writers, politicians, teachers, and professors at the beginning of the second half of the 20th century. Besides discussions, it provided a congenial locale for reading newspapers. Literary people such as Balakr̥sṇa Sama, Lakshmi Prasad Devkota, Janaklāl Śarmā, and many other renowned Nepali intellectuals of that time were regular visitors. After Sankrityayan's trip to Nepal in 1953 and after the above-mentioned article had appeared, a copy of the journal found its way to the tea shop (Ātreya 2066a VS and J. Śarmā 2052 VS) when such an assortment of writers, including Devkota himself, were present. Devkota was immediately drawn to the title, 'Nepālī Mahākavi Devkoṭā' (Nepal's Master Poet Devkota) and read the whole article then and there. Towards the end, Devkota stopped short at the following lines:

> देवकोटा नेपाली के पन्त-प्रसाद-निराला तीनों हैं, इसमें अतिशयोक्ति नहीं है। निराला के कुछ दूसरे गुण भी उनमें मौजूद हैं, यद्यपि उतनी मात्रा में नहीं। निराला को राँची ले जाने की बात ही भर कितनी बार उठी, किन्तु जब देवकोटा को घरवालों ने विक्षिप्त समझ राँची चलने के लिए कहा, तो उन्होंने जरा भी आपत्ति नहीं की और राँची के पागलखाने में कुछ दिन रह भी आए।

[33] In the Bhādra-Āśvin 2010 VS issue of the Nepali journal *Pragati* (J. Śarmā 2052 VS: 47).

> It is not an exaggeration to say that Devkota is a combination of Prasad-Pant and Nirala.[34] He also has some of Nirala's secondary qualities, but not to the same degree. The issue of taking Nirala to Ranchi was raised [with him] many times, but when Devkota's family told him to go to Ranchi, thinking him mad, he agreed without the least objection; and he stayed for some days in the Ranchi madhouse. (Sankrityayan, in *Ājkal,* May 1953: 87)

Devkota became very angry and his face turned red. He was not happy that Sankrityayan had been informed about his time in Ranchi. He pointed his finger at Janaklāl Śarmā and said, 'You are one fool leaking information to another fool,' knowing that Śarmā was close to Sankrityayan and could have been the only conduit. Then he stormed out.

That night Devkota wrote his plaintive poem in his continuing fit of anger, and that calmed him down. Early the next day Śarmā was invited to listen to the poem at Devkota's house. In the place where he had written 'your Mahāpaṇḍit Rāhul [is] my great fool [तिम्रा महापण्डित राहुल मेरा मूर्ख]', Śarmā requested him to take out the name 'Rāhul' and said 'mahāpaṇḍit' would be enough. Devkota agreed to do so.[35]

Mad (Pāgal)[36]

Surely, my friend, I am mad,
that's exactly what I am!

I see sounds,
hear sights,
taste smells.
I touch things thinner than air,
things whose existence the world denies,

[34] Jaya Shankar Prasad, Sumitranandan Pant, and Surya Kant Tripathi Nirala were three pillars of 20th-century Hindi literature.

[35] For details, see J. Śarmā (2052 VS: 41–7).

[36] The English translation and the glossary items related to the poem in the footnotes are taken from Hutt (1993: 53–6). Hutt's footnotes are indicated by '(H)'.

Things whose shapes the world does not know.
Stones I see as flowers,
pebbles have soft shapes,
water-smoothed at the water's edge
in the moonlight;
as heaven's sorceress smiles at me,
they put out leaves, they soften, they glimmer
and pulse, rising up like mute maniacs,
like flowers—a kind of moonbird flower.
I speak to them just as they speak to me,
in a language, my friend,
unwritten, unprinted, unspoken,
uncomprehended, unheard.
Their speech comes in ripples, my friend,
to the moonlit, Gangā's shore.
Surely, my friend, I am mad,
that's exactly what I am!

You are clever, and wordy,[37]
your calculations exact and correct forever,
but take one from one in my arithmetic,
and you are still left with one.
You use five senses, but I have six,
you have a brain, my friend,
but I have a heart.
To you a rose is a rose, and nothing more,
but I see Helen and Padminī,
you are forceful prose,[38]
I am liquid poetry;
you freeze as I am melting,
you clear as I cloud over,
and then it's the other way around;
your world is solid, mine vapor,

[37] Sankrityayan had been well trained by the Arya Samaj to deliver effective speeches.

[38] Sankrityayan was known as a prose writer, having hardly any poems to his credit.

your world is gross, mine subtle,
you consider a stone an object,
material hardness is your reality,[39]
but I try to grasp hold of dreams,
just as you try to catch the rounded truths
of cold, sweet, graven coins.
My passion is that of a thorn, my friend
yours is for gold and diamonds,
you say that the hills are deaf and dumb,
I say that they are eloquent.
Surely, my friend,
mine is a loose inebriation,
that's exactly how I am.

In the cold of the month of Māgh I sat,
enjoying the first white warmth of the star:
the world called me a drifter.
When they saw me staring blankly for seven days
after my return from the cremation *ghāṭs*,[40]
they said I was possessed.
When I saw the first frosts of Time
on the hair of a beautiful woman,
I wept for three days:
the Buddha was touching my soul,
but they said that I was raving!
When they saw me dance
on hearing the first cuckoo of Spring,
they called me a madman.
A silent, moonless night once made me breathless,
the agony of destruction made me jump,
and on that day the fools put me in the stocks!
One day I began to sing with the storm,

39 Sankrityayan was a materialist and realist; Devkota a romantic and theist.

40 A *ghāt* is a stepped platform beside a river where Hindus take their daily baths and where the bodies of the dead are cremated (H).

the wise old men sent me off to Rānchī.[41]
One day I thought I was dead,
I lay down flat, a friend pinched me hard,
and said, 'Hey, madman, you're not dead yet!'
These things went on, year upon year,
I am mad, my friend,
that's exactly what I am!

I have called the ruler's wine blood,
the local whore a corpse
and the king a pauper.
I have abused Alexander the Great,
poured scorn on so-called great souls,
but the lowly I have raised
to the seventh heaven on a bridge of praise.
Your[42] great scholar[43] is my great fool,
your heaven my hell,
your gold my iron, my friend,
your righteousness my crime.
Where you see yourself as clever,
I see you to be an absolute dolt,
your progress, my friend, is my decline,
that's how our values contradict.
Your universe is as a single hair to me,
certainly, my friend, I'm moonstruck
completely moonstruck, that's what I am!

I think the blind man is the leader of the world,
the ascetic in his cave is a back-sliding deserter;
those who walk the stage of falsehood

[41] Rānchī is [where] the mental asylum in Bihār, northern India [was located] (H).

[42] Ātreya (2066b VS: 78) conjectures that this possessive pronoun 'your' refers to Janaklāl Śarmā.

[43] 'Rāhul' was taken out here. 'Great scholar' is the translation of mahāpaṇḍit, the title conferred on Sankrityayan by the Kāśī Paṇḍit Sabhā (see Appendix 4). Mahāpaṇḍit is also used ironically in the meaning of *mahāmūrkha* (great fool) (Ātreya 2066b VS: 572).

I see as dark buffoons,
those who fail I consider successful,
progress for me is stagnation:
I must be either cockeyed or mad—
I am mad, my friend, I am mad.

Look at the whorish dance
of shameless leadership's tasteless tongues,
watch them break the back of the people's rights.
When the black lies of sparrow-headed newsprint
challenge Reason, the hero within me,
with their webs of falsehood,
then my cheeks grow red, my friend,
as red as glowing charcoal.
When voiceless people drink black poison,
right before my eyes,
and drink it through their ears,
thinking that it's nectar,
then every hair on my body stands up,
like the Gorgon's serpent hair.
When I see the tiger resolve to eat the deer,
or the big fish the little one,
then into even my rotten bones there comes
the fearsome strength of Dadhīchī's soul,[44]
and it tries to speak out, my friend,
like a stormy day which falls with a crash form Heaven.
When Man does not regard his fellow as human,
all my teeth grind together like Bhīmsen's,[45]
red with fury, my eyeballs roll round
like a half-penny coin, and I stare
at this inhuman world of Man
with a look of lashing flame.

44 According to the Mahābhārata, the magical 'diamond-weapon' of Indra, the god of war, was made from a bone of the legendary sage Dadhīchī (H).

45 Bhīmsen 'the terrible' was the second of the five Pāṇḍava princes and was described in the Mahābhārata as an enormous man of fierce and wrathful disposition (H).

My organs leap from their frame,
there is tumult, tumult!
My breath is a storm, my face is distorted,
my brain burns, my friend, like a submarine fire,
a submarine fire! I'm insane like a forest ablaze,
a lunatic, my friend,
I would swallow the whole universe raw.
I am a moonbird for the beautiful,
a destroyer of the ugly,
tender and cruel,
the bird that seals the fire of Heaven,
a son of the storm thrown up
by an insane volcano, terror incarnate,
surely, my friend, my brain is whirling, whirling,
that's exactly how I am!

APPENDIX 4

Rahul Sankrityayan's Felicitation Certificate

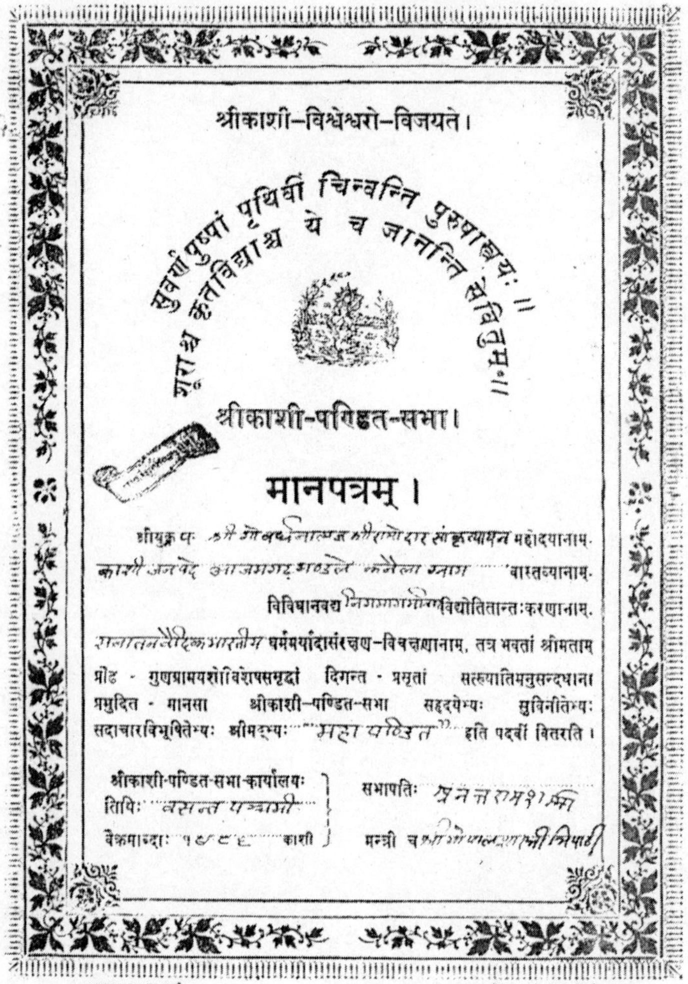

श्रीकाशी–विश्वेश्वरो–विजयते।

गुणाश्च सुवर्णपुष्पां पृथिवीं चिन्वन्ति पुरुषास्त्रयः। कृतविद्याश्च ये च जानन्ति सेवितुम्॥

श्रीकाशी–पण्डित–सभा।

मानपत्रम्।

श्रीयुक्त पं० श्री गोवर्धनात्मज श्रीरामोदार सांकृत्यायन महोदयानाम्,
काशी जनपदे आजमगढ़ मण्डले कनैला ग्राम वास्तव्यानाम्,
विविधानवद्य निगमागमैः विद्योतितान्तःकरणानाम्,
सनातन वैदिक भारतीय धर्ममर्यादासंरक्षण–विचक्षणानाम्, तत्र भवतां श्रीमताम्
प्रौढ - गुणग्रामयशोविशेषसमृद्धां दिगन्त - प्रसृतां सत्ख्यातिमनुसन्दधाना
प्रमुदित - मानसा श्रीकाशी–पण्डित–सभा सहृदयेभ्यः सुविनीतेभ्यः
सदाचारविभूषितेभ्यः श्रीमद्भ्यः "महा पण्डित" इति पदवीं वितरति।

श्रीकाशी-पण्डित-सभा-कार्यालयः
तिथिः वसन्त पञ्चमी
वैक्रमाब्दाः १९८९ काशी

सभापतिः
मन्त्री च

Figure A.1 Rahul Sankrityayan's Felicitation Certificate

Source: Image made available to the author by Ratna Sundar Śākya in 2008, and printed with the permission of Jaya Parhawk, daughter of Rahul Sankrityayan and Kamala Sankrityayan.

Kāśī-viśveśvarais victorious
Three kinds of men can pick the golden flower which is the Earth:
Warriors, scholars, and those who know how to serve.

Śrī Kāśī Paṇḍit Sabhā

Felicitation Certificate

Mr. *Rāmodār Sāṅkr̥tyāyan*, son of Mr. *Govardhan* [and] resident of Kāśī *janapad* (district), Azamgarh district, *Kanailā* village, who has studied in depth and whose soul is irradiated by the various faultless [forms of] ancient and modern knowledge, [and being] one who skilfully protects India's *sanātan vaidik* religion and customs—mature, talented, well reputed in his own locality and in foreign countries—upon such a modest, kind-hearted man adorned with good conduct the *Kāśī Paṇḍit Sabhā* with joyful spirit confers the title "*mahāpaṇḍit*".

The office of the *Kāśī Paṇḍita Sabhā*

Date: Vasanta pañcamī — President: Anant Rām Śarmmā

1989 V.S., *Kāśī* — and Adviser: Śrī Gopāl Śāstrī Tripāṭhī

APPENDIX 5

A List of Doctoral Theses on Rahul Sankrityayan

Below are listed twenty-six doctoral theses on Rahul Sankrityayan. Of them,[46] twenty-three relate to Sankrityayan's literary output, two to his involvement in the peasant movement (S.Nos 22 and 26) in Bihar, and another to the process of altering his identity (S.No. 25). The sign '◆◆' following English translations of titles indicates works I was able to access. The name of the university is not mentioned when not known; in that case, then, the place-name indicates the place of study. Twenty-five theses were written in Hindi in India, and one in German in Germany. All English translations of the titles are mine.

All dissertations were written and/or published after the demise of Sankrityayan in 1963. The first one was completed in 1965. After the publication of the twelfth dissertation in 1975 there is a gap of sixteen years until 1991, when Hildegard Fischer published an analysis of Sankrityayan's historical novel *Siṃh senāpati* and made a translation of it from Hindi into German.

A huge loss to Hindi literature was felt following Sankrityayan's loss of memory (in December 1961) and eventual death (in April 1963), and in response many researchers became inspired to study his life and work. From 1965 to 1975 many fruits of these studies were published, followed by the lull. After a decade or so, however, the topic attracted renewed interest, the reason being that in 1993–4 Sankrityayan's centennial anniversary was looming, with anticipated celebrations in India and many other countries. The last decade of the 20th century continued to produce many dissertations on Sankrityayan along with many other non-academic works. Numerous Indian journals dedicated volumes to Sankrityayan, and many symposiums were organized both in India and abroad. Some centennial anniversary volumes[47] were also

[46] The twenty-one titles without the sign '◆◆' are courtesy of *Abhinav Kadam* 1 (16–17), edited by Jayaprakash Dhumketu (December 2006–November 2007), pp. 535–6.

[47] Some of the centenary volumes on the works and life of Rahul Sankrityayan that have come to my notice are:

1. *Mahapandit Rahul Sankrityayan Birth Century Volume*, Buddha Dharmakar Sabha, August, 1994.

published upon the occasion. The Indian government issued a commemorative postal stamp in 1993. In this way, the grand celebration of his centennial anniversary in and outside India encouraged people to continue work on Sankrityayan. Further, India's Kendrīya Hindi Saṃsthān [Central Hindi Organization] established the Mahapandit Rahul Sankrityayan Award in 1983 to honour two writers every year for outstanding contributions to Hindi travel literature and research relating to Hindi literature, respectively.[48]

---

2. *Mahapandit Rahul Sankrityayan Birth Century Volume*, Maha Bodhi Society, Calcutta, 1994
3. *Sāptāhik Hindustān*, 30 August 1992 (Birth Century Volume)

Among the centennial anniversary celebrations are:

1. Mahapandit Rahul Sankrityayan Birth Century Program, 9 April 1993, organized by UP Hindi Sansthan, Lucknow and Hindustan Academy, Allahabad.
2. Rahul Sankrityayan Memorial National Workshop, 27–28 March 1992, organized by Hindi Sahitya Sammelan, Allahabad.
3. Rahul Memorial Seminar, 23–25 March 1993 Allahabad.
4. Rahul Birth Century Celebration, 9–14 April 1993, Bhaktapur, Kathmandu.
5. Rahul Sankrityayan Seminar, Ministry of Culture, UP, India (date not known).
6. International Seminar on Rahul Sankrityayan: A Multi-Dimensional Personality, 27–28 April 1993, Maha Bodhi Society, Calcutta.
7. Jivan Yatra—eine Pilgerreise durch Religionen & Kontinente [Jivan Yatra—A pilgrimage through religions and continents], photo exhibition, 20–21 November 1994, organized by Indian Cultural Center, Berlin and South Asian Institute, Humboldt University Berlin.
8. Jivan Yatra—eine Pilgerreise durch Religionen & Kontinente [Jivan Yatra—A pilgrimage through religion and continents] photo exhibition, 5–10 December 1994, organized by Humboldt University and Center for Asian and African Studies Academy of Sciences Berlin at the South Asian Institute, University of Heidelberg, Germany.
9. Mahāpaṇḍit Rāhul Sāṅkṛtyāyan Pratiṣṭhān [Mahapandit Rahul Sankrityayan Foundation] was founded in Delhi in 1995, and has organized a 'Rahul Lecture Series' every year since.

[48] Twenty-nine scholars were awarded from 1993 to 2007. See www.hindisansthan.org (accessed on 6 June 2012).

Table A.1 below presents the dissertations on Sankrityayan in chronological order of publication/completion.

Table A.1 Theses/Dissertations on Rahul Sankrityayan

S.No.	Title of the Thesis	Researcher	University/ Place	Year
1.	*Rāhul kā kathā sāhitya* [Rahul's Fictional Literature]	Subodh Chandra Saksena	Lucknow University	1965
2.	*Rāhul Sāṅkr̥tyāyan kā kathā sāhitya: kahāniyā̃ aur upa-nyās* [Rahul Sankrityayan's Fictional Literature: Stories and Novels]	Gauri Shankar Sharma	*Not known*	1966
3.	*Rāhul Sāṅkr̥tyayān ke kathā sāhitya kā adhyayan* [A Study of Sankrityayan's Fictional Literature]	Prabhakar Mishra	Kurukshetra	1966
4.	*Rāhul jī kā kathā sāhitya* [Rahul's Fictional Literature]	Makhanlal Sharma	Agra	1967
5.	*Hindī yātrā sāhitya ko Rāhul Sāṅkr̥tyāyan kī den* [The Contribution of Rahul Sankrityayan to Hindi Travel Literature]	Sushila Rani Garg	Agra	1969
6.	*Mahāpaṇḍit Rāhul Sāṅkr̥tyāyan ke sr̥jnātmak kathā sāhitya kā saiddhāntik adhyayan* [A Theoretical Study of Mahapandit Rahul Sankrityayan's Creative Fictional Literature]◆◆	Gokarna Nath Shukla	Navalpur	1970
7.	*Rāhul Sāṅkr̥tyāyan kā sr̥jnātmak sāhitya* [The Fictional Literature of Rahul Sankrityayan]	Sudesh Kumari Vasadev	Delhi	1970
8.	*Mahāpaṇḍit Rāhul Sāṅkr̥tyāyan: sr̥jnātmak sāhitya kā adhyayan* [A Study of Rahul Sankrityayan's Creative Literature]	Khelchandra Anand	Punjab University, Chandigarh	1970

(*Cont'd*)

Table A.1 (*Cont'd*)

S.No.	Title of the Thesis	Researcher	University/ Place	Year
9.	*Kathākār Rāhul Sāṅkr̥tyāyan: ālocnātmak adhyayan* [Fiction Writer Rahul Sankrityayan: A Critical Study]	Dinesh Chandra Chaturvedi	Uttar Pradesh	1971
10.	*Rāhul vāṅmay kā adhyayan* [A Study of Rahul's Literary Work]	Surya Kumar Yog	Vishvabharati, Kolkata	1973
11.	*Rāhul jī ke lalit kalā par sāmyavād kā prabhāv* [The Influence of Communism on Rahul's Fine Art]	Vishvanath Shulka	Merath [Meerut]	1974
12.	*Rāhul jī ke gadya sāhitya kā śailīgat adhyayan* [A Stylistic Study of Rahul's Prose]	Gupteshvar Nath Upadhdhyay	Aligarh	1975
13.	*General Simha: Interpretation und Übersetzung eines historischen Romans / von Rahul Samkrtyayan.* (In German) [General Simha: Interpretation and Translation of One of the Historical Novels of Rahul Sankrityayan]◆◆	Hildegard Fischer	Humboldt University, Berlin	1991
14.	*Rāhul Sāṅkr̥tyāyan ke yātrā sāhitya kā samagra adhyayan* [An Inclusive Study of Rahul Sankrityayan's Travel Literature]	Kalpana Sahay	Kumaon	1992
15.	*Rāhul Sāṅkr̥tyāyan ke upanyāsõ mẽ sāmājik tatvajñān* [Social Theoretical Thought in Rahul Sankrityayan's Novels]	Anjali M.M.	Kerala	1992
16.	*Rāhul Sāṅkr̥tyāyan kī sāmājik evaṃ aitihāsik dr̥ṣṭi* [The Social and Historical Vision of Rahul Sankrityayan]	Meena Kumari	Shimla	1992

(*Cont'd*)

Table A.1 (*Cont'd*)

S.No.	Title of the Thesis	Researcher	University/ Place	Year
17.	*Rāhul Sāṅkr̥tyāyan ke kathā sāhitya mẽ pragatiśīl cetnā* [Progressive Consciousness in Rahul Sankrityayan's Fictional Literature]	Dinesh Kushvah	Banaras Hindu University, Varanasi	1992
18.	*Rāhul ke kathā sāhitya mẽ samsāmyik prāsaṅgiktā* [The Contemporary Relevance of Rahul's Fictional Literature]	Vibha Pathak	Varanasi	1995
19.	*Rāhul Sāṅkr̥tyāyan ke upanyāsõ mẽ mārksvād* [Marxism in Rahul Sankrityayan's Novels]	Shivraj Dhanpat Singh	Jhansi	1995
20.	*Mahāpaṇḍit Rāhul Sāṅkr̥tyāyan ke upanyāsõ aur kahāniyõ mẽ parilakṣit sāmājik cetnā* [The Social Consciousness Depicted in Rahul Sankrityayan's Novels and Short Stories]	Kumaran A. Senthil	Bangalore	1998
21.	*Rāhul Sāṅkr̥tyāyan ke kathā sāhitya kā mūlyāṅkan* [An Assessment of Rahul Sankrityayan's Fictional Literature]◆◆	Madan Rai	Delhi	--
22.	*Rāhuljī: Bihar kā kisān āndolan* [Rahul: The Peasant Movement in Bihar]	Urmileś	Jawaharlal Nehru University, New Delhi	1978–80*
23.	*Rāhul Sāṅkr̥tyāyan kā yātrā sāhitya: Ghumakkaṛ śāstra* [The Travel Literature of Rahul Sankrityayan: *Ghumakkaṛ śāstra*]	Janaki Pandey	Bhagalpur	2000
24.	*Rāhul Sāṅkr̥tyāyan kā kathā sāhitya: cetnā ke vividh pravāh* [Rahul Sankrityayan's Fictional Literature: Different Currents of Consciousness]	Ravidhra Chudamani Patil	Kohalpur	2005

(*Cont'd*)

Table A.1 (*Cont'd*)

S.No.	Title of the Thesis	Researcher	University/ Place	Year
25	*Mahāpaṇḍit Rāhul Sāṅkṛtyāyan ke vyaktitvāntaraṇ kī prakriyā* [Rahul Sankrityayan's Practice of Altering His Personality]◆◆	Abhijīt Bhaṭṭācārya	Calcutta University, Kolkata	2005
26	*Rāhul Sāṅkṛtyāyan: bhārtīya mukti āndolan ke apratim yoddhā* [Rahul Sankrityayan: An Unequalled Warrior of the Indian Independence Movement]◆◆	Harerām Pāṇḍeya	Jai Prakash University, Bihar	2011

Source: Author.
Notes: * Urmileś (1994: Foreword).

APPENDIX 6

Chronology of Prominent Events in Rahul Sankrityayan's Life[49]

9 April 1893	Birth at grandparents' village of Pandaha in Azamgarh district in Uttar Pradesh
1899–1901	Primary education in Urdu school
1904	Married to Ramdulari by his parents
1907	First fled home, going alone to Calcutta
1909	Fled home to Calcutta for the second time
1910	Undertook a pilgrimage to the western Himalayas before going to Banaras and starting studies there
1911–12	Studies in Banaras
September 1912	Became a Vaishnava sadhu in Chapra, Saran district, in the state of Bihar; acquired a new name, Ramudar Das
July 1913	Fled Chapra for south India
1913	Reached Tirumishi and was again initiated as a Śri Vaishnava sadhu, given the name Damodarachari
1914	Headed back north to Ayodhya, and gained entry to a Vedanta school
October 1914	Fetched back home by his father, for his final longer stay in the parental home
1915	Entered Ārya Musafir Vidyālaya in Agra, and gained a reputation as a Arya Samajist zealot and an iconoclast
1915	First Hindi article appeared in Bhāskar, directed against bogus sadhus

[49] For an outline of Sankrityayan's life see the section titled 'An Outline of Sankrityayan's Life' in Chapter 1 of this work.

1916	Undertook advanced studies in the Sanskrit department at Lahore Dayanand Anglo Vedic (DAV) College
1917	Met his father for the last time in Azamgarh. Took a vow not to return to his home district of Azamgarh until he was fifty years old
1920–1	Travelled to various places in India and studied Mīmāṃsā and Vedanta philosophies in Tirumishi
1921	Entered politics and joined the Congress party in Chapra
January 1922	Was arrested while chairing a meeting of the District Congress Committee in Chapra and sent to Baksar jail for six months.
December 1922	Participated in the Gaya congress and campaigned on behalf of the future Swaraj Party, while also pushing to have the Bodh Gaya Temple handed over to the Buddhists
March–April 1923	Travelled through Nepal to participate in the Śivarātri festival
April 1923–April 1925	Imprisoned for two years in the Hazaribagh jail, and wrote his first book (the Utopian novel *Bāisvī̃ sadī*)
1927–8	Took up a teaching post in Sanskrit at Vidyālaṅkāra Pariveṇa in Sri Lanka, where he immersed himself in Buddhist texts; earned the title Tripiṭakācārya
1929–30	Undertook first journey to Tibet, entering from Nepal, and was accorded the title 'mahāpaṇḍit' by the Kāśī Paṇḍit Sabhā from Banaras
22 June 1930	Initiated as a Buddhist monk in Sri Lanka, receiving a new name, Rahul Sankrityayan
December 1930–November 1931	Took part in the satyagraha, visited many historically important places including Karachi, Mohenjo-Daro, Harappa, and Sarnath

1932–3	Went to London as a religious representative of the Maha Bodhi Society; also visited France and Germany
March 1934	Set off for Tibet via Kalimpong
1935	Visited Malaya, Japan, Korea, Manchuria, Iran, and the Soviet Union
1936	Undertook third journey to Tibet via Nepal
1937	Visited Russia for a second time at the invitation of the Soviet Academy (upon Stcherbatsky's suggestion) to teach Sanskrit at Leningrad University
22 December 1937	Married Ellena Narvertovna Kozerovskaya in Leningrad
1938	Made fourth journey to Tibet
December 1938	Became a member of the Congress Socialist Party and organized a peasant satyagraha, was imprisoned for a few months
5 September 1938	Birth of his son Igor in Russia
1939	Became a member of the Bihar Communist Party
February 1940	Arrested and spent the next twenty-nine months, from 1940 to 1942, in the Hazaribag and Deoli jails
1942	Travelled to different parts of India for both political work and literary meetings
July 1945–July 1947	Served as a professor at Leningrad University
1947–8	Was elected president of the All-India Hindi Literary Conference in Allahabad
December 1947	Was dismissed from the Communist Party of India; learned that he was suffering from diabetes
December 1950	Took marriage vows with Kumari Kamala Pariyar
1953	Birth of his daughter, Jaya
1955	Birth of his son, Jeta

1958	Travelled to Burma and China; awarded Sāhitya Vācaspati by the Hindi Sāhitya Sammelan
1959–61	Headed Department of Philosophy at Vidyālaṅkāra University in Sri Lanka
11 December 1961	Suffered memory loss in Calcutta
1962–3	Underwent medical treatment in India and Russia
14 April 1963	Died at his Darjeeling house at the age of seventy
1963	Posthumously awarded the Padma Bhushan by the Government of India

RAHUL SANKRITYAYAN'S WORKS

In Hindi

1931. *Buddha caryā*. Sarnath: Mahabodhi Sabha.

1942a. *Bauddh darśan*. Allahabad: Kitab Mahal.

1942b. *Darśan digdarśan*. Allahabad: Kitab Mahal.

1946. *Merī Jīvan Yātrā* [*MJY*]. Allahabad: Kitab Mahal.

1950. *Ādi Hindī kī kahāniyā̃ aur gītẽ*. Patna: Rahul Pustak Pratisthan.

1952. *Bauddha saṃskṛti*. Calcutta: Adhunik Pustak Bhavan.

1956. *Mahāmānav Buddha*. Lucknow: Buddha Vihar.

1957a. *Dohā koś* by Siddha Sarahapād, edited and re-translated by Rahul Sankrityayan. Patna: Bihar Rastra Bhasha Parishad.

1957b. *Jinkā maĩ kṛtajñ* [*JMK*]. Allahabad: Kitab Mahal.

1957c. *Navdīkṣit bauddh*. Lucknow: Buddha Vihar.

1960. *Siṃhal ghumakkaṛ Jayavardhan*. Delhi: Rajpal and Sons.

1961. *Siṃhal ke vīr*. Allahabad: Kitab Mahal.

1963. *Dharmaratna 'Yami'*. Kathmandu: Shankar Bahadur K.C.

1990 (VS). *Tibbat mẽ savā varṣ* [*TMSV*]. New Delhi: Sharada Mandir.

1994. *Pā̃c bauddh dārśnik*. New Delhi: Vani Prakashan.

1995. *Yātrā ke panne* [*YKP*]. New Delhi: Bharatiya Prakashan Sansthan.

1998a. *Kanailā kī kathā*. Allahabad: Kitab Mahal.

1998b. *Rāhul-vāṅmaya: Jīvan yātrā*, 4 vols, edited by Kamala Sankrityayan. Delhi: Radhakrishna Prakashan. Vol. 1 (*MJY-1*); Vol. 2 (*MJY-2*); Vol. 3 (*MJY-3* and *MJY-4*); and Vol. 4 (*MJY-5* and *JY-6*).

2003. *Jīne ke lie* [*JKL*]. Allahabad: Kitab Mahal.

2004a. *Bhāgo nahī̃ (duniyā ko) badlo* [*BNDB*]. Allahabad: Kitab Mahal.

2004b. *Ghumakkaṛ śāstra*. Allahabad: Kitab Mahal

2004c. *Kārl Mārks*. Allahabad: Kitab Mahal.

2004d. *Rāṣṭrabhāṣā Hindī*. Delhi: Radhakrishna Prakashan.

2004e. *Ṛgvaidik ārya*. Allahabad: Kitab Mahal.

2005a. *Islām dharm kī rūprekhā*. Allahabad: Kitab Mahal.
2005b. *Jay yaudheya*. Allahabad: Kitab Mahal.
2005c. *Siṃh senāpati*. Allahabad: Kitab Mahal.
2005d. *Vismr̥t yātrī*. Allahabad: Kitab Mahal.
December 2006–November 2007a. 'Ambedkar: Navdīkṣit Bauddh'. *Abhinavkadam* 11(16–17): 33–42.
December 2006–November 2007b. 'Buddh kā darśan', *Abhinavkadam* 11(16–17): 27–32.
December 2006–November 2007c. 'Dā. Ambedkar: Vajrādapi Kaṭhorāṇī'. *Abhinavkadam* 11(16–17): 31–32.
2006a. *Bāisvī̃ sadī* [*BS*]. Allahabad: Kitab Mahal.
2006b. *Sone kī ḍhāl*. Allahabad: Kitab Mahal.
2007a. *Eśiyā ke durgam bhūkhaṇḍõ mẽ*. Delhi: Bharatiya Prakashan Sansthan.
2007b. *Volgā se Gaṅgā*. Allahabad: Kitab Mahal.

In English

1970. 'Buddhist Dialectics'. *Buddhism: The Marxist Approach*. Delhi: Peoples Publishing House.
1984. *Selected Essays of Rahul Sankrityayan*. New Delhi: Peoples Publishing House.

In Sanskrit

1943. *Pramāṇavārttikam* (*Svārthānumānaparicchedaḥ*) by Dharmakīrti, edited and completed by Rahul Sankrityayan. Allahabad: Kitab Mahal.

OTHER WORKS

Hindi, Nepali, Sanskrit, and Newari Books and Articles

Ācārya, Narendra Dev. 2010. *Rāṣṭrīytā aur samāvād*. New Delhi: National Book Trust.
Ātreya, Viṣṇurāj. 2066a VS. 'Rāhul, Rā̃cī, Devkoṭā ra pāgal kavitā'. *Nepālī* (200): 566–74.
———. 2066b VS. *Ek Devkoṭā anek āyām*. Kathmandu: Himalaya Book Stall.
Bajrācārya, Madan 'Sen'. 1989 [1109 Nepāl Saṃvat]. *Lok mye munāmi Māndās Tulādharyā jīvanī*. Kathmandu: Nepalese Folklore Society.
Bhaṭṭācārya, Abhijīt. 2005. *Mahāpaṇdit Rāhul Sāṅkr̥tyāyan ke vyaktitvāntaraṇ kī prakriyā*. Calcutta: Anand Prakashan.

Bhaṭṭācārya, Rāmkṛṣṇa. 1993 (January–March). 'Rāhul kī vaicārik yātrā: Buddha se Mārks tak', *Samkālīn sṛjan* (15): 105–12.

Bhaṭṭarāī, Ghaṭarāj. 2051 VS. *Pratibhāi pratibhāra Nepālī sāhitya*. Kathmandu: Ekta Books Distributors.

Bhārtīya, Bhavānīlāl, ed. 1987a. *Svāmī Śraddhānand granthāvalī 8*. Delhi: Vijaya Kumār, Govindarām Hāsānand.

———. 1987b. *Svāmī Śraddhānand granthāvalī 11*. Delhi: Vijaya Kumār, Govindarām Hāsānand.

Bhikṣu Sudarśan. 2022 VS. *Nepāle Rāhul*. Kathmandu: Nepal Bharat Sanskritik Kendra.

Brahmānand, ed. 1971. *Rāhul Sāṅkṛtyāyan: vyaktiva evaṃ kṛtitva*. Delhi: Hariyana Prakashan.

Caṭṭopādhyāya, Baṅkimcandra. 2006. *Ānand maṭh*. Delhi: Rachana Prakashan.

Caturvedī, Paṅkaj. 2011. *Ātmkathā kī saṃskṛti*. New Delhi: Vani Prakashan.

Chudal, Alaka Atreya. 2068 VS. 'Rāhul Sāṅkṛtyāyan ra Bāisvī̃ sadī'. *Racanā* 5(117): 34–40.

Gandhi, M.K. 2003. *Satya ke prayog athvā ātmkathā*, translated by Kashinath Trivedi. Ahmedabad: Navjivan Trust.

Gautam, Paṅkaj. December 2007–November 2008. 'Rāhul Sāṅkṛtyāyan aur bhāṣā-samasyā'. *Abhinavkadam* 12(18–19): 239–47.

Ghimire, Mādhav. 2060 VS. *Kinnar kinnarī*. Lalitpur: Sajha Prakashan.

Ghimire, Rocak. 1994 (January–February). 'Mahāpaṇḍit Rāhul Sāṅkṛtyāyan ko Nepāl sambandha'. *Madhuparka* 26(9): 29–33.

———. 2056 VS. *Samjhanāmā phakriekā thũgāharū*. Lalitpur: Sajha Prakashan.

Giri, Narayan. 2066 VS. *Viṣvako rūprekhā*. Kathmandu: Rajan Timilsina and Narayan Giri.

Kauśalyāyan, Bhadant Ānand. 1992. 'Dambadiu paṇḍitumā: Vidyālaṅkār mẽ darśan ke mahācārya'. *Sāptāhik Hindustān*, 30 August, p. 4.

K.C. Surendra. 2065 VS. *Nepālmā kamyuniṣt āndolanko itihās* (*pahilo bhāg*). Kathmandu: Vidyarthi Pustak Bhandar.

Lāl, Kaśmīrī. 2006. *Rāhul Sāṅkṛtyāyan kā kathā sāhitya*. Ludhiyana: Unistar.

Mācve, Prabhākar. 2005. *Rāhul Sāṅkṛtyāyan*. New Delhi: Sahitya Akademi.

Mammaṭa. 1981. *Kāvyaprakāśaḥ: sāhityacūḍāmaṇi-sudhāsāgara-sahitaḥ*. Varanasi: Kashi Hindu Vishvavidyalaya.

Miśrā, Kṛṣṇa Candra. 1993. 'Nepāl aur Nepālī ke sacce mitra: Rāhul Sāṅkṛtyāyan'. *Sāhityalok* (Kathmandu: Hindi Department, Tribhuvan University) 11(1): 1–4.

Mule, Guṇākar. 1993. *Svayaṃbhū mahāpaṇḍit*. New Delhi: Rajkamal Prakashan.

———. 1998. *Mahāpaṇḍit Rāhul Sāṅkṛtyāyan: jīvnī aur kṛtitva*. New Delhi: National Book Trust.

Nāgārjun. 1983. *Annahīnam kr̥yāhīnam·*. Delhi: Vani Prakashan.

Nepāl, Jñānmaṇi. 2057 VS. *Paṃ Hemrāj Śarmā: unkā kr̥ti ra samīkṣā*. Dang: Mahendra Sanskrit Vishvavidyalaya.

Pāṇḍeya, Anil Kumār, ed. 2006. *Dūsrī duniyā sambhav hai*. New Delhi: Rāhul Sāṅkr̥tyāyan Pratiṣṭhān.

Pāṇḍeya, Harerām. 2011. *Rāhul Sāṅkr̥tyāyan: bhārtīya mukti āndolan ke apratim yoddhā*. Delhi: Mekhala Prakashan.

Parmānand, Bhāi . 1932. 'Ek jel se dūsre jel mẽ'. *Haṃs* 2(7): 17–19.

Pāṭhak, Gajendra. 2005. *Hindī navjāgraṇ*. Varanasi: Vishvavidyalaya Prakashan.

Pokhrel, Mādhav Prasād, and Suman Dhakāl, eds. 2060 VS. *Janaklāl Śarmā kā saṃsmaraṇ*. Lalitpur: Sajha Prakashan.

Prasād, Rājendra. 2007. *Ātmkathā*. New Delhi: Sasta Sahitya Mandal.

Prasāī, Narendrarāj. 2007. *Nārīculī*. Kathmandu: Nai Prakashan.

Rahbar, Haṃsrāj. December 2006–November 2007. 'Rāhul Sāṅkr̥tyāyan ek śāndār śāhbalūt'. *Abhinav kadam* 11(16–17): 278–81.

Rāy, Madan. 1997. *Rahul ke kathā sāhitya kā sāmājik sandarbh*. New Delhi: Radhakrishna Prakashan.

Rākeś, Rāmdayāl. 2003. *Nepāl ke Hindī lekhak*. Varanasi: Prachya Prakashan.

Rimāl, Aravinda. 2062 VS. *1997 dekhi 2017 sāl: ek avalokan*. Kathmandu: Tanka Prasad Acharya Smriti Pratisthan.

Rimāl, Gopāl Prasād. 2062 VS. *Āmāko sapanā*. Lalitpur: Sajha Prakashan.

Śākya, Ratna Sundar. 1998/99 (December/January). 'Rāhul ko Tibbat yātrā'. *The Himalayan Voice*. Kathmandu: The Himalayan House: 52–5.

———. 1993. *Bauddha r̥ṣi Mahāprajñā*. Kathmandu: Nepal Press.

———. 1994. *Bauddha jagat kāsmādaraṇīya vyaktitvaharū: dosro bhāg*. Kathmandu: Mandas Memorial Publication.

———. 2000. *Bauddha jagat kā smaraṇīya vyaktitvaharū: tesro bhāg*. Bhaktapur: Vajirayani Lumanti Prakashan.

———. 1992. *Bhikkhutrayī: Rāhul Sāṅkr̥tyāyan, Ānand Kauśalyāyanra Jagadīś Kaśyap*. Bhaktapur: Dharmodaya Sabha.

———. 2046 (VS). 'Rāhulayā vyaktitva'. *Anandabhūmī* (Kathmandu: Ananda Kuti Vihar) 17(2): 17–21.

Sama, Bālkr̥ṣṇa. 2026 VS. 'Paśubali'. *Rūprekhā* 10(4): 13–15.

———. 2054 VS. *Mero kavitā ko ārādhanā*. Lalitpur: Sajha Prakashan.

Sankrityayan, Igor Rahulovich. December 2006–November 2007. 'Merī Yaśodharā mā̃ Yelenā Sāṅkr̥tyāyan'. *Abhinavkadam* 11(16–17): 295–307.

Sankrityayan, Kamala. 1971. 'Rāhul sāhitya'. In *Rāhul Sāṅkr̥tyāyan: vyaktitva evaṃ kr̥titva*, edited by Dā Brahmānand, pp. 57–67. Delhi: Haryana Prakashan.

———. 1995. *Mahāmānav mahāpaṇḍit: saṃsmaraṇ*. New Delhi: Radhakrishna Prakashan.

Sankrityayan, Kamala. 2025 VS. 'Mahāpaṇḍit Rāhulle mahākavi Devkoṭāsãga bhet garnuhũdā'. *Bhānu* 5(12): 431–6.

Sankrityayan, Kamala, and Ravelcand Ānand, eds. 1982. *Rāhul Sāṅkr̥tyāyan ke śreṣṭh nibandh*. Delhi: Nagari Printers.

Śarmā, Buddhadev. 2059 VS. 'Rāhulsãga rumallīdā'. *Juhī* 22(2): 20–1.

Śarmā, Janaklāl. 2023 VS. *Lalitkalā ra sāhitya*. Kathmandu: Educational Enterprise.

———. 2052 VS. *Mahākavi Devkoṭā: ek vyaktitva duī racanā*. Lalitpur: Sajha Prakashan.

Śarmā, Viṣṇu Candra. 2002. *Samaya sāmyavādī*. New Delhi: Vani Prakashan.

Śāstrī, Omprakāś Śarmā. 1971. 'Rājbhāṣā Hindī aur Rāhul Sāṅkr̥tyāyan'. In *Rāhul Sāṅkr̥tyāyan: vyaktitva evaṃ kr̥titv*, edited by Dā. Brahmānand, pp. 84–8. Delhi: Haryana Prakashan.

Siṃh, Nāmvar. 2006. 'Bhāgo nahī̃ (duniyā ko) badlo'. In *Dūsrī duniyā saṃbhav hai*, edited by Anil Kumār Pāṇḍeya, pp. 20–33 (lecture delivered at India International Centre, New Delhi on 15 November 1995). New Delhi: Mahāpaṇḍit Rāhul Sāṅkr̥tyāyan Pratiṣṭhān.

Siṃh, Vīrendra. 1995. *Mahāpaṇdit Rāhul samagra mūlyaṅkan*. Jayapur: Panchashil Prakashan.

Śivrānī Devī. 1932. 'Merī giraftārī'. *Haṃs* 2(7): 97–8.

Snātak, Vijyendra. 2004. *Hindī sāhitya kā itihās*. New Delhi: Sahitya Akademi.

Sotī, Vīrendra Candra. 2006. *Ārya evaṃ ārya saṃskr̥ti*. Delhi: Pratibha Prakashan.

Śreṣṭha, Dayārām, and Mohan Rāj Śarmā. 2063 VS. *Nepālī sāhitya ko saṅkṣipta itihās*. Lalitpur: Sajha Prakashan.

Śreṣṭha, Dhīrkumār. 2067 VS. *Bāisaũ śatābdī*. Kathmandu: Airavati Prakashan.

Śreṣṭha, Kr̥ṣṇamān. 2046 VS.'Rājnītiko pahilo pāṭh'. In *Dharma Ratna 'Yami' smr̥ti grantha*, pp. 74–5. Kathmandu: Krishna Printers.

Śukl, Rāmeśvar. December 2006–November 2007. 'Navsaṃskr̥ti puruṣ: Rāhul-jī'. *Abhinavkadam* 11(16–17): 192–6.

Tivārī, Rāmcandra. 2007. *Hindī kā gadya-sāhitya*.Varanasi: Vishvavidyalaya Prakashan.

Tivārī, Udayanārāyaṇ. 1971. 'Rāhul-jī kā vyaktitva'. In *Rāhul Sāṅkr̥tyāyan: vyaktitva evaṃ kr̥tit*, edited by Dā. Brahmānand, pp. 209–16. Delhi: Hariyana Prakashan.

Tripāṭhī, Śailendra Kumār. December 2006–November 2007. 'Ḍāyrī ke panne aur Rāhul'. *Abhinavkadam* 11(16–17): 197–201.

Tulādhar, Rīnā. 2064 VS. 'Sugat saurabh mahākāvya ra bauddha darśan'. *Śāradā* 1(11): 74–8.

Urmileś. 1994. *Rāhul Sāṅkr̥tyāyan: sr̥jan aur saṅgharṣ*. New Delhi: Vani Prakashan.

Urmileś. December 2007–November 2008. 'Itihās kī tah mẽ manuṣya kī sṛjanśīltā kī talāś'. *Abhinav kadam* 12(18–19): 43–50.

Vaidya, Nirañjan Govinda. 2002. 'Mahāpaṇḍit Rāhul Sāṅkṛtyāyan kī śatvārṣikī par 'sraddhā suman'. In *Rāhul Vimarṣ*, edited by Rājendra Rāy, pp. 37–9. Patna: Nepali Vidya Bhavan.

Yādav, Nareś. 2009. *Kṣitij: Bhāg 1*, 3rd edition. New Delhi: National Council of Educational Research and Training.

Yami, Dharmaratna. 1993. '*Nepāl ko Rāhul-jī kī den*'. *Sāhitya lok* (Kathmandu: Hindi Department, Tribhuvan University) 11(1): *ka*.

Newspapers, Periodicals, and Commemoration Volumes or Issues in Hindi

Ājkal. May 1953. New Delhi,

Āzād Hind. 1942–3. Berlin.

Haṃs. 1932, 2(7). Varanasi.

Jansattā. 9 April 1993. New Delhi.

Navbhārat Times. 4 April 1993.

Rāhul Vimarś. 2002. Patna: Nepālī Vidyā Bhavan.

Sāhityalok. 1993. Hindi Department, Tribhuvan University, Nepal

Sāptāhik Hindustān. August/September 1993. Pandaha, India.

Journals, Periodicals, Special Volumes, and Commemoration Volumes in Nepali

Bhānu. 2025 VS (trimonthly). Kathmandu.

Dharma Ratna 'Yami' smṛti grantha. 2046 VS. Kathmandu.

Gorkhapatra. 1923–present (weekly and later daily). Kathmandu.

Kantipur (daily) Kathmandu.

Madhuparka. 1994, 26(9; January–February). Kathmandu.

Nepālī (trimonthly) (200). Kathmandu: Madan Puraskār Pustakālaya.

Rūprekhā. 2026 VS (monthly). Kathmandu.

Śāradā. 2064 VS. Kathmandu.

Suskerā. 2027 VS, 1(2). Kathmandu.

English Books, Articles, Dissertations, and Commemoration Volumes

Ahir, Diwan C. 1993. *Himalayan Buddhism Past and Present*. Delhi: Sri Satguru Publications.

Ahir, Diwan C. 2010. *Buddhism in India: Rediscovery, Revival and Development*. Delhi: Buddhist World Press.

Aiyar, R.P., and L.S. Bhandare. 1945. *The Congress Caravan: The History of the Indian National Congress and of India's Struggle for Swaraj 1885–1945*. Bombay: National Youth Publication.

Allinger, Ewa. 2001. 'Narrative Paintings in 12th–13th Century Manuscripts: An Examination of Photographs Taken by Rāhula Sāṅkrityāyana at the Ṅor Monastery'. *Tibet (Journal of Bengal Art)* 6: 101–15.

Aloysius, G. 2009. *Nationalism without a Nation in India*. New Delhi: Oxford University Press.

Amin, Shahid. 2003. *Event, Metaphor, Memory: Chauri Chaura, 1922–1992*. Berkeley: University of California Press.

Anderson, Benedict. 2006. *Imagined Communities: Reflections on the Origin and Spread of Nationalism*. London: Verso.

Arnold, David. 2004. 'The Self and the Cell: Indian Prison Narratives as Life Histories'. In *Telling Lives in India: Biography, Autobiography and Life History*, edited by David Arnold and Stuart Blackburn, pp. 29–53. Delhi: Permanent Black.

Arnold, David, and Stuart Blackburn. 2004. 'Introduction'. In *Telling Lives in India: Biography, Autobiography and Life History*, edited by David Arnold and Stuart Blackburn, pp. 1–28. Delhi: Permanent Black.

Arya, Krishna Singh, and P.D. Shastri. 1987. *Swami Dayananda Saraswati: A Study of His Life and Work*. Delhi: Manohar.

Bapu, Prabhu. 2013. *Hindu Mahasabha in Colonial North India, 1915–1930: Constructing Nation and History*. London: Routledge.

Bandurski, Frank. 1994. 'Übersicht über die Göttinger Sammlungen der von Rāhula Sāṅkr̥tyāyana in Tibet aufgefundenen buddhistischen Sanskrit-Texte (Funde Buddhistischer Sanskrit-Handschriften, III)'. In *Untersuchungen zur Buddhistischen Literatur*, edited by Frank Bandurski, Bhikkhu Pāsādika, Michael Schmidt, and Bangwe Wang, pp. 9–126. Göttingen: Vandenhoeck and Ruprecht.

Bayly, Christopher A. 1998. *Origins of Nationality in South Asia: Patriotism and Ethical Government in the Making of Modern India*. Delhi: Oxford University Press.

Bechert, Heinz, and Jens-Uwe Hartmann. 1998. 'Observations on the Reform of Buddhism in Nepal'. *Journal of the Nepal Research Centre* 8: 1–30.

Berglund, Henrik. 2004. *Hindu Nationalism and Democracy*. Delhi: Shipra Publications.

Bhattachan, Krishna B. 2005. 'Nepalese Buddhists' view of Hinduism'. *Occasional Papers in Sociology and Anthropology* 9: 47–62.

Billig, Michael. 1999. *Banal Nationalism*. London: Sage Publications.

Blaikie, Norman. 2007. *Approaches to Social Enquiry: Advancing Knowledge.* Cambridge: Polity Press.

Brass, Paul. 1974. *Language, Religion and Politics in North India.* London: Cambridge University Press.

Brown, Emily C. 1975. *Har Dayal: Hindu Revolutionary and Rationalist.* Arizona: The University of Arizona Press.

Chalmers, Rhoderick. 2002. 'Paṇdits and Pulp Fiction: Popular Publishing and the Birth of Nepali Print-Capitalism in Banaras'. *Studies in Nepali History and Society* 7(1): 35–97.

———. 2003. '"We Nepalis": Language, Literature and the Formation of a Nepali Public Sphere in India, 1914–1940. Unpublished PhD thesis, School of Oriental and African Studies, University of London.

Chatterjee, Partha. 2011a. 'Nationalist Thought and Colonial India'. In *The Partha Chatterjee Omnibus.* New Delhi: Oxford University Press.

———. 2011b. 'The Nation and Its Fragments'. In *The Partha Chatterjee Omnibus.* New Delhi: Oxford University Press.

Chattopadhyaya, Debiprasad. 1975. 'Introduction'. In *Papers of Th. Stcherbatsky,* edited by Debiprasad Chattopadhyaya, pp. i–xxiv. Soviet Indology Series, no. 2. Calcutta: Indian Studies Past & Present.

Chaturvedi, R.P. 2010. 'Mahapandit Rahul Sankrityayan'. In *Great Personalities.* Agra: Upkar Prakashan.

Chowdhory, Hemendu Bikash, ed. 1994. *Mahapandit Rahula Sankrityayana Birth Centenary Volume.* Calcutta: Buddha Dharmankur Sabha.

Chudal, Alaka Atreya. 2014. 'Embodying Nepal's Geography: Imagery of the Earth and the Sun in Nepali Poetry'. *Pandanus' 14: Nature in Literature, Art, Myth and Ritual* 8(2): 47–64.

Dalmia, Vasudha. 1997. *The Nationalization of Hindu Traditions: Bhāratendu Hariścandra and Nineteeth-century Banaras.* Delhi: Oxford University Press.

———. 2010. 'Introduction: Hindi, Nation and Community'. In *Nationalism in the Vernacular: Hindi, Urdu and the literature of Indian Freedom,* edited by Shobna Nijhawan, pp. 33–63. Ranikhet: Permanent Black.

Dange, S.A. 1985. 'Literature and the People'. In *Marxist Cultural Movement in India: Chronicles and Documents 1943–1964,* edited by Sudhi Pradhan, pp. 3–30. Calcutta: Pustak Bipani.

Das, Sisir Kumar. 1995. *A History of Indian Literature 1911–1956: Struggle for Freedom—Triumph and Tragedy.* New Delhi: Sahitya Akademi.

Dasgupta, Subrata. 2007. *The Bengal Renaissance: Identity and Creativity from Rammohun Roy to Rabindranath Tagore.* Delhi: Permanent Black.

Denzin, Norman K., ed. 1994. *Handbook of Qualitative Research.* California: Sage Publications.

Desai, A.R. 1954. *Social Background of Indian Nationalism*. Bombay: Popular Book Depot.

Diwakar, R.R. 2001. *Bihar through the Ages*. Bombay: Orient Longman.

Dwivedi, Mahavir Prasad. 2010. 'The Present State of Hindi', translated by Sujata Mody. In *Nationalism in the Vernacular: Hindi, Urdu and the literature of Indian Freedom*, edited by Shobna Nijhawan, pp. 350–70. Ranikhet: Permanent Black.

Eakin, Paul John. 2008. *Living Autobiographically: How We Create Identity in Narrative*. Ithaca: Cornell University Press.

Fischer, Hildegard. 1990. *General Simha: Interpretation und Übersetzung Eines Historischen Romans von Rāhul Sāṅkr̥tyāyan*. Wiesbaden: Harrassowitz.

Fischer-Tiné, Harald. 2004. 'National Education, Pulp Fiction and the Contradictions of Colonialism: Perceptions of an Educational Experiment in Early-Twentieth-Century India'. In *Colonialism as Civilizing Mission: Cultural Ideology in British India*, edited by Harald Fischer-Tiné and Michael Mann, pp. 229–47. London: Wimbledon Publishing Company.

Fisher, James F. 1997. *Living Martyrs: Individuals and Revolution in Nepal*. Delhi: Oxford University Press.

Gaenszle, Martin. 2002. 'Nepali Kings and Kāśī: In the Changing Significance of Sacred Centre'. *Studies in Nepali History and Society* 7(1): 1–33.

———. 2006. 'Nepali Places: Appropriations of Space in Banaras'. In *Visualizing Space in Banaras: Images, Maps, and the Practice of Representation*, edited by Martin Gaenszle and Jörg Gengnagel, pp. 303–23. Wiesbaden: Harrassowitz.

Gandhi, Sonia, ed. 2004. *Two Alone, Two Together: Letters between Indira Gandhi and Jawaharlal Nehru 1922–1964*. New Delhi: Penguin Viking.

Garzilli, Enrica. 2001. 'A Sanskrit Letter Written by Sylvain Lévi in 1923 to Hemrāja Śarmā along with some Hitherto Unknown Biographical Notes (Cultural Nationalism and Internationalism in the First Half of the 20th Century: Famous Indologists Write to the Raj Guru of Nepal—No. 1)'. *Journal of the Nepal Research Centre* XII: 115–49.

Geertz, Clifford. 1973. *The Interpretation of Cultures: Selected Essays*. New York: Basic Books.

Gellner, David N. 1992. *Monk, Householder, and Trantik Priest: Newar Buddhism and Its Hierarchy of Ritual*. Cambridge: Cambridge University Press.

Gellner, Ernest. 1987. *Nations and Nationalism*. New York: Cornell University Press.

Gerke, Barbara. 1995. 'Rahulji's Quest for Tibet'. Paper presented at the International Seminar on the Life and Works of Rahul Sankrityayan at the University of St Petersburg, Russia, October/November 1995.

Ghosh, Suresh Chandra. 2002. *Civilisation, Education and School in Ancient and Medieval India, 1500 B.C.–1757 A.D.* Frankfurt am Main: Peter Lang.

Gopal, Priyamvada. 2009. *The Indian English Novel: Nation, History, and Narration*. New Delhi: Oxford University Press.

Gould, William. 2005. *Hindu Nationalism and the Language of Politics in Late Colonial India*. Delhi: Cambridge University Press.

Grant, Patrick. 2009. *Buddhism and Ethnic Conflict in Sri Lanka*. Albany: State University of New York Press.

Gupta, D.N. 2008. *Communism and Nationalism in Colonial India 1939–45*. New Delhi: Sage Publications.

Gupta, Sumitra. 2005. *Impact of Arya Samaj on Society, Education and Indian Freedom Movement*. Varanasi: Kishori Vidya Niketan.

Haithcox, John Patrick. 1971. *Communism and Nationalism in India: M.N. Roy and Comintern Policy, 1920–1939*. New Jersey: Princeton University Press.

Harder, Hans, ed. 2010. *Literature and Nationalist Ideology: Writing Histories of Modern Indian Languages*. New Delhi: Social Science Press.

Hobsbawm, Eric J. 1990. *Nationalism since 1780: Programme, Myth, Reality*. Cambridge: Cambridge University Press.

Hoy, David C. 1982. *The Critical Circle: Literature, History and Philosophical Hermeneutics*. Berkeley: University of California.

Hutchinson, John. 1987a. *The Dynamics of Cultural Nationalism: The Gaelic Revival and the Creation of the Irish Nation State*. London: Allen and Unwin.

———. 1987b. 'Cultural Nationalism, Elite Mobility and Nation-Building: Communitarian Politics in Modern Ireland'. *The British Journal of Sociology* 38(4): 482–501.

———. 1999. 'Re-Interpreting Cultural Nationalism'. *Australian Journal of Politics and History* 45(3): 392–407.

Hutt, Michael James. 1993. *Himalayan Voices: An Introduction to Modern Nepali Literature*. Delhi: Motilal Banarasidas Publishers Private Limited.

Jaffrelot, Christophe. 1999. *The Hindu Nationalist Movement and Indian Politics: 1925 to 1990s*. New Delhi: Penguin.

———. 2007. 'Introduction'. In *Hindu Nationalism: A Reader*, edited by Christophe Jaffrelot, pp. 3–25. New Jersey: Princeton University Press.

Jayasawal, K.P. 1984. 'Lost Sanskrit Works Recovered from Tibet'. In *Selected Essays of Rahul Sankrityayan*, by Rahul Sankrityayan, pp. ix–xix. New Delhi : Peoples Publishing House.

Joireman, Sandra F. 2003. *Nationalism and Political Identity*. New York and London: Continuum Press.

Jones, Kenneth W. 1989. *Socio-religious Reform Movements in British India*. Cambridge: Cambridge University Press.

———. 2006. *Arya Dharm: Hindu Consciousness in 19th-Century Punjab*. Delhi: Manohar.

Jordens, J.T.F. 1978. *Dāyānanda Sarasvatī: His Life and Ideas*. Delhi: Oxford University Press.

Khan, Abdul Jamil. 2006. *Urdu/Hindi: An Artificial Divide: African Heritage, Mesopotamian Roots, Indian Culture & British Colonialism*. New York: Algora Publishing.

King, Christopher R. 1995. *One Language, Two Scripts: The Hindi Movement in Nineteenth Century North India*. Oxford: Oxford University Press.

King, Robert D. 1998. *Nehru and the Language Politics of India*. Delhi: Oxford University Press.

———. 2001.'The Poisonous Potency of Script: Hindi and Urdu'. *International Journal of the Sociology of Language* (150): 43–59.

Kohn, Hans. 1948 *The Idea of Nationalism*. New York: The Macmillan Company.

———. 1955. *Nationalism: Its Meaning and History*. Princeton, New Jersey: Van Nostrand.

Kopf, David. 1979. *The Brahmo Samaj and the Shaping of the Modern Indian Mind*. Princeton, New Jersey: Princeton University Press.

Krishna, Gopal. 1966. 'The Development of the Indian National Congress as a Mass Organization, 1918–1923'. *The Journal of Asian Studies* 25(3): 413–30 (http://www.jstor.org/stable/2051999, last accessed 9 February 2016).

Kuppusamy, T.S. 1992. 'Hindi'. *Buddhist Themes in Modern Indian Literature* [seminar papers]. Madras: Institute of Indian Studies, publication no. 18: 111–22.

Lal, Guru. 1944. 'Hindustani—Lingua Franca for India'. *Āzād Hind* (3/4): 23–7.

Law, Narendra Nath, ed. 1949. *Sphuṭārthā abhidharmakośa-vyākhyā of Yaśomitra*. London: Luzac and Co.

Levine, Sarah, and David N. Gellner. 2008. *Rebuilding Buddhism: The Theravada Movement in Twentieth-Century Nepal*. Delhi: Orient Blackswan Private Limited.

Lewis, Todd T., and Subarna Man Tuladhar. 2007. *Sugatasaurabha: An Epic Poem from Nepal on the Life of the Buddha by Chitadhar Hṛdaya*. Harvard University: The Department of Sanskrit and Indian Studies.

Low, D.A. 2004a. 'Introduction: The Climactic Years 1917–47'. In *Congress and the Raj: Facets of the Indian Struggle 1917–47*, edited by D.A. Low, pp. 1–45. Delhi: Oxford University Press.

———, ed. 2004b. *Congress and the Raj: Facets of the Indian Struggle 1917–47*. Delhi: Oxford University Press.

Machwe, Prabhakar. 1978. *Rahul Sankrityayan*. New Delhi: Sahitya Akademi.

Mandelbaum, D.G. 1973 (June). 'The Study of Life History: Gandhi'. *Current Anthropology* 14(3): 177–206. (http://www.jstor.org/stable/2740760, accessed on 6 July 2012.)

Manjapra, Kris. 2010. *M.N. Roy: Marxism and Colonial Cosmopolitanism*. Delhi: Routledge India.

Masselos, Jim. 2005. *Indian Nationalism: A History*. New Delhi: New Dawan Press.

Mathur, Subh. 2008. *The Everyday Life of Hindu Nationalism*. New Delhi: Three Essays Collective.

Mendel, Arthur P., ed. 1965. *Essential Works of Marxism*. New York: Bantam Books.

Mookerjee, Girija. 1942. 'Political Influence of Some Indian Writers'. *Āzād Hind* (7/8): 56–63.

Much, Michael Torsten. 1988. *A Visit to Rāhula Sāṅkṛtyāyana's Collection of Negatives at the Bihar Research Society: Texts from the Buddhist Epistemological School*. Vienna: Arbeitskreis für Tibet u. Buddhist Studien, University of Vienna.

Muller-Vollmer, Kurt, ed. 1990. *The Hermeneutics Reader*. New York: Continuum.

Nehru, Jawaharlal. 1996. *The Discovery of India*. New Delhi: Oxford University Press.

———. 2004. *An Autobiography*. New Delhi: Penguin Books.

Nijhawan, Shobna. 2012. *Women and Girls in the Hindi Public Sphere: Political Literature in Colonial North India*. New Delhi: Oxford University Press.

Orsini, Francesca. 2010. *The Hindi Public Sphere 1929–1940: Language and Literature in the Age of Nationalism*. New Delhi: Oxford University Press.

Overstreet, Gene D., and Marshall Windmiller. 1959. *Communism in India*. Berkeley and Los Angeles: University of California Press.

Özkrimli, Umut. 2000. *Theories of Nationalism: A Critical Introduction*. Macmilllan Press.

Pandeya M.R., and P. Molnar. 1988. 'The Distribution of Intensity of the Bihar–Nepal Earthquake, 15 January 1934 and Bounds on the Extent of the Rupture Zone'. *Journal of Nepal Geological Society* 5(1): 22–44.

Pathak. S.K. 1994. 'Rahul Sankrityayan: A Tibetan Lexicographer'. In *Mahapandit Rahula Sankrityayana Birth Centenary Volume*, edited by Hemendu Bikash Chowdhury, pp. 27–30. Calcutta: Buddha Dharmankur Sabha.

Patten, Alan. 1999 'The Autonomy Arguments for Liberal Nationalism'. *Nations and Nationalism* 5(1): 1–17.

Pradhan, Sudhi, comp. and ed. 1985. *Marxist Cultural Movement in India: Chronicles and Documents 1943–1964*. Calcutta: Pustak Bipani.

Prasad, Bimal. 1999. *Pathway to India's Partition*. New Delhi: Manohar.

Pruthi, R.K. 2004. *Arya Samaj and Indian Civilization*. New Delhi: Discovery Publishing House.

Rahman, Tariq. 2011. *From Hindi to Urdu: A Social and Political History*. Karachi: Oxford University Press.

Rai, Alok. 2007. *Hindi Nationalism*. New Delhi: Orient Longman Private Limited.

Rai, Amrit. 1991. *A House Divided*. Oxford: Oxford University Press.

Raj, Prakash A. 1994. *Portraits & Photographs from Nepal*. Kathmandu: Nabeen Publications.

———. 1996. *Brahmins of Nepal*. Kathmandu: Nabeen Publications.

———. 2003. *Profile of a Nepalese Writer: Life and Work of Prakash A. Raj*. Kathmandu: Nabeen Publications.

Renan, Ernst. 1939 [1882]. 'What Is a Nation?' In *Modern Political Doctrines*, edited by A. Zimmern, pp. 186–205. London: Oxford University Press.

Roberts, Brian. 2002. *Biographical Research*. Buckingham: Open University Press.

Roy, M.N. 1940. *Gandhism: Socialism: Nationalism*. Calcutta: Bengal Radical Club.

Sarkar, Sumit. 1984. *Modern India 1885–1947*. Delhi: Macmillan India Limited.

Sengupta, Sagaree. 1994. 'Krishna the Cruel Beloved: Hariscandra and Urdu'. *The Annual of Urdu Studies* 9: 82–102.

Shackle C., and R. Snell. 1990. *Hindi and Urdu since 1800: A Common Reader*. London: School of Oriental and African Studies.

Shafer, Boyd C., 1955. *Nationalism: Myth and Reality*. New York: A Harvest Book.

———. 1974. *Faces of Nationalism: New Realities and Old Myths*. New York: Harvest Book.

Sharma, R.S. 2009. *Rethinking India's Past*. New Delhi: Oxford University Press.

———. 2012. 'Rahul Sankrityayan and Social Change'. In *Recording the Progress of Indian History: Symposia Papers of the Indian History Congress 1992–2010*, edited by S.Z.H. Jafri, pp. 209–23. Delhi: Primus Books.

Singh, Lata. 2012. *Popular Translations of Nationalism Bihar 1920–1922*. Delhi: Primus Books.

Smith, Anthony D. 1975. *Nationalism: A Trend Report and Bibliography*. The Hague: Mouton.

———. 1998. *Nationalism and Modernism*. New York: Routledge.

———. 2000. *The Nation in History: Historiographical Debates about Ethnicity and Nationalism*. UK: Polity Press.

———. 2010. *Nationalism*. UK: Polity Press.

Smith, Sidonie, and Julia Watson. 2003. *Reading Autobiography: A Guide for Interpreting Life Narratives*. Minneapolis: University of Minnesota Press.

Smith, William Roy. 1938. *Nationalism and Reform in India*. London: New Haven, Yale University Press.

Srivastava, Sanjay. 2005. 'Ghummakkads, a Woman's Place, and the LTC-walas: Towards a Critical History of "Home", "Belonging" and "Attachment"'. *Contribution to Indian Sociology* 39(3): 375–405.

INDEX

Abhidharmakośa, 153, 153 n. 30, 156–8, 160, 185
Ājkal, 58, 268 n. 14, 284
Akhil Bhārtīya Hindi Sāhitya Sammelan, 19, 81, 204, 218
Akhil Bhārtīya Kisān Sabhā, 197, 199 n. 16, 200
All-India Muslim League, 12
Ambedkar, B.R., 14, 134 n. 3, 163 n. 48, 168 n. 55, 175, 255, 255 n. 8
Amritananda, 134 n. 3, 174–5, 175 n. 69
Amvāri satyagraha, 79, 198
Anderson, Benedict, 17, 20, 26–7;
  nation, 18;
  'imagined community', 20, 120
Ardhkathānak, 43
Ārya Musāfir newspaper, 112
Ārya Musāfir Vidyālaya, 67–8, 95, 99–104, 106, 112, 300
Arya Samaj, 2, 5, 8, 11–12, 15, 17–19, 25–6, 37, 67–74, 87, 95–6, 101, 104, 105–9, 121, 128–9, 132, 143, 145, 245, 249–50, 252, 271, 286;
  Ārya *bhāṣā* (language of the Aryans), 202, 202 n. 21;
  and Buddhism, 5, 138, 244;
  and child marriage, 89–90;
  and education, 22, 91, 94, 96–9;
  and Hindi, 202–4;
  and nationalism, 108, 110–11;
  in politics, 94–5, 244;
  as a religion, 108–9;
  Sankrityayan's comparison with Buddhism and communism, 137–9;
  Sankrityayan's involvement in, 273 n. 23;
  śāstrārth, 94, 103
asahyog āndolan, 70–1, 73
autobiography and biography:
  definition, 44, 49;
  as popular literature, 47, 49, 82

Bāisvī̃ sadī, 42, 73–4, 112, 115 n. 36, 119, 120–8, 130, 192–3, 202, 221–2, 238, 249, 301;
  about Nepal 29, 238, 241 n. 62, 266, 130
Bajpeyi, Nand Dulare, 44
Bauddh darśan, 162
Bauddha saṃskṛti, 163
Bhāgo nahī̃ (duniyā ko) badlo, 22 n. 33, 214, 226, 230, 235, 250 n. 4
Bhāratvarṣ, 124–5, 249, 251
Bhārtī bhāṣā, 124–6, 124 n. 46
Bhattarai, Muralidhar, 38, 58, 58 n. 23, 238, 279, 280–3,
Bhoj Datt, Pandit, 99, 103
Bodhananda, Bhadanta, 142–3, 143 n. 7
Bodh Gaya, 100 n. 16, 143–4, 147;
  Maha Bodhi Temple proposal, 119;
  temple, 73, 145, 147 n. 16, 301. *See also* Maha Bodhi Temple

Stark, Ulrike. 2007. *An Empire of Books: The Naval Kishore Press and the Diffusion of the Printed World in Colonial India*. Ranikhet: Permanent Black.

Subedi, Abhi. 1999. *Ekai Kawaguchi: The Trespassing Insider*. Kathmandu: Mandala Book Point.

Tagore, Saumyendranath. 2001. *Rammohan Roy: His Role in Indian Renaissance*. Kolkata: Asiatic Society.

Tewari, Ramesh Chandra. 1983. 'Socio-Cultural Aspects of Theravaada Buddhism in Nepal'. *The Journal of the International Association of Buddhist Studies* 6(2): 67–93.

Trautmann, Thomas R. 1997. *Aryans and British India*. Berkeley: University of California Press.

———. 2005. *The Aryan Debate*. New Delhi: Oxford University Press.

Vajpeyi, Ananya. 2012. *Righteous Republic: The Political Foundations of Modern India*. Cambridge, Massachusetts: Harvard University Press.

van der Veer, Peter. 1994. *Religious Nationalism*. Berkeley: University of California Press.

Vyas, M.R. 1942. 'What is India?' *Āzād Hind* 1(1): 11–14.

Whelpton, John. 2011. *A History of Nepal*. Delhi: Cambridge University Press.

Wolpert, Stanley A. 2002. *Gandhi's Passion: The Life and Legacy of Mahatma Gandhi*. Oxford: Oxford University Press.

Zavos, John. 2000. *The Emergence of Hindu Nationalism in India*. New Delhi: Oxford University Press.

Zwick, Peter. 1983. *Nationalism and Communism*. Colorado: West View Press.

Dictionaries

Bahri, Hardev. 2009. *Bṛhat śikṣārthī Hindī-Aṅgrejī śabdkoś* (vols 1 and 2). Delhi: Rajpal and Sons.

McGregor, Ronald Stuart. 2006. *The Oxford Hindi–English Dictionary*. Oxford: Oxford University Press.

Pradhan, Babulall. 2000. *Ratna's Nepali–English–Nepali Dictionary*. Kathmandu: Ratna Pustak Bhandar.

Turner, R.L. 1980. *A Comparative and Etymological Dictionary of the Nepali Language*. New Delhi: Allied Publishers Private Limited.

Online Resources

Oxford Dictionary	http://www.oed.com/
Shabdkosh English–Hindi Dictionary	http://www.shabdkosh.com/
Nepali Date Converter	http://www.rajan.com/calendar/

INDEX

Abhidharmakośa, 153, 153 n. 30, 156–8, 160, 185
Ājkal, 58, 268 n. 14, 284
Akhil Bhārtīya Hindi Sāhitya Sammelan, 19, 81, 204, 218
Akhil Bhārtīya Kisān Sabhā, 197, 199 n. 16, 200
All-India Muslim League, 12
Ambedkar, B.R., 14, 134 n. 3, 163 n. 48, 168 n. 55, 175, 255, 255 n. 8
Amritananda, 134 n. 3, 174–5, 175 n. 69
Amvāri satyagraha, 79, 198
Anderson, Benedict, 17, 20, 26–7;
  nation, 18;
  'imagined community', 20, 120
Ardhkathānak, 43
Ārya Musāfir newspaper, 112
Ārya Musāfir Vidyālaya, 67–8, 95, 99–104, 106, 112, 300
Arya Samaj, 2, 5, 8, 11–12, 15, 17–19, 25–6, 37, 67–74, 87, 95–6, 101, 104, 105–9, 121, 128–9, 132, 143, 145, 245, 249–50, 252, 271, 286;
  Ārya *bhāṣā* (language of the Aryans), 202, 202 n. 21;
  and Buddhism, 5, 138, 244;
  and child marriage, 89–90;
  and education, 22, 91, 94, 96–9;
  and Hindi, 202–4;
  and nationalism, 108, 110–11;
  in politics, 94–5, 244;
  as a religion, 108–9;
  Sankrityayan's comparison with Buddhism and communism, 137–9;
  Sankrityayan's involvement in, 273 n. 23;
  śāstrārth, 94, 103
asahyog āndolan, 70–1, 73
autobiography and biography:
  definition, 44, 49;
  as popular literature, 47, 49, 82

Bāisvī̃ sadī, 42, 73–4, 112, 115 n. 36, 119, 120–8, 130, 192–3, 202, 221–2, 238, 249, 301;
  about Nepal 29, 238, 241 n. 62, 266, 130
Bajpeyi, Nand Dulare, 44
Bauddh darśan, 162
Bauddha saṃskṛti, 163
Bhāgo nahī̃ (duniyā ko) badlo, 22 n. 33, 214, 226, 230, 235, 250 n. 4
Bhāratvarṣ, 124–5, 249, 251
Bhārtī bhāṣā, 124–6, 124 n. 46
Bhattarai, Muralidhar, 38, 58, 58 n. 23, 238, 279, 280–3,
Bhoj Datt, Pandit, 99, 103
Bodhananda, Bhadanta, 142–3, 143 n. 7
Bodh Gaya, 100 n. 16, 143–4, 147;
  Maha Bodhi Temple proposal, 119;
  temple, 73, 145, 147 n. 16, 301. *See also* Maha Bodhi Temple

Brahmo Samaj, 11–12, 11 n. 21, 93–4
Buddha and Marx, 140
Buddha caryā, 162, 173 n. 66, 262, 266

Chauri Chaura incident, 72, 72 n. 42, 73, 119, 191–2
Communist movement in India, 191, 200 n. 16
Communist Party of India, 1, 38, 81, 189, 190, 196, 200, 204, 218, 244, 247, 250, 253, 302;
in Munger (Bihar), 197
Communist Party of Nepal, 234–5
Congress party (Indian National Congress), 71–3, 71 n. 40, 95, 104, 116, 119, 121, 128, 124, 145–7, 190–2, 194, 197, 197 nn. 11–12, 213, 226, 301
Congress Socialist Party, 79, 196, 302, 196 n. 9, 197 n. 11
cultural identity, 10, 14–5, 20, 110, 124, 185, 247, 251
cultural nationalism, 14, 26–7, 59, 134, 284, 253, 253 n. 7
Cwasa Pasa (Friends of the pen), 172–3, 172 n. 63

Dahlke, Paul, 161, 161 n. 45
Dakkhinī Hindī kāvya dhārā (A collection of Dakkhini Hindi poetry), 217
Damodarachari, 66, 300
Darśan digdarśan, 42, 43 n. 8, 79, 162, 200 n. 18, 234
Das, Chittaranjan (C.R. Das), 13, 72, 191
Das, Ramudar (Rahul Sankrityayan), 66, 68, 75–6, 300
DAV school/college, 68, 95, 98–99, 114, 301
Dayananda, 12–13, 21, 48, 55, 93–6, 98–9, 102 n. 17, 104 n. 22, 105, 108, 129, 137–8, 143, 186, 202–3, 202 n. 21, 249
Devanagari: for Urdu, 23, 204, 206 n. 9, 211, 242;
for Newari, 231
Devkota, Lakshmi Prasad, 58, 184, 238, 259, 268, 276, 284–5, 287 n. 39;
Pāgal (The madman), 38, 58, 268, 284, 285
Dharmacharya, Dharmaditya, 168–9, 169 n. 57
Dharmalok, Bhikkhu, 150, 171 n. 61, 175, 258, 261–2
Dharmakirti, 59, 154–8
Dharmapala, Anagarika, 76 n. 48, 143, 146, 148, 148 n. 17, 168, 175
Dharmodaya Sabha, 175
Dwivedi, Hazari Prasad, 251 n. 5
Dwivedi, Mahavir Prasad, 46, 47 n. 15

Fick, Richard, 153, 161
Fouché, Alfred, 153

Gandhi, Mahatma, 13–14, 42, 35 n. 46, 44 n. 13, 68, 71 n. 40, 72, 72 n. 42, 73–4, 97, 114–15, 115 n. 35, 117, 118, 118 n. 38, 119, 146, 186, 191, 221, 225, 256, 273;
autobiography, 42, 44, 46, 48–9, 84–5;
and Buddha, 186
Gandhi Vidyālaya, 97–8
Gaya congress, 72–3, 115 n. 36, 119, 142, 145, 147, 185, 191–2, 273, 301
Geertz, Clifford, 17, 25;
cultural impact on the concept of man, 25;

culture in the making of a person, 244, 256;
notion of culture, 244, 256;
Ghumakkaṛ śāstra (The wanderer's manual), 6, 6 n. 12, 55–6, 298
ghumakkaṛī (wandering), 6, 27, 55–6, 82, 85

Haṃs autobiography issue (January–February 1932), 44–5
Harishchandra, Bharatendu, 14, 43, 232
Hindi nationalism, 15, 24, 127, 189, 190, 202–3, 218, 221, 240, 245
Hindi–Urdu controversy, 206
Hindu nationalism, 11, 98, 108, 117
Hindu nationalist sentiments, 12
Hindū Sabhā, 13, 110, 146 n. 13
Hindustani, 211–5, 202 n. 20, 212 n. 32
Hridaya, Chittadhar, 169 n. 57, 172, 172 n. 65, 173, 175, 184, 259, 262, 268
Hutchinson, John, 17, 253
nationalism, 253
cultural nationalism, 27, 254

Indian nationalism, 10–11, 13, 28, 62 n. 32, 107–8, 138, 243

Jain, Banarsidas, 43
Jaysawal, Kashi Prasad, 146, 155 n. 34
Jay yaudheya, 23, 164
Jīne ke lie (In order to live), 42
Jinkā maĩ kr̥tajñ (To whom I am grateful), 56

Kangri, Gurukul, 90 n. 1, 98–9
Kāśi Paṇḍit Sabhā, 76, 288 n. 43, 301, 293
Kauśalyāyan, Ānand, 76–7, 133 n. 2, 175, 175 n. 69, 253
Kawaguchi, Ekai, 31, 56, 150, 150 nn. 22–3, 153, 160, 160 n. 44, 161, 161 n. 46
Kisān Sabhā, 197, 199, 200
kisān satyagraha campaign, 1, 79, 302
Kitayama, Junyu, 161
Kozerovskaya, Ellena Narvertovna, 78, 158, 218, 302
Krishnatirth, Bharti, 41, 146 n. 13

La Vallée-Poussin, Louis de, 156, 156 n. 38–9, 160
Lekh Ram, Pandit, 99, 100
Leningrad University, 78, 80, 157 n. 42, 201, 218, 253, 302
Lévi, Sylvain, 153, 155, 158, 181, 232 n. 52
Lüders, Heinrich, 158, 160

Madhya Eśiā kā itihās (The history of Central Asia), 81
Maha Bodhi Society, 76–8, 144 nn. 10–11, 148, 148 n. 17, 153, 168, 227, 224, 250, 294 n. 47, 302
Maha Bodhi Temple, 14, 73, 119, 142–7, 147 n. 16, 185, 192
Mahāmānav Buddha (The great man [who was] Buddha), 57, 162
Mahapad Nayak Mahastavir, 75–6
mahāpaṇḍit (great scholar), 38, 76, 183 n. 82, 285, 288 n. 43, 293, 301
Mahastavir, Dhammaloka, 133
Mahavamsa, 133 n. 2, 133–4, 162
Mānav samāj (Human society), 42–3, 79, 200, 235
Mere asahyog ke sāthī (My friends from the non-cooperation movement), 57

Merī jīvan yātrā (*MJY*), 5 n. 11, 28, 32 n. 42, 36, 39, 43
modern education in colonial India, 11, 96–7
Muru monastery, 75, 151

Nāgārjun, 165, 165 n. 52, 229
Naravil Dharma Ratna, Bhikshu, 148
Narendra Dev, Ācārya, 12, 152
national history, 17, 48
nationalism in India, 9–11, 16 n. 26, 111
Navdīkṣit bauddh (Neo-Buddhists), 163, 163 n. 48
Naye bhārat ke naye netā (New leaders of new India), 57
Nepāl-bhāṣā Pariṣad, 172
Nepāl-bhāṣā Sāhitya Sammelan, 173–4
Nepal Buddhopasak Sangh, 169
Nepal Buddhopasika Sangh, 169

one cultural soul, 29, 37, 167, 176, 177 n. 70, 179, 186–7
Otto, Rudolf, 153, 160

Pā̃c bauddh dārśnik, 162
Pandey, Kedarnath, 53, 60, 62, 84, 278
Parmānand, Bhāī, 44, 106, 113 n. 31, 146 n. 13
Pathak, Ramsharan, 52, 59, 61, 65
Pelliot, Paul, 161,
Pramāṇavārttika, 154–9, 154 n. 33, 227–8, 228 n. 50, 274
Prāntīya Kisān Sabhā, 197
Prasad, Jaya Shankar, 45, 224, 268, 285 n. 34
Prasād, Rājendra, 44–5, 119, 146–7, 147 n. 16
Premchand, 44–6, 44 nn. 12–13, 45, 46, 116 n. 36, 255
primordialism, 25, 27
print capitalism, 20–21, 30, 226
prison literature in India, 41–4, 50
progressive writers, 45, 230

Rhys Davids, Caroline Augusta Foley, 160–1
Roy, M.N., 41, 191
Roy, Ram Mohan, 11 n. 21, 12, 93–4, 97
Rūs mẽ paccīs mās (Twenty-five months in Russia), 51–3, 80, 225
Russian Revolution, 37, 69, 78, 91–2, 96, 111–13, 119–21, 128, 221

Saddharma-Pundarika, 153
Sahu, Dharmaman, 32 n. 42, 58, 150, 169–70, 169 n. 56, 170 n. 58, 172, 175, 259, 262–3, 266
Sama, Bālakr̥ṣṇa, 258, 260–1, 261 n. 2, 284
sāmyavādī duniyā (egalitarian or communist world), 112, 141
Samye monastery, 152
Sankrityayan, Rahul:
  as Arya Samajist, 3, 7 n. 17, 8, 17–19, 28, 34 n. 45, 38, 50, 67, 74, 100, 104, 107, 112–14, 116, 119, 123 n. 45, 128–9, 138, 164 n. 49, 187, 190, 246, 257, 273, 286 n. 37, 300 (*see also* Arya Samaj)
  and *bhārtīyatā* (Indianness), 1, 19, 20, 92, 127, 193, 206–8, 212, 239, 244, 249, 251–2;
  and bhārtīyatā and Hindi, 216, 242;
  and bhārtīyatā for unity, 254;
  on Buddhism and communism, 137, 141;

communist literature or works on communism, 68–9, 191, 120, 140, 229–35;
and concept of *ek jātīyatā* (single cultural entity), 20, 109, 111, 115, 124–5, 127–8, 202, 249, 251, 254–6;
and cultural unity, 206;
and Dayananda, 96 n. 12;
dismissal from the communist party, 38, 189, 202, 204, 206, 240, 242;
in dress, 20, 126–8, 250, 254;
as a fervent nationalist, 18, 128;
on Hindi and Devanagari, 18, 23, 61, 81, 203, 208, 211, 231, 240, 247;
on Hindi–Urdu controversy, 206;
on Hindustani, 211, 214–16;
on Indianizing Islam, 1, 20, 250;
and Marxist theory and communism, 141–2, 192, 195;
nationalism, 19, 23, 27, 37, 62, 59, 92–3, 105, 108–9, 134, 234, 239, 253, 256;
nationalist sentiment, 10, 15, 17–18, 25, 27–8, 31, 35–9, 73, 81, 78, 89, 91–3, 100, 105, 107, 111, 114, 140, 145, 146, 189, 210, 244, 245–8, 257;
on Nepal, 226–7, 283;
Nepal for him, 167;
progressive works in Nepal, 235, 236;
as a progressive writer, 1, 240, 253, 298;
as a Sanskrit teacher, 133, 148;
involvement in satyagraha, 76;
travelogues, 223, 225, 263, 30, 33, 46, 51–2, 55, 83, 122, 160 n. 44, 165 n. 51,
on Urdu, 24, 61, 81, 204–5, 211–15, 242, 251

Sankrityayan, Kamala, 2 n. 3, 32 n. 41, 46, 49, 51, 53, 63 n. 33, 82 n. 52, 83, 87, 151 n. 26, 167, 223 n. 45, 251, 259, 265–8, 292;
as Kumari Kamala Pariyar, 81, 268, 302

Sanskrit, 13, 24, 33 n. 43, 45, 51, 58–9, 61–3, 65, 67–8, 74–5, 78–80, 82, 91, 94, 96, 98, 101, 121, 122, 130, 135, 145, 150 n. 23, 151–5, 156 n. 38, 159, 173 n. 66, 176, 180, 182 n. 82, 184, 202–3, 212, 215–6, 216 n. 33, 221, 223 n. 45, 227, 231–2, 232, 240, 245, 250, 259, 260, 271, 272 n. 22, 275, 277, 281, 301, 302

Śāntarakṣita, Ācārya, 152

Sarasvatī (Hindi journal), 46–7, 47 n. 15, 67, 221

Śarmā, Janaklāl, 3, 32 n. 42, 166, 184, 259, 264–7, 266 n. 9, 284, 285, 288

satyagraha, 1, 17, 71, 72 n. 42, 114, 119, 198, 228, 301–2;
at Amvāri (*see* Amvāri satyagraha)

Satyārthprakāś (*The Light of Truth*), 94–6, 203

sevā (service): to literature, 22, 38, 190, 219, 221, 222, 224;
to the country 219–21, 221, 222

Shamsher, Chandra, 169, 174, 183 n. 85, 265, 272, 273 nn. 23–4

Shamsher, General Mohan, 170

Sharma, Hemraj, 32 n. 42, 34 n. 44, 58, 155, 155 n. 35, 155 n. 37, 180, 183 n. 85, 184, 188, 232, 259, 270, 273, 275, 275 n. 27, 276

Shrestha, Pushpa Lal, 126, 184, 235, 238, 278
Shri Nivasa, Bhikshu, 144
Siṃhal ke vīr (Sri Lankan heroes), 162
Siṃhal ghumakkaṛ Jayavardhan, 162
Siṃh, Mohan Bikram, 234, 234 n. 55
Siṃh Senāpati, 6, 23, 43 n. 8, 79, 92 n. 4, 164–6, 200 n. 18, 250 n. 4, 294
Singh, Fatte Bahadur, 172–3
Smith, Anthony D., 17;
  nationalist sentiment, 17;
  nationalism, 17;
  soft primordalist, 26;
  about Benedict Anderson, 27
Soviyat bhūmi, 122
Stcherbatsky, Theodor Ippolitovich, 78, 78 n. 49, 153, 156 n. 38, 156 nn. 40–1, 157–8, 157 n. 42, 160, 223 n. 45, 302
Suzuki, Daisetsu Teitaro, 161
Swaraj Party, 72, 72 n. 42, 191–2, 301

Theravada Buddhism in Nepal, 168–9, 174
Theravada movement in Nepal, 29, 37, 175, 181, 236
Tibbat mẽ bauddh dharm (Buddhism in Tibet), 154, 163
Tibbat mẽ savā varṣ (One and a quarter years in Tibet), 153 n. 30, 160 n. 44, 223 n. 44, 233, 269
tripiṭakācārya (master of the Tripitaka), 7 n. 17, 75, 148, 301
Tucci, Giuseppe, 155, 232, 274
travelogues in Hindi literature, 46, 55

Vaidya, Jagatman, 168
Vaidya, Niranjan Govinda, 126, 234
Vidyālaṅkāra Pariveṇa, 8, 25, 74, 82, 133, 134 n.3, 148, 152, 301
Vidyarthi, Kedarnath (Rahul Sankrityayan), 68
Volgā se Gaṅgā (From Volga [to] the Ganges), 6 n. 12, 42, 43 n. 8, 79, 200 n. 18, 211 n. 31, 250 n. 4
Vajraḍākatantra, 75
Vaijñānik bhautikvād, 42
Viśva kī rūprekhā (An outline of world history), 42, 43 n. 8, 79, 200 n. 18, 235, 241,
Vismr̥t yātrī, 165

World Fellowship of Buddhists (WFB), Fourth General Conference of, 175

Yami, Dharmaratna, 32 n. 42, 58, 58 n. 23, 87, 172 n. 65, 184, 231, 236, 238, 259, 263–4, 264 n. 6, 265–8, 279, 281, 283
Yashpal, 3, 165

ABOUT THE AUTHOR

Alaka Atreya Chudal is a senior lecturer at the Department of South Asian, Tibetan and Buddhist Studies, University of Vienna, Austria. Earlier she has taught at Nepal Sanskrit University, Kathmandu, Nepal. She is also a littérateur who writes in Nepali and Hindi. Her research interests span book history in nineteenth- and twentieth-century northern South Asia, intellectual history of north India and Nepal with a focus on the autobiographical self in Hindi and Nepali literary studies, as well as modern and contemporary Hindi and Nepali literature.